Opera Omnia

Volume III

Christianity

Part One
The Christian Tradition

(1961–1967)

Opera Omnia

I. Mysticism and Spirituality b13424804
Part 1: Mysticism, Fullness of Life — b13759681
Part 2: Spirituality, the Way of Life

II. Religion and Religions b13759905

III. Christianity
Part 1: The Christian Tradition (1961–1967)
Part 2: A Christophany   2004 faith meets faith

IV. Hinduism
Part 1: The Vedic Experience: Mantramanjari
Part 2: The Dharma of India

V. Buddhism

VI. Cultures and Religions in Dialogue
Part 1: Pluralism and Interculturality
Part 2: Intercultural and Interreligious Dialogue

VII. Hinduism and Christianity

VIII. Trinitarian and Cosmotheandric Vision

IX. Mystery and Hermeneutics
Part 1: Myth, Symbol, and Ritual
Part 2: Faith, Hermeneutics, and Word

X. Philosophy and Theology
Part 1: The Rhythm of Being
Part 2: Philosophical and Theological Thought

XI. Sacred Secularity

XII. Space, Time, and Science

Opera Omnia

Volume III

Christianity

Part One
The Christian Tradition
(1961–1967)

Raimon Panikkar

Edited by Milena Carrara Pavan

ORBIS BOOKS
Maryknoll, New York 10545

ORBIS BOOKS
Maryknoll, New York 10545

Fathers and Brothers
MARYKNOLL™

Founded in 1970, Orbis Books endeavors to publish works that enlighten the mind, nourish the spirit, and challenge the conscience. The publishing arm of the Maryknoll Fathers and Brothers, Orbis seeks to explore the global dimensions of the Christian faith and mission, to invite dialogue with diverse cultures and religious traditions, and to serve the cause of reconciliation and peace. The books published reflect the views of their authors and do not represent the official position of the Maryknoll Society. To learn more about Maryknoll and Orbis Books, please visit our website at www.maryknollsociety.org.

Library of Congress Cataloging-in-Publication Data

Panikkar, Raimon, 1918–2010, author.
    Christian tradition / Raimon Panikkar ; edited by Milena Carrara Pavan.
      pages cm. — (Christianity ; part one) (Opera omnia ; volume III)
    Includes bibliographical references and index.
    ISBN 978-1-62698-159-1 (cloth)
    1. Christianity. 2. Christianity—Philosophy. 3. Theology. 4. Philosophical theology. I. Carrara Pavan, Milena, editor. II. Title.
    BR121.3.P36 2015
    230—dc23
                                                                            2015023952

Series Foreword

All the writings it is my privilege and responsibility to present in this series are not the fruit of mere speculation but, rather, autobiographical—that is, they were first inspired by a life and praxis that have been only subsequently molded into writing.

This *Opera Omnia* ranges over a span of some seventy years, during which I dedicated myself to exploring further the meaning of a more justified and fulfilled human lifetime. I did not live for the sake of writing, but I wrote to live in a more conscious way so as to help my fellows with thoughts not only from my own mind but also springing from a superior Source, which may perhaps be called Spirit—although I do not claim that my writings are in any way inspired. However, I do not believe that we are isolated monads, but that each of us is a microcosm that mirrors and impacts the macrocosm of reality as a whole—as most cultures believed when they spoke of the Body of Śiva, the communion of the saints, the Mystical Body, *karman*, and so forth.

The decision to publish this collection of my writings has been somewhat trying, and more than once I have had to overcome the temptation to abandon the attempt, the reason being that, though I fully subscribe to the Latin saying *scripta manent*, I also firmly believe that what actually matters in the final analysis is to live out Life, as witnessed by the great masters who, as Thomas Aquinas remarks in the *Summa* about Pythagoras and Socrates (but not about Buddha, of whom he could not have known), did not write a single word.

In the twilight of life I found myself in a dark forest, for the straight path had been lost and I had shed all my certainties. It is undoubtedly to the merit of Sante Bagnoli, and of his publishing house Jaca Book, that I owe the initiative of bringing out this *Opera Omnia*, and all my gratitude goes to him. This work includes practically all that has appeared in book form, although some chapters have been inserted into different volumes as befitted their topics. Numerous articles have been added to present a more complete picture of my way of thinking, but occasional pieces and almost all my interviews have been left out.

I would like to make some practical comments which apply to all the volumes:

1. In quoting references, I have preferred to cite my previously published works following the general scheme of my publications.
2. Subject matter rather than chronology has been considered in the selection, and thus the style may sometimes appear uneven.

3. Even if each of these works aspires to be a self-sufficient whole, some ideas recur because they are functional to understanding the text, although the avoidance of unnecessary duplication has led to a number of omissions.
4. The publisher's preference for the *Opera Omnia* to be put into an organic whole by the author while still alive has many obvious positive features. Should the author outlive the printer's run, however, he will be hard put to help himself from introducing alterations, revisions, or merely adding to his original written works.

I thank my various translators, who have rendered the various languages I have happened to write in into the spirit of multiculturalism—which I believe is ever relevant in a world where cultures encounter each other in mutual enrichment, provided they do not mislay their specificity. I am particularly grateful to Milena Carrara Pavan, to whom I have entrusted the publication of all my written works, which she knows deeply, having been at my side in dedication and sensitivity during the last twenty years of my life.

R.P.

Contents

ABBREVIATIONS

Hindū Scriptures

AB	*Aitareya-brāhmaṇa*
AV	*Atharva-veda*
BG	*Bhagavad-gītā*
BU	*Bṛhadāraṇyaka-upaniṣad*
CU	*Chādogya-upaniṣad*
IsU	*Īśa-upaniṣad*
JabU	*Jābāla-upaniṣad*
JaimUB	*Jaiminīya-upaniṣad-brāhmana*
KaivU	*Kaivalya-upaniṣad*
KathU	*Kaṭha-upaniṣad*
KausU	*Kauṣitaki-upaniṣad*
KenU	*Kena-upaniṣad*
MahanarU	*Mānārāyaṇa-upaniṣad*
MaitU	*Maitrī-upaniṣad*
MandU	*Māṇḍūkja-upaniṣad*
Manu	*Mānava-dharmaśāstra*
MB	*Mahābdārata*
MundU	*Muṇḍaka-upaniṣad*
PaingU	*Paiṅgala-upaniṣad*
RV	*Ṛg-veda*
SB	*Śatapatha-brāhmaṇa*
SU	*Śvetāśvatara-upaniṣad*
TB	*Taittirīya-brāhmaṇa*
TMB	*Tāṇḍya-mahā-brāhmaṇa*
TU	*Taittirīya-upaniṣad*

Christian Scriptures

Ac	Acts
Col	Colossians
Dan	Daniel
Dt	Deuteronomy
Ep	Ephesians
Ex	Exodus

Ez	Ezekiel
4 Ezra	Fourth Ezra
Gal	Galatians
Gn	Genesis
Hag	Haggai
Heb	Letter to the Hebrews
Hos	Hosea
Is	Isaiah
Jas	James
Jb	Job
Jg	Judges
Jn	John
Jon	Jonah
Jos	Joshua
Jr	Jeremiah
Lk	Luke
Lv	Leviticus
Mc	Micah
Mk	Mark
Mt	Matthew
Nb	Numbers
1 Co	First Letter to the Corinthians
1 Jn	First Letter of St. John
1 Kgs	First Kings
1 Pet	First Letter of Peter
1 Sam	First Samuel
1 Th	First Letter to the Thessalonians
Ph	Philippians
Pr	Proverbs
Ps	Psalms
Qo	Qohelet
Rev	Revelation
Rom	Letter to the Romans
Si	Sirach
Song	Song of Songs
Tt	Titus
2 Co	Second Letter to the Corinthians
2 Mac	Second Maccabees
2 Pet	2 Peter
2 Tim	Second Letter of Timothy
Ws	Wisdom

Others

Adv. haer.	Irenaeus, *Adversus haereses*
BC	Biblia catalana
BJ	Bible de Jérusalem
Caes.	Plutarch, *Caesar*
Categ.	Aristotle, *Categories*
C. gentes.	Thomas Aquinas, *Contra gentiles*
CIC	*Codex Iuris Canonici* (Code of Canon Law)
Conf.	Augustine, *Confessions*
De div. nom.	Dionysius, *De Divinis Nominibus* ("On the Divine Names")
De myst. theol.	Dionysius, *De mystica theologica* ("On Mystical Theology")
Denz.	Heinrich Denzinger, *Enchiridion Symbolorum*
De sacram.	Ambrose, *De sacramentis*
Dom. VIII post Pentec.	*Roman Missal,* Eighth Sunday after Pentecost
Ench. Symb.	*Heinrich Denzinger, Enchiridion Symbolorum*
Epist.	Basil, *Letters of St. Basil of Caesarea*
Epist. ad Eph.	Ignatius Antioch, *Epistle to the Ephesians*
Epist. ad Parthos	*Augustine, In Epistolam Joannis Ad Parthostractatis Decem*
Epist. in I Cor.	John Chrysonstom,
Ex Officio Smi. Sti	*Ex Officio Smi. Sti.Ati* n. 71
Expos. in Ioan.	Eckhart, *In Ioannis Evangelium Tractatus*
Fragm.	Heraclitus, *Fragments*
Fragm.	Philolaus of Kroton, *Fragments*
Homil. Pasch.	Cyril of Alexandria, *Homilia Paschalis*
In Cant.	Bernard, *In Canticum Canticorum Expositiae*
In Ezech.	St. Gregory the Great, *Homilia in Ezechielem*
In Iohan.	Augustine, *In Iohannis Evangelium Tractatus*
In Iohan.	Cyril of Alexandria, *In Iohannis Evangelium*
I Sent.	Bonaventure, *Commentaria in quatuor Libros Sendendiarum*
KJ	King James Version
Knox	Knox Bible
Met.	Aristotle, *Metaphysics*
NácarColunga	Nácar-Colunga Bible
NEB	New English Bible
NJB	New Jerusalem Bible
NRSV	New Revised Standard Version
PG	J.-P. Migne, *Patrologiae Cursus Completus.* Series Graeca, Paris, 1857–1866
Phileb.	Plato, *Philebus*
Phys.	Aristotle, *Physics*
PL	J.-P. Migne, *Patrologiae Cursus Completus.* Series Latina, Paris, 1844–1855

Quaest. Disp.	
de Pot. Dei	Thomas Aquinas, *Quaestiones Disputatae de Potentia Dei*
RV	Revised Version
Serm.	Bernard of Clairvaux, *Sermones de diversis*
Strom.	Clement of Alexandria, *Stromata*
Sum. theol.	Thomas Aquinas, *Summa Theologiae*
Theat.	Plato, *Theaetetus*

INTRODUCTION*

Littera enim occidit
Spiritus autem vivificate.[1]

2 Co 3:6

All the great religions have their holy books. This is a characteristic they all share, even though it cannot be said that all religions have the same conception of *holy* with regard to their Scriptures. The Christian thought concerning this is summed up in the complex and meaningful concept of *inspiration.*[2] This word, taken in its deepest sense, indicates that God is acknowledged as the author of the Bible,[3] while the hagiographer may quite correctly be called an author for the fact that he freely compiled his text on the basis of his own temperament and his own knowledge.[4]

The Holy Scripture, then, contains the revelation[5] of God to mankind (this, of course, from a Christian standpoint), but the Bible as such is neither the revelation[6] itself nor does it contain the complete revelation.[7]

Rather than tackling these problems now, however (which are mentioned here merely to help us focus on the question at hand), let us return to the previous problem—the relationship that exists between the Bible and Christianity. In what sense is Christianity the religion "of the Book," of the Bible? Can we know and deduce Christianity, from the Bible alone? What, after all, is Christianity and what does it draw from the Scripture?

1. *What is Christianity?* Christianity is a simple name with a very definite meaning, and this meaning is precisely the *concept* of Christianity. Many stop here and mistake *Christianity* for the *concept* of Christianity. While these people may have a concept of Christianity that is correct and, at least to a certain extent, true, to them it remains always and only a concept, an idea, or, if you like, an ideal, an essence. They never, in

---

  * Revised version of "La posizione della Sacra Scrittura nel Cristianesimo," in *Maya e Apocalisse. L'incontro dell'induismo e del cristianesimo* (Rome: Abete, 1966), 157–64. Translated by Geraldine Clarkson.

  [1] The letter, in fact, kills and the spirit gives life.

  [2] See 2 Tim 3:14–16; 2 Pet 1:20–21; 3:15.

  [3] See Council of Trent, sess. IV (*Denz.,* 783) and Vatican Council I, sess. III (*Denz.,* 1787).

  [4] See Vatican Council I, *loc. cit.* (also *Denz.,* 1952, 2294, etc.).

  [5] See Vatican Council I, sess. III, 2 (*Denz.,* 1785–1788).

  [6] See Heb 1:1–2, *in Filio,* εν υιω. Christ in his *being* is the full revelation, manifestation (αποκαλυψις, φανερωσις) of God; not only in His words or teachings nor only in His actions.

  [7] See Jn 16:12–15; 21:25; Mk. 9:37–39, etc.

any case, penetrate the concept to the extent of reaching the very heart of the thing, the *res significata* (as St. Thomas of Aquinas points out), and so they miss this vital and mysterious reality (a reality that is always transcendent and, consequently, a mystery) that lies at the very heart of the concept. To them Christianity is a doctrine, a creed, conceived precisely as a series of formulas that they generally call dogmas and interpret as intellectual statements relating to given aspects.[8]

This is not to say, of course, that Christianity does not *have* its own doctrine, or its own *Weltanschauung*. We are merely emphasizing here that it is far more than all this, far more than a concept, an essence, or a series of formulas or dogmas.

If Christianity is truth (and this is precisely what it claims to be), then it must be Reality itself, since truth is much more than the mere adequacy of the intellect to the thing[9], and much more also than the pure precision of our understanding of reality. The truth, in fact, is not primarily an essence, but rather an existence[10] and, *ultimately*, exists only where the essence is fully and wholly existence—in other words, in God.[11]

The Christian message came down to us—*sunkatabasis*—not only so that we might know better the true nature of reality or understand the real and final structure of the universe, but also, and above all, in order to save us, to help us *become* what we truly *will be*.[12] In other words, Christianity or, rather, the Christian *status*, is the condition of pilgrimage, the real condition of the wandering universe on its path back to God (*plerōma*).[13] It is the whole structure of beings that are moving toward their reconstitution (*apokatastasis*).[14] It is the ontic growth of all the sparks of Being—all the members of the mystical Christ[15]—toward the fullness of Light that is the whole Christ.[16] It is the temporal life of Christ on earth, in the innermost part of every being, in the hearts of all men of goodwill.[17]

---

[8] For example, God is the judge, the resurrection of the flesh, etc.

[9] Aristotle's *adaequatio rei et intellectus*.

[10] The Sanskrit word for truth, *tattva,* is far more effective than the Greek concept of αληθεια in expressing the basically existential character of truth, which is not a discovery of the mind, a gnoseological result, an extraction of what was hidden in the δοξαι (opinions) of things; it is what truly *is*. God, and God alone, is the Truth, because He is *tattvam asi,* YHWH, *Ego sum qui sum.*

[11] When Pilate asked Jesus what truth was, Christ gave him the most exact answer. (Yet the Roman governor, and many others with him, did not understand Jesus's answer, because they did not understand him). The silent figure of Christ before Pilate was the living Truth (Jn 18:38)—"I am the Truth" (Jn 14:16; see also Jn 1:17).

[12] Christianity or, more exactly, the church, is historically an *event*, and psychologically could be considered a *doctrine*, but ontologically it is the *revelation* of the true existential framework of Being, and ontically it is the *wandering existence* itself and fullness in God in the afterlife. (See 1 Co 15:28.)

[13] See Jn 1:1–6; Col 2:9; Ep 11:23; 3:19.

[14] See Ac 3:21 and its interpretation in the "Fathers of the Church."

[15] See Gal 3:28.

[16] See Ep 4:13.

[17] See Jn 6:57–58; 15:5ff.

2. *The Christian doctrine.* Since Man is an intellectual being, equipped with consciousness and free will, Christianity also has an intellectual aspect (though this is only a part of it) with two dimensions: one theoretical, dogma, and the other practical, moral. These two make up what is called the Christian doctrine.

This doctrine is the divine-human locution—or the revealed expression—of the unutterable truth and rests in the Christian community (*ekklesia*) itself. The Christian doctrine is not, however, the rigidly rational statement of some truth, or even a final and specific formulation of certain facts. All formulations invariably use defined concepts, and all concepts are the fruit of a given culture and are valid only within the particular horizon in which they were conceived and used, in the same way as the simple, basic mathematical law of intervals.[18]

We cannot deny, however, that there exists a Christian doctrine, however different it may be from the dialectical and logical unfolding of a rational system deriving from a central axiom.[19] This explains how we can claim that the Christian doctrine, though sufficient in preserving Man from substantial errors, is neither complete, nor finished, nor concluded,[20] much less static, petrified, and crystallized once and for all.

The truth is always the same and the profound meaning of Christian dogmas— that which lies beyond the concepts and represents Christian reality—remains constantly unique and unchangeable, but the conceptual structure, the systematic framework within which the various parts of this ineffable reality are arranged, are as contingent as the historical cultures that mankind traverses.[21] We might go further, in fact, and say that Christianity itself, like Jesus[22] and like every Christian,[23] is not only a pilgrim and a wanderer but also an evolving being, growing upward to reach the church in the heavens, where God will be all in all.[24]

3. *The sources of Christian doctrine.* What, then, are the origins of Christian doctrine? The Christian community (the Church) as the continuation of Christ himself is, on the earth, the final source of this doctrine.[25] And since it is ontic reality that lives its own life, that grows and moves to return to the supreme Origin of everything, it can have no other criterion of truth outside itself.[26]

---

[18] This does not mean there cannot be universal concepts with a general human value, but it is unlikely for this kind of eternal value to be postulated a priori.

[19] The Christian doctrine has developed in a purely existential and historical way on the basis of circumstances, by emphasizing now one point and now another, depending on the vital and pastoral need to correct or prevent or react in the face of unilateral explanations or negations of the Christian Mystery, without ever following any "logical/systematic" order.

[20] Such an idea is not conceivable for the revelation, the fullness of which is Christ himself, who, being God, is infinite, and therefore neither closed nor limited.

[21] This problem, in its entirety, is very clearly defined in Christianity. It is known as the "homogeneous evolution of dogma."

[22] See Lk 2:52, etc.

[23] See Ep 4:13.

[24] See 1 Co 15:28.

[25] See Ep 5:1ff.; Rev 21:9, etc.

[26] See Jn 12:12ff.; Rom 12:5; Gal 3:28; Col 1:24, 28; Ep 1:23.

This means that the source of the Christian doctrine is far from any form of individual interpretation or any bizarre statement from any type of authority. Only the Christian mind, therefore, by reflecting on the reality of the church, seeks to express in conceptual forms its real nature. Christian *gnōsis* (in the orthodox sense of the word, as it was used in the Patristic Age) is, by nature, not without a certain internal hierarchy; what concerns us here, however, is not so much the unfolding of Christian *gnōsis* (principles of hierarchy, Holy Spirit, orthodoxy, etc.) as the material (so to speak) from which the Christian spirit must draw its consequences and build its doctrine.[27]

4. *Scripture and Tradition.* The Christian doctrine is the product of an intellectual effort born of faith or, if you like, the effort made by the Christian intellect in order to formulate a *Weltanschauung.* The source can only be reality, as seen in the light of the full human intellect. This *gnōsis* is achieved thanks to all the possible existential sources of knowledge.[28]

The *specific* and characteristic doctrine of Christianity must be sought in a unique yet twofold economy (*oikonomia*)—the Holy Scripture and tradition. These are not two separate sources of information but two aspects of the same reality. The first is the written word and the second the spoken word of the same Holy Spirit that inspires both the holy author and the living witness.[29] The first emphasizes the essential dimension and the second the existential dimension of the very same economy of salvation. Each one is the key to interpreting the other—not in the sense of a rationalistic "vicious circle" but rather a *vital circle*, a bearer of mutual light.[30]

Since the Bible exists as a given fact, tradition, though it has a certain priority over Scripture (*evangelium ante evangelia*), has no value if it is separated from the Bible. Tradition is the vital development of the living Christ—his Message—and, at the same time, the existential interpretation and fulfillment of His words and actions.[31] A large part of these words and actions, however, have been recorded in writing, and "the Scripture cannot be broken."[32]

---

[27] For the very fact that, ultimately, the sacrament of the church is identified with the Mystery of Christ, it represents something more than the mere juridical structure of the church; indeed, being the ultimate manifestation of the church, it is in a certain sense the key to understanding the full meaning of Christianity.

[28] See the same idea in the *Bhagavad-gītā,* IV.34, and also the wonderful metaphor of the *Mahābhārata* II.55.I.

[29] See Mt 10:19–20; Lk 12:12, etc.

[30] The Scripture-tradition relationship does not refer to a revelation of the type "partim in sacris libris et partim in sine scripto traditionibus" [partly in sacred writings, partly in oral traditions] but rather "totum in sacra scriptura et iterum in viva traditione" [wholly in the sacred Scriptures, and also in the living tradition]. See, regarding this particular theological problem, the interesting discussion held on the subject at the Second Vatican Council.

[31] Tradition does not represent the entire sum of Christian accomplishments. Neither does it claim that the praxis of Christians has always been immaculate, perfect, and in a word, Christian. (See Mt 7:21–23; Lk 13:26–27, etc.)

[32] Jn 10:35.

5. *The Meaning of the Scripture.* On the other hand, the Bible without tradition could not be called Holy Scripture or Christian Scripture. It could only be considered as an ordinary book, of a more or less profound content, that each may interpret according to his own temperament and in which each may, by projecting on it his own particular *apriorisms*,[33] discover what he chooses.

Like any other holy book, the Bible cannot be approached, without reverence, from the outside, nor from a viewpoint that is purely specific and individualistic. Any book, in fact, can only be truly understood if we are able to grasp the underlying intention of its author.[34] To believe that every human expression may be understood in itself, separated from all reference to its author and from any anthropological relationship (whether individual or sociological) would be to fall into the most extreme form of rationalism.[35]

In reading the Scriptures I must, of course, strive to grasp their true meaning, to understand their vital message; at the same time, however, I cannot leave to others that which represents the experience of a personal quest. Yet this personal fulfillment may only be attained if I enter into ontological communion with the author; if I believe, I read the holy book while fully respecting the tradition and vitally placing myself within it.[36] This is an attitude of human[37] and Christian[38] nature.

---

[33] As the well-known idiom says, "The devil may quote scripture for his own purpose" (see Mt 6:6; Lk 4:10–11, etc.).

[34] And, in this case, the author is God. We need, therefore, the help of the Holy Spirit to understand his Message (see Jn 14:26).

[35] It is not, perhaps, strictly necessary to know the author and his environment in order to understand the meaning, for example, of the words "five fruits on the tree," but if the hagiographer speaks of *logos*, love, peace, etc., then it is a completely different matter. A certain kind of understanding can be communicated through concepts or written words, but only a human being can understand another, if by *understanding* we mean something more than the knowledge of the anatomical and rationalistic infrastructure of a thing. From a purely philosophical point of view, it can be proved that the necessary condition for understanding lies in the sharing of essence (a dog may understand a man only to the extent of what they have in common and not with regard to that which is specifically human). Only faith can "understand" the Christian Bible.

[36] This does not at all mean that I cannot keep my own personal opinions and original ideas, but only that my personal discovery and my own opinions belong to and enrich the tradition.

[37] Every human expression—especially if it refers to subjects of the utmost importance and directly concerning the person—is merely a means of communication for reaching a transcendent alterity that can only be grasped if we are in tune with the whole existential Source (or Cause).

[38] This is common, in fact, to Catholics and Protestants alike. Protestants believe so strongly in the need to read and understand the Bible in the context of the Christian community that they claim every *bona fide* reader is inspired by the Holy Spirit. The Protestant is not alone; the Spirit of Christ breathes within him. He is a living member of the community and, therefore, the tradition. Catholicism does not deny this fact but corrects any possible abuses

Having made these observations, let us now summarize the relationship existing between Christianity and the Bible:

1. Christianity, for the very fact that it is far more than a mere doctrine, cannot be fully contained in any book.

2. Since Christian doctrine is living and dynamic it cannot be contained and congealed by the statements of any book.

3. Christian doctrine, as the human expression of divine revelation, cannot in any way contradict the main document inspired by the revelation, that is, the Bible.

4. Since the Bible is the written expression of a living message, it can only be fully and truly understood if we place ourselves within the living tradition in which the Divine Spirit itself blows.[39]

5. Since the Bible is the book that carries a simple and ineffable divine message, the Mystery of Christ, the message it contains cannot be understood by enucleating or developing certain maxims isolated from their context, but must be assimilated in its entirety.[40]

6. Since the Bible was written to help mankind on its path to salvation it must be considered, going beyond its scientific-historical character, as a spiritual, mystical, and religious book and not a scientific and rationalistic work from which it is always possible to logically draw other deductions and other consequences.

*

This large volume, *III: Christianity*, comprises two parts.

The first part deals mainly with *the Christian tradition*. It begins with a book dating back to 1963 (*Humanismo y Cruz*), in which I present the cross as the center of the Christian message. Despite its somewhat outdated language I thought it would be worth including it in the *Opera Omnia* because its expresses the form of spirituality that was taking shape in that period, of which the book remains an important testimony. This is followed by a series of writings, in chronological order, beginning from the first period of my priestly commitment and continuing through my full maturity.

---

and misunderstandings of it, completing the idea of community also from a truly human and historical perspective while, at the same time, remaining one with its mystical sense.

Here on earth, in fact, the only spirits that exist are incarnate.

[39] We do not need to remind the reader that "the Spirit blows where it pleases" (Jn 3:8) and that the conception of the church presented in this essay is of an ontological nature, without any other limits (see Jn 10:6).

[40] The Bible is neither the "constitution," nor the "canon law," nor even the sacred code of the laws of Christianity.

SECTION I
HUMANISM AND CROSS[*]

---

[*] Original text: *Humanismo y Cruz* (Madrid: Rialp, 1963). Translated by Carla Ros.

1

THE HUMAN SYNTHESIS[1]

Et verbum caro factum est.

Jn 1:14

Theory (Integral Anthropology)

Ecce homo!

Jn 19:5

In the Middle Ages, human beings were considered microcosms, worlds in miniature. Nowadays, this idea has been individualized; it has been interpreted from a nominalist point of view, and we tend to say that every person is a world. Because we do not have a unified conception of the microcosm that each human being is, everyone is said to build their own world in their own way. Strictly speaking, the human microcosm is the most complete world there is—though not the most perfect. All scales of being are represented in the human cosmos; the union between all that exists takes place in it; it is the point of encounter of the entire universe, the intersection of everything that is real. In humans there is body, soul, spirit, and divinity. (In humans in grace, the latter is given by participation, and in Jesus Christ—true man—it is given by His very nature.) Why is it strange, then, that after the fall—after losing grace—human beings, who participate in the kingdoms of matter, of soul, of the intellect and of God, are the most complex and paradoxical beings in creation? To be precise, the world is a *mesocosmos*, and the purpose of synthesis is more to search for the place of the cosmos in humans and for the place of humans in God, than only to find the place of humans in the cosmos.

The first task of human synthesis must consist, then, in reestablishing order insofar as possible. For this, we need, precisely, to develop an *integral anthropology*. Integral does not mean finished, but rather formally complete, in the sense that it considers the entire human being for the restoration of the *intra* (microcosmos) and the *inter* (mesocosmos) orders.

---

[1] [Editor's note: Part of this article appeared in *Arbor*, an important Spanish cultural magazine of the postwar period, of which Panikkar was deputy editor for several years and in which he published many of his articles.] *Arbor* 1 (1944): 5–40.

3

We distinguish the subjective order—which we call also personal—from the objective one. Personal order in the human microcosm is fulfilled by holiness; it is an order that, in a *fundamental* minimum, coincides with the objective, but which is not necessarily mistaken with it. The latter is what a complete science of the human being must develop.

In the classical conception of the Middle Ages, people were primarily interested in God. It has been said that they spoke of God referring to everything and of everything referring to God. The focus of their efforts of synthesis was much simpler than in modern times. Being basically interested in God, when lowering their gaze to creatures, they placed themselves almost automatically in the real order, although it would be perhaps better to say that, being imbued with the objective order of things, they were, above all, interested in God. Present-day human beings—perhaps because they feel disconnected from everything, as we pointed out at the beginning—are primarily interested in themselves; they have turned themselves into a set of problems, and nowadays it is essential that any attempt at synthesis begins with human beings. We cannot study human beings descending from God; when faith has been lost, it is first necessary to ascend to Him. Only those who know themselves to be children of God can begin by contemplating Him, but those who inside feel a constitutional split and a permanent anxiety must necessarily begin with their own selves. The only starting point and the first matter is the human being, the complete human being, which includes the historical human being. When human beings, basing themselves on their intellect, reverted to God and then attempted to understand the universe through a theocentric vision, it is understandable that they did not cultivate anthropology as such and that the definition of the human being as a rational animal was already sufficient. Even if all of this were true, modern human beings have possibly forgotten it, and we must first restore their confidence in their own intellect so that they may once again admit God. Additionally, their confidence in their own reason must not come from a mere theory of knowledge—since understanding the gnoseological problem as something isolated and independent of everything else is not the correct approach—but rather from a complete anthropology.

What, then, is the human being? The basis of the entire microcosmic order, both in its entitative aspect as well as in its operative one, must emerge from the answer to this question—an answer founded on the person's complete being, which cannot be defined solely in terms of the elements of a natural system.

Postponing the outline of an integral anthropology for another occasion, we will only be able to keep moving forward if we invert the required order in the discussion of a synthesis and we also disregard the *entitative aspect* of the human being. To be precise, instead of looking for the constitutive elements of the human being and using them to establish an ontological order for people's being and doing, we will only deal with their *operative aspect*, considering the different human manifestations as emerging from a radical unity. This is possible, in the first place, because the data are there: science, art, culture, technology. . . . In the second place, because the goal, human beings' ultimate end and that of all their actions, is also well-known—though its foundation and the extension of its ontological influence to the smallest details of the person's being is left for a future task. Every operation is fruit of the entity of a being; we will only be able to obtain an authentic synthesis when we can truly say that every activity is the fruit of an inner plenitude that produces it and not only the manifestation of one partial aspect of human nature.

We said that the ultimate meaning of human life is already known, and what remained was to make it come to fruition. We saw that the only possible synthesis, if it was to be a complete and perfect synthesis, consisted in the possession of God, and in seeing Him and all things in Him. From there we deduced that the path to synthesis is one of coming closer to God, until we are able to see with His very eyes and judge things with His own criteria. This path must be a process of complete sanctification of human beings and, therefore, also of their intelligence. For intelligence, sanctification lies in Truth; not in one parcel of truth, but rather in the complete Truth, whose intellectual possession necessarily implies love. Therefore, in the same way, the life of the human being must be to serve God—to give Him glory—bearing in mind that putting oneself at God's service denotes something *essentially* different from any other service. Service indicates servitude, subordination, working for another's end, not one's own, even if both of these ends may partially coincide. On the other hand, to serve God is certainly to reign. There is no *real* limitation whatsoever in human beings who are harmoniously developing their potential while serving God, and in creatures, service to God coincides with perfection.

Furthermore, with this we have an extrinsic criterion—the only one that can be used before establishing an anthropology—of the rectitude of something's activity, seeing if it really serves God. In addition, it is a real guide in the activity of a being. Obviously, this criterion alone is not enough, because there is an evident danger of making leaps and believing that something leads to God, when actually it does not serve Him. The best way of approaching God is for each being to perfect itself in its own sphere, without any ambition of premature conclusions and syntheses; faith in God must show in our confidence in things. And the *paradox* is that God is served by being loved.

In order to divide human activities in some way, we begin with a consideration of the essential aspect of human beings. Human beings are personal beings. Their strength is personality. Person and personality acquire their full dimension in the social sphere. Thus, we first have to consider human beings in their individual aspect and then in their social one.

Humans as Individuals

Human beings, placed between God and the world and participating in both, manifest an accumulation of activities—whose crystallization constitutes culture, which, to a certain extent and exclusively for methodological purposes, can be grouped according to what predominates in them: sentiment, intellect, or will, which can be considered the trilogy that composes the human spirit. We are not going to discuss which of these ingredients has primacy, or even their adequate division. Suffice it to admit that, despite possible interferences and the imprecision of limits, these three fields of human manifestation exist.

Sentiment: Art

Artem nemo odit nisi ignarus.

Without examining the philosophical problem presented by beauty, we can, nevertheless, assert that the main anthropological ingredient of art is human sensibility, crystallized in any external manifestation.

The world is filled with hidden connections, only manifest to a sensitive temperament able to apprehend them. Human beings penetrate the world that surrounds us in very different ways. From one extreme of seeing things as unrelated to the other extreme of seeing God *in* things, including the stage of seeing God *through* his medium, through things, there is an unlimited range of experiences.

The mystical interpretation of the world lies here, as does a great portion of its symbolic vision. Even Christian symbolism needs a considerable dose of affective knowledge. Things fulfill something of God; they are, in a certain way, symbols, images, divine fulfillment. Nature is a sign, the symbol of an invisible reality. Human beings use words in order to denominate their ideas. God uses things in order to signify them. The world thus appears as a manifestation of God. Knowing all of this is not enough; we must experience it in order to truly know it. An artist is one who knows how to read the book that is reality.

Leaving mysticism aside—which is a different question altogether—it is obvious that human beings possess a sense that apprehends all those deeper connections of whose existence they have a *pre-sentiment*. The universe has a rhythm—that cannot be intellectually apprehended. That is why Man turns to feeling—a rhythm that discovers unsuspected links that are not exactly causal.

Myth comes from the human need to possess a synthesis; and this is why myths lose ground to the extent that sciences expand and deepen a series of analytical connections. Nonetheless, myths have their own mission: *Mythos* and *Logos* are both necessary to comprehend the universe.

Artists live in the world. One could say that beauty is their Aristotelian transcendental, and feeling their Kantian transcendental.

Art's mission is to show the beautiful, bring the intimate connections between things to life by means of the sensitive forms with which it appears to want to apprehend the spirit. Art will be all the more profound when, by means of the Beautiful, it makes us guess the latter's internal connection to Truth and Goodness—whether this union is independent of the human spirit or not. Art elevates because it unifies. Its evil lies in its disconnection from the rest of the spheres of culture. Its mission consists in revealing human sentiment and channelizing them toward a complete synthesis; this in no way means that it must become a mere propagandist at the service of some preconceived notions. We are referring to the conclusions of art itself, not to the artist's intentions. Authentic art, without intentions of any kind, leads to God. It is altogether another thing to ignore that humans are fallen beings and that they may find aesthetic pleasure in the wicked and even in the ugly, that is, that they may believe that evil is beautiful.

The artistic world considers itself *misunderstood* by the rest of mankind, and it is true that many people have no sense of the artistic because they believe it to be *extravagant*; you could say they have a restricted vision of art (which many artists, incidentally, share). Art must preserve its universality and be conscious that its mission is to sing the glory of God "for the wonders he has done." And all humans are capable of artistic emotion, because all humans are capable of love. When a simple mortal falls in love, he becomes something of an artist, because he harbors an accumulation of experiences that surpass any adequate means of expression. And an artist is one who feels the inadequacy between the real and the ideal; this is why, if a strong artistic temperament does not lead to God, socially the artist is considered a misfit, a bohemian.

Light is the form under which the artist, like the mystic, desires God, Light of the universe, who illuminates the *shadows* of the world as well as the blackness of the dark night of the soul.

The artist is concerned with a noble and important task in the construction of a human synthesis. Scientists use their intelligence to progressively dominate reality, to gradually get closer to the truth: scientists *discover*. Technicians, by means of their will and the goals they set, apply their knowledge to practical life, they model culture: technicians *invent*. Artists give life to this entire apparatus. They bestow beauty and illusion to the entire assembly and to its parts; they apply their sensibility to the search for a nonsensitive truth; they make the beauty of the sky descend to the earth. Artists *create*.

It is disappointing to perceive, in the human lives of our times, so much authentic value that is so disconnected, so much suffering and so little sense of the fruit and mission of pain, so many good—even heroic—tasks that are so badly understood and taken advantage of. It is religion's task to give life meaning, but making us feel this is still the role of art. Suffice it to mention the importance of the story in contributing to a mature human vision of the world. We could say that that which is human—truly human—must be its maximum criterion, even before the beautiful. The world, God's vestige, cannot be contemptible.

Reason: Science

Deus scientiarum Dominus.

1 Sam 2:3

The fundamental categories here are truth and reason.[2] In the dawn of Western civilization, all products of human intelligence were referred to as science or philosophy, indistinctly. The truth that humans attained with their thought, as

---

[2] [In the beginning of this section he refers to the three fields of human manifestation as sentiment, intellect, and will. In this discussion, however, reason, rather than intellect is discussed as the second manifestation.]

opposed to what was offered by feelings, was called scientific truth, philosophical truth. A stick submerged in the water at an angle is not broken, even if it looks that way; future inspection shows us that the stick is intact, and science tries to explain the cause of this optical illusion. All knowledge of causes can, strictly speaking, be called scientific. Before long, the particular sciences split from science/philosophy, in a process that we cannot detail here. In the concatenation of causes that our intellect discovers, some are close and some remote. Every time the immediate causes of a group of phenomena were discovered, a new science emerged. Philosophy was left with the last causes.

The factual situation of the present gives us a multitude of sciences with stronger or weaker links to other sciences, but without a visible hierarchy among them, or any kind of manifest internal unity, or even an external one in the minds of those who cultivate them. How to reduce all sciences to a unity? It is not about *reducing* them to unity, but rather about *finding* this unity. If science looks for truth, truth is what will guarantee its unity. That said, truth is the reality of things, and we will have diverse types of sciences according to which type of reality or which one of its aspects our intellect considers. Depending, thus, on the type of reality that is considered, either experimental sciences, or spiritual sciences, or philosophical or theological ones will emerge. Depending on the depth with which our spirit penetrates into the natural world, depending on the degree of abstraction—detachment—with which we regard concrete matter, all matter except for quantity, or absolutely all, we will have the physical sciences, the mathematical ones, or the philosophical ones, respectively.

We are not attempting to establish here an exhaustive and adequate division of the sciences, but rather to point out, in a programmatic manner, the issues that come into play in a scientific synthesis.

A synthesis of all sciences may be called a *system*. It has two main chapters: the connections of the sciences among themselves, their mutual concatenation—that is to say, the establishment of an internal order—and the ends of Science in general, its global meaning, its mission—that is to say, the establishment of a system in the cosmic order, its place in human life.

We have spoken about the division of sciences. Only what is previously whole can be divided. It is just as important to perform a sound division as it is to perform a sound multiplication that we can use as proof. If the historical process has been one of division—of separation and disintegration—of the sciences, the current process is one of integration. As sciences are already divided—unfortunately also in the figurative sense of the term—what is the point of view of each science, and what is the depth with which it apprehends reality? The answer to this question will allow us to assign certain coefficients of extension and of security, respectively, to each science, which will be the key to elucidate the connections between them.

There are many types of connections. Some are essential. Every science has a series of essential connections to the other sciences; these connections are constitutive, in the sense that one science uses the conclusions of another as its principles. Alternatively, other connections are merely indirect; yet others belong to pure vicinity, with occasional contacts; others are instrumental, in the sense that one science uses another as an instrument for its own development. Thermodynamics has an essential connection to mechanics, an instrumental one to mathematics, one of vicinity to acoustics, and a completely indirect one to geology. Two connections are particularly interesting to point out: Every science has an instrumental relationship to logic and an essential one to philosophy. This explains its privileged situation. This idea is merely outlined here.

The second capital problem of a system is its order as a whole, its mission. Science is one method of knowledge. But it is not the only one. It lies in the middle between inspired, mystical knowledge and sensitive, animal knowledge, just as Man lies between God and the world. It is, thus, advisable to delimit its connections with other methods of knowledge beforehand. All the problems between science and faith, philosophy and theology, reason and mystical illumination, belong here.

Nevertheless, science is the typically, specifically, human method of knowledge. This appreciation allows us to put it in its place within human life without having to study all previous issues exhaustively. Science is a type of knowledge; it is the food of understanding; it is the life of the intellect here on earth, since the human intellect is rational, that is to say, scientific. What is the mission of reason in human life? It is, undeniably, that of helping Man discover his ultimate end, and even that of cooperating in its achievement. How can science help save human beings, perfect them, make them happy, give glory to God? Only by fulfilling its specific end, which is the attainment of truth. Therefore science must try to know the maximum amount possible and in the best way it can—being conscious, however, that this knowledge is the discovery of God in the intimate texture of creation, be it in its material, spiritual, or even purely mental creatures. Creation is a canticle, and science must, at the very least, make an effort to discover its melody.

It is not only about science giving glory to God, but rather human beings, through science, must also glorify Him. As soon as science discovers any given truth, it implicitly discovers God; furthermore, science ontologically supposes God, in the sense that, without God, science would not be possible. But additionally, science, as a human product, must give glory to God through the priesthood of man, that is to say, for the reference to God made by the scientist who cultivates it or the mere mortal who takes advantage of its fruits. The scientist is the priest of truth, just as the artist is that of beauty, and every religious human being, that of goodness. It is not enough, then, for science to lead implicitly to God; in fact, science does not lead anywhere. It merely discovers the truth through much effort, and after many mistakes; rather it is scientists who, in their uninterrupted asking, must know that they always end up in God and in the divine Will that made things this way and not another. And it is not necessary for the scientist to cover all the other sciences until he reaches the primary cause; in the essential connection of each science with philosophy, every scientist has a bridge to reach God.

Scientists create an intellectual world that provides decisive support to a complete synthesis. The scientific aspect of the world is an important ingredient in their plenary vision. And, analogously to artists, they run the risk of one-sidedness. If, due to their excessive anxiety, artists see shadows where there are realities, scientists, due to their excessive confidence in their own methodology, see very simple solutions—in both of its meanings—where mystery reigns. Their risk is extrapolation, be it formal (or methodological), by believing that their methods can be applied to all reality, or material, by supposing that the whole world has a similar structure to the one branch of knowledge that they cultivate. Generally, the man of science is satisfied with clarification instead of explanation, and he mistakes clarity for evidence. We have not necessarily explained a phenomenon just because we have its mathematical expression, even if we can measure it and predict it; even if nothing else about it interests us. The *how* of a thing is not the *why*, and the scientist, being only interested in the former, can easily fail to differentiate them.

The history of each science confirms this fully, so much so that this criterion has even influenced philosophy. During practically four centuries, a great portion of European philosophy has lived immersed within mathematicist molds that suffocated it. Even in order to scientifically validate a conclusion, to stay within the course of data, the scientist who interprets it must have a vision of the whole, a synthesis that is broader than that of his exclusive field of investigation. This is not about pulling specialists away from their own fields. It is about making them see the connection, the multiple bonds that exist between their own terrain and the whole. In this sense, the more specialized one becomes—the deeper one has penetrated into a particular science without losing the sense of whole—the more universalist, the "wiser," one will be.

It is significant that in the West we call people who are prominent in one discipline *wise*. In Greece, wisdom was the heritage of philosophy. The sciences split from philosophy and they took wisdom captive. We no longer call the philosopher—the one who makes sense of the totality—wise, but rather the eminent scientist. In the East, the wise and the saintly are still united; they still understand that mysterious bonds make all humans powerful before God, who is also master on earth.

If the intellect is the noblest part of humans, its perfection—vision of God—will also be the goal of all humans. We already said that the perfect synthesis consisted in this. It would thus seem that humans could best prepare themselves on earth to join God through their intellect; yet true wisdom is given to the humble, to those who love much and not to those who know a great deal. This is the human paradox. This is why, whoever wants to save their soul must hate it, and whoever wishes to know divine wisdom must be a saint. Original sin broke human synthesis, altering the order of our being. Nevertheless, there must be a more or less harmonious path, even on earth. To clear this path is the mission of Christian synthesis.

It will have been obvious that I have used the word "science" in its classical conception, and the term "scientist" in its current sense of cultivator of the natural sciences. It would now be appropriate to speak of the role of the other sciences, and especially of philosophical synthesis, but this would require a separate, monographic study of its own.

Will: The Ideal

Deo servire regnare est.

If it is through intellect—as we have said—that we join God in the "homeland," in the "path," it is through will, through love, through charity that we join Him.

If feelings produce art and reason science, human will, because it is free, is capable of tending toward more than one object. If beauty and truth are the two poles of art and science, then goodness, power, and pleasure are the goals of will. Up until now we have spoken of the artistic and the scientific worlds. We will now have to introduce the religious world, governed by goodness as the supreme value.

If the synthesis of reason has been called *system*, the synthesis of will could be termed *ideal*. The ideal is the unification of all the conscious operations of a will. Founded on an integral anthropology, the human ideal that unifies all of Man's aspirations must emerge, that which gives a meaning to all the values toward which our will is drawn. This will, together with the ideal, is what takes the results of science and applies them toward its own end, thus creating technology. Modern civilization patently shows that current technology has not been created because of an ideal—because of a full ideal. Material progress, instead of *being useful* for humans, for their spiritualization, for their perfection, has often *used* humans to enslave them. Technology has often ceased to make sense. For much of humanity, the commercial and industrial worlds, which are inherent parts of the technological world, have acquired supremacy in fact and in law. The words of St. John of the Cross are incomprehensible for the modern world: that a person's one sole spiritual thought is worth much more than the entire material universe.

In any case, the justifying principle of the human ideal must be universality. The ideal does not calm—its full realization is unattainable in this world—but it must guide, direct, and give meaning to all human activities. Everything must fit into an authentic ideal; no human value must be insignificant. The study of each one of the indicated types must be the work of maturity, which cannot be achieved right now. The fullest human synthesis is fulfilled in the ideal. Four years ago, I wrote somewhere, "We have spoken extensively about the fertility of ideas, yet scarcely considered that this fertility consists in the fact that an idea can be identified with a person and then it is called an ideal; from that moment on, the force of person-ality—*höchstes Glück der Erdenkinder* (Goethe)—prevails, and through that vital force, the idea triumphs."

Humans in Their Social Aspect: Community

Humans are not timeless beings; culture and history weigh down upon them. The meaning of history and the meaning of culture are also fundamental in any conception of the world. Precisely what little there is written on an integral synthesis is about the interpretation of culture or of history.

Once we have described the categories around which the individual being of every person revolves, we can try to discover the meaning of their collective manifestations. Because people are governed by Providence, the way in which human beings have developed their lives—faced their destinies in the past and face them in the present—cannot be the mere result of an unconnected series of will and circumstance: rather we could say that individual forces and movements are the result of a decomposition—albeit free—of the total directive force, of the resulting one.

Disintegration is also a feature of present-day culture. "Primitive" human beings and children share an excess of unity in their conception of the world; their unity is mythical. For them, the portrait, the name, and the person, for example, are the same; they attribute responsibility to things, and so on. Modern human beings, on the other hand, are guilty of the opposite; they separate the work of intelligence from will, they atomize their lives, they divorce their sciences from their practical lives, they believe that an action that is humanly evil can be economically or politically good. "How is it that they go to Mass, and yet they are evil?" This is the first religious scandal for our children. The end—the End, within cosmic order—most certainly conditions the means. The thing is that the means cannot be justified by the ends—in plural—by particular ends that are disconnected from the order of the world. Humans are not supposed to judge the utility of any event. Their intelligence can only guide them in matters of truth or goodness. That is why only the person of faith, the one who, consequently, has faith in God, can affirm the usefulness of truth against all the appearances of our myopic sight. The optimist, the one who can fully affirm human culture, is the religious person.

Culture is essentially temporal; it is concerned with the terrestrial goodness of human society. Nonetheless, if a supernatural destiny intrudes into a person's life, it will have to be taken into consideration. The order of personality must be reflected in the order of society. The material must be subordinated to the spiritual, though not with a blind and primitive subjection. Human beings, including their supernatural destiny, are unities. And culture must be at the service of the complete person.

Elaborating the postulates of a culture that is Christian, founded on an authentic anthropology, belongs to an integral synthesis.

There is a providentialist interpretation of history that could be called *stunted* or *minimalist*. It consists in saying it all and at the same time not saying anything. It is limited to succinctly postulating a Providence that rules the destinies of human beings and later ignores this affirmation. If it exists, and it is God, this truth cannot be a mere factor that partially impregnates the conception of history; nonetheless, this does not exempt us from trying to find out if we possess any means to know the intentions that this Providence may have about humanity. The cultivation of history, even—and precisely—as knowledge of a constitutive dimension of the human being, must culminate in a theology—a theology of history.

*

The meaning of the human being will appear in all its plenitude after a study "from within" of that which we have merely pointed to extrinsically here. Not being able to show the diverse aspects of a thing by one sole intuition is one of the limitations of our rational spirit. This compulsory division often provokes serious obstacles for a synthetic vision. Human anxiety will never be satisfied here on earth. The contemplative human beings who have risen highest in the vision of the Mystery are the thirsty par excellence.

To take on the anxiety-ridden preoccupations of the common people and attempt to elevate them to the authentic anxiety that pulsates beneath all appearances of daily vulgarity is another mission of human synthesis. God is present in all of His creatures, not only in those that are highest in the order of beings. God is transcendent to the world, and that is why His relationship to it is not exclusively through the last ring of the admirable cosmic order, but rather directly in each being, and personally in each person.

Praxis: Life

Et fides sine operibus mortua est.

Jas 2:26

The transmutation of elements is a fact. Some have even claimed to be able to create gold in their laboratories, but this had no influence on the commercial and economic lives of the peoples: the synthesis was not industrial. Up to this point, we have tried to point out the necessary operations to fulfill a synthesis of the laboratory. We still need to see if this synthesis is industrial, that is, if it yields efficiency, if it is worth putting into praxis. Obviously, and let me stress this point, any sort of industrial synthesis will be less efficient, not only than a theoretical one, but even than one obtained in the laboratory. Furthermore, the "head"—the beginning—of the operation is frequently not very useful.

The mere fact of cultivating a particular science without losing sight of its function in the whole is enough for the acquisitions of that science to be, for this very reason, comprehensible in a scientific synthesis, in a system.

The problem of the world is a problem of (saintly) people, of grace. Its solution and its very proposal are fully supernatural. But within the natural order, one of the most important factors is the intellect, ideas. Ultimately—and as ordinary instruments of the supernatural order—ideas rule the world. So then, the path to synthesis consists in contributing to forging, rediscovering, or simply—most of the times (as *nihil sub sole novum*)—putting into updated circulation the ideas which, both because of their internal dialectics as well as because of the willingness of Providence, can lead humanity toward its authentic destiny. That is to say, expose the Christian intellectual solution to the problems of today's life.

It is not as much about writing the *Summa scientiarum*—which the world is not mature enough either to produce or to assimilate—as it is about showing the spirit the way to the living channels of the Christocentric vision of things, getting it out of the dead paths and putting it into a path that leads to God. Grace and the expansive force of ideas itself will already help it advance toward the end.

In order to live, human beings need some anxieties, they need tension, to aspire to something that they do not yet have: a hope, an ideal. In one word, they need *faith*. This is simply about giving them authentic objectives, real problems, vital preoccupations.

The living faith gives the ultimate solution. The first mission consists in posing the *authentic* problems of modern human beings. The task to be fulfilled is reduced to filling in the void between the first proposal and the ultimate solution. Great thinkers have always developed their science with an inspirational extra-scientific idea, not directly guided by the value truth, but rather by the value goodness. Thinking is born, if not from action, from the desire for action.

To truly live present-day life and the Christian faith fully, and to have sufficient intellectual training, are the prerequisites to achieve a unification of the sciences in practice.

All of this does not imply that we must always deal exclusively with philosophical-theological questions. Human culture, because it is the work of human beings, has an atomic structure, and there is no insignificant cultural atom. The greatest danger of a synthesis is reaching premature conclusions. This is why we must never be in a hurry. Partial truths must gradually come together due to internal demands. A favorable cultural atmosphere is needed, one that is open to synthesis. This is what should be pursued first of all. The physical conditions of chemical synthesis make this possible.

Consequently, there is room here for the efforts of the scientists who hope to expose the true fruits of their science, consisting both in methodological detail or the partial aspect of truth discovered, as well as in its integration within a harmonic synthesis, which anyway requires a previous knowledge of the scientific fact. This is why it is more necessary to generalize than it is to divulge.

This is also why there is room here as well for those who feel the noble desire to clarify the meaning and the mission of our existence in its multiple and complex dimensions: theological, philosophical, historical, judicial, scientific, technical, cultural, and so on, thus facilitating interchanges of the respective points of view and the version, in nontechnical language, of the preoccupations that are proper to each branch of human knowledge, often misunderstood by those unversed in that particular science, in order to achieve fruitful comprehension, the cornerstone of a true synthesis of human knowledge, by means of mutual contact.

After that, the first practical step we must take is dialogue, the collaborative work between specialists from diverse sciences. This is the contact that appeared necessary for synthesis. The direction of philosophy will impose itself by itself. The truth is strong enough to open up its own way, if there are no illegitimate intentions. Science will reconcile with philosophy, and the latter with theology. The human being's work in all culture—in all cultivation—is precisely this: to cultivate. The growth and the fruit of what is cultivated ultimately depends on the germinal force of the seeds. If one sows living doctrine, it will bear fruit. The work can be limited to the intellectual plane, even in practical problems. The rest will come as a consequence.

2

INTELLECT AND ITS PRAXIS[1]

Dilectio Dei honorabilis sapientia.

Si 1:14

One of the *radical*—and this is a fitting metaphor—theses of *Arbor* that gradually penetrates our intellectual subsoil could be called honorability or, if you prefer, intellectual honesty: "honor is the patrimony of the soul and the soul belongs only to God," and it could be formulated by saying that all the activity of our intellect must emerge from an inner plenitude.

Otherwise, when it separates from our true life, it degenerates into a distasteful cerebral secretion with deadly fruits, despite a possible spellbinding cover, an *extrinsic* good intention or even unilateral and partially valuable results. Human beings are a unit, and despite our brilliant civilization, the cancer of the scientific spirit destroys this unity. Our declining era of rationalism has taken much too seriously the idea that the truth of a thing lies in a concise, rational judgment that is disconnected from the whole. Truth also has its rights, but these are found within reality itself, beyond rational dialectics. The real truth, and this is a redundancy, transcends the world of essence in order to lead to the existential.[2] Truth is the mediating bridge between essence and existence. It is not a banality that it has been revealed to us that truth *exists* and that it *is* the Person of the ontic Mediator between God and things.[3]

Beings *are* insofar as they are truth, and they are *truth* insofar as they are "thought" by Christ, that is, He who has *made* all things. That is why one cannot "know truth" if one does not *remain* in His λόγοζ. "Quando cor nostrum visitas—Tunc lucet ei veritas" (Hymn to the Most Holy Name of Jesus). "I am the truth," and if "the law was *given* through Moses, grace and truth have *come* through Jesus Christ." *Sed de hoc satis.*[4]

---

[1] Published in *Arbor* 87 (1953): 316–24, and in *Neues Abendland* (November 1995): 643–48.

[2] This will turn out to be what St. Thomas has already said. Cf. J. Pieper, *Philosophia negativa* (Munich: Kösel, 1953), 18.

[3] On the meaning of truth in the Gospel according to John, see A. Wikenhauser, *Das Evangelium nach Johannes* (Regensburg, 1948), 148ff.

[4] For another *granum salis* on this problem, see R. Panikkar, "Die existenzielle Phänomenologie der Wahrheit," in *Philosophisches Jahrbuch des Görresgesellschaf* (Munich, 1956), 27–54.

The Three Planes of the Intellect's Honesty

I must be authentic. That is to say, I must be myself: "honest," according to both classical and popular Spanish theological language. Yet if the life of my intellect must be authentic, this requires a very profound honesty. If I have a true intellectual calling, I must discard even the real possibility of falling into the external temptation of working, of writing something just in order to obtain a post, in order to accumulate one more merit, in order to be liked by such and such a person. This would not be lack of honorableness, rather maliciousness—and not intellectual, but human. I think it is great that we want to find career opportunities for degrees in the humanities, but it seems to me that whoever undertakes or fails to undertake any such studies because of the "opportunities" they afford sullies their spirit and renounces a true vocation. And the same can be said of the real sciences. The great danger of gaining a degree in "science" is that the career opportunities are much too close. Intellectuals are not technicians; this is why they can work on Sundays, because their occupation is not a τέχνη with an end extrinsic to itself. Strictly speaking, if they consider it a job, they are undeserving mercenaries who do not observe the holy feasts. But this is not my topic. . . .

I am referring to an honesty that is intrinsic to intellectual work itself. And even here, there is room for different planes of depth. I will disregard the first, which is professional honesty. It is obvious that in my intellectual occupation I must proceed with order, with pulchritude, I must quote with fidelity; I must not deceive, pretend that I know or have read what I do not know or have not read; I must not fall into that puerile vanity of feigning erudition or into that graver still intellectual sin of plagiarism, of copying. This is all very clear.

Now I turn to a deeper plane. The first sin, that of the mercenary, is only human and does not belong solely to the mind; it is human ambition itself that has assassinated a possible intellectual vocation. The second fault, that of scarce professional honesty, is primordially a sin of intelligence—which has let itself be vanquished by vanity, comfort, ambition, and so forth—and only supplementarily of the entire human being. Here, in the third plane, is where what is human, the entire human being, is once again reunited with the intellect. It is properly an intellectual sin. If it is not a sin against the Holy Spirit, it comes very close as it is a sin against the spirit. It is simply about the concupiscence of the mind, the voluptuousness, sometimes painful, of letting myself be carried away by a simple dialectic without bearing the underlying reality in mind; it is about letting my ideas be disembodied from my life with the excuse that they may become more elevated, purer or even more apologetic or convenient for other ends, as if what I had to redeem were not my own existence. It is about an intrinsic insincerity of my intellect in my life, of a guilty dichotomy between my mind and my heart, my intelligence and my love—more specifically, between my ideas and my ideals. Let me explain myself.

The Separatism of Reasons,
the Specific Temptation of the Authentic Intellectual

There are humans who eat to live, as we are also a body, while others live to eat, as if they were merely a body. There are people who work to live, as life is work; there are people—I repeat—that think, investigate, write, study, to live, as life is thought, study, investigation; but there are people who live to think, to write, to investigate, who take care of their brains like singers take care of their throats, who cultivate their ideas as dancers do their muscles. And this, even though it may give marvelous partial results, is a disorder that always takes vengeance and can even grow to become sin (*pneumolatry*).

I must purify my intention. Human life—human, I say, not animal, not vegetable—is thinking activity, willing movement; it is to know and to love. The spirit has a life—participation in the Life of He in whom life was—that consists of knowledge *and* love (here, as in the Trinity, the copulative conjunction is essential). If these are disconnected, if they do not both serve the same Lord—loving God with all of our mind and knowing Him with all of our love (and this is what the first and only commandment consists of)—if we love *for* our own selves and want to know *for* our own selves, we introduce the source of all evil into our spirit. Classical asceticism has only accentuated the dangers of love for oneself. It is now time to recall the dangers of self-knowledge, of the humanist γνῶθι σεαυτόν, which are not lesser. Intellectuals cannot look for their perfection in subjective good intentions. Rather they must aspire to the objective perfection of the human spirit (conquering self-love, overcoming self-knowledge), as far as possible.

In other words, a cripple can be a saint; so can a merchant and so can a "primitive" person, the integral perfection of their spirit notwithstanding. This is where divine mercy shines brightest, when it gathers and saves the fragments of the Mystical Body of its Son. (There are many mansions in the house of the Father.) But whoever has as a mission to work with their intellect cannot ignore the real hierarchy of things and the demand to sanctify themselves "in the truth." Their approach to Christ, their salvation, must pass through their intellect. The faith of the rough man is only good for the rough man. Intellectuals are required to have something more than good will, something more than good intentions. They are required to fill the intended with real, that is, true, content; they are required to reach the maximum activity of the spirit and recapitulation of their own lives, which Christian terminology has called *contemplation*. I do not mean to say that less is asked of "others," as if they were an inferior class. There are no two Christian paths, just as there are no two types of human beings. I only wish to recall that "to whom much is given, much will be required."

The permanent scandal of our current culture consists in the fact that humans, cultivating that faculty for which they are specifically human, in the image and likeness of God, have distanced themselves from Divinity. The evil of our civilization is that intellectuals have ceased to be contemplative; they no longer see God *in* things, and because of this, their gaze becomes more superficial, their wisdom becomes shallow and statistical experience, their science is transformed into technique; their integral knowledge of theology—even in the Aristotelian and Platonic sense—degenerates into the rational knowledge of philosophy. "Modern philosophy" only wants to know in order to have "power" over the rest of humans or in order to dominate nature. This is why it results in impotence.

It is not my place now to say that contemplative humans are those who have been unified, who live in harmony, all of a piece—because they rest in being—toward their integral end. Rather I must once again turn to the disorder of the intellect.

This is where temptation and, consequently, my purpose, emerge. Why do I study? What is the meaning of my activity, which we can call intellectual work, if you will? It is not, certainly, that of earning a living or of being successful in a public examination. Neither is it to attain the fame of a wise man or the prestige of having written many books or of being an authority in my field. I do not look for σόφα for its ἐξουσία. Neither do I work, study, or investigate—the contemplation of truth is not a means—*in order to* do great good for humans, *for* a determined apostolate, or *to* reach an ideal. All of this may come in addition, and it is not bad, but it is neither what I am looking for, nor the specific temptation of the authentic intellectual.

This temptation has had catastrophic effects on the rationalist European mind of these past centuries. And it still does so with many intellectuals of our time, as it is the specific temptation of human reason. It is based on the fact that it only studies in order to know what is studied, segregating this from reality; it only investigates in order to dominate the particle that is investigated; it disconnects the world of essence from that of existence so that my reason may run more freely without being held back by reality; it falls into the separatism of reason; it disconnects my intellectual activity from my life; it excommunicates my intellect from my existence; it falls into an idealist ambush and I get tired of *thinking* reality—which slows me down, dominates me, and conditions me. Therefore I linger over the *thought* thing, which does not curb my desire for independence. *Cogito cogitatum.* Then I am sure that I am not making a mistake, but I am not going outside of myself. And formal lack of error is not yet the truth.

The temptation is subtle, as is the Evil One. To put it more bluntly: I feel within myself the incentive to work in order to be able to write a book, to study in order to attain knowledge of a problem or discern a solution. I experience the claims of an intellect, which would like to determine reality and feels the humiliation of having to understand by composing and dividing. Simply put, I feel attracted by the autonomy of the creature, and in my spirit, the original temptation of knowing, from my point of view, anthropocentrically, the science of good and evil resonates.

The known autonomous formulas: art for art's sake, science for science's sake, and so on, are often adduced with the laudable intention of defending these values in the face of the illegitimate intrusions of unsustainable heteronomies; but, taken in themselves, they are also not valid, as the logical subjects of these affirmations of tautological appearance—art, science, knowledge, love, and so forth—are *ontonomically* connected to a substantial reality, Man, from which they cannot be divided, while the predicates are full of a merely dialectic autonomous content.

Yet all of this is not correct. Basically because reality is not in the essences, rather it *is* an existence. The mind that succumbs to the aforementioned temptation then discovers its own nudity, which it has provoked by undressing itself from God, by disconnecting from *Being*. Therefore my spiritual activity is not my life. My existence continues still, somehow "re-ligated" to its Foundation, while my intellect is spending all its capital letting itself be taken by its own intellectual voluptuousness. Then my mind descends along the slope of the inauthentic. It penetrates into the path of an infrahuman life, I lose myself in disquisitions that are increasingly further away from reality, and I have no other solution but that of gradually deifying my own intellect and turning it into a dialectic god, certainly infinite, but incapable of breaking the enclosure of the rational and of producing—creating—one sole existence. One simple flower is more powerful, as it cannot be produced by reason and yet it *is* able to produce other flowers.

Symptoms

Absence of contemplation, lack of rest in the being, in the *esse*, lead me to nervousness and haste. It is natural that I cannot be calm or able to stop until I have discovered some foundation for my life. Then not only am I anxious, but I let myself be dominated by unease and by that intellectual vice that medieval authors understood so deeply and they called *curiositas*, and which we could translate as dilettantism, indiscretion, and being fickle, or, with greater etymological fidelity, as "intellectual preoccupation."[5]

I pry into everything hastily and nervously. When I come across an idea, or a thought comes into my head, almost before I can even think it—live it—I have already written it down, obsessed with the objective of taking advantage of it, of making it fit in somewhere, like hurried tourists or people keen on photography who have ruined their own taste because they can only see through the camera lens. When I read a book I no longer assimilate what the author wants to say, but only that which interests me as a stimulant, as suggestive for my own book or for me in general. In this same order of things, though on an inferior plane, we find the case of those who do not know how to listen, who only know how to talk or, in any case, how to listen to themselves.

---

[5] See the beautiful text by St. Bernard, *In Cant.* 36, 6, quoted in the apostolic letter *Unigenitus Dei Filius* by Pius XI (March 19, 1924): "Sunt qui scire volunt—animadvertit S. Bernardus—eo fine tantum ut sciant, et turpis curiositas est; . . . et sunt item qui scire volunt, ut scientiam suam vendant, verbi causa pro pecunia, pro honoribus, et turpis quaestus est; sed sunt quoque qui scire volunt ut aedificent, et caritas est; et item qui scire volunt ut aedificentur, et prudentia est." See etiam *S. Bernardi sententiae* 19 (*PL* 183, 751).

The curiosity to which I alluded earlier—vanity of the intelligence—has nothing to do with so-called scientific curiosity, which is a participation in that constitutive θαυμάζειν of our spirit that admires the reality of things with intellectual passion.

Another symptom is the shortsighted obsession with making the most of time in a merely pragmatic sense, looking toward a determined end, as if the profound—and Christian—sense of time were in my future and not in my present. Eternity is not in the future. These people must always find themselves busy in one *task* or another because they do not know how to *be*. They project, but their projectiles are empty. It is all gunpowder; there is no bullet.

A worse symptom—very severe, in fact—is intellectual envy, not so much toward those who prevail due to a valid idea but rather toward those who have said or discovered the same thing as one has thought oneself. The latter do not communicate in the being; they will never be able to understand the Communion of the Saints. That is why they are distraught when others have—and publish—the same ideas they had previously thought of themselves but had not written down yet. Later they will fight for intellectual property rights. This is the gentrification of intelligence. They have forgotten that true originality is not in *saying*, but in *being*. Only if my being is unique will I, perhaps, be able to say something, provided my word becomes sacrament.

*

I prefer not to give any examples of lack of intellectual honesty. I fear somebody may think I have ceased to carry out my own soul searching in order to write down an accusation. I have no right to judge anybody, but only to discover the secret desires of the "old man"[6] who sometimes cries out for lost privileges.

Proposal

Intellectual honesty. Authenticity in my intellectual life. I am concerned about the problems of the spirit because they inspire passion in me vitally, not because I want to give some kind of lesson or teach anyone anything. To resist the temptation of the professor. "You have only one teacher." *Contemplata adiis tradere* is the true role of teaching, according to the Angelic Doctor. But this "tradition" can only take place by means of life. The "Master" called us "friends." Without friendship, no teachings are the *tradition* of life, but rather simple *translation*, and consequently, *treason*. In order to teach us His doctrine, Christ sent us His Spirit, which inhabits within us.

Thus my life must be the tradition of what I see, the expression of what I love. My investigation cannot be a violation of the seclusion of being, but rather a silent listening, an active obedience to the reality that reveals itself to me.

---

6 See Ep. 4:22.

Writing is not selfishness for me, but rather necessity and a means of authenticity, because writing, the crystallization of thought, is part of my life. I do not live and take care of myself (and there are scrupulous intellectuals who wash their hands twenty times) in order to think and to love; rather my life, my own life, is thought and love. If I have anything to say to the world, Providence will make sure that I say it, if I do not place any obstacles in the way. If it is not my mission to be a prophet, it is enough for me to be a man. St. Paul said that he did not place value on his soul over and above his I.[7]

Many years ago, I worried because I could not publish the thick books I had written for lack of actual time to make the final corrections or due to other reasons. A good friend made me realize that anything that could be of value in all of those still unpublished works was still gravitating in my present life, if it was authentic. And I now understand the personal purification and the catharsis of time when someone waits many years for the testimony of their existence. The price of the testimony—μαρτύριον—is one's own life.

But there is still more. What one lives, what one says, is what remains, is what endures, is what influences in the *regressus* of all things to God, through Christ. What one simply writes down is consumed by moths and by dust; what one etches onto people remains in eternal life—that is to say, precisely the opposite, in this ontological order, to what is usually upheld: "Verba volant, scripta manent!" Better off flying! says a Spanish heraldic coat of arms. "Do not amass . . ." more than the authentic, ultimately because any other kind of saving is impossible; "do not worry about your life," in short, because worry destroys it.[8]

Summary

One cannot *do* science, much less cultivate the sciences of the spirit, in the same way that one manufactures anilines or elaborates essential oils. Philosophy, authentic wisdom, which after Christ is true theology, is not a dialectic stunt over and above any given object, nor are the humanities a series of clever somersaults over and above some interesting subject. My investigation must be part of my life, and I must not live *to* study, or discover, or know. Rather I must feel the need to study, to engage in intellectual activity, as an ingredient of my life; I must write, that is to say, etch the terrestrial Book of Life with a hard stylus, with my own life rather than with my pen.[9] Years ago, those people who burned their own writings seemed to me to be demented or lacking common sense. I am now beginning to understand them. . . .[10]

---

[7] Ac 20:24.

[8] See the ultimately Catholic posture of D. H. Lawrence. Cf. the introduction by Aldous Huxley to his *Selected Letters* (Penguin Books), no. 759, p. 14ff.

[9] See 2 Co 3:1ff.

[10] See the deep motives that St. Thomas gives as to why Christ did not write down his doctrine. *Sum. theol.* III, q. 42, a. 4.

One last criterion, one symptom, and one piece of advice: eliminate intellectual haste, which is different from intensity, as if life were measured by material velocity or our own temporality by the amount of times the Earth revolves around the Sun. The important thing—and in this case also the urgent one—is to live, to live authentically, to make an effort to live consciously, and to know how to express this in order to help life itself, that is to say, to contemplate.[11]

Not to give my ideas—these have no value whatsoever, and even less force; they are not testimony—but rather my life. Charity requires that you lay down your life for your friends. And this is also true for intellectuals: they must give their lives to others, they must substantialize their activity as far as possible, turning it into life. Only thus can they be saved. They must not worry about writing any kind of apologetics, but rather *be*, in any case, even in their own thought, an apologia—better yet, testimony. Truth need not be defended. It does not need propaganda (it is thirty years and twenty centuries of hidden life!)[12] It does not need guardians. On the other hand, I need to live it, to fulfill it in me in order to be.

Preaching consists in this, and not in propaganda—similar to commercial advertising. For my life, I need truth. I am, insofar as I am true—sinners are not, insofar as sinners, said the Angelic Doctor—and, in turn, truth reigns in the world insofar as people incarnate it. Man is not the light, but he must give testimony of it;[13] that is to say—and this is not a play on words—he must become transparent, thin, as St. John of the Cross would say.

Perhaps what I wanted to say at the beginning when I affirmed that all of my professional activity must emerge from a plenitude of inner life is now better understood; it must sprout, like a mature fruit, from an authentic internal vitality. I must also be able to say, about my own ideas, like Christ, "My teaching is not from myself; it comes from the one who sent me."[14] I am much better than my actions and all my activity; but, complementarily, this intellectual work of mine must not be a simple technique, my own manufacture, but rather, even in a degree more eminent than in artistic creation, a little bit of my heart, a piece of my soul, a part of my life. In the meantime, while the gestation is under way, I am quiet, I suffer, I mature, I pray. . . .

---

[11] "Ad hanc etiam [sc. ad contemplationem] omnes aliae operationes humanae ordinari videntur sicut ad finem. . . . ut sic, si recte considerentur, omnia humana officia servire videantur contemplatibus veritatem." Thomas Aquinas, *C. gentes*. III.37.6ff.

[12] "Quae autem sunt, a Deo ordinata sunt"—τεταγμέναι εἰσίν, Rom 13:1. Everything that is—αἱ δὲ οὐσαι—is put in order by God, or, as St. Thomas puts it, audaciously moving the punctuation: "quae a Deo sunt, ordinata sunt." *C. gentes*. III.81. It is not necessary, then, for us to organize too much.

[13] See Jn 1:8.

[14] Jn 7:16.

3

FREEDOM OF THOUGHT[1]

Ubi autem Spiritus Domini ibi libertas.

2 Co 3:17

We believe it appropriate to state, from the beginning, the specific problem that is going to be treated, so that it may be clearly isolated from many of the other problems to which it is intimately connected. We are not referring to freedom of expression, or freedom of opinion, or freedom of the press and propaganda, not even to freedom of consciousness. Rather, what we wish to exclusively study is *freedom of human thought* itself. The sole value of this study may lie precisely in this attempt to focus on the problem.

Proposal

In libertatem vocati estis.

Gal 5:13

When Western culture disregarded God—this is a historical fact—not exactly denying His existence, at first, but by being unfaithful to the extrinsic demands that arise from divine existence and essence for every created being—if God exists and is God, He cannot cease to have repercussions and an intimate influence on the most lowly atom of people's being and doing—Man had to base his life on himself, and consequently he turned to its most noble ingredient: reason or thought. This has been the slow and painstaking task of philosophers ever since Descartes—*cogito, ergo sum*—or since his nominalist precursors, if you will.

This attempt, which was initially formulated in a purely theoretical manner, constitutes the well-known critical problem; later it descends to the other layers of human culture, specifically to the political and social orders, and crystallizes in the classical formula of the French Revolution: the Declaration of the Rights of Man, so that, at most, we may only speak of the *recognition* of his rights and obligations.

Humanity believes it has the duty—and also the right—to revise its own values and dogmatically define what these "rights of man" must be. It is understandable

---

[1] From a talk at *Conversaciones Católicas Internacionales*, San Sebastián, September 1948.

that, among these, the first place be occupied by the right to a full development of the specific faculty that makes humans human: thinking.

So, what are the rights of thought? This question, identical in its human basis to that of the critical problem, and both of them subsidiary to the disengagement of human culture from God and from theology, is the one we have been formulating with the equivocal expression of *freedom of thought*.

*

Leaving aside the historical study of the vicissitudes that the issue of freedom of thought has undergone—sufficiently and amply dealt with to date—we will have to reflect on the latent philosophical problem that this question entails. Only then will the disorientation disappear, even among Catholics themselves, produced by merely proposing the problem. We cannot, in fact, approach the deep, latent problem of the mission of our thinking faculty as a mere issue of "freedom of thought."

It is necessary to make an effort, and this is the task of the intellectual, to break the structure of a proposal that obeys a series of unacceptable and outdated presuppositions. This is the reason why it is necessary to go back to the origins of current thought, because we do not wish to merely contradict one thesis by affirming its opposite, but rather to attack it from the roots, in its very formulation. This is why it is not enough to say that freedom of thought is something good in itself—who would doubt this?—but rather that it is detrimental to society, or that it harms higher interests, and so on. It is inappropriate and imprecise to speak of "freedom of thought," not because rational beings are not free, but because the alleged reality to which the concept expects to refer is nonexistent. Thought is not "free," in the same way that it is neither round nor heavy, nor is it properly good or bad.

Only if my being is thinking, if being is thought, may I attribute to it characteristics and properties that belong to other spheres of being. The last premise of this proposal and the climate within which it makes sense is rationalism.

When theology ceases to be relevant in Western culture and there is a consequent split in the unity of human knowledge, reason comes to occupy the foremost place in people's lives, and it must do what it can to discover the truth. Reason thus becomes the only criterion of truth—and therefore of salvation—and, as the ultimate judge of what is true and what is false, it claims to be the guide and savior of humanity.

But reason can only admit as true that of which it is sure—this is the first step from objective to subjective obedience—and it can only be sure of what it sees clearly and distinctly. Yet this evidence is essentially individual. My evidence will be my truth, and I will not be able to admit any criteria of authority or any light superior to that of my own reason. I will certainly—irrationally!—trust that *my* truth will also be seen with the same certainty by my neighbor, but there is no other means of communicating this, if my neighbor does not agree. My reason will be my supreme norm. This is why mistakes become highly scandalous, and why, consequently, Descartes relegates them to the sphere of will.

Yet the presence of error keeps torturing philosophers, and they will finally come to the point of relativizing truth. My reason is as valid as my neighbor's, and so is my evidence. Reason, on the other hand, is irrevocable and the only criterion of truth. There is no alternative but to allow absolute freedom to individual thought, as there is nothing superior that can regulate its operation or on whom it depends. From here it is but one step to idealism, on the one hand, and another step to the skeptical point of view that truth does not exist or that it is inaccessible to the human mind, on the other.

The political and sociological consequences of "liberal" doctrines all lie here. Philosophy put the mines in the field as well as the explosive charge. Knowing who set the fuse and who lit it will be of little consequence later.

It is true that a certain line of thought wants to react against this radical subjectivism and individualism. It is objective idealism. But since its ultimate premise is staunch rationalism, it limits itself to affirming the opposite theses without overcoming the problem. Reason, then, will be the only criterion of truth, but not individual reason—rather objective, deified thought, in which human beings participate at a greater or lesser degree of enlightenment. This reason will be absolutely free, but it will possess its own dialectics that people will necessarily have to obey. Whoever knows the process of reason in the world will dominate it. This is the transition from Hegel to Marx and to historical materialism.

We can now understand why liberal and Marxist forces clashed in the fields of culture and of action.

The Catholic Doctrine

Quia tu es qui liberas ab omni malo.

Ws 16:8

The doctrine of the Church maintains the true balance between the two extreme, exaggerated, and unilateral postures.

It is wrong to deny reason its rights and privileges, as it is equally wrong to exalt it unconditionally. There are two orders of knowledge, one natural and the other supernatural; the former is of reason, the latter, of faith. This twofold order cannot be overlooked in favor of one or the other (Pelagius, Baio, Jansen, etc.), but neither can it be fully unified, since the state of Man on earth will always be that of *viator*, pilgrim and traveler. That said, this twofold order is hierarchized and it is the purpose of human beings in this world to tend to its unification (see *Denz.*, 1795).

There is, then, an order of truths and even of certainties that differ from those faith provides us with (see, for example, *Denz.*, 558). Furthermore, not only is there a natural noetic order, but in the same religious sphere our reason alone, without any revelation and, therefore, without faith, can know a great amount of religious truths (cf., for example, *Denz.*, 1022, 1391, 1622, 1627, etc.). By itself, reason can acquire certainty of the existence of God (see, for example, *Denz.*, 1785–806, etc.), divine nature and attributes (*Denz.*, 1670), the soul's spirituality and immortality (*Denz.*, 1627), its freedom (*Denz.*, 1650) and all the *preambula fidei* in general (*Denz.*, 1171, 2025, etc.)

In addition, the use of reason *precedes* that of faith (cf. *Denz.*, 1651), and thus philosophy plays a fundamental role in the acquisition of truth (cf. *Denz.*, 1670). Reason has a certain autonomy and full responsibility within its own sphere (*ontonomy*), but it preserves a certain mandate even above and below its specific sphere of action, in the sense that it continues, at all times, to be the specifically human cognitive instrument.

But, at the same time, reason is neither omniscient nor omnipotent in Man. It is not the *only* means of knowing the truth, and with regard to religious truths, it is not even the main one (cf. *Denz.*, 1616ff., 1709, 1806, 1915, etc.), so that reason must submit itself to uncreated truth because it is not absolutely independent (cf. *Denz.*, 1642, 1708, 1789, 1810).

Human reason often errs and makes mistakes. As a result, there is a certain moral necessity for revelation even of the religious truths of the natural noetic order (cf. *Denz.*, 1618–34).

Human reason *is not independent*, and this is why it must be denied *absolute* freedom of opinion, speech and writing (cf. *Denz.*, 1614, 1666, 1674, 1679, 1690, 1779, 1877, 1932). Human reason is not "free" to believe, think, and say whatever it wants because its mental patterns are dependent on a superior form of knowledge that is faith, because Man's reason is not absolute and his will is damaged or, at the very least, dispossessed. Reason is not free because only the entire human being is free, and reason is not the entire human being as rationalism would have it. Ontic human wealth very much surpasses the merely rational. Man, in a word, is a contingent and finite being whose existence has been given to him, and *he is not in a position to make an autonomous declaration of his own rights.*

This is the precise and concrete doctrine of the Church. Doctrine that does not contradict the fact that, in the practical sphere, tolerance toward those who hold different opinions is advisable—and even necessary.

The Liberation of Thought

Et veritas liberabit vos.

Jn 8:32

The time has come for Catholic intellectuals to exercise this audacity of the spirit, which should really be their own, not only to *defend* the teachings of the Church, but also to free themselves from the yoke of four centuries of rationalist philosophers and turn themselves into the *makers*—fulfillers—of a new—and old—positive Christian vision of the world.

We must certainly liberate human thought, which does not mean we have to emancipate it from truth and faith, but rather free it, precisely, from the tyranny of reason.

This problem presents a twofold aspect: one is doctrinal and theoretical. It is simply the problem of the dependence or independence of reason. It is about the entire problem of Christian philosophy and of the noble philosophical—perhaps also Kantian—effort of looking for a place for faith, of finding a positive limit to reason. We are only interested in the proposal of this aspect here, not in the practical and political one.

Can we give the human beings who live in society absolute freedom of opinion? The theoretical solution we have mentioned is quite simple. It is not about limiting anybody's freedom, because it is reason itself that postulates a service and demands to be connected to a hierarchical order in which it does not occupy the very highest place. Thought in itself is not independent; it is not free, one could say, forcing the word a little. We could say that we must free it, if you will. Thought—like everything human—also needs a Redeemer.

On this issue, the Church has produced a series of documents of a disciplinary nature but full of very profound doctrinal content that has often escaped Catholics themselves. But there is still more. The classical encyclicals *Mirari vos* (Gregory XVI, 1832), *Immortale Dei* and *Libertas* (Leo XIII, 1885 and 1888) are not the richest on a theological level, rather it is the Vatican Council I itself, and more specifically the celebrated third chapter of the constitution *Dei Filius*, that provides a more profound doctrine on the role of thought in the life of Man and, therefore, on its freedom.

The heart of the matter lies not so much in a political and practical problem of method as in a vision of the intellectual life of Man on earth, and specifically the role of reason in human life.

Human knowledge is rational par excellence; yet is not exclusively rational. It is sustained by other types of knowledge and exceeded by faith as a superior form of knowledge. The formula of philosophy as *ancilla theologiae* does not represent a barbaric and despotic expression of a clerical and theocratic age: instead, it indicates that the role of reason—the instrument of philosophy—is not precisely that of the champion and discoverer of truth to guide us through this world and *save us*, but rather that its role is auxiliary, though valuable and indispensable. Reason possesses autonomy in its own field—ontonomy—but without lethal separatisms.

Simply put, reason is not independent, as the formula *freedom of thought* would have us believe within the liberal culture that forged it.

Theology was attacked for not being a free science as it received its principles from elsewhere than reason. Besides the fact that this objection supposes nothing less than ignorance of what faith claims to be, philosophy itself has currently overcome the rational conception that only ascribed the title of science to what claimed to be completely free of assumptions.

Thought is free as soon as it determines itself in an intrinsic principle: truth within reach of reason, but only imperfectly insofar as there is another truth inaccessible to it that we are given by faith. This is why thought is free in its own sphere, but this sphere is not that of complete human life on earth. The field of reason is not the real area in which Man's life moves. That is why to attribute absolute freedom to reason is to condemn human beings, as it means enslaving everything that is not reason within them. Human thought will be that much freer, in its correct sense, the more dependent it is on truth, its supreme norm.

Because human thought is inserted within a natural and supernatural cosmic order, it is doubly dependent on both orders.

*

The natural dependency of reason is *ontological*, on the one hand, and *historical*, on the other.

Because of the former, our thought depends first and foremost on things themselves—unlike in idealism—on the external object that triggers our thinking activity. This activity, through its own laws, also constrains reason to submit itself to things. In the second place, it depends on countless external, though nevertheless ontological, criteria that do not constitute the internal structure of our thinking but rather limit it externally. Our intellectual and discursive capacity is limited; our perspectives are, necessarily, partial, and so forth.

Furthermore, there are influences of the historical, contingent, concrete, and circumstantial type. These influences can also be internal, such as our special temperament, character, and so on, or merely external, such as the environment, cultural climate, the temporal cycle in which one exists, and so on. Present-day philosophy knows much about this, and psychoanalysis perhaps even too much.

*

The dependency of our reason in the face of the supernatural order is also twofold. Reason thus finds itself informed—illuminated, according to the Vatican Council I—by faith.

The first dependency is habitual and profound by virtue of sanctifying grace. Our intellect participates, by means of faith, in God's own self-knowledge, and thus our intelligence reaches the region of the supernatural.

The second dependency refers to its single acts and is more accidental; it influences us constantly in our intellect, as an active, though extrinsic, principle. These are particular graces and inspirations.

*

Thanks to this multiple dependency and its harmonic framework, reason can perform its task. *Its category is not freedom, but truth.* Only true thought is free, because it *achieves freedom through truth*. Only truth liberates thought and the actual thinking subject, as freedom does not mean absolute and irrational uncertainty, but spiritual order.

Freedom is not a supreme value but a functional one, and it must, therefore, be in relation to the *good* that conditions it. Freedom exists in will and not in intelligence, even though the intellect is the root of freedom, insofar as only intelligence possesses knowledge of the end and of the means that lead up to it, which permit freedom of will.

Attaining this alleged freedom of thought means truncating and mutilating Man. Man in fact (not thought) is properly free, and so he will become freer and freer as each of his integral parts will harmoniously and hierarchically fulfill its own mission.

Nobody thinks of claiming complete freedom for our lungs, making them independent from the rest of our organism. Instead, the more dependent and linked they are to the totality of the human body, the freer they are. Furthermore, in order for Man to be able to breathe—that is, to think—freely, it is necessary for him to live in an environment that is healthy and free of miasmas and atmospheric pollution. Freedom of thought is a lethal cancer that is the fruit of rationalism. If Man were merely reason, we could then give this freedom greater meaning, since Man would then be really free; but to defend the separatism of one part of the human being, *mistaking independence with freedom*, is to commit a crime against Man himself.

Freedom of thought in the "liberal" sense claims that we must let individuals think whatever they *want*. But what do individuals want to think? Either they will want to think the *truth*—and for this they will let themselves be influenced by it and they will be disposed to avidly capture all of its manifestations, wherever they may come from—or they will want to think what they deem convenient by virtue of extra-intellectual interests, good or bad. In one case or the other, thought is dependent. If its interests are crooked, it will also fail in the acquisition of the truth.

Man is given his existence, and his reason, and he must conquer freedom by obeying the intrinsic laws of his being. Ultimately, only truth will set us free.[2]

*

The consequences of this are already self-evident. Individual human thought is infallible in its dialectical functioning, in such a way that, even if we wanted to, we could not force it to believe in absurdities. But it is not the supreme norm of truth. Therefore, individuals cannot rely exclusively on their reason—on its free examination—in order to decide on their own beliefs and convictions by themselves.

This may be humiliating for Man, who believed he was independent of God and master of his own destiny. But this does not make it less true that in order to put themselves on the path to conquering true freedom, people must accept that true freedom is not freedom of thought, but rather freedom of truth and of our very own being: being children of God.[3]

---

[2] See Jn 8:32.
[3] See 1 Jn 3:2.

4

On Theology and the University[1]

Ο λόγος του θεού ού δέδεται

2 Tim 2:9[2]

The Transcendence of the Problem

This issue is being discussed in Spanish public life and in Catholic life all over the world.[3] This time, significantly, we are not lagging behind, and I would like to recall—appropriately or inappropriately, I do not know—some principles that seem to me essential for the correct formulation of the question. Speculation also has its rights, but I do not want to insist now on the importance and transcendence of the poor, disdained θεωρία. The only thing I will say is that prudence—even political—is, above all, an intellectual virtue.

Nowadays everybody recognizes that one era is ending and another beginning, and furthermore, we have the conviction—and the experience—that ideas govern the world, though with a minimum discrepancy of one generation, a tribute that all human beings who live in this *subcrucial* world pay to time, death, and humility. Therefore, this problem that now concerns Spain has a singular importance and transcendence. And we may perhaps need a good dose of intellectual audacity in order to face up to an unavoidable series of consequences that may be somewhat distant from the current state of things but that obviously derive from Christian principles and that, furthermore, have been traditional within the Church. Are we not saying that a new world is beginning? There is intellectual cowardice that is more catastrophic than military defeats.

It has already become commonplace to say that our current civilization is paganized, that there is a divorce between the modern world and the remaining Christian world, that there is a fatal abyss between the clerical and secular milieus

---

[1] A summarized version of this study was published in *Revista de Educación* 16 (1953): 79–82.

[2] *Verbum Dei non est alligatum.* "Theo-logy" cannot be bound.

[3] The general topic of the World Congress of Pax Romana celebrated in Canada in September 1952 was about the "mission of the University," and the main problem discussed was the Church/university relationship.

within Christianity itself. All of this may be true: the structures have changed, as have the very ways of thinking and even the spheres of interest. But if we do not wish to be satisfied with negative criticism, utopian longing for an irreversible past, or the temporary remedies of simple healers or witch doctors, we must delve into the region of ideas itself, into the ultimate foundation of our culture, into the theological roots of the problem.

Ultimately there is a serious problem involving both theology, as it is about the shaping of human values through faith, and Christian culture itself, whose future depends, in part, on the verdict of this question.

What Theology Is

As far as the negative is concerned, all believers agree: The evil of present-day society lies in the disengagement between religion and earthly life. We also agree on the positive: unity must be *restored*, the split must be *repaired*, or even more precisely, human beings must be *redeemed*, Redemption must be reenacted and applied, and we must make its fruits descend to all of the activities of Man and society.

So then, one of the means, and there must also be agreement here, consists in getting theology—the science of God (divine *Logos*)—to inform and impregnate earthly culture, the science of men (human *logos* and *ethos*). And descending even further—and I am confident that there are also no great discrepancies here—it is obvious that the best way to achieve this—*hic* and in a *nunc* of a few years—is by once again establishing the unity of the "Universitas litteratum," the synthesis of culture, under the supremacy of theology.

But theology—after having been isolated for so many years (there are Christians who no longer recognize its features) and having deteriorated in its confinement—is not an application form with Latin recipes which, if conveniently applied, yield the solution to every problem. Theology—*teologia viae*[4]—the kind of theology that is on a pilgrimage, and theologians know this well, is not an elixir that has been manufactured beforehand and given to us to cure all ailments. True theology accompanies Man in his pilgrimage on earth, and it is nothing but the worship that Man—who is, after all, an intellectual being—that his mind, his λόγος, if you wish to be more precise, renders to God by listening to His message and trying to decipher it. "Love is the cause of the Revelation of the mysteries," says the Common Doctor in a verdict that can be applied to God and to Man, to the natural and to the supernatural.[5]

Speculative theology itself, according to St. Thomas—but is there any reason to take refuge in the Angelic Doctor?[6]—is a *normal* expansion of faith, of real faith, *quaerens intellectum*, which looks for the understanding of reality, the spiritual

---

[4] See Thomas Aquinas, *Sum. theol.* I, q.1, a.2.
[5] Thomas Aquinas, *Super Ioannem* XIV.4.
[6] See, e.g., *Sum. theol.* I, q.1, a.4, 5.

adoration of the Mystery and not the approval or benevolence of routine; it is δόγμα, not δόξα.

Theology is not, therefore, either a metaphysics of the supernatural nor a simple pastoral and pious experience cloaked in science *ad usum clericorum*, but rather the total human effort—intellectual, if you wish, which is not a synonym of *rational* but more one of *spiritual*—to understand and grasp the meaning of God's revelation. Christian theology, which is the fullness of theology, culminates in the union with Christ, the maximum manifestation of God, and comes down, here on earth, to the loving intellection of the complete message, incarnate not only in the doctrine but in Christ himself.[7] Theology is supernatural, that is to say, it is charismatic wisdom. It essentially implies faith, a free gift of God. Theology is *intellectus fidei*, and since the object of Christian faith is Christ, bearer—χαρακτήρ, figure—of the fullness of Revelation, theology is *intellectus Christi, sensus Christi* in its purest ontological signification (νους, διάνοια).[8] Yet this *intellectus fidei*, the basis of what will unluckily be called speculative theology, is not disconnected from the *auditus fidei*, the source of so-called positive theology.[9] *Fides ex auditu*,[10] and the intellect is only applied to hear better.

Theology, Responsibility of the Whole Church

This is the Catholic, universal sense of theology, and this is how the Church has always taught and defended it (see the foundational bulls of medieval universities as an example!), according at least to those who think that theology is neither the prerogative nor the privilege of the clergy, but rather a requirement for the Christian mind. The priest has a special obligation to know theology—in order to be able to fulfill his marvelous "ministry of the word"[11]—but not an exclusive right. To want to monopolize theology would be that awful sin condemned by the Gospel: "Woe to you, scribes and Pharisees, you hypocrites, who close the kingdom of Heaven to men! Neither will you go in yourselves nor do you allow others to go who want to."[12] This is why the Church hierarchy, which considers itself responsible for Christ's teaching mandate,[13] has always deemed its own educational role, the teaching of people from elemental catechism to the highest speculation, as one of its most basic duties.

---

[7] See the theological definition we are given of Christ in Heb 1:3. And of us: Rom 8:29.

[8] See 1 Co 2:16 and the marvelous text of 1 Jn 5:20. To know and to be. This is true theology!

[9] See the authentic Scholastic mentality in M. D. Chenu, *Introduction à l'étude de Saint Thomas d'Aquin* (Paris: Vrin, 1950), 60.

[10] Rom 10:17.

[11] See what the Apostles say about their own task in Ac 6:4.

[12] Mt 23:13.

[13] See Mt 28:19.

The Church maintains and guarantees the purity of this theology, and it guides human efforts to reach the comprehension of the total Christ.[14] In any case, the Church is not only hierarchy. The Church is the Church and the hierarchy is the hierarchy of this Church, Mystical Body of Christ, to which even the angels belong.[15] The most visible maximum authority of the Church[16] insistently recalls this highly elemental and tautological affirmation, which is sometimes forgotten. Through baptism we are members of the Church, and now that the fear and the danger of the Protestant exaggeration of the "royal priesthood"[17] of every Christian has passed, the traditional doctrine that everyone who is baptized is a "minister of Christ" and responsible for the church is once again repeated to us.[18]

Theology is obviously the Church's concern. Furthermore, there can be no authentic Christian theology outside the Church, and a theologian's personal investigation is an act of the entire Church community, of that family in which "everybody carries another and is in turn carried by the other."[19] But this does not mean that theology must be the exclusive occupation of the hierarchy or of priests, monks, and religious people. We have been told by Pope Pius XI that the theological culture and education of Christian intellectuals must be, at the very least, as good as their professional knowledge. And this means something. "The laity must urgently come to take part, in some way, in the Church's hierarchical apostolate."[20] And one cannot participate in an apostolate without knowing what one has to hand. Saying that theology is a clerical science is just as false as affirming that carrying out mental orations is a privilege of the religious. And some decades ago, in certain circles, both of these things seemed to be so.

Theology and University

This very same principle of Catholicity, of the Church's ecumenicity and therefore of theology, can also be illuminated from another side of the question. If theology must be universal because it is "Catholic," the university must be Catholic because it is university, *uni-versitas*.

---

[14] See Ph 3:12.

[15] See Thomas Aquinas, *Sum. theol.* III, q.8, a.4.

[16] See, for example, Pius XI, letter to the patriarch of Lisbon.

[17] 1 Pet 2:9.

[18] "This apostolic work, carried out according to the mind of the Church, consecrates the layman as a kind of 'Minister to Christ' in the sense which St. Augustine explains as follows: 'When, Brethren, you hear Our Lord saying: where I am there too will My servant be, do not think solely of good bishops and clerics.' You too in your way minister to Christ by a good life, . . . by preaching His Name and teaching to whom you can." Pius XII, *Summi Pontificatus* (October 20, 1939). See also *Mediator Dei* (November 20, 1947).

[19] St. Gregory the Great, *In Ezech.* II.1.5, recalling the sublime Pauline statement in Gal 6:2.

[20] Pius XI, *Letter to the Episcopate of the Philippines* (January 18, 1939).

This is why their mutual connection is much more profound than a merely juridical approach to the matter could suppose.

It is a constitutive relationship, in such a way that university, without theology, betrays its most intimate essence.

From here emerges an internal nexus between university and Church since, as we have seen, theology is an activity of the Church.

And finally, the relationship is reciprocal, since theology as such also calls for a university.

There are three serious, though timeworn and traditional affirmations that we will briefly expose.

The University Requires Theology

Not only is there a significant historical motive that bears witness to the fact that theology is essential to the university, but the integral concept of the university itself also requires the vital presence of theology within it.

In fact, if the university aspires to be something more than a factory of degrees or a disheveled mosaic of disciplines; if the university aspires to be something more than an institute of technology; if the university aspires, thus, to be a true *universitas*, which incorporates *unitas* and *diversitas* (philologists forgive me!), then it must form the individual man for a diversity of occupations that used to be called liberal and are called intellectual today.

Only theology can provide this unity within diversity, both in reference to human beings (α) as well as to the concerns of the sciences themselves (β).

(α) With regard to the subject, our time period, which is responsible for the experience of failure and the collapse of the myth of Man as an autonomous—bourgeois—and detached being, does not have great difficulty in recognizing not only that when man wants to be an angel, he is a beast,[21] but also that when he contents himself with being rational, thus naturally human, he also acts like a beast, because human beings have been called to be something more than mere human nature; and this calling, this vocation, has repercussions in the deepest part of their being, making them unable to live in an alleged state of pure nature.

Man cannot be formed without knowing him, but nothing "is truly and fully human except what is Christian."[22] This is why only religion—that is, faith, and consequently theology—is the sole lead for an integrally human formation. The consequences of this are within our reach. . . .

(β) It is also impossible to find a synthesis of human sciences if these are abstracted from theology. Human knowledge does not allow itself to be integrated into any natural unit. Our century has also become disenchanted with the naïve rationalism

---

[21] Let us recall Pascal's famous declaration: "L'homme n'est ni ange ni bête, et le malheur veut que qui veut faire l'ange fait la bête." *Pensées* (ed. Brunschvicq), n. 358.

[22] Pius XI in his last Christmas message, in 1939, few weeks before his death.

that promised people it would eliminate mystery; consequently, the philosophy of our times is, whether consciously or unconsciously, looking for the lost sapiential nature that it can only recuperate by integrating itself in theology, that is to say, by ceasing to be a pretentious supreme science and turning to a higher service.[23] The imprint of the supernatural has also reached the human intellect and, consequently, "religious truth is not only a part of general knowledge, but its precise condition."[24] *Philosophia ancilla theologiae* because reason must be guided by faith.

Human reason can handle many things, but on its own it cannot make the university fulfill its mission of synthesizing all domains of science into a harmonic unit.[25] If this unit is not the intrinsic unity that only theology can attain—unless philosophy is idealized and science is reduced to an anemic and disembodied world of essences—then we fall into the artificial unification of the university at the illegitimate service of totalitarian or nationalist political interests. Only theology is able to guarantee the authentic freedom of the university. The entire history of European nationalism is good proof of this.

Thus, if the university desires to be an authentic and integral university, it needs the binding and synthesizing—better still, liberating—role of theology; only truth shall make us free.[26] This is how the Church and tradition have always understood it.

In any event, theology thus understood cannot be one subject among many others; but it must also not be deprived—with this excuse—of its scientific nature. On the other hand, we cannot expect to impose it upon every professor either. This is why theology must be present in each faculty as a center of irradiation that reaches the hearts and minds—and the encephalon—of all university members, including professors. (The specific way of achieving this is not the issue here.) But at the same time, in order to discover these internal links, in order to elaborate this Christian vision of science, in order to shape the human life of our generation—not that of the thirteenth or sixteenth centuries—we urgently require its immanent justification as well as a theological laboratory, let us call it a faculty, where this work is carried out in positive symbiosis with the other faculties. What is more, only then will theology cease to be a useless queen dethroned from the sciences: it will be able to direct the spiritual life of humanity with the superiority granted to transcendent

---

[23] "Philosophica scientia," as St. Bonaventure puts it in a lapidary way: "via est ad alias scientias; sed qui ibi vult stare cadit in tenebras" (*Collationes de septem donis Spiritus Sancti*, IV.12 [ed. Quaracchi, V.476]).

[24] J. H. Newman, *Naturaleza y fin de la educación universitaria* (Spanish translation; Madrid, 1946), 125; partial translation of *The Idea of a University* (London: Basil Montagu Pickering, 1873).

[25] "University does not only mean juxtaposition of faculties that are foreign to one another, but rather synthesis of all objects of knowledge . . . modern progress, increasingly advanced specializations, make this synthesis more necessary than ever. . . . To fulfill this synthesis, as far as possible, is the purpose of the university." Pius XII in his last—and often quoted—*Speech to the Representatives of the Catholic Institutes of France*.

[26] See Jn 8:32.

authority. Only then does the Christian have the right to overcome—and even, for that matter, to scorn—the terrestrial.[27]

It is very instructive to observe that the birth of universities in India was entirely parallel to the genesis of Western university knowledge. There too, both in the early and celebrated University of Taxila (the old *Takṣhaśilā*), already existent in the seventh century before Christ, and in the most famous university of India, Nalanda, knowledge was unified by religious concern and it was all integrated within a broad theology, as religious *Weltanschauung*. There, too, teaching begins alongside the temples and monasteries, and is accomplished through direct contact between masters and disciples. And then, later on, the *āśrama* or *gurukula* (from *guru*, master) acquires a certain autonomy and turns into the university proper.[28]

The Catholic University

If theology is a function of the Church and an essential constituent of the university, it evidently follows that "it needs the Church for its integrity"[29] (that of the university). If humanity has a supernatural destiny and the Church is responsible for its attaining this destiny and the trustee of the means to do so, consequently the entire classical doctrine of the Church's rights of teaching emerges.[30]

So, after everything we have said, the following observations appear to be quite obvious.

The Catholic university is not, primarily, a restrictive denomination, as if *Catholic* were merely a limiting adjective for the noun *university*, a peculiar type of university; conversely it is the fullness of university, it is the universal university, that has developed all the potential it contained within it. When we speak of the rights of Catholics, we often forget that our rights are universal because of a twofold title of creation and redemption. We must not lose sight of the ideal, nor of the rights, even when we find ourselves in situations very distant from the right order of things.

However, this does not imply that there does not exist a more restricted meaning of a Catholic university. It does exist, but even then it is not synonymous with a clerical university or "religious" in the canonical sense of the word. Certainly, a Catholic university means *ecclesiastical*, but this term, summarizing so much

---

[27] This atmosphere is still patent within the golden stones of the building of the glorious University of Salamanca—whose official funeral will take place on the day they turn it into a museum—in one of whose classrooms one can still read, "Theologiae sacrae qua, rerum divinarum cognitione hominum mentes imbutae, terrena despiciant, coelum votis petant, beatamque iam nunc incipiant vivere vitam."

[28] See the interesting work of S. R. Dongerkery, *Universities and Their Problems* (Bombay: Hind Kitabs, 1948), 16ff.

[29] Newman, *Naturaleza*, 33.

[30] See the encyclicals by Leo XIII, *Immortale Dei* (November 1, 1885); *Libertas* (June 20, 1888); *Sapientiae Christianae* (January 10, 1890); Pius XI, *Divini illius Magistri* (December 31, 1929), etc.

implicit reasoning—taken in its double sense—is where the confusion has its roots. In everyday language, in the living language of this current age that is drawing to a close, *ecclesiastical* has become a synonym of *clerical* (and *clerical* has acquired a somewhat pejorative nuance), but the secular also form part of the *ecclesia*.[31] *Nos utique sumus Ecclesia*.[32]

The specific trait of the Catholic university is not, therefore, that it is run by clergy, but rather that it is "in-formed," shaped by the Church.[33] This shaping presents two aspects. One, judicial, by means of which the Church—and here is where the hierarchy must intervene—has control of such a university in matters of its jurisdiction. And another aspect, essential in nature, by virtue of which a Catholic university is not a university in which religion is taught *in addition to* science and in which antireligious manifestations are prohibited, but rather one in which theology intrinsically (but this is redundant) "in-forms"—in the same way that charity informs, invigorates, the other virtues of a Christian in grace—the different disciplines of human knowledge. The true problems of Christian culture lie here, and not elsewhere.

Theology Calls for a University

We still have to clarify one more statement that complements the earlier ones. Until now, we have said that the university needs theology and, consequently, the Church. ("The Church is responsible for the salvation of the City."[34]) Well, then, we now add that theology, in turn, needs the university.

The damage caused to Western culture by theology's banishment has been frequently and profoundly studied, but the decline and anemia that the sacred science has suffered in its secular confinement has been less commented upon, despite the numerous pontifical testimonies[35] that confirm this and urge us to, once again, connect to that theology of the past that had not yet divorced from the university. It is significant that it is not recommended that we return to those precious *Summae*

---

[31] Pius XII says that lay believers—please take this seriously—"are in the front line of Church life; through them the Church is the animating principle of human society. Therefore, they in particular ought to have an ever-clearer consciousness not only of belonging to the Church, but of being the Church, that is to say, the community of the faithful on earth under the leadership of the Pope, the common Head, and of the bishops in communion with him" (*Allocution to the Consistory*, February 20, 1946).

[32] St. Peter Damian, *Sermon 72, in dedication Ecclesiae* (PL 144.909).

[33] Pius XI, *Divini illius Magistri* (1929), 77; John XXIII, *Prima Romana Synodus* Vatican City: Typis Polyglottis Vaticanis, 1960), art. 326.

[34] Cardinal Suhard, *Le Prêtre dans la Cité* (Paris, 1949), 43.

[35] The testimonies are countless: the encyclical *Aeterni Patris* (Leo XIII, August 4, 1879); the "motu proprio" *Doctoris Angelici* (Pius X, June 29, 1914); the encyclical *Studiorum Ducem* (Pius XI, June 29, 1923); the encyclical *Humani Generis* (Pius XII, August 12, 1950). For the testimonies from Alexander IV (1254) to Pius X (1914), see J. J. Bertheir, *Sanctus Thomas Aquinas "Doctor Comunis" Ecclesiae* (Rome, 1914).

and *Commentaries* of the sixteenth and seventeenth centuries, apparently more developed than those of the thirteenth century. But this is a very complex problem that we are not interested in reviving here.

The truth is that authentic theology, in fact, calls for the "in-formation" and even the transformation of all human values and knowledge, and it does not tolerate being disconnected from life and culture. Theology is not an arcane and esoteric science, "for nothing is hidden but it will be made clear, nothing secret but it will be made known and brought to light."[36] God is neither an object for a museum nor the monopoly of a few. Neither God nor theology can be relegated to the ambit of the sacristy or of the clerical.[37] And this has always been the criteria of the Church, which created the universities for that. "The Church cannot shut itself up, lifeless, in the depths of its temples and thus abandon the mission that divine Providence has entrusted to it, that of forming the complete man," said the Supreme Pontiff.[38]

If the mere natural sciences need to be fertilized by theology, the latter needs the entire world as a field in order to develop. Certainly, the theologian receives his object—revelation—from God Himself through the Church and elaborates it in the supernatural light of faith; but both revelation, which needs natural materials, as well as faith, which has an impact on reason, require the cultivation of the human, of the humanities, if you wish, even of culture, as an indispensable requisite for the understanding of the divine Message. In the end, God manifests Himself to human beings. This must be properly understood; it is not about defending a refined civilization as necessary for theology—it will always be true that revelation is made to the small and the humble[39]—but rather an authentic spiritual culture, which is also necessary to understand the parables of the gospel.

For a twofold reason, theology needs the university, considered the collective place of the cultural vectors of an epoch.

1. On the one hand, because in order to develop a Christian vision of science and of the world, we must know both of them in their concrete and existential reality. The philosopher can perhaps deal with pure and "rootless" essences, but the theologian can never cultivate disembodied speculation. Theology is essentially wisdom of salvation for the concrete man. This is an urgent task for the theology of our time, and for this it not only needs knowledge of science but also dialogue with the entire world. The revelation of God to men is not a divine exhibition of His greatness to belittle us and stress His own transcendence, but rather a communication of His love to elevate us to Him and unite Himself with us. This is the very reason why theology looks for all human values wherever they may lie, to take the message of redemption and its profound transformation to them.

---

[36] Lk 8:17.

[37] It is a cultural fact that not so long ago the name of God could not be pronounced in science: it was reserved for the scientist's own beliefs.

[38] Pius XII, *Speech to the New Cardinals*, February 20, 1946.

[39] See Mt 11:25; Lk 10:21, etc.

But for this, it must know them intimately. And it is then that theology itself expands and acquires its full integrity and its saving function.[40]

2. But there is another reason, more profound than the previous one, through which theology cries out for help from the university (understood, as we have said, as the exponent of the culture of an epoch) to constitute itself fully in theology. An integral theology cannot happen outside the university. An encapsulated theology, without any contact with the world and with reality—even the historical one—cannot be a λόγος του θεου, as *Verbum Dei non est alligatum*,[41] the Word of God cannot be secluded, no matter how artistic the cloister in which we wish to confine it.[42] There was a time—not over as yet—in which there was an attempt to confine theology to monasteries and convents, but nowadays the barriers of this sad imprisonment are already being taken down. St. Paul himself speaks of a "barrier of separation" that we must break down.[43]

In fact, theology needs all of human culture, crystallized in the university, because the very concepts on which all theology will build its enormous edifice are the concepts that the culture of each time lends to it. The inspired authors and Christ himself are no exceptions to this law: they speak with the language and the concepts of the culture of their time.

Theology will later make the colossal effort of purifying all of these concepts and transcending them analogically. This is the great problem of the *analogia fidei*, which it sometimes seems we forget and seek to substitute with a formal *analogia vocis*. If theology does not want to degenerate into a mere *repetitorium* of formulas, it cannot ever separate itself from the cultural reality in which it lives; that is to say, it cannot separate from the university. Furthermore: it alone has enough vital power to create a university around itself. This has been the Christian phenomenon—of the past and the present centuries, for example—in which Theology, after having been exiled from the existing universities, has created a cultural world around itself (pontifical universities, "Catholic" universities, seminaries, etc.).

Yet this is not the normal path, that of creating a small protoplasm with which to be able to exchange vital substances. Theology cannot enclose itself in a small parcel of culture or of society, because its mission is to penetrate the bloodstream of all humanity. And for this, present-day theology cries out for its original union with universities.

---

[40] Saint Bonaventure speaks of a "prostitution of the spirit" referring to "*scientia sine devotione.*" Something similar could be said with regard to *Theologia sine scientia.*

[41] 2 Tim 2:9.

[42] Those who fear this use of the Scripture should recall that St. Thomas defends that "omnis veritas quae, salva litterae circumstantia, potest divinae scripturae aptari, est eius sensus." *Quaest. Disp. de Pot. Dei* q. 4, a. 1.

[43] Ep 2:14.

Militant Theology

This is the living and perennial struggle of the theology of the militant Church. The theology of the pilgrim man on earth, member of a Church that is ready for battle, must forge itself in struggle. *Pectus facit theologum!* Furthermore, in this full contact with the world, theology constantly renews itself, and the world, in turn, receives and lives off the uniting energy of theological wisdom. This can be said to have been the constant tone of all pontifical documents of the modern epoch on priestly culture.[44]

Mature people of the older generation are so alarmed by the modern world's process of secularization that it is understandable that they cannot truly believe that what we are dealing with here is the opposite, ascending movement. Let us not fear that theology will become secularized when it comes into contact with the world. This "terrible" word, "secularization," was divested of all of its virulence when it was baptized by the Church and even assimilated into its ascetic language. There are Christians who sanctify themselves, even more, who live a life of perfection *in saeculo*, in the world.[45] But this is not only a judicial measure; it also implies the maturity of the Church with regard to its connections with this *aeon*. All of this requires a profound theological effort. This is the very voice of hierarchy[46] and of Scholastic tradition.

Culture, for a Christian, is none other than the human instrument that is available to him to apprehend the meaning of revelation and, consequently, of his own life. And if we must rise up to God—*per ea quae facta sunt*[47]—through creatures, and the Lord speaks to us through creatures, theology cannot ignore the knowledge of any created being, not only to illuminate it with a new light, but also to prosper thanks to the contribution of a new creature of the Most High. All things are a reflection of the divine λόγος.

---

[44] See, for example, Pius XI, *Ad Catholici Sacerdotii Fastigium* (December 20, 1935); and Pius XII, *Menti Nostrae* (1950), etc.

[45] See the transcendental Apostolic Constitution of Pius XII, *Provida Mater Ecclesia* (February 2, 1947).

[46] "Yes, be present everywhere, on the front lines of the struggle of intelligence, in the hour in which it makes an effort to consider the problems of man and of nature in the new dimensions which are now at hand," Pius XII reminded Catholic intellectuals at a World Congress of Pax Romana (August 19–26, 1950).

[47] Rom 1:20.

5

ON THE CHRISTIAN MEANING OF LIFE

Realism and Microdoxy

Theological Realism in Culture[1]

I could exemplify my assertions indefinitely, and even arbitrarily, as it would be the same to mention the latest movie or any theatrical production, as well as the deaf—and subterranean—Spanish discussion on the Catholic university, and the world of novels, art, or history.

But what use is it to me if a story culminates in God and everything ends well and "edifyingly" if God is not also the beginning and motor, if it does not also originate in God? If I acknowledge that theology is the queen of sciences, why must I keep it at a distance, as if it were the esoteric princess of the *universitas* of our culture? Why is an inauthentic apostolate afraid of truth and the light of day? Why should we ascribe the adjective "Christian" to things and to human activities instead of finding a more valuable substantive nucleus that would show its *existential* thirst for redemption?

Interestingly enough, estimations of the morality of any cultural work are almost always expressed in the negative: the absence of affirmations or situations that could offend Man's upright sentiments, . . . and they usually forget the positive aspects, its connection to God, its profound aspect of truth or of error. There is nothing as immoral as error, and a truncated truth presented as a whole—for example, the mentality of a Romantic novel or a trivial movie—is a flagrant, immoral lie.

I want to state the following: If we truly wish to collaborate in the construction of a Christian culture, the good intentions of a sermon are not enough, nor is writing an edifying work. On the other hand, neither can we stand idly by and merely go with the flow; it is not enough to well-meaningly—and naïvely—clothe our thirst for the apostolate using "modern" and "current" forms. Let me make it even clearer: We cannot achieve anything positive, lasting, and above all, true with mere patches, scaffolding, or injections. Let whoever reads understand. Christian culture will be Christian if, to begin with, it is true.

---

[1] Published in *Arbor* 64 (1951): 595–97, with the title *Etiquetas cristianas y realismo teológico en nuestra cultura.*

I would like to commend a simpler and truer method. Less diplomacy, less strategy—less fear and false prudence—and more courage and sincerity. I would like to cry out for the return of authentic and singular realism, of true and exclusive reality such as it *is*. I believe theological realism must be the keynote of a renewed Christian culture. Things are *one* way, and they do not hold up any other way.

This is not about demonstrating anything or about writing thesis novels, rather simply about showing, discovering, making it possible to discover the profound and real dimension of things. It is about falling more in love with the whole truth and putting our hope—active and operating virtue—on this truth.

There is no need to moralize our literature by drawing a veil over it or cutting it up—strange and sad symbolism of those who are incapable of anything else. Rather we must penetrate deeper into human, personal, social, historical, and economical situations, and ultimately discover God; if He exists, He must have a direct, decisive, and *ultimate* influence on all the events of the universe. It is one thing to go to God by means of a short-circuit based on a pedantic name that exempts us from looking for the passionate second causality, and another to disconnect these immediate causes from their first divine Mover.

It is difficult to explain myself in a few words. I believe the Christian style of our nascent epoch must be realism, an authentic realism that attempts to see things as they are, and coming from God, if possible. And I call this realism—this new style of the Christian era that is humbly and flourishingly being reborn—theological because only a misty ray of faith, like an ultraviolet light, can reveal to us the intimate and real structure of the things and situations of the created world.

There was a time in which the much debated and problematic impossibility of experiencing supernatural grace was used as an easy excuse to disregard the study of God's intimate action in the created world. Along with this and other, more serious neglect, God began turning into a superfluous hypothesis.

If God's universal causality is true and must become manifest in any of Man's constructions that aspire to sustain itself in reality, of even greater importance is the factual ontic and historical primacy of Christ as a point of attraction—or of repulsion—of all people considered individually and collectively. This cosmic Christ in which everything rests and because of whom all things have been made has varied the very structure of this hypothetical human nature, and consequently, any cultural development that does not consider the Christian axiological shift may be very "moral" for a good humanist, but it contains the greatest of immoralities, as whoever is not with Him is against Him.[2]

I repeat that it is not about invoking Providence inappropriately in order to explain our failures or justify our laziness; it is not about *placing* God in everything, but rather about *finding* him—*ab intra*—in all things, and discovering the intimate plot of events and of beings, in whatever measure we can, with the help of faith, since reason—theological realism—cannot help us here. If faith gives us a fuller and

---

[2] Mt 12:30.

more exact vision of the world, why do we have to ignore it with the excuse that not everyone accepts it? When we carry out apologetics before those who do not believe, then we can do without faith; but with our brothers and within a Christian culture we cannot clip our own wings. There also exists a duty of charity toward Christians; there is also the best of all apologetics, which is to show the fullness of the Christian vision of all things. When faith is not used, it is not utilized. It also becomes atrophied.

This is not the place to lay the foundation for and explain this theological realism, but only to proclaim it as the new *style* of the nascent Christendom of our times. And I say "to lay the foundation for and explain," although it might be better to say "discover and obtain," since an intrinsically Christian vision of things has not yet been achieved. A synthesis between the specifically natural—for example, the mission of the lawyer, the doctor, the engineer, the employer, and the Christian worker *as such*—and the supernatural is yet to be achieved. And the only route to construct this integral anthropology is to live an inner fullness that gradually reveals the Christian solution through supernatural connaturality—consonance—with problems, but also step by step, patiently, and above all, within our being.

Microdoxy[3]

Once formulated, a critique has finished its task, and now is not the time to routinely and somewhat sadistically repeat the critique of our times. Rather, it is time to move on and examine our conscience, which is something that can be done daily and is never an obstruction.

What I am about to say may be a cliché, but it may also be motive for some serious reflection: People read novels instead of theology because novels are more exciting. And by *novel* we tend to understand the conflict—conveniently seasoned and disguised—between a few elemental instincts. Isn't the story underlying theology—that is, the Christian *kerygma*, and not some moralizing veneer to a Pelegianist plot—thrilling and marvelous? Why should the unforeseen events of human life and the great adventures of terrestrial existence, seen from God's point of view, seen with the utmost clairvoyant eyes of faith, turn out to be boring and monotonous? Could heaven also be, perhaps, for those who think so, a boring place?

I do not wish to fully deal with this matter right now, but will concentrate on only one point. Forgive me for not giving any examples, but I believe the general situation to be more interesting than any particular anecdotes. I am referring to the atmosphere of *microdoxy* created by intellectual fear and prudence of the flesh, which paralyzes the laudable efforts of those who wish to illuminate through their faith—*orthodoxy*—and impregnate all manifestations of human life through their Christian spirit.

---

[3] First published in *Arbor* 67/68 (1951): 532–34, as *El miedo intelectual y la prudencia de la carne.*

I once promised a friend that I would write a book in which I would only use authentic ideas of St. Thomas, who would nowadays be judged as dangerous, daring, and a little less than heretical by many, both within the field of "Thomist" philosophy as well as in that of theology—or any other Doctor of the Church for the experiment.

We complain that Catholics trail behind present-day culture, but when some of them, with the utmost good faith—and they have proven this—want to deal with problems authentically and immediately, they are attacked by zealous defenders of routine, using the sacred words of tradition, prudence, and orthodoxy.

Culture—and especially the Church, which is a living organism—grows and develops. Many factors intervene in this growth. One of them is ideas. When ideas first appear in the public light, they are still imperfect, as they have yet to grow and develop; if nothing else, they have to adapt, fit together in the harmonic totality to which they belong. We seem to have forgotten the "convenience" of heresy, as St. Paul once stressed.[4] It seems today as if only the faithless could be audacious and venture opinions—I say opinions and not dogmas—that will need to be corrected and refined in serene discussion, but that discover forgotten aspects of reality. Let no one object that everything has already been said because, even if such an assumption were true, the personal and nontransferable task of assimilating and knowing that same reality would always remain. The marvelous Thomist theses, kept within the pages of a closed book, will not save me unless I have digested them for myself and I have incorporated them into my own thinking.

A Christian must be careful not to fall into heresy—although it is not up to his neighbors to judge him—but he is entitled to imperfection, and I would also add (please do not misunderstand me) that he has a right to make mistakes. Faith is boldness of life, according to a classic patristic expression, and this boldness leads to the most portentous visions of reality. "Why are you so frightened? Have you still no faith?" (Mk 4:40). Even greengrocers squabbled and fought over the *Filioque* during the time when theologians lived, died, and were deported because of a simple iota of the Law.

The Christian is not a mere spectator, less still a judge, of all that happens in this world, but rather a real and responsible actor of what occurs in it. But the most serious illness of modern Christian conscience is that in the theological mind of many—and I say mind, *mens*, νοῦς, and not routine, imagination—the urgent and troubling questions presented to men of our time do not even seem to be problems. Whenever somebody attempts to introduce these questions into the arena of theological discussion, the false prudence of the flesh emerges, which has taken over the intellect and spirit of those who do not realize the gravity of the present moment and who do not tolerate that what has been "so simply and clearly" repeated in the Latin theses of the manuals *ad usum Delphini* be expressed differently. Afterward, of course, when the loud voices of those who have amplified a problem or exaggerated

---

[4] 1 Co 11:19.

an issue emerge from the other side, we must quickly defend the *treasure* we had hidden for fear of moths, dust, and even the air. I was once told, "In the Church, 'the good' either become heretics or they gentrify" (or they become saints, I added). This was wrong, but it expressed that alluded air of microdoxy in which many of the best spirits of our time suffocate.

I repeat, I do not want to be asked for examples; I am merely going to transcribe one paragraph of a prologue written in 1947 by a bishop of the Catholic Church, so that we may meditate on whether a similar air would be advisable or not in the spiritual climate of Spain: "There are certainly some sentences among your pages that I would not have written; I do not agree with you on every point, yet I have not felt wounded, I have not suffered on any occasion while reading your book, I truly felt I was part of the Church and a true son of hers. On the other hand, at other times, one may read perfectly orthodox writings where one can tell that the author knows Denzinger quite well and that he protects himself from any condemnation (or at least that he could always manage to escape from any threat of condemnation, as all his words present an acceptable meaning), and nevertheless everything sounds false. The *ecclesial sense* partakes in a kind of superior aesthetics of which the Holy Spirit is the Master."

I hope that nothing more is understood than what is written. I do not seek the licentiousness of heretics; rather I recall the freedom and the active responsibility of the children of God. I am not trying to justify a superficial and irresponsible essay, nor am I attempting to sustain that any bright, fleeting—unilateral and immature— idea deserves to be published and be immediately considered. When someone dares to publish something, they must have thought about it a lot; even conversations themselves are full of responsibility. There is no right in defending—and even less publishing—truncated truths, incomplete viewpoints, simple irresponsible essays, hypotheses that have not been matured. But this does not mean that one must lead a scrupulous intellectual life, full of fear and anxiety, never daring to directly and passionately—that is, humbly and realistically—face problems. With the wisdom of the Shepherd, Leo XIII said, "We must let the wise have time to think and to make mistakes"—even to rectify, one could add.

In the sacred exercise of his supreme teaching, Pius XII wrote a text of which I dare to highlight a part, in which he taught and reminded us of the need for *true* prudence—science of the saints (Pr 9:10)—in face of the pernicious novelties that proliferate in our world; at the same time he did not omit to admonish us to find in the Catholic doctrine all the profundity and expansive power of the truth. This can only be done if one becomes passionate—and humbles oneself—for the mysteries of our faith. Furthermore, "With regard to new questions, which modern *culture* and *progress* have brought to the foreground, let them engage in most *careful research*, but . . . let them not think, indulging in a false 'irenism,' that the dissident and the erring can happily be brought back to the bosom of the Church, if the *whole truth* found in the Church is not *sincerely taught to all without corruption or diminution*" (*Humani Generis*, August 8, 1950).

The Paradigmatic Sense of Life among Early Christians[5]

Once we have outlined the vital and concrete aspect of Christian life for modern Man, we could indirectly complete it by turning to the study of the posture held by the first bearers—bon vivants, we could say, if this term had not been so corrupted—of the Good News. The *contrast* with their epoch was not the only thing that made them realize the novelty they were introducing into the world; their great fidelity to their vocation—which is analogous to that of the current Christian world—and a specific divine grace also made them into the creators of what, to put it a certain way, could be called the principles of a *Christian culture*.

The only thing we are interested in showing now, in a general vision, is how the *Christian meaning of life*, of common and concrete human life, emerged from the clash between an inner life produced by grace and an exterior life conditioned by paganism. It is obvious that this meaning is ultimately given by Jesus Christ, but here our concern is not to study what it is absolutely, but rather to partially—and only in a few points—examine how it has been interpreted, how the first Christian generations experienced it.

Nevertheless, it is fitting to insist that this *function of exemplarity* that the early Church exercised does not imply an inferior position of the current Church; on the contrary, it supposes a more advantageous situation since today's Christianity also possesses the example of early Christendom, which the former did not have. We must not forget that those early Christians also experienced frustrated attempts and strong temptations. It is a mistake to believe a priori that the early Church lived in better times than those we live in now. This would presume a false conception of the Church. There is no living, healthy, and young organism that ceases to continually progress in order to revert to previous states. And the Church is the organism responsible for spreading divine life throughout the world; there is no way we can maintain that it has reached old age yet. Christian optimism is little less than a dogma. *Confidite, ego vici mundum.*[6]

Yet it is obvious that the first Christian centuries represent a model, a paradigm, for many situations of our current epoch. We are merely trying, in a hasty vision of synthesis and of summary, to relive the dominant atmosphere of this time, which was sufficiently rich and long to allow room for directions that are contrary or different from the current of thought expressed here.

Finally, we must point out that we do not in any way intend to naturalize Christianity. It is essentially supernatural. What is underlined is the naturalness of this supernatural stance. The more human people are, the better they accept the irruption of the supernatural without stridency or mutilations of any sort, as being human is not an obstruction for being Christian—on the contrary. And yet there is an infinite distance from Christian to pure human nature.

---

[5] Published in *Arbor* 11 (1945). See "Revista de Filosofôa," *Arbor* 8 (1944): 141–45 and 154–61.

[6] Jn 16:33.

Human Science

Human science is one of the cultural products where the clash we alluded to earlier was revealed in a more pressing and less studied way. By virtue of their insertion in a preexistent cultural world, patristic thinkers were forced to distinguish between a divine science—the science of divine things—which is in direct relation to God and to eternal health, and the profane science of human affairs.

Due to the historical circumstances of the gestation of such a new worldview, one can understand that the main intellectual task of the Christian sage consisted in incorporating all the cultural heritage that we would today call sciences of the spirit to the science of salvation in an attempt to Christianize these. Along with a positive theological development, to a great degree independent of previous cultures, this constitutes the main mission the Church Fathers carry out and of which they are conscious. It is thus logical that that part of pagan culture that is inadmissible and irreducible to Christian principles be labeled diabolical and malign science, to be avoided by all Christians, such as, for example, the pagan mysteries and the practical religious systems of the first centuries of our era.

But what we are especially interested in here is Christianity's position as regards the profane sciences, in the face of what we would today call *physical sciences* in the broadest sense. Patristic thinkers are conscious of the existence of a profane science.[7] If the latter exists, it is because there are intellectual—scientific—activities that are indifferent and alien to the mission of the Church. Must Christians ignore these occupations? The question is serious, since it comes to question whether being Christian completely transforms Man or not. It asks whether there is something of interest to Man as such, as a unit—not insofar as he possesses within himself the most varied inclinations, including those that are merely animal—and that is not of interest to Christians. This is what is meant by speaking of the "intensive Catholicity"—universality—of Christianity. Theoretically, it seems that the Christian must only be concerned about collaborating in redemption, incorporation into Christ, both his own as well as that of his neighbors. It is St. Augustine's wish to know nothing besides God and his soul.[8]

It is the cry of Simeon the New Theologian: "Leave me alone, hidden in my cell. . . . Let nobody knock on my door. Let nobody raise their voice. Let nobody visit me. What is there for me to look for outside my cell? What good does the world have to offer? What can anybody on the outside still bring me? Nothing, in truth!" Nevertheless, there are many who hold different opinions to this author of the Byzantine era.

So, then, the issue we have presented logically reverts to another theme: Is there really anything that is related to Man and that is not modified by the fact of redemp-

---

[7] St. Jerome's doubts about whether he could be a Christian and a Ciceronian at once are well known, as are those of St. Augustine about whether he must burn his profane books or Christianize them, etc.

[8] *Soliloqui* I.2.7.

tion? That is to say: *Are there any human values that are not redeemed?* Patristic thinkers know full well that redemption has been universal and that all of creation has been freed from the oppression of the Prince of Darkness. "When someone reaches purification," says St. Paul the Hermit,[9] "everything becomes subordinate to him, as it was to Adam in Paradise before the Fall." This liberation from the devil and from the disorder of our nature, which gives rise to the awareness of a *new creation*,[10] is precisely what lays the foundations of the new meaning that the early Christians give to life. It is the voice of the Precursor that all humanity will see the salvation of God[11] and the very cry of the Redeemer: *Ecce ego facio nova*, already prophesied by Isaiah,[12] which is repeated in St. Paul[13] and that constitutes the "exceedingly trustworthy and true words" of the revelation of the Apocalypse;[14] it is the science of Christianity. And the very mission of the Precursor consisted in the *renovation* of all things.[15] The early Christians are conscious of the mission they had been given by the Apostle: *instaurare omnia in Christo*,[16] and the Church Fathers ontologically interpret this instauration,[17] or, strictly speaking, *recapitulation* of all values—even terrestrial—in Christ. One of the first acts of the Redeemer, at the beginning of his public mission, was to withdraw into the desert for forty days and be with wild animals.[18] The miraculous fishing,[19] the curse of the sterile fig tree,[20] the power over the storms,[21] and so on, also show that Christ exercised his power over the entire infrahuman world because it also was under his redeeming influence.[22] After that, the question we have formulated must also be answered negatively: in fact, there are many human activities not yet livened by the breath of the New Spirit, and the mission of Christianity will precisely consist in cooperating to introduce the fruit of redemption in them, since this mission, initiated in Christ, continues and consummates in his Church *ad recapitulanda universa*.[23]

---

[9] PG t. 65, col. 381.

[10] 2 Co 5:17.

[11] See Lk 3:6.

[12] Is 43:19.

[13] 2 Co 5:17.

[14] Rev 21:5.

[15] Mk 9:11, literally, in Greek: "will once again reestablish things in their pristine state." Redemption essentially possesses the attribute of repair, in the popular, material sense that this word has nowadays.

[16] Ep 1:10.

[17] For example, St. Irenaeus, *Adversus haereses* I.10.1.

[18] Mk 1:13. See the wonderful article by Friedrich Pater, "Das Tier und die ewige Liebe," *Hochland* 47, no. 3 (1955): 244–77.

[19] Jn 21:6.

[20] Mk 11:21.

[21] Mk 4:39.

[22] This is also the reason why matter is suitable as an instrument of grace in the sacraments.

[23] Iren., *Adv. haer.* For St. Gregory of Nyssa, for example, man is not only the "image of

Now then, it is not so much about a theoretical disquisition as it is about a practical stance in face of the physical sciences of those early centuries. And with regard to this science one can maintain the same reproach that St. Paul directs toward the sciences of the spirit: the fact of having proved unable to find God.[24] Physical science, almost exclusively astrology at that time, is not in itself bad, even if, in actual fact, it has not guided men to the path that leads to God; this is why the early Christians wholeheartedly feel that "vain are all those who are unaware of God"[25] no matter how wise they may seem in the eyes of the world—as, if they "are capable of acquiring enough knowledge to be able to investigate the world, how have they been so slow to find its Master?"[26]

It is in no way forbidden to devote oneself to the physical sciences, but early Christianity reminds its adherents of the true mission these types of sciences defend and the dangers they entail.[27] St. Augustine points out that there are many more interesting and more urgent things than the study of the material world, even if "not everyone who dedicates themselves to the study of Astrology falls into superstition, nevertheless it hardly contributes to knowledge of the Holy Scripture since, by virtue of its method, which is alien to the fear of God—secular, as we would say today—it constitutes more of an obstacle."[28] It is a science that is cultivated outside the Church, and therefore it is of little use for the attainment of eternal life.[29]

And, despite this, the early Christians are perfectly aware that one of the tasks that is incumbent upon them is that of Christianizing all human manifestations *ab intra*. This desire could not be fulfilled in depth in the then limited field of physical science, since it had very little significance as a science as such, and on the other hand, it thrived as an extra-scientific superstition used to foretell events, dominate people, and restrict freedoms. As such, it makes sense that the Church condemns it.[30] On the other hand, the Church's confidence of being the bearer of a doctrine and of a life that can assimilate all positive values found on earth is noticeable with regards to pagan culture, which was then flourishing.

This *awareness of superiority*—which does not imply a position of pride, but rather one of faith—of the early Church may perhaps find its most vigorous extra-biblical form in that solemn saying by the apologist St. Justin, written barely a century after the death of the Lord: *"Whatever things were rightly said among all men, are the*

God, of a perfect beauty," but also the instrument and channel through which all material creation is spiritualized and joins God.

[24] Rom 1:20.

[25] Ws 13:1.

[26] Ws 13:9.

[27] See K. Prümm, *Chritentum als Neuheitserlebnis* (Herder: Freiburg in Breisgau, 1939).

[28] *De diversis quaestionibus* 45.

[29] For a more in-depth analysis of St. Augustine's conception with regard to the "mathematici," cf. L. C. P. J. De Vreese, *Augustinus en de Astrologie* (Amsterdam; doctoral dissertation, Maastricht, 1933).

[30] See Denzinger, *Ench. Symb.* 35, 239, 240.

property of us Christians."[31] Christians demand the right that the Apostle has given them, in the name of the Master: "*Omnia vestra sunt.*"[32]

Clement of Alexandria does not want his philosophy to have anything in common with the impiety of the Epicureans: "What I call philosophy is neither Stoicism, nor Platonism, nor Epicureanism, nor Aristotelianism, but rather an *expanded* recollection of all the good things these schools have said about the doctrine of Justice and Piety."[33] One really needs an unshakeable certainty—the kind only faith can give—in the germinal strength of the doctrine of Christ to be able to declare that one is in possession of a universal criterion of truth, capable of recognizing truth wherever it may lie and of unifying everything in synthesis. And, on the other hand, it is significant that none of its numerous enemies, at that time, branded Christianity as eclectic, but rather as unilateral and intransigent.

This *awareness of superiority* in the face of cultural manifestations finds its immediate source in the elevated concept Christianity has of man.[34] Man must be important if God has elevated him to His authentic son and if there really exists a man, one of our race,[35] who is equal to us and, at the same time, true God. Man as the goal of creation, as its king and, therefore, as superior to the world, is a purely Christian idea—which will later hypocritically scandalize the Renaissance. *Omnia subjecisti sub pedibus eius,* says the Psalm;[36] the first man had already received custody over all things from God.[37] Christians cannot refuse this right, which St. Paul himself again ratifies, though recording that it is not yet exercised in point of fact even by the Son of Man.[38] This is why redemption of the universe is carried out through Man. The Hellenic Man, on the other hand, is not above the world, but rather thoroughly immersed in it, as one of its particles, more or less noble, depending on the philosophical system. Post-Aristotelian and Latin pantheism follow this same line; for Plotinus[39] it was an outrageous blasphemy that Christians considered themselves superior to the stars.

There is a well-known saying in a sermon on the Nativity of the Lord by that saintly pope of the fifth century that expresses the same feeling of extolling human dignity: "Christian, acknowledge your dignity, and since you became the consort of divine nature,[40] refuse to return to old baseness by degenerate conduct. Remember the Head and the Body of which you are a member."[41] Aside from its theological foundation—Man is the son of God and all irrational creatures are ordained to

---

[31] *Apologia* II.13.

[32] 1 Co 3:22.

[33] Clement of Alexandria, *Stromata* I.VII.37.6.

[34] See Thomas Aquinas, *Sum. theol.* I, q.115, a.4, ad 3, and I–II, q.77, a.1.

[35] Ac 17:28.

[36] Ps 8:8. This entire psalm is a canticle to man.

[37] Gn 9:3.

[38] Heb 2:8.

[39] See Prümm, *Chritentum,* 40.

[40] 2 Pet 1:4.

[41] Leo the Great (Leo I), *Sermones* 21.

God, as a supernatural end, by means of the human being—this point of view has a biblical echo with a strong influence on the first Christian centuries: Man is so important, he is so valuable, we would say today, that the Divinity itself treats him with respect. The scientific centuries will admire the *gentleness*[42] and *precision*[43] with which God set up the universe; in contrast, this early Christian time rhapsodizes when it sees the *reverence* with which Divine Wisdom treats Man: *Cum magna reverentia disponis nos.*[44]

The Christian ascetic sense of this age also rests on the same conviction, on the same *superiority complex*. Arnobius the Younger, writing to Gregoria, a palatine lady of the fifth century—a letter that is a paradigm of the Christian vision of the everyday life of a married woman—provides the following as the basis of an ascetic plan of life and of the struggle against internal, external, and intermediate enemies, if her own brutal husband could be referred to as such: "I value myself above any other goods, as all of these, together, are not worth as much as I am. I have not been created for them, rather they have been created for me."[45] *The ascetic is the true lord.* This is why Christian asceticism is positive, why its vision is majestic and glorious. Christians can afford the luxury of spurning the world—if they do not have a God-given mission to fulfill in it—because they are its owners; they may even reject it, because they are very much above it. "The world in its entirety, including the totality of goods and treasures, is not worthy of the son of God,"[46] who knows that one mere goodness of the supernatural order is greater than all the goodness of the entire universe.[47]

On the other hand, the aforementioned *superiority complex* does not consist in exporting the values that Christians—the ascetic—have renounced here, on this earth, to the other world. It is not some kind of reaction due to resentment, as would have us believe some piteous manifestations of the nineteenth century lacking any living faith, "audacity of the spirit," as was felt by all primitive Christendom in the wake of Clement of Alexandria.[48] And this is so, in the first place, because, in this evaluation, Christians do not renounce any positive human value, but only evil, or, more specifically, disorder; and in the second place, because it is not a reaction that compensates a terrestrial inferiority complex, but rather, more precisely, the attitude of the early Christians is eminently positive and imbued with *terrestrialness.*

---

[42] "Disponit omnia suaviter" (Ws 8:1).

[43] "Omnia in mensura et numero et pondere disposuisti" (Ws 11:21).

[44] Ws 12:18.

[45] See the collected texts, L. Welsersheimb (ed.), *Kichenväter an Laien* (Herder: Freiburg im Breisgau, 1939), 93.

[46] M. J. Scheeben, *Die Herrlichkeiten der göttlichen Gnade* (Herder: Freiburg im Breisgau, 1941), 1:86.

[47] Thomas Aquinas, *Sum. theol.* I–II, q.113, a.9, ad. 2.

[48] *Strom.* II.4.

Terrestrialness

Early Christians know they are foreigners *on* earth, as their homeland lies in heaven; but they do not feel foreign *to* the earth, as they consider themselves truly men and more fully so than those who have not received the ultimate mark of the human being—to the extent that St. Irenaeus considers as a full man only the one who has been elevated by grace.[49] Although not as explicitly, the rest of the Church Fathers share this opinion.

The already alluded-to position of someone like Clement of Alexandria, for example, in the face of contemporary culture, clearly shows the value of *terrestrialness* that we are now interested in underlining. Christianity is not satisfied with possessing the truth by eminence. Rather it aspires to form a thought that is as powerful and as concrete as any existing philosophy or conception of the world and, of course, much more complete than any of those.

Certainly, the end of Christian life is in the afterlife, as its conclusion; but in the interregnum, in the transition, the end is also present as the real final driving cause, communicating to all our actions not only a direction and an efficacy in order to reach the goal, but also an authentic and self-sufficient *meaning*. This is why we speak of the Christian meaning of this life and not of its mere end. The end certainly specifies action, but it is extrinsic to it. The meaning is in the action itself. There is considerable difference between giving alms out of duty and kissing someone out of love. There are actions that drive to an *end* because they make *sense*. What tells novices apart from masters is that the former, in their incipient fervor, want to disregard actions that are full of meaning in order to limit themselves to what they believe will lead them directly to the end, forgetting that they are complex beings and that the *unum necessarium* also has its parts.

During these early times, the memory is still very much alive of Jesus's reproach to his disciples—precisely to his own disciples—for having been shocked at Mary's "beautiful deed" in Bethany, pouring expensive ointment over his head.[50] On the other hand, we need merely recall the *maturity* of such a passionate temperament as that of St. John Chrysostom[51] or that of Clement of Alexandria, who, not letting himself be intimidated by the exaggerations of false gnōsis, cultivates an intense orthodox Gnosticism and who, with a mature vision of the cosmic order—of the cosmological axiom—and a head start of many centuries, solves the medieval problem of Man's *natural* love for God above everything else.

---

[49] *Adv. haer.* V.8.2.

[50] Mt 26:10. In the Greek text we can see that Jesus defends her precisely for having carried out a *beautiful* task (καλον).

[51] Thus, for example, he believes that most of the work of the monk "is based on a good physical disposition; so that if the body is not robust, everything that remains is desires, since it is not possible to put it into practice" (*De Sacerdotio* VI).

We have specified *maturity*, and this is certainly another of the characteristics of this epoch, despite how paradoxical this may seem at first glance for those accustomed to portraying early Christian times by a superhuman anchoritism and a cruel ascetic. It is another thing altogether that faith then was alive enough not to fear what frightens the cowardly and pusillanimous faith of some modern Christian environments. We must eschew both extremes: that of considering the beginning of Christianity in a purely human way and consequently judging its development as a kind of gradual humanization of an exaggerated primitive intransigence, and also that of attributing an exclusively supernatural beginning to it, spurning the human element on which divine action rests.

And early Christianity had to fight precisely against this twofold tendency, in the form of excessive spirituality on the one hand and coarse materialism on the other. But this is not the place to describe, even summarily, the struggles of the nascent Church against different heresies. Nevertheless, we hope the following reflection on one of the implicit premises of the Christian position described above will be enough.

We spoke of the *meaning* of life, as opposed to the simple *end*. Ultimately, what makes it possible for human life, for Man's actions to have a meaning as well as an end, is the *body* or, to put it another way, human unity, composed of soul and corporeality. If we were pure spirit, our actions would certainly have an end; but not that complex thing—in which beauty, comfort, feeling, elegance, and so on intervene—that is referred to as the *meaning* of an action and that makes it properly human. There were certainly those who said, for example, in these initial centuries of Christianity, that marriage should be banned as it did not lead to and was of no use for Man's ultra-terrestrial end; but they did not understand that the union of a man and a woman, besides possessing an end, also primarily possesses a meaning.[52] These people were excluded from the community as heretics. The passionate Augustine's doubts about sacred music are characteristic of this, though he finally accepts it because it does possess a meaning.[53]

Patristic thinkers are conscious that, not only the ground, but also the form of life is valuable—that is to say, we must give ourselves to God with elegance, as God only loves joyful givers,[54] and are very aware that we are men, not angels, and have a body destined for a glorious resurrection. But these allusions to this important problem of a Christian anthropology can suffice.

This world is valued much more highly by Christians than by any other system of the early centuries; the latter are characterized by that very weariness and desire for redemption that imbued most of the philosophies of that time with religious and magical traits. Redemption took place at a specific and unrepeatable moment in time, and only one concrete interval of time is available for each man to carve out one's eternal destiny—hence the importance that Christianity gives time, and

---

[52] Jn 2:18.
[53] See Augustine, *Conf.* I.10.33.
[54] 2 Co 9:7.

the fact that it bestows dignity to Man and the value of unicity and irretrievability
to the events that occur on earth, and breaks the chain of the temporal cycles that
had enslaved almost all philosophical systems. Eternal values are at stake in eternal
temporality. The terrestrial is so important because it is full of eternity, and in such a
way that these two things cannot separate. "Neither the essence nor the substance of
creation," says St. Irenaeus,[55] "is annihilated: just the form of this world passes away."[56]

This *terrestrialness* also finds itself informing the meaning of Christian asceticism. "For he is alone religious," says Clement of Alexandria,[57] "who serves God
rightly and immaculately in human things." It seems, then, at first glance, that the
most immediate consequence of falling in love with the novelty that Christianity
introduces would be the unilaterality—sublime, if you wish—that only values
the "one thing needed";[58] but the early Christian generations, who have fallen in
love with Christ not by virtue of a psychological process in the face of a noble and
attractive newness, but rather by the power and grace of the Holy Spirit, are above
myopic rationalist explanations, and being very aware that Mary of Bethany chose
"the better *part*," they do not forget that contemplation is none other than that: a
"*part*" of the *whole* of Christian life. This is why Christianity's first step in the face
of the world seems to be, "Nothing interests me"; but the second, which completes
the first, appears immediately: "Everything interests me again—because of Christ."
This is why the apostolic calling, rather than dying a thousand deaths, is to conquer
a thousand worlds. Thus with faith, with this "having chosen life,"[59] the world is no
longer a danger from which to flee, but rather an enemy to defeat.[60]

This *terrestrialness* is a value consciously delimited by the early Christians.
Therefore, when they found themselves with the newness of their doctrine and the
historicity of their crucified God in the face of the traditional and well-rooted pagan
cults, they resorted to making the antiquity of their God known, a God who is identical to the YHWH of the Old Testament; with this they prevented the prejudice
of the "Gentiles" who did not want to abandon their family traditions and customs.
Our God is the God that your families formerly worshipped, the early Christians
could say. Appropriately, the mature experience and the deep human meaning of
the Old Law constitute one of the sources of the *maturity* of the New Law to which
we alluded earlier. It is the same attitude that St. Paul adopted toward the unknown
God.[61] And if the Apostle failed in the Areopagus, it happened because the value
of terrestrialness should not dominate more than the Divine, since Christianity is
supernatural, despite everything; conversion is the work of grace, and the means,
sufficiently disproportionate, *ut non evacuetur Crux Christi*.[62]

---

55 *Adv. Haer.* V.36.
56 See 1 Co 7:31.
57 *Strom.* VII.1.3.4.
58 Lk 10:42.
59 *Strom.* II.4.
60 See Jn 17:15.
61 Ac 17:23.
62 1 Co 1:17.

The Christian Testimony

The study of the early Christians' position in relation to *death* is intimately related to the aforementioned characteristic of terrestrialness, as well as to their interesting conclusions about the sense of *life*. In other words, the *tension* that current Christians feel between their faith and the world, in patristics—and here lies a new function of exemplarity of this epoch—takes the form of the relation between the here and now and the other world. In order to be able to apprehend the complete Christian meaning of *this* life, it will be necessary to previously consider the magnitude of the meaning of the *other* life.

Martyrdom and monasticism emerge as the two initial fruits of this epoch, and at first glance they seem to demonstrate that patristics was directed solely and exclusively toward the other life. Nevertheless, this scheme is much too simple—and inexact, not because it is simple, but because of its *excessive* simplicity—and has distorted the true meaning of those two undeniable products of early Christianity.

A martyr is not a suicide victim who is tired of this life and longs to move on to the next as soon as possible, nor a dreamer who ignores the value of present life; the martyr is a witness, a testimony, a testifier on *this* earth and in *this* life, even if the collateral is his own. Precisely because life is so valuable and so appreciated, the martyr's human testimony is irrefutable. Martyrs undeniably yearn to die, but not simply to die *tout court*, rather to die *because of* Christ and, furthermore, *for* Christ and his Church, not *for themselves*. Martyrs do not die *in order to* go to heaven, but rather in order to serve Christ in his Church, by giving their own blood in *imitation*—and here lies the ultimate raison d'être of martyrdom—of their Master who died to save the world.[63] This is why the martyr, unlike the soldier who dies *for* his homeland, dies *with* Christ. The martyr is the Christian who participates bloodily in the redemption. This is why the early Christians considered martyrs the perfect believers, because they were the most exact imitators of the Crucified. And we have proof of this in the Catholic doctrine on the baptism of blood,[64] superior to that of water.[65] Anyone who loses their soul will find it.[66]

By the same token, when martyrdom ceases to be common, Christians will look for a substitute in monasticism and, more primitively, in solitary life, though Clement of Alexandria already distinguishes between the spirit that animates the monk and the loner, and its material realization, which is inadvisable—and impossible—for everyone.

What modern language means by being an apostle and the vocation of the apostolate, patristics expresses as being a martyr and having a vocation for martyrdom. What the Church needs is not vociferous supporters, but rather testimonies and testifiers of its divine mission. And it is a categorical fact that many conversions of pagans

---

63 Mt 10:24–26.
64 See Cyprian, *Espistula ad Iubaianum* 21; Cyril of Jerusalem, *Catecheses* III.10.
65 See Thomas Aquinas, *Sum. theol.* III, q.66, a.12 (and ad 1).
66 Mt 10.39.

were closely influenced by the spectacle of the superhuman magnificence offered by the martyrs who died as testimonies of the Divinity of Jesus Christ. "See how they love one another!" Tertullian tells us that the Gentiles exclaimed, dumbfounded in the face of the unprecedented outbreak on earth of a love incomprehensible for the natural faculties.[67] Christians are ready to die, if necessary, not only for God, but also for their brothers.[68]

The novelty of Christian martyrdom and its essential distinction from any similar type of death appears quite blatantly if one reads the theological and exegetical debates between the main masters of Judaism in Lydda on the subject of Hadrian's persecution.[69] The rabbis' most severe conclusion consisted in saying that, threatened with the death penalty, a faithful Israelite could tolerate anything, except public idolatry, murder, or incest.[70] For the Christian, martyrdom does not pose any kind of exegetical problem, as it is not alien to his vocation; it is a mere realization of a very real possibility that he has had to have from the moment he was introduced into baptismal waters, effectively dying to himself.

But this is not the place for an exhaustive study on martyrdom or for any sort of prejudgment of non-Christian martyrdom. Later, the Jews themselves proved to be much more rigorous on many other occasions. Thus, in the third century, the obligation of martyrdom was defended before the slightest transgression of the Law, provided it was done publicly.[71] The Old Testament narrates true cases of "Christian" martyrdom; for example, that of Eleazar and the seven Maccabees brothers.[72] Martyrdom may also take place outside Christianity.[73] What we are interested in pointing out here is that in all these cases martyrdom is an exception, whereas for Christianity it is both normal and natural.[74] Thus, for example, in regard to Eleazar, a martyr because he refused to eat forbidden meat, we find, in the first place, the legal sense of duty in keeping with the nature of the pact with God characteristic of Jewish religiosity.[75] Furthermore, Eleazar scorns this life.[76] He definitely feels his age and does not want to enact the pretense they propose (of eating nonforbidden meat, making "as if" it were forbidden meat) to avoid dishonoring his old age, giving

---

[67] *Apologeticum* 39.

[68] 1 Jn 3:16.

[69] See Strack-Billerbeck, *Kommentar zum Neuen Testament aus Talmud und Midrasch*, vol. 1, *Das Evangelium nach Matthäus* (Munich: Beck, 1922), 22ff.

[70] See T. Soiron, *Die Bergpredigt Jesu* (Freiburg: Herder, 1941), 199ff.

[71] Ibid., 201.

[72] 2 Mac 6:18ff.

[73] See, for example, the case of Al-HallAj, theologically studied by J. Maréchal, *Études sur la Psychologie des Mystiques* (Paris: Desclée de Brouwer, 1937), 2:487ff.

[74] See Lk 14:26–27, and even more, Mk 8:34–35.

[75] 2 Mac 5:30.

[76] 2 Mac 6:25.

the young a bad example,[77] and falling into the hands of the Almighty if he does not die as one should.[78] The eldest of the seven Maccabees also tells the tyrant that they are willing to die before breaking the laws of their people's God.[79]

But even if these testimonies from the Old Testament are magnificent and prefigure those of the New Law, we still do not find among them death as redemption and as a path. Ignatius of Antioch's "I will willingly die for God"[80] has not yet arrived; nor has the first martyr Stephen's prayer[81]—in imitation of the Master's[82]—for those who stone him, in gratitude for the good they paradoxically do him. "I now begin to be a disciple,"[83] wrote Ignatius, who aspired to nothing more than to be God's wheat, ground by the teeth of beasts in order to become the pure bread of Christ.[84] His Love was crucified,[85] and he asks the Romans to please grant him the opportunity to imitate the passion of his God.[86]

Martyrdom is connatural to Christians. Furthermore, it is connatural to Christianity: blood is one of Christ's three testimonies on earth.[87] In the collective struggle against the mystery of iniquity and the prince of lies, the kingdom of God needs the testimony of the blood. "The kingdom of Heaven has been subjected to violence, and the violent are taking it by storm."[88]

Monasticism and life in solitude are analogously governed by the principle of the imitation of Jesus Christ, though this in no way implies contempt toward the world as God's creation. The doctrine of the superiority of the life referred to as mixed over the purely contemplative one dates from the time of the early Church. St. Gregory the Great already considered "preachers" to be much superior to married people and even to virgins;[89] and St. John Chrysostom, who writes an entire treatise on the priesthood, another one on virginity, and a third one more specifically against those who challenge monastic life,[90] is, on the other hand, a passionate defender of the perfection of laypeople, and he insists that they can practice the same virtues as monks, as the same laws apply to the former and the latter, with the sole exception

---

[77] 2 Mac 6:24.

[78] 2 Mac 6:26.

[79] 2 Mac 7:2.

[80] *Epistula ad Romanos* IV.1.

[81] Ac 7:60.

[82] Lk 24:34.

[83] *Epistula ad Romanos* V.3.

[84] *Epistula ad Romanos* IV.1.

[85] Pseudo-Dionysius the Aeropagite cherished this maxim by the "divine Ignatius" and therefore kept it alive in the Christian tradition. See *De divinis nominibus* IV.12.

[86] *Epistula ad Romanos* VI.2.

[87] 1 Jn 5:8.

[88] Mt 11:12.

[89] *In Ezech.* II.4.6.

[90] *De sacerdotio* (*PG* 48.623–92); *De virginitate* (*PG* 48.533–96); *Adversus oppugnatores eorum qui ad monasticam vitam inducunt* (*PG* 47.319–86).

of matrimony. One of the goals of prayer—St. Augustine will say in an epistle to a widow named Proba—is that of infusing the other acts of our lives—and active life—turning them into prayer. The mission of contemplative life is to inform and fill active life with meaning and fullness, thus achieving the perfect Christian life, which fulfills the union between action and contemplation.

If the martyr is a witness and monasticism is a substitute for martyrdom, it follows then that the monk—despite its etymology[91]—will also be a certain type of testimony. This is why even if monasticism is a special institution, its spirit exceeds the pure limits of the monastery. Monasticism is immersed in terrestrialness, and for this reason it coincides with the spirit of Christian life in the world. Although the limits between laypeople and monks existed, they were not the legal ones that we have today, nor were they as stereotyped as they are now. Everyday Christian life had the value of testimony, too. Mutual love and the fascinating picture of an integral humanness presented by the early Church constituted, toward the world, the unimpeachable testimony of the truth of its message. The entire life of a Christian, like Christ's, consists in giving testimony of the truth to the world.[92] The Sanhedrin were looking for a "false testimony against Jesus" in order to condemn him.[93]

Additionally, Peter publicly calls himself and those who are with him witnesses—martyrs—of the resurrected Christ.[94] And the Precursor's actual mission simply consisted in bearing witness.[95]

Christian life demands that we be *martyrs* in every sense of the word. Being conscious of this responsibility toward the world, of being those who had to bear witness of the Truth, like their Master, explains the fact of martyrdom as an ordinary social phenomenon during the first three centuries. Those who had come to testify that Christ was God[96] were not going to keep quiet, and those who knew they were called to a new life were not going to be shocked by the persecutions. This is not to say that there were no defections. Some did not have the courage to be martyrs, but they never considered martyrdom a possibility that was alien to Christianity.

Perhaps it is not out of place at this point to dispute an idea whose strength lies in its excessive diffusion and that frankly contradicts the panorama we have outlined here. It is commonly held that the perfection of laypeople was not of much concern either in antiquity or in the Middle Ages, as people concentrated their attention on monks alone, and apparently decisive evidence is usually put forward to support this idea: the fact that there exist no treatises on spirituality for those living among people in the world. Moreover, an authority such as St. Francis de Sales is conscious

---

[91] It comes from μοναχός, which means alone, only, solitary; from the root μεν.
[92] Jn 18:37, which could be translated as "to be a martyr for truth."
[93] Mt 26:59. Looking at the Greek text, we could say that they tried to make Christ a pseudo-martyr.
[94] Ac 3:15.
[95] Jn 1:7.
[96] Ac 4:20.

of being an innovator in the field of Christian action due to the fact that he writes for the people of the world.[97]

We must say, in the first place, that the absence of such guides for simple Christians down the path of virtue is not as complete as we are sometimes led to believe.[98] But in second place, and more importantly, we must bear in mind that the fact that is cited as proof only confirms the thesis presented here that there were not two spiritualities, not because laypeople were ignored, but rather because the division between monks and the simple believer—which has caused so much damage during the past centuries—did not exist; as if the former were the real followers of Christ and the latter second rate Christians. The work of the saintly Bishop of Geneva was directed precisely to repair this division.

The Church never believed in such a separation. Even today it is very wary of identifying the classical life of perfection of the three evangelic virtues with the essence of so-called religious life, and it is even warier of equating the degree of perfection of Christians with the "state" to which they pertain. "Books on spirituality written by monks were also used for the edification of the simple believers,"[99] for the plain reason that neither did the latter feel disconnected from the only doctrine and the only goal of perfection to which every Christian is called,[100] nor did the former consider themselves to be superior or more saintly than the latter. But this is not the place to analyze the essence of the monastic calling, or to deny that there is one state that is more perfect than another. Many people still read and absorb the *Imitatio Christi* even if a lot of time has passed after the Middle Ages, and the book was written by and for monks and no longer responded to the more universal patristic scheme of perfection. The attitude of the true Christian *gnōsis*, in the face of heterodox Gnosticism, confirms this same consciousness.

The life of the early Christians can be judged as a life lived facing our sister death. It is death that gives us the meaning of life. But death is the beginning, not the end. To live facing death is *morti-fication*. Life, as the continuous flow that it is, must be comprehended by means of some fixed point. Death is one of these. But how does death give life meaning? By *placing* all the values that appear in it *in a certain order*. In considering the static repose of death, we will see which values remain and which vanish or have a merely passing function. Life, then, will be judged according to how order and death are judged. Life will be a preparation for death insofar as death means the beginning of another life. This means that this life is conditioned by the other.

---

[97] See his preface to his *Introduction to Devout Life*.

[98] An interesting and well-documented renovation of these ideas is expected in the new chair of *Théologie et historie de la spiritualité*, which E. Gilson and A. Combes so conveniently created in the Catholic Institute of Paris (in the 1943–44 academic year).

[99] P. Pourrat, *La Spiritualité Chrétienne*, vol. 1, *Des origines de l'Église au Moyen âge* (Paris: Gabalda, 1943), XIII.

[100] See Mt 5:48.

But if the other is eternal and true life, if it has a much greater fullness than *this one*, that *other* life will make *this one* participant of its wealth and transcendence. This is why Christian life, which is based on the afterlife, is, as such—as terrestrial life—fuller, richer, more of a life than the merely terrestrial life of the man who does not live in faith. No other life on earth possesses the tension and vitality that the authentic Christian life does. "In me lies all hope of life."[101] Christian life on earth represents the marriage of time and eternity; moments are temporal, and at the same time they have eternal transcendence and a causal effect with regard to the other life.[102]

There will undoubtedly exist, therefore, aspects of human life—because Man's βιος is a complex of the diverse ontological spheres in which Man participates—that correspond to purely animal or natural sectors of human beings themselves and which will have to yield to the greater development of the seeds of superior life that Man possesses. This is what asceticism consists of, in the culture—and, like any cultivation, somewhat arduous and somewhat artificial—of the inferior life of Man so that the divine seed deposited in its subsoil bears fruit.

Therefore, in patristics, this is not about "fleeing from the here and now toward another world as fast as possible," as Plato advises,[103] but rather about taking advantage of this life to the best of one's ability in order afterward to live in the afterlife more intensely, more perfectly, and forever.

There is nothing strange, then, about the here and now—as such—being somewhat despised. The aforementioned bishop Arnobius wrote that "we do not have this life as a *prize*, but rather as a *test*." This summarizes the patristic conception of present-day life. We must not aspire to enjoy it, as if that were the reason why we have it; rather we must live it in order to deserve the other life. The Pauline recollection of the sports competition and the prize, as parables of present and future life, are clearly sources of this conception.[104] As a result, our current life possesses all the intensity of an exam, all the emotion of a test, and all the interest of a competition in which the prize is infinite. In the midst of the ascetic exaggerations of the first anchorites, this truly human *desire* to win a competition and attain a prize vibrates. With profound human feeling, St. Augustine cries out that "some grief may then be justified, but none of it loved"[105] as such, given that if something can be justified it means it is good, and if it is good, then it can and must be loved.[106] We, the redeemed, have in Christ's Passion a truer and more genuine reason for joy than for pain, says St. Leo the Great.[107] *O felix culpa*, sings the liturgy.[108]

---

[101] Si 24:25 (in the *Vulgate*).

[102] See my *Patriotismo y cristiandad* (Madrid: Rialp, 1961), 143ff., where this idea is further developed.

[103] Plato, *Teeteto* 176B.

[104] 1 Co 9:24.

[105] *Conf.* III.2.4.

[106] *Conf.* X.28.2.

[107] *Sermones* IX.

[108] In the *Exultet* of the Easter vigil.

The Christian Meaning

However, together with all these rationalizations, the early church feels the madness of the cross, and it becomes inflamed with love for its crucified God. There is no lack of writers who, unable to sustain the enormous tension of Christian life in the world, upset the balance and abandon all human means to try to live closer to the cross.

This is not the place to pass judgment on all of these attitudes, nor to describe the extrinsic novelty of Christianity, the cross, or its intrinsic innovation, grace.

The Christian's mission is to praise the Lord. Basil, father of Eastern monasticism, and Benedict, head of Western monks, construct their respective rules for the life of perfection based on this truth. Perhaps today's Christianity is not sufficiently aware of the greatness that being admitted into God's praise represents, of what it means that God takes pleasure in the canticle of the human heart, even if it is constantly repeating itself. This new task for Man is the result of his elevation to a new sphere, superior to that of the merely natural. The rational being—and the history of religions proves this—understands that the Divinity takes delight in Man's works, in the fruit of his actions, in his sacrifices, but we hardly fathom that mere loving contemplation of His perfections or the spontaneous effusions of our spirit can give glory to God.[109] And only the authentic children of God are admitted in the prayer of praise. This is the consciousness of Man's divine dignity to which we alluded earlier as characteristic of the patristic age.

This praise, manifesting itself through the most diverse human activities, is, then, what emerges as a consequence of the way of understanding life in early Christian culture. This praise involved the whole man. No human value was denied, because Christians did not admit that there was any such value that could not be in Jesus Christ, *perfectus homo*.[110] Thus, the newness of the hymn that the Church asks Christians to sing lies in the new hymn[111] of their very existence, in daily praise shaped through the uninterrupted work of personal perfection, which is neither alien nor independent from the perfection of the entire universe.

This is the great lesson of the early Christians that we are interested in highlighting: the affirmation of everything human because the whole man has been redeemed; this is why praise of God emerges in all the orders, states, and occupations of life. And this is why, even if it seems paradoxical, *naturalness* is a distinguishing facet of Christian life on earth. And this is why the greatest Christian revolution of all time in the face of the pagan world is the sanctification of ordinary existence. This is the teaching that early Christianity transmits to us with urgency. Ultimately it is about the enhancement and supernatural reshaping of classical human virtues. It is the

---

[109] The contemplation of Hindu religiosity, for example, is a means for man's perfection and his union to God, but much less a tribute of praise, a *sacrificium laudis*.

[110] *Symbolum Athanasianum* (*Denz.*, 40).

[111] Ps 32:3.

nucleus of authentic Christian theandrism. The patristic age is a humanly divine age, while the fifteenth and sixteenth centuries intended to establish a divinely human era. But we did not set out to establish comparisons here.

All of the meaning of Christian life is contained in this single line from the Prince of the Apostles:

Sed communicantes Christi passionibus, gaudete.[112]

Missionary Action[113]

This is not about developing a missiology—a task that, however, is urgent—nor about fixing directives for a missionary action—also a pressing obligation—but only about showing that a full Christian meaning of life requires missionary action in an *essential* and *constitutive* way.

In fact, Christianity is essentially dynamic because ultimately it is life, and all of life is dynamism . . . activity. On the other hand, it is not so clear that this dynamism must necessarily result precisely in missionary action—one more proof of the obscurity that generally surrounds the concept of missionary action.

Present-day Christian life still has a weakened sense of *Church-consciousness*, even if less so now than in previous times. The proposal itself of the missionary problem is precisely a sign of this weakness, and the serious attempts at a solution are, on the other hand, the exponents of a gradual resurgence.

The Church is something more than the hierarchy. Every faithful Christian is also the Church, an integral part of it. At the same time, the Church is something more than a pure means to save souls. There is a triumphant Church, as much Church as the militant one. Furthermore, the Church worries not only about souls but also about the entire man; there is nothing human that is alien to it, given that it is the society of those people who, in one way or another, participate in the fruits of redemption. This is why Christianity has not only an individual destiny but also a collective one, which is why nobody can dissociate themselves from the community—excommunicate themselves—without ceasing to be Christian.

Christian life, then, is a personal and collective adventure on earth. God did not wish—nor does human nature itself allow—to elevate Man and give him a new life in an individual and spiritually solitary way. The sacraments require a concurrence that is human and divine, individual and social, and moreover, material and spiritual. Men need each other—and they need the Son of Man—in order to reach God. Total isolation is heresy; perfect anchoritism has been condemned. Spiritual rickets, like any anemia, is a consequence of a life enclosed within the four walls of one's own egocentric interests, and to air the room, it is not enough to extend this *ego* to a small group, party, chapel. . . .

---

[112] 1 Pet 4:13.

[113] Published in *Revista Española de Pedagogia* 5, no. 19 (1947): 393–99.

It is impossible to live a Christian life without believing in the communion of the saints, without living the life of the Church, not only in the judicial sense, or even in its exclusively visible aspect, but rather at its most profound and real onto-logical level. The Church is something more than its body, and it does not identify either with its structure or with its morality.... The Church exists wherever Christ is present, Cardinal Newman said.[114] But the presence of Christ is not a subjective or sentimental phenomenon, but a real and authentic fact that modifies the very structure of our soul. The imprint of a God on its creature cannot be a fact of no consequence.

Christian life *with* and *in* the Church cannot ignore the actual problem of the establishment of the Church in the world, and this is, ultimately, the missionary problem. It has been written, no doubt with good intentions though dismissing the essence of the missionary problem, that "the jungle is as much the territory of the mission as is the suburb or the café." It is here that the classical objection that there is no need to *go* on missions emerges, as we have these at home, and that a well-ordered charity begins with oneself, and so on. In the first place, it is not about *going* on missions, but rather about *being* a missionary. Furthermore, the aphorism—of pagan origin—about order in charity is not completely true. Charity that is well ordered starts with God, continues through his works, and passes—quite speedily—through oneself and ends with one's neighbors.

But, first and foremost, the issue is another, as it is not even a question of charity understood in that restrictive sense of the quoted aphorism. Missionary activity as such is not the same thing as apostolic action. In addition to everything we have already said, the Church is a visible, external society that, being the vehicle of salva-tion for humankind, is still not to be found throughout the world, as a matter of fact. There are places where the Church does not yet exist with the necessary external life to achieve its mission in a normal and ordinary manner. No Christian *can* ignore this fact or its consequences. Christianity is essentially universal; it is constituently catholic and ecumenical.

We can draw two consequences from this: the first, that every Christian problem that is not proposed in ecumenical terms is wrongly or, at the very least, only partially proposed; and the second, that all Christian life that does not vibrate in unison with all the palpitations of the Mystical Body of Christ is not authentic or solid.

It is interesting to note how the action of divine grace in simple and uncultivated souls gradually leads them to concerns that are not only apostolic but specifically missionary. Christians do not have an exclusively individual goal. In other words, their personal end is not an individual end since they are connected to the rest of creation, as priests or as neighbors. Endowed with a priestly mission with reference to the infrahuman world, Man must help it to attain its ultimate end. In relation to the other human beings, as a neighbor, he cannot detach himself from them, and

---

[114] John Henry Newman, *Sermons Bearing on Subjects of the Day* (London: Longman, 1918), 354.

his personal destiny is framed within the specific goal of generations, peoples, races
... as well as within the general goal of humanity as a whole. In the same way that
the essence of religion presumes a you-I relationship, it also supposes a collective
link: you-us. The ultimate reason is that my *you*—the *you* of my prayer and my
religion—is the same as my neighbor's *you*, and therefore, *in Him*, in this *you*, we
are all united and we are all brothers.

This is why the missionary problem is so important. It represents the overcoming
of the small egocentric ideals in which many well-meaning Christians drown. It means
relating fully to the Church itself, as an integral part of it, in its preoccupation to
spread throughout the world in fulfillment of its mission and Christ's mandate. It is,
furthermore, an indication of vitality, of a spirit of expansion and development, which
automatically eliminates the old-fashioned attitude of thinking about the past and
yearning for better times. It is the ambition for growth, as every healthy organism does.

Considering the problem from this point of view, it is understandable that
missionary action is unavoidable for every Christian. It simply means positioning
oneself in the real and authentic dimension of Christian life. Nobody can say the
Lord's Prayer, "Our Father ... ," without thinking about the *us* of those who recognize God as Father and the *us* of those who do not recognize Him yet. In other
words, missionary activity is the action of the *entire* Church, and therefore, every
Christian participates in it.

This missionary dimension is really implicit in any Christian action, and it would
be desirable if it were also carried out consciously. This is not about going to the forest
to convert the infidel, but rather about consolidating oneself in the Church so that it
may expand—besides the fact that the Church's principal missionary field of action
is not in the jungle, but rather in such advanced civilizations as the Western one.

It has been said that "without the collaboration of our professors from Europe
we will not beat Buddhism."[115] It is not *missionaries* who are the promoters of the
Church's geographical growth on the planet, but rather the Church itself—and
every believer along with it. In our Catholic consciousness, because of habit,
attitude, time, and indifference, the schism and heresy implanted in the core of
Christendom do not wound us any longer. St. Teresa of Avila, for example, felt the
apostasy of "the Lutherans" in the depths of her soul, not to mention the concern
and preoccupation of the early Church for the schisms and heresies of the time. Let
us recall, for example, the reaction in the face of Arianism and compare it with our
own "spirit of compromise and indifference" regarding the fact of Protestantism.
We have considered it a stable and natural fact, and we have not felt it like a thorn
in the flesh of the Church—that is, *our* flesh—but for its disappearance we have the
unavoidable duty of work and prayer. This does not eliminate—on the contrary, it
presupposes—charity and embracing all those Christian values that have remained
outside the Church. In the same way, we do not feel as strongly as we should about
the fact that after twenty centuries of Christ's mandate to roam the entire earth, the

---

[115] Pierre Charles, *Missiologie* (Paris: Desclée, 1939), 15.

Church is only fully and historically established in one-fifth of it.

Christians are responsible for the world, as, ultimately, they are its master. A great portion of humanity's destinies weigh on every Christian life. Christians cannot disengage themselves from any human problem: *Et carnem tuam ne despexeris.*[116] Naturally, this responsibility is neither complete nor full; but it is no less true because of that. The Christian vocation sometimes looks unbearable to us. We are children of God; we are destined to be God though without losing our personality, but we yearn for the animal life of our infra-nature. The yearning for "the onions of Egypt"[117] of "the good old days" is nothing but human.

The missionary action is intimately linked to this consciousness of universal mission that every Catholic must possess.

The activities of Catholics cannot be alien to the Church's preoccupations. And it is not asking too much of all Catholics to ask them to break the iron circle of their selfish interests, even if they do not consider them illicit, in order to live with greater fullness the lives of children of God to which they have been called. As early Christianity perfectly understood in the second century, what the soul is to the body, Christians are to the world.[118] But this obligation to be the world's vital principle, salt of the earth, is unavoidable for any simple believer. The sublimity and responsibility implied in simply being Christians has become devalued, even within our most religious environments.

The greatest ontological differentiation among men, among created beings, passes through the line drawn by baptism. Nobody is born a Christian; rather we must be reborn through water and the Spirit in order to become so. On occasions we have wanted to make Christianity manageable—as if it were some sort of load and not a dignity—reducing the burdens and obligations of the simple faithful to a minimum and reserving the integral Christian life for others, as if they were some sort of specialists. One thing is the problem of the *state* of perfection and another altogether that which we have pointed out here of the obligation of every simple Christian believer to fully and integrally live their Christianity. If Man were not elevated to a supernatural plane, if grace were not an authentic reality, if the gifts of the Holy Spirit were not seeds of heroism, we would have to think about creating an easy Christianity, suitable for people that are "poorly endowed" or the "common" people; but in the face of the supernatural world we are all in an identical situation. We must have no fear—that is, lack of faith—in proposing all the strength and vigor of their divine calling to the Christian people. Truth will set us free,[119] precisely because it will make us strong enough to be so.

Missionary action, as such, is the Church's very breath; it is the unavoidable result of its expansive force. The Church would cease to be the Church of Christ, the only

---

[116] Is 58:7.

[117] A popular saying—in Italy, at least—coming from Nb 11:5.

[118] See the celebrated *Letter to Diognetus.*

[119] Jn 8:32.

means of salvation for humanity, if it ceased to be catholic, that is, universal; and the same is true for every Christian believer. And while the Church's catholicity is not also geographical, the radical imperfection of that which is being built, the pain of gestation of that which is becoming, will weigh upon the militant Church, as it does upon every one of its members.

This is the reason why prayer is needed, and missionary prayer; this is the reason why this intimate contact with God is essential for every Christian—with Christ the Redeemer of all mankind, as there is no other possible way of participating in the epic adventure of Man's pilgrimage on earth. They will say that we attempt to turn every believer into a contemplative. This is not, rigorously speaking, true, but there is no need to fear. As a matter of fact, isn't prayer, according to the unanimous opinion of all of theology, an essential constituent of Christian existence?

Only thus, moreover, will we avoid the danger of intellectual stagnation, so regrettable in itself and because of its consequences. In its living contact with other religions, the Church will find seeds of truth and new aspects with which to enrich its doctrine and the concrete fulfillment of its very life in each man. The incorporation of Eastern wisdom in Catholic theology is one of the most fertile consequences of the missionary spirit. In our Western countries, we can see a reduction in that intellectual boldness that, for example, the patristic age, especially in the East, possessed to such a great degree, to be able to build and live grandiose cosmic visions of redemption, the Church, humanity, and so on. The West has lost sight of the forest, to some extent, because of the lushness of its trees.

Ultimately, this is something more than a consequence. Until the Church is *also* external, stable, and authentically extended throughout the world—this and nothing else is the end of all missionary activity—we will not be able to say that it has reached its full spatial development, and along with this, one of the dimensions of its fullness. Thence the radical imperfection to which we alluded. We refer to the authentic Church and not to an organization. Not only is the militant Church unfinished in time and in the hearts of men, but also in space. If the development and temporal maturity of an organism come along somewhat naturally, the constant and free efforts of its own members—ultimately guided by the Spirit of Christ, soul of the Church—are necessary for the spatial development of the Church.

The affirmation that the Church is ontologically the end of creation and that which gives all history its ultimate meaning seems increasingly less exaggerated, even if we do not yet comprehend and live it in its actual depth. If it were true, the consequences for Christians are incalculable, and the importance of missionary action is patent. The latter is nothing but the collaboration of all Christians in the historically and geographically expansive movement of the Church. This is a move-ment of growth that is not and cannot be in the hands of a few, especially chosen, but rather it is a task that concerns the entire Church as such, even if the external, material work—that of establishing the Church in places where it is not yet perma-nently founded—belongs to a few people in particular. In the early Church there were special charismas—apostles, prophets, doctors, and others—but the one of missionary did not exist, because it is not a special task, but rather the Christian mission *itself*. The entire Church on earth bears the name "militant."

Therefore, missionary action is simply one of the channels of the natural and compulsory overflowing of the Church itself, and of each one of its members along with it—as the Church is not an abstract entity. It is a necessary manifestation of our fullness of inner life; this is the reason why it is also a thermometer for taking its temperature. Missionary *doing* is a simple fruit of Christian *being*. At its heart, it all boils down to beginning, down here, the ontological unfurling of our supernatural possibilities, which will culmi'nate with the super-fullness of our being when we become Gods.[120]

Extra Ecclesiam Nulla Salus[121]

Ε'Εν ἄλλῳ οὐδενὶ ἡ σωτηρία.

Ac 4:12

Proposing the Sociological-Christian Problem

The old classical axiom of true theology, "*extra ecclesiam nulla salus*," not only has an eschatological and individual meaning, but also a mundane magnitude, of the here and now, sociological. *Salus*, salvation, means something more than the life of the other world (attained perhaps by means of a good confession at the last moment), more than a life that is considered independently of the values of this world, as if it were not created by God and saved by Christ—indeed, made by Christ. Salvation means complete redemption, the healing, that is, the sanctification—that begins in this *saeculum*—of all beings, including material ones (dogma of the resurrection of the flesh). *Salus* indicates the health of all human structures: by perfecting (better yet, saving) them, we will be able to reach the full development of our entire personality, that is to say, our ultimate end, as this end is not only the well-being of the superior part of our soul but also the divine fullness of all our being.

This is why the *ecclesia* is not only a mere nurse of humanity who applies the best medicine to the "poor creatures" so that after this "vale of tears" they may achieve, at the very least, comfort and a greater joy in the "other life" as a reward. The Church is not *only* an external, visible, judicial structure, nor can it simply be identified with the hierarchy. The Church is reality as it develops, it is the Body of Christ that is forming itself, mysterious, temporal, for now, still becoming, with sighs and pains, but already aiming, truly on its way. Only the Church can join the dispersed fragments of Being that, at some point, will *be* in their fullness.

---

[120] See 1 Jn 3:2.

[121] The original German version, with the subtitle *Die innere Unzulänglichkeit einer nicht-christlichen Welt*, appeared in *Neues Abendland* 10, no. 5 (1955): 159–266.

The role of the Church does not end in the sacristy or in a rigorously religious field. Inasmuch as it is catholic (ecumenical), it has the precise task of saving the world, of returning it to God by Christ, little by little, in time, patiently, fully pervading it.

Our real and historical world, without the Church, is not only unsustainable because it would be incomplete or imperfect, lacking only a sort of external complement, but also because the terrestrial structures themselves and their foundations crumble if they are not supported and sustained internally by the Church. In other words, a fragment of the world may exist, perhaps, outside the Church, but not this, our *world*. The world is none other than the still developing Church, and it can only exist when it is on the path, when it is moving toward its end. As soon as it stops or it closes in on itself, it collapses.

When wheat and weeds grow together for some time, it can seem that only the weeds have consistency on their own; but the only reason they grow is because they are rooted on Christian earth. An antiecclesiastic world only exists thanks to the Church itself.

Therefore, what we are affirming here is that the exclusivity of salvation that the Church has always claimed for itself is not a moral exclusivity, but rather an ontological one; not only individual, but also sociological. Outside the Church there is no being (who is properly a not-yet-being) who can attain its complete-being. There is no culture, society, or world with any lasting consistency outside the Church. We *only* wish to sketch out the sociological side of the issue here.

What we have stated may perhaps seem harsh for whoever does not yet think in *Christian* and whose *intellectual* life is an external compromise with the categories of rationalist thinking. We have all grown too accustomed to indulging in apologetics, and this way we allow our genuinely Christian thought to become atrophied. We will try to show an example of Christian thought by means of a specific case.

The Theological Bases

In order to avoid making mistakes we must first explicitly state the theological bases, at least briefly.

If we take Christocentric thought seriously, we must overcome a way of thinking that is frequently affected and rationalist (we do not hereby wish to deny the legitimate rights of rational thought). The first requirement of the new epoch that is now beginning is a μετάνοια, a change of γνῶσις, a conversion of the νοῦς, a transformation of our fundamental classical categories—and doing this with full consciousness that such a *conversio* does not mean a break with tradition, but rather its true and exact continuation.

From a purely rational standpoint, we must recognize the essential distinctions as valid, but we must also bear in mind that these do not refer to the entire reality of existence. We wish to underline that the *existential* unity that we are stressing here must in no way hold back on the *essential* duality.

Let us briefly indicate the threefold problem that should be discussed here, that is to say, the theological investigation of the pairs of concepts: natural-supernatural, man-Christ, world-Church.

Let us recall that there is no pure nature, that only Christ is the perfect man, and that the ontic end and the supratemporal definitive future of the world is the Church. Additionally, the order of creation—at least that which we know—and therefore "creation" itself is only one part, one partial aspect of the existential order, of the true regeneration of all beings by Christ. Just as all manifestations of the Old Testament must be understood in light of the definitive revelation of the New Testament, so must we here not only complete but also examine and understand the beginning of Genesis as the beginning of the Gospel according to John: Christ is the ontic mediator—that is to say, beings, the "made" things, are precisely *being(s)* because they participate in Christ.

The Dualist View

There is a certain opinion about terrestrial realities that distinguishes between a natural order that rests on itself, that is self-sufficient although it is *immediately* dependent on God, and a supernatural order that is considered in general as a mere gratuitous continuation of the natural ends, even if it is attributed a certain, though not necessary, final perfection of nature. Worried about not ignoring the *gratuitous* nature of grace, sometimes one tends to accentuate the elevation of purely natural things to a supernatural plane more than the renovation and existential unity of reality that such a renovation implies.

According to this criterion, Christians would be inhabitants of two worlds, citizens of two cities. Generally, the famous work by St. Augustine is quoted mistakenly as a clarification, according to which an otherwordly *civitas Dei*, as the empire of love and happiness, would fight against an earthly *civitas diaboli*, that is, the sinful and selfish world.

Undoubtedly, Christians also have to live in this world. As human beings, they find themselves in the "profane" plane, and as Christians they try to harmonize the latter with the "sacred" way of living. The problem is very complex and cannot be outlined briefly. Let us extract one partial problem from the complete set of problems.

With the growing decline of faith in Europe, when people stopped seeing the complete, integral truth in the Catholic doctrine, they turned to a more general and more fundamental base for the understanding and unification of humankind. The narrowness in which the medieval conception must have appeared, removed from its context and transferred to modern culture, and its identification with Christian culture "as such" also contributed to making people believe in the partiality of Catholicism. And so there appeared, for example, a merely moral religion, without dogmas, and then its paradigm, the so-called natural religion, seen as an anthropological invariant that, according to the needs of cultures, epochs, and so on, could turn into the different positive religions.

The "modern" mentality of the present makes a similar mistake when it wants to build an ecumenical order on a *natural right*. Man's elemental rights could be recognized by each man as such, it was believed, and on this basis Catholics could subsequently found their Christian rights. But this pure humanity does not exist. It can certainly be developed, but always as an abstraction, a *determined* natural right, that can later be the basis for positive Christian rights. But those fundamental rights are not based on "nature," but rather on Man's real existence. The numerous current points of view on this problem could be enough to expose its thoughtlessness. Since "nature" does not exist, each of us adorns it with different rights according to our own conception of the world. A quick glance at the life of the people of Israel in the Old Testament shows that no secularized natural law is in force there.

According to the dualist opinion, there is such a thing as a "profane," "natural," "mundane," "worldly" order, which exists in itself and for itself, without any relation to Christ. The Christian task—that is, the role of the Church (here almost always likened to the hierarchy)—would reside in taking advantage of the culture for its own ends and seeing that it did not take a direction that could cause harm to the supernatural and eschatological interests of Christianity.

Outside the Church there would then be a kind of human salvation, a provisional, not definitive salvation that could facilitate the achievement of supernatural salvation. Dualism also believes it is possible that there is a world that is internally structured outside the Church, since, according to this hypothesis, all the natural structures of this earth possess their *autonomy*. This is the conception of all *humanisms*.

The Internal Dialectic of Culture

What the dualist opposition we have just described means may not be untrue. But the tacit assumptions on which it is founded and with which it is formulated are not sustainable: they are neither Christian nor existentially true.

We must also renounce an analysis of these assumptions here (for example, of the pairs of concepts: temporary-eternal, secular-ecclesiastic, profane-sacred, human-Christian), and we must be satisfied with displaying the thesis. We will merely indicate the factual insufficiency of humanism's dualist concept.

Since we have not spoken of the ontological dimension of the problem here, we will leave the metaphysical critique of the being considered as autonomous aside, and we will try to show, through the existential destiny of human culture itself, the real insufficiency of a world that ontologically is not Christian. It is obvious that by "world," we do not refer to the *saeculum* (universe) in itself, but rather the set of secularized structures of a "world" closed off to divine transcendence and impervious to divine immanence.

The internal dialectics of culture demonstrate that a dualist separation is not possible, and that an independence of the natural sphere (i.e., autonomism) is not real.

In the first place, the supposedly "purely natural" culture is so saturated from *above* and from *below* by religion and transcendence that any autonomism turns out to be impossible.

From *above*, insofar as all culture includes a religious or, more exactly, a theological impulse. Not only is our spirit animated in its fullest degree by a desire for God, but also every human being, every concrete human life possesses a certain nostalgia for God that penetrates into the tiniest and slightest structures of the world. If we separate the human values, even in their lowest degrees, from their ultimate end, a breach is produced that gradually transforms into a fracture. And this artificially created situation always takes vengeance.

A culture that is purely natural is not only incomplete but also impaired and convulsive, unable to achieve its specific and immediate end. Man is a unit and cannot be divided without difficulty; that is to say, if I wish to achieve a value in isolation, just for the sake of it, I am in an unfavorable position to truly do it. If I wish to become "somebody" only because of my self-love, I will easily fall into ridicule; if I wish to have fun at all costs, this will be hard for me to achieve; if I desire a determined triumph too much, I will probably not achieve it. These are only partial examples; the greatest example is the one of the actual end of culture. The latter wishes to make Man happy and complete, and it does not achieve it.

From *below*, culture also depends on Man's integral—not natural—existence. If the impulse of culture does not take Man's ultimate end into account, it ends up not even being culture—not only because culture does not achieve its end in this way, that is, it does not procure human perfection (that is its first reason) for Man, but also because it makes Man's internal structures inconsistent and forces them to collapse. If I aspire to a certain *comfort*, for example, without bearing in mind my factual existence (which only theology clarifies for me)—in other words, if I attempt to fulfill a natural cultural value with full autonomy (perhaps only limited by the external direction of my impulse aiming at higher roles)—then I am not satisfied, which drives me to looking for the same value elsewhere with greater force, even if a certain success may have led me to a superficial result. What I have expected of *comfort* was not what I needed, and in the midst of the greatest comfort, not only do I feel unsatisfied, but even uncomfortable.

If I live for success, it will not bring me what I wish for, even if I could achieve it, because my internal structures are affected and altered by existential disorder. What is boredom sometimes, for example, but the dialectical internal result of the vertical search for pleasure? What are certain wars if not the simple consequence of a selfish peace? Technology, for example, considered as an absolute end, leads to the enslavement of Man, and is more likely to weaken him. Much can be achieved with machines, yet Man is impoverished and debilitated if he turns into the mere instrument of a power idolized for itself.

Not only from above and from below—as merely natural culture is not stable because it does not meet its ends and human structures fall into disorder or are altered—but also from *within* does the internal dialectics of culture show us that it destroys itself if it does not tend toward Christianity. That is to say, not only is the naturally desired goodness not achieved (and because of this I destroy myself internally), but also goodness itself (once separated from its existential connection to reality) ceases to be goodness and is transformed into futility.

All human values degenerate if the orthogonal projection of our pretensions falls on them, that is to say, if we desire them immediately for themselves. We absolutize them, then, and this is why they are destroyed, because by their essence, they are relative. That is, if I expect a cultural value to be the only end, even assuming I was successful, what I achieve would not be valuable. Success, *comfort*, intellectual culture, personality, technique, and so on are no longer positive values.

*

One may perhaps object that these thoughts could apply to an atheist culture, but that there could, in any event, be a natural religious culture that does not necessarily have to be Christian.

As we will clarify later on, there are multiple Christian cultures, and if we consider them all, one reaches the conclusion that non-Christian cultures are not stable in themselves, they are not based on Man's factual existence, and therefore they entail the seeds of decomposition and degeneration. They are not even religious cultures, as there is no religion independent of Christ.

Furthermore, even if our reason alone *is able* to know the existence of God, a *merely* rational culture, even if it recognized God (since it cannot limit itself to a stratification of pure essences), would not recognize the true existential reference of the cultural values to God, and it would postulate only a world of pure nature that does not correspond to the real world. (Let us recall the integral secularization of Christianity carried out by Marxism.)

Although a natural and abstract nature recognizes the existence of God, it cannot help the real man. A culture in Rousseau's sense is not a true culture, and it slowly leads to barbarism.

In the real world, faith, grace, sin, conversion, salvation, humility, hope, obedience, the angel and the devil, and so on play a decisive role. A merely natural and rational culture cannot even perceive these values adequately, less still direct and shape them inwardly; it lacks the absolute, uncreated, supernatural Love that continuously and uninterruptedly scrutinizes and penetrates the world.

Christian Affirmations

As Man, then, is more than human nature, a merely natural culture is untenable. In a word, an exclusively natural world is not human, and consequently it is not justified. In other words, mere humanism leads Man to degeneration and destruction. Either a culture is on the right path and results in a Christian culture—that is, it leads to a Christianity (not precisely, however, in the medieval sense)—or it degenerates into barbarism. The real Man is more than "man," and that is why he reduces himself to an animal if he contents himself with being "a mere man." The real man is destined (condemned, the incredulous would say) to be God, a child of God; if he does not accept his destiny with love, he cannot be saved as Man.

Extra ecclesiam nulla salus. Outside the Church the world does not have a definitive consistency, with all of its values, because only within the Church does Man fully become Man, because only the Church sustains the ultimate foundations of human existence. Any order of beings that is stripped of its ultimate base is left empty, without foundation—finally, without *being*, so that it collapses.

In this way, our formula also expresses that, in fact, without the ultimate supernatural and existential foundation of human order, there can be no real world, because salvation does not only mean the health of the soul in the afterlife, but also the reestablishment, the liberation of the whole man, whose true life has already begun in and with this world. There is no natural order of the world over which, using it as a foundation, a Christian world could be built. The Christian order is neither a continuation nor a partial modification, nor a simple perfection of the natural, but rather a rediscovery, a renovation of the original situation by means of the redemption (therefore, of the cross); more precisely, a renovation of true reality, which is simultaneously on the way and in the fall. In other words, what is Christian is found on the plane of the existential, and what is truly existential is found in direct relationship to Christ.

This classic Christian principle—*extra ecclesiam nulla salus*—has nothing to do with a narrow, closed conception. "Anyone who is not against you is for you,"[122] Christ once said. He also said, "Anyone who is not with me is against me."[123] Anyone who is not against the Church is, in a way, inside the Church. The Church is something like the "geometrical place" of Christ's message: it is the true communion of the saints, to which every man can belong insofar as he does not fight against it. The Church is wherever there is a participation in Christ. This participation can have three different degrees, corresponding to the triple kind of baptism. Let us apply them to culture.

In the first place, a culture can be pre-Christian (which is, however, a way of being Christian) whenever it truly shows an *obediential potentiality* toward Christ; that is to say, when culture is sustained by an invisible force in the achievement of an order and in the realization of certain values and rights that causes it to remain unsatisfied and maintains it open toward a deepening of its structures, it finds itself *in via*, on the way toward a Christian fullness. But this order cannot be attained voluntarily, and once the "sign of contradiction"[124] of the cross has appeared in its bosom, it is no longer feasible. And nevertheless, there are still pre-Christian cultures nowadays, as the message of the cross has not yet reached them. The foremost sin of the epoch we misleadingly call the Renaissance was the desire to return to a good and natural world. They lacked the courage to decide either for or against the cross.

---

[122] Lk 9:50.

[123] Mt 12:30.

[124] See Lk 2:34.

Second, a culture can be called *para-Christian* if it shows a *positive potentiality* toward Christ. It will not always be possible, or even advisable, to introduce a complete Christian order. It may then be enough that the culture does not bar the way toward its culmination and maintains awareness of its provisional nature and insufficiency. The danger appears when this culture isolates itself or separates itself and claims absoluteness. But so-called openness is not mere knowledge of imperfection and incompleteness, rather a positive indication for the real preparation of another order. Natural reason and natural will alone cannot achieve this. This is why Christian grace is necessary, even if it may often be invisible.

Third, a culture can be simply called *Christian* when it is actually Christian—that is, when it allows itself to be internally imbued by the ultimate and only supernatural end of human life. But this does not mean that such a Christianization be complete or that such a culture be perfect, or that such a Christian world be univocal and uniform, as if there were no great space for human freedom and for defects as well. There is room for multifaceted pluralism in each one of these groups, without excluding the latter.

With this we have perhaps clarified the full magnitude of that doctrinal axiom. Certainly, salvation already begins here on earth, and it embraces all human values that are necessary for the complete development of the personal being. And yet the Church is not *only* that which is merely visible. Christ's Body extends beyond that, without this meaning that it may be disconnected from its visible corporeality. This can be testified from the point of view of the Church. Our dogmatic axiom must not be ideologically opposed to the doctrine, condemned by the Church, according to which *extra ecclesiam nulla conceditur gratia* (God bestows no grace outside the Church). And since it is also dogmatically affirmed that without grace there is no possible supernatural salvation, we may conclude that the two subjects of the same name, *ecclesia*, do not signify exactly the same thing in both sayings. Outside the Church of the sacraments, outside the visible Church (the Church of the Jansenist heresy) there *is* the grace of Christ; outside the total Church, on the other hand (ontological doctrine), there is no salvation because this pure and true Church is Christ himself. Consequently, there is no intermediate link: *et non est in alio aliquo salus*.[125]

Outside the *Church* there is no *salvation*: once the two concepts have been clarified and expanded, we can say that outside Christ, ontologically and, therefore, personally and sociologically, no authentically human value can stand, and that happiness in this world, insofar as it is possible and insofar as it is directed to the complete and real man (and not only to one part, a fragment of this being), is only found in Christ. Only in Christ can Man attain his perfection, not only that of his soul, but also that of his complete and unitary physical-spiritual being. And the Church is the Body of Christ, the true Christ who still grows on earth in wisdom, age, and grace before God and men.[126]

---

[125] Ac 4:12.
[126] Lk 2:52.

6

Overcoming Humanism[1]

Quia quod hominibus altum estabominatio est ante Deum.

Lk 16:15

Man cannot live without ideas, and every culture is characterized by the more or less explicit hegemony of a determined set of concepts, even though sometimes it is not concepts that prevail, but rather words. Every culture implies the unanimous acknowledgment of certain indisputable axioms for its own historical existence. When these "dogmas" cannot have a precise objective content, they are "nominalized," and thus appears the authority of the word, that of the "slogans" that everybody interprets in their own way. This is the eschatological self-defense of a culture that is collapsing. And this is, in part, our topic of interest here, which we would like to exemplify with one specific case.

One of these words in our epoch is *humanism*. As a term it has achieved undeniable prestige, and the most diverse systems attempt to take advantage of it, claiming its patronage in order to subsequently fill it with the most diverse content. When a culture does not recognize real *dogmas*, it must accept *voices* in order to subsist.

This article does not intend to be an *onomatoclastic* outburst. Let the word remain, but let it do so with a precise content, and above all, let us strip it of the kind of monopoly it attempts to hold over everything human. Human-*ism* is not a synonym for human. When we defend that Christianity is not a humanism, we do not mean that Christianity is inhuman, rather that it is incompatible with the humanistic distillation that is common to all the different humanisms. We do not wish to deny humanism, rather to overcome it.

This should be sufficiently clear, but to avoid any historical confusion or nationalistic exegesis I wish once again to emphasize that this article refers to the philosophical-cultural aspect of the humanism of our times and that it does not take a stand in the face of any political or national interpretation, a task that, on the other hand, would be quite commendable and convenient for someone else to undertake.

---

[1] The original article, published in *Arbor*, no. 62 (February 1951) with the title *El cristianismo no es humanismo*, provoked a series of studies for and against its thesis. See, for example, *L'Osservatore Romano* (August 13/14, 1951); *Arriba* (Madrid), April 13, 1951; June 8 1951, etc. That same year I wrote a few notes that I have now incorporated into the main article, which is otherwise preserved in its entirety.

79

The following is another preliminary caution: We are well aware of the imperfect and somewhat fervent style of the pages that follow. We are absolutely convinced of the importance of this issue, as ultimately we are expressing none other than the very Christian meaning of life in the current situation we have been given the opportunity to live; but this very consciousness prevents us from arguing against all those who, with much greater merits, find themselves in the cultural arena of our times. We do not seek controversy, but rather collaboration, and it is precisely in this sense that we would like to offer this investigation to "Christian humanists" in the event that it could become an incentive of sorts for them, as well as give them the opportunity to secure themselves in the common task and live, above all else, that authentic Christian existence that continues to be foolishness for some and scandal for others, but eternal life springing out of living waters for those who, having laid down the saddlebag and the staff, have placed themselves on the way to the invisible city in which *nox ultra non erit*.

Terminological Clarification

In order to make what we are about to say easier to understand, we will adopt the following nomenclature, justification for which seems obvious to us from a Christian perspective:

Man: The complex existential reality of human beings as they appear in this world. (They are not nature or merely fallen nature, since the influence of the second Adam, as well as that of the first, gravitates over "Man.")

Christian: Man participating in divine nature (by virtue of the forgiveness of the original stain and the realization of his supernatural vocation).

Grace: That "plus" that makes Man Christian (without going into greater disquisitions about its essence).

Human nature: The principle of operations of that part of Man that corresponds to the abstraction obtained through the mental operation of abstracting from Man both the "imprint" of his supernatural calling as well as the "stain" of his original fall. (This operation is possible under the assumption that our rational reason has not been essentially affected by any of the mentioned factors and that it is the criterion of what is natural.)

Supernatural: The principle of operations of Christians as such. (It possesses greater consistency than human nature insofar as it is not a principle that has been abstracted from some fiction, but rather from an existing reality.)

Human existence: The act of Man's concrete existence. (That is to say, of the existing man, who is neither purely natural nor supernatural.)

Christianity: Christ's reality insofar as through its actual ecclesial life and its present doctrine it transforms man into a Christian. (In what follows, to make its relationship with humanism clearer, we will stress the doctrinal aspect of Christianity.)

Humanism: That cultural attitude that tends toward the perfection of Man insofar as human nature or, at most, insofar as Man.

Christian humanism: That humanism that claims to come from Christian principles themselves.

The Role of Contemporary Humanism

Today humanism is a topical subject.

Pius XII[2]

A great many Catholic intellectuals have paid abundant tribute to this word. They speak of *Christian humanism*, yet this does not demonstrate the internal compatibility of both concepts. This position appears to be the last act of tribute of Catholics to a culture that, if it does not die out yet, is already changing and clearly fermenting.

The age of classic apologetics has passed. Attacks on the Christian faith have, to a great degree, already divested themselves of their rationalist garments. There are very few people interested in contradicting or challenging proofs that "demonstrate," even though they do not convince if one is not spiritually prepared. Christian humanism presents itself as the last concession in face of the a-Christian spirit of our epoch. But perhaps it is an excessive compromise.

There is no reason to object to the urgent precept of charity, crystallized in comprehension, adaptation, and incarnation. We must always adapt to everyone, not following some uninspired need to adapt, but rather to win them over to Christ. And Christ is more than a man. Christian humanism may be a provisional platform for combat and it may, perhaps, even be a good tactical stratagem, but I believe that it lacks a firm base—that it is strictly unstable. Perhaps it would be better to recall the antihumanistic foolishness of Christian preaching, so that Christ's cross does not become inane.[3] The law of the cross, scandal for the Jews and nonsense for the Greeks, cannot be reduced to any humanism.

In the face of an austere and not very human posture that is held by some Christians who are far removed from this earth, many have adopted the opposite reaction: making Christians forget their true homeland and their purest ultra-terrestrial hopes. One excess does not justify the other.

---

[2] Reply to the homage given him by the International Congress of Humanistic Studies, on September 25, 1949. The pope does not approve of humanism here. In addition, he seems to say that what is good about it, it has in common with the Middle Ages.

[3] See the beautiful article by P. Eucharius Berbuir, O.F.M., "Gloria Dei," *Das Formalprinzip der Fundamentaltheologie* 8, no. 2 (1953): 106–18, showing, among other things, how even from a strictly dialectical point of view, only an ontologically Christian reason is able to do apologetics.

On the other hand, we cannot deny that even if Man is not the center of the world, he is the window through which we can lean out onto it, and therefore the subjective point of departure for any philosophical conception of reality.

But even if Man is the most immediate problem, he is not, however, the most important one. The preoccupation for that which is human does not have to be Man's greatest concern. The Western spirit has been gradually falling into intellectual narcissism as it has refused to carry out Man's most proper action: to worship God. And worship implies *holocaust*, "total sacrifice." Any humanism that aspires to be intrinsically Christian would have to offer itself in holocaust, and it would destroy itself in this process. If Man were nothing more than man, he could not resurrect. This would be an ontological lesion of the principle of noncontradiction.

More than following the general trend of a heterodox philosophy and trying to put orthodox patches on it, the Christian solution must emerge from the fullness of a supernatural life that sincerely and authentically brings up the problems that are presented to contemporary men. Because of this, many of today's Christian thinkers are starting to doubt the possibility of a Christian humanism,[4] but still too attached to the prevailing cultural milieu, they rarely dare to recognize that they misinterpret the basic conception of humanism by wanting to Christianize it.

Christian culture cannot always follow whatever trends are in style, borne by excessive adaptationism that leads to a disorientation of the Christian people and that is a sign of trailing behind the movement of culture with the naïve urge to be up to date. We all recall such well-intentioned, and even sometimes true, sayings such as, "Christ was the first communist," "True democracy is Christian democracy," "Authentic existential philosophy is Thomism," "The only complete humanism is Christian," "The real socialism is that which is advocated by papal encyclicals," "True liberalism is evangelical," and so on. All of this is true if we can invert the sayings and turn the predicate into that which is Christian within the parcels of truth disseminated throughout the world.

Let no one object that there is a good and inoffensive prephilosophical cultural humanism, as an evaluation of all that is human and an interest in the anthropo-logical. In the first place, this seemingly harmless posture presupposes a metaphysical basis that could very well turn out to be heterodox; there were Christians who were communists and Nazis in good faith because they did not go deeper into the respective principles. In the second place—I repeat—we cannot mistake humanism with some kind of monopoly over everything human. We may misuse words sometimes, but they may also take vengeance.

As we have already stated, none of this denies that humanism, and specifically the plea for a Christian humanism, could be a strategic point of departure for the

---

[4] "C'est une question de savoir s'il y a un humanisme chrétien." H. de Lubac, "L'idée chrétienne et la recherche d'un homme nouveau," in *Etudes* (October 1947): 3 (the article continues in the following issue, in November). See also L. E. Palacios, *El mito de la nueva Cristiandad* (Madrid: Rialp, 1951).

conquest of truth. In fact, we cannot ignore the positive role fulfilled by humanism in the face of an inhuman materialism, for example. But we must emphasize that defending the rights of the human person is not characteristic of humanism or even its monopoly. And furthermore, those rights are not absolute either.

From a practical point of view, Christian humanism may be a bastion that preserves a minimum Christian spirit in the face of Christian Marxism, and it could perhaps be the point of departure for a true Christianization of the world. But we cannot confuse medicine with health, an imposed surgical amputation with bodily integrity. Additionally, a simple anticommunist posture—implicitly accepting the Marxist point of view—would not take us very far. And this is another of the dangers of a Christian humanism that is opposed to an atheist humanism. Moreover, we are not dealing with a strategic problem now but rather with a speculative consideration about Christianity as such and its demand for a however imperfect incarnation in the present epoch. This is why we have insisted that this is about a radical and ontologically Christian proposal, to which, unfortunately, part of the modern Western mentality is not accustomed. Greek Oriental Christianity, for example, acknowledges our thesis as immediate evidence. (The danger there is exactly the opposite. Christianity is not angelism either.)

The Western Christian mentality of the past few centuries has been so preoccupied in engaging in a dialogue with the faithless and in adapting to the situation of the "humanist" man that, to some extent, it has lost the sense of Christian radicalism—and what is more, of the Christian scandal. It has inherited a great deal of the reverential awe of someone like Descartes for theology, which made him—and makes us—practically leave it aside, and it still continues to contribute to the servile fear of someone like Jansen toward the world of faith. So, it prefers to call itself humanist—*Christian* humanist, it goes without saying—rather than simply calling itself Christian.

With all this, we are not denying that there has been a certain evolution in the conception of Man within the very history of Christianity. Humanism represents the reaction of autonomy in the face of the heteronomous posture of a previous epoch that appeared to have forgotten that Man possesses a consistency and a personal consciousness of his own. Humanism seems to us to have perhaps been the necessary step for the awakening of the individual and of individual consciousness that had not yet emerged from *collective consciousness* with regards to a series of aspects of reality. The humanistic phase of Western humanity represents the period in which reason acquires its independence in the face of superior forms, such as faith, and inferior forms, such as instincts. Strictly speaking, reason facilitates discernment between the different forms of knowing and later allows their integration into a mature synthesis. The birth of philosophy as something different from theology is also intimately connected to humanism.

The step toward an *ontonomy*, both of men and of society, and even of human reason itself, has occurred by means of the reaction of humanist autonomy against the preceding heteronomy. Some of the *felix culpa* could very well be applied to this reaction. It is not, therefore, a matter of going back in history or ignoring the services rendered by the humanistic and philosophical period of European culture; but we do not want to stagnate in an attitude that only makes sense as reaction, or to idolize humanism as has so often been the case. The case with humanism is similar to the case with Protestantism, with which it is culturally linked: it makes sense as protest and reaction, as reform (of something else), but it collapses when it tries to be "substantive" and to support itself.

Thus everything we will say to oust humanism must be interpreted in function of the historical dynamism of the present, which urges us not to linger on—and even less to substantiate—a cultural form whose main mission has already ended, not so much because heteronomy in its multiple forms has disappeared from the planet, but because the ontonomy of the different spheres of beings which we are already able to discover makes the use of the simple unilateral humanist reaction inappropriate; the latter only takes us to the opposite extreme, as more than one current political form can testify.

Definition

Man is the measure of all things.
Protagoras, *Fragments* 1

Wanting to provide a definition of humanism that is not purely formalist is a useless enterprise, as a real definition would latently imply a determined meaning of Man that not all humanisms would accept. The real definition of humanism is a function of anthropology that, in turn, is in debt to metaphysics. This does not mean that humanism can be a prioristically defined as of an abstract and elaborated metaphysics, but rather that any humanism must ultimately be founded on a metaphysics or identify with it.

All humanisms not only connote an interest in everything human, but they also one way or another postulate Man's primacy and his central position for us in the universe of being. Man's priority over being—which, ultimately, the former discovers for us—is the latent characteristic of all humanisms. Essentially this is about the primacy of Man's thought over his being, which is the foundation of all idealism.

Humanism is the separatist attempt of a man who wants to constitute himself as master of his own self and who does not accept having to account for his behavior to anybody else. Humanity is the supreme moral law. Let us recall Kant's ethical attitude. And from there it is but a small step to Hegel, Feuerbach, Comte, and Marx.

Even more succinctly, humanism can be defined as the *anthropocentric attitude of life*. Humanism means accepting all that is human *insofar as human* and evaluating it positively. "What an agreeable (beautiful, grand, and pleasant) thing Man, insofar as Man, is," says Menander.

It is true that some have spoken of a theocentric humanism, but if Christian humanism is a concept whose internal consistency is problematic, theocentric humanism is a contradiction in terms.

It is obvious that everything depends on the definitions that are given, but it would make no sense to postulate extraordinary meanings for terms of such general use as humanism. One thing is a theocentric anthropology—theological, if you wish—and another a theocentric humanism. In humanism, Man's primacy over everything else must shine through, and this is the basic meaning of the word that emerges spontaneously as soon as we cease to exercise any violence upon it. Furthermore, here lies the social and collective importance of words that suggest and create a determined climate, even sometimes against the intentions of those who have created them. (Another sad example of terminological disorientation is offered by the expression "freedom of thought.")

A theocentric humanism would not be a humanism because it would displace the center of gravity from Man to God. The firm support of reality, the basis of our lives and object of our interest, would be the divine being and not the human being. It is not a coincidence that the humanism that is called theocentric results in an absolutist personalism that reduces God's rights and turns the human person into the absolute center of salvation. Genuine humanism eliminates any theocentrism. Christianity certainly possesses a theocentric attitude, but it is not humanist. Christians know that neither their autonomy nor their criteria are absolute. Humanism's unappealability is incompatible with the complete submission—worship—of Christians for their Creator. Christianity is immanently open to transcendence. And this is precisely how Man conquers his freedom and defends his dignity.

Not every defense of human dignity entails humanism, unless one calls humanism any reflexive attitude man may have when facing a problem. But then there would be no human posture or culture that was not humanism, and saying *humanism* would be the same thing as saying *Man* or *human*. Conversely, humanism presumes that only Man is capable of defending his own dignity.

If it did exist, theocentric humanism would represent the same aberration as those spiritual lives that have turned the supernatural—for example, the Eucharist—into a simple means for their own selfish perfectionism, exclusively to solve their problems of chastity, for example. It would be a humanism that has discovered God and accepts Him because this seems like an essential piece of its system, but it is ultimately subordinated to the unappealable court of human reason. Man would grant God the "grace" of recognizing Him as God.[5] This

---

[5] In a parody of the humanist mentality that gave rise to what is significantly called *theodicy*, we could say that the good Leibniz, upon seeing that everything is subject to the court of reason, had the brilliant idea of orchestrating the great—as well as "methodical"—comedy of summoning God so that He could obediently descend to the court of reason and submit Himself to the examination that the learned men of the time wished to perform upon Him.

type of humanism would be, at most, a theistic humanism, as we will see later on, but not a theocentric one.

Protagoras's ancient formula rigorously expresses the humanistic pretension: *Homo mensura*. A philosophical stance compatible with Christianity would say: *Homo mensurans* (Man as measuring), and revelation would add, *utpote mensuratus* (insofar as he himself is measured), but never *mensura*, criterion, pattern, foundation of things. But let us not forget: we will be measured by the measures we use.[6] If we measure God with our own standards, and humanistically we have no other, by such standards shall we be measured.[7]

Despite our reiterated wariness not to identify humanism with any human attitude, because we then find ourselves little less than facing a petition of principle (outside humanism there would only be room for the inhuman), it is understandable that—by virtue of a dialectics that is internal to any doctrine—if a doctrine affirms that it is true, it must consider wrong those that do not share the same opinion in the same field. It is understandable, therefore, why the humanist atheist, for example, says that he is the only real humanist, without recognizing that others are also humanists, that is, denying them even the right to call themselves so. The atheist humanist will say that the Christian humanist is not a humanist, and the Christian will retort asking according to what is humanism a priori denied the possibility of being theocentric and even Christocentric, as true humanism is only and exclusively his; and that if there is any difficulty in admitting the thesis of Christian humanism it is because the adversary harbors the prejudice that humanism is essentially centered on a human nature that is closed in itself.

This defense, though essentially fair, must nevertheless pay its due by abandoning the thesis itself, because saying there is no humanism other than the Christian one is equivalent to saying that the specific difference "Christian" exhausts the entire genre "humanism," so that everything is reduced to asserting that Christianity is the truth and that it is the only one that contains a true doctrine about Man. If there is no other humanism besides the Christian one—since a false humanism cannot be

---

We can imagine Leibniz confidently nudging and whispering to the good clergy—clearly shocked—he had invited to the ceremony: "Do not be the least bit alarmed. You will see that God will emerge triumphant from this test and we will give Him a unanimous 'Excellent'; this is the real 'justification' of God." Since then, as we are sure of the results—by virtue of something foreign to reason with which the seriousness and value of the test is invalidated— "theodicy" has taken over even in those curricula that claim to follow he who, when pressed to write a "philosophy," wrote the best of his theology and, without much spirit of compromise, entitled it *Summa contra Gentiles*.

[6] Mk 4:24; Mt 7:2.

[7] "Quidquid recipitur ad modum recipientis recipitur," says a classical aphorism. Christian humanism receives Christianity *ad modum recipientis*, which is Man. It certainly turns Christianity into humanism, but makes it incompatible with Christian orthodoxy. What we need to know is if it has not left out that which makes Christianity truly supernatural and transcendent—because this exceeds it.

called so—the problem collapses at its very base. It then becomes merely a terminological issue. If Christian humanism *by definition* means Christianity, there is not much to discuss.

The broadest nominal definition of humanism seems to be the one that defines it as that attitude that seeks the perfection of Man qua Man. It is obvious that if we supress the reduplication "qua," we destroy humanism, since we identify it with any attitude seeking the perfection of Man—that is, with every healthy and not pathologically degraded human position. That said, what does the perfection of Man qua Man consist of? Depending on the answer given to this question, we will have the different types of humanisms. Only thus can this discussion make sense without turning into a mere nominal dispute.

Humanism and Christianity

Sine tuo Numine
Nihil est in homine.
(*Sequentia Pentecostes*)

Christianity cannot be a humanism because it cannot be anthropocentric, ultimately because it is not man who makes himself Christian. Furthermore, no concept of Man satisfies it. It is obvious that a non-Christian concept of Man is unsuitable for this problematic and nonexistent Christian humanism. But the Christian concept of Man is also unable to support Christian humanism, since for Christianity Man is more than simply man, and his factual human structures are intrinsically modified by the irruption of the supernatural. The Christian man is not a humanist. *Ego dixi: dii estis.*[8]

Humanism constitutively tends toward human immanence, while Christian anthropology must inexorably defend Man's transcendence, not only in his destiny, but also in his very constitution. Man's ultimate end is not his own happiness. *Gloria Dei vivens homo*, stated St. Irenaeus of Lyon in a phrase some have liked to interpret humanistically—human values are not absolute, human perfection is not the goal of our lives, nor is love of oneself the ultimate of our loves, and so on. Briefly, Man's center of gravity is not found in himself, culturally, morally, or ontologically. All of these theses are in blunt unconformity with any humanism.

So far, the heart of our argument has consisted in asserting that humanism is essentially anthropocentric while Christianity is not and cannot be so. The critique to this thesis from a Christian point of view does not deny the second part of our statement, but it does refute the first one. The argument could be as follows: A merely rational and strictly philosophical analysis can come to prove human beings' contingency and perhaps even the insufficiency of reason itself; it indisputably leads to the demonstration of the existence of a God who, by definition, then becomes

---

[8] Ps 82:6.

the base and foundation of the human being, thus making humanism theocentric. In the human search in pursuit of Man's perfection, the latter comes upon God, and once He is found, Man cannot help but worship Him as such. From there, Christian humanism is but a step away, they say. Man can only fully perfect himself within Christianity. Therefore—it is argued—Christian humanism exists, and it is the only authentic humanism.

Our answer is this: *First*, even in case all this could be accepted theoretically—despite the heavy latent philosophical problems in such an attitude—a theoretical discovery of God of this sort would not mean that "the task of integrally human perfection"[9] from a factual and practical point of view, that is, as a task of perfecting, could be carried out effectively with such a humanism. To accept this would be to fall into the most anti-Christian idealism. Such a theocentric humanism would always be impotent in leading Man and carrying out his process of perfection; the discovery of a void is not synonymous with being able to fill it. Christian humanism would then be something exclusively negative that limits itself to recognizing human insufficiency and impotence.

Second: A humanism of this sort is not, strictly speaking, theocentric, but rather simply deist. Its point of departure, and even more so its center, is and continues to be Man, and even when it achieves knowledge of a Supreme Principle, everything is based, like the great "humanist" figure in Nebuchadnezzar's dream, on the feet made from the clay of our own reason. In order to be theocentric we must begin with God Himself—that is to say, we must have a religion, and what is more, a revealed religion. Nobody can jump over their own shadow, and Man cannot expect to be theocentric while it is not the θεός Himself that reveals Himself and places Himself in the center of human affairs. Christian humanism's aspiration to be theocentric without thus aspiring to be revelation clearly shows that it is in fact humanism, and that perhaps it is not incompatible in its explicit results—something different from its implicit and fundamental principles, which is what is at stake here—with the formulations of Christianity, but this is not enough to unequivocally call it a Christian humanism.

Third: Let us imagine that humanism has been able to become deist and accept as a hypothetical concession that it has also been able to realize the extraordinary pirouette of displacing Man's center of gravity to God and that we find ourselves before a veritable theocentric humanism. The leap that, nonetheless, would still have to be made transcends all possibilities, not only humanistic, but also natural. Without the supernatural and free gift of faith we cannot recognize and accept Christ the way that Christ wants to be recognized, which is what Christianity believes. No matter how much we delve into Man's insufficiency, how deep we go into human nature, how much we wish to spiritualize and existentialize, humanism alone, on its own, will never be able to cross the threshold of faith and establish itself in Christian

---

[9] This is how O. N. Derisi intelligently defines humanism ("Cristianismo y Humanismo," *Sapientia* 20 [1951]: 135–40).

territory. Were we to reject the idea that humanism is essential and constitutively natural, we would no longer know what humanism is.

Some will say that Christian humanism does not need to be strictly supernatural itself and that it is enough for it be open to faith or to supernatural revelation in order to justifiably be called Christian. This is true, but then the difficult thing is to still call it humanism if it receives its orders from some transcendent place that it is banned from entering. Obviously it is not enough to recognize that Man is more than Man in order to consider humanism positively open toward Christianity.

In fact, this bonus must either be integrated into the concept of Man—and then we consider the second concept ("Christian") as the most adequate one—or it is not integrated into the previous concept of Man—and then a consequent humanism has no other option but to reject such a bonus. In addition, these well-intentioned philosophical considerations can make us assume that the novelty introduced by Christianity is reduced to the introduction of a more or less sublime bonus, and we forget that the Christian modification is radical—and mortal for all of humanism.

Below we will not refer directly to Christian humanism, but rather to humanism in general. The verification of our thesis is manifold.

*

Phenomenological

The fact that a man, left to his own devices, cannot behave like a man is a common phenomenon. Not only are there temptations that human beings alone cannot overcome because of overwhelming external pressures, but they also succumb to these due to a seed of internal disorder that is rooted in their very nature. In this respect, theology speaks of the dogma of original sin, of the free gift of final perseverance, and of the inability to obey natural law in its entirety without God's special assistance. Phenomenologically speaking, we can assert that Man possesses a thirst for happiness and for salvation that he cannot quench on his own, that human existence possesses a peculiar instability in the goodness—no matter how specific—that it wants though it cannot achieve. *Video meliora proboque, deteriora sequor.*[10]

Man specifically, as humanity in general, left to his own strength, suffers from a radical disorientation in his life because of his inability to achieve what he would truly like to achieve, if he does not realize that his own will is weakened by the rise of other powers and inclinations. Humanism, which attempts to extract light and strength to guide Man from human immanence itself, is impotent to lead Man toward the attainment of his end. This is why humanism holds a secret rivalry against God.

In fact, a simple glance at humanist culture reveals a latent resentment toward God. Seeing things from Man's point of view, through humanistic eyes, it seems as

---

[10] Ovid, *Metamorphoses* VII.19. See the enigmatic and transcendental Pauline affirmations, Rom 7:14ff.

if Creation's plan had failed, and God is unconsciously blamed for not having done things better. Many of the problems that are posed have no solution because they are pseudo-problems that emerge from considering Man the measure of all things and the center of the universe. Spanish Jews were also shocked at not being able to cross the Strait of Gibraltar—as they had previously done in the Red Sea—when they were banished by the Catholic monarchs.

The sin of intellectual envy runs skin-deep in humanistic culture. It causes a latent spiritual scandal in our era with which we justify our mistakes: since things are already going badly—we reason—it matters little that we personally upset the theoretical order a little more. Humanism is secretly envious of God and of the absolute, and this makes it incompatible with the Christian virtues of humility, justice, and charity. Humanists believe they have rights that they do not possess and they forge for themselves a narcissistic perfection that draws them away from He who demands abnegation, self-hatred, and the cross to follow Him and achieve eternal life.

Likewise, the relativity of all human values appears to be an experimental anthropological law, in such a way that these values emerge with greater freshness and vigor when they are overcome and not sought as ends. A technique that is too perfect degrades, sensual licentiousness becomes torture, the desire to have fun engenders boredom, and so on. Human values are all there to be overcome. These and analogous facts transcend all humanism.

Philosophical

Humanism is not a philosophical system, although it presupposes one. It is more like a cultural attitude in which Man—and consequently human perfection—occupies, at the very least, the psychological center of interest. This psychological context implies a specific gnoseological position that is characteristic of humanism. Humanism needs to be able to believe in Man, and for this it needs human beings to be founded on themselves, if not metaphysically, at least epistemologically. If Man is not the supreme being, he must at least be the ultimate tribunal in the cognitive order. This is why all humanism is latently idealist, even when it hypostasizes the reason in a Supreme Being or when it wishes to appear in realist garb. Ultimately, the man of humanism must be criterion of truth since he must somehow justify everything.

This egocentric psychological attitude of "modern" Man comes from the vital loss of God as beginning, end, and foundation of our lives. In the sixteenth century, human reason becomes independent from faith as the superior form of knowledge; theology becomes consigned to an honorific primate with Descartes, who divests it of its status as science and, relegating it to the sphere of the practical, makes it ineffective and impotent to direct philosophy. Man then becomes his own judge, and his reason the court of last resort.

The philosophical foundation of humanism is rationalism. One implies the other. Only if my reason is the sole criterion of truth will Man be the measure of all things.

And vice versa, if primacy belongs to Man, it is because he possesses a faculty that allows him to judge all things without it being judged by anybody. The main philosophical issue of humanism is critical philosophy, since in this radically anthropocentric humanist attitude, Man must be founded on himself. This is why the gnoseological problem is the first thing presented to humanism, before any other philosophical approach. Before going outside himself, Man must justify the validity of his own instrument. That said, Who must he justify it before? Definitely before his own self; but then, by accepting what he takes to be the point of departure as facts, the problem is solved. And this is where the critical problem of modern philosophy has, in the end, led to.

In point of fact, however, the human intellectual horizon, although true, is complete neither in extension nor in intensity. There is a positive limit to reason. Reality overwhelms and surpasses us. Human intelligence is limited and must let itself be conditioned by reality, that is, it must freely and rationally perform an act of submission and subjugation.

The problem is indeed complex. After the loss of innocence, Man cannot return to a paradisiac state; neither can the modern mentality take itself back to a precritical phase. Furthermore, the need to found oneself on oneself appears to be an inseparable characteristic of reflexive knowledge (truth is no longer in the correspondence between the concept and the thing, but rather the adaptation of the object—already a conceptual one—of the thing to the mind). Once Man becomes conscious of himself up to this point, that is to say, once he gets the science of good and evil, he can no longer escape himself, unless he actually throws himself into the arms of a transcendence that gives him direct vision of things. Perhaps the gnoseological enlightenment of the early Christians was philosophically weak—and it is certainly so once critical doubt has started to gnaw at the human minds—but anthropologically, that is, as an existential human attitude, it was the only one possible at the time: either Man's knowledge is a participation in an enlightenment in which he is simultaneously the enlightened and the enlightener, or we fall into the pit of self-justification which, even if realized, entails humanist anthropocentrism, which is quite clearly insufficient. A great deal of existentialism lies precisely in once again posing the problem from its very foundation in order to try to find a way out that will inevitably lead to or will be founded on nothing—that *nothing* from which God, in the beginning, created heaven and earth, as an existentialism that wants to call itself Christian will say; but this is to end where the problem begins. . . .

Moreover, Man's axiological evaluation is also imperfect, and therefore no humanist ethical foundation can be drawn from humanism. Man knows how to distinguish good from bad, but with many limitations. Goodness, like truth, is hidden in the being, and Man can only reveal its secrets tenuously.[11]

---

[11] Let us recall the beginning of chapter 3 of the Vatican Council's constitution *Dei Filius*: "Cum homo a Deo tamquam creatore et Domino suo totus dependeat et ratio creata increatae Veritati penitus subiecta sit, plenum revelanti Deo intellectus et voluntatis obsequium fide praestare tenemur." *Denz.*, 1789. Neither human intelligence nor will are supreme norms.

Additionally, all of this has sociological repercussions. A natural hierarchy of values is not Christian. Christianity has not come to be a supplement for Man and, consequently, to perfect social order. Rather it transforms human beings and alters social values. In short, there is no humanism that can digest the affirmations of the Sermon on the Mount.

Theological

A certain human self-sufficiency and autonomy that are incompatible with the Christian foundations of life are essential for humanism. Original sin has destroyed the possibility of a Christian humanism, and supernatural elevation has even taken from Man the positive sense of an exclusively human existence. For Christians, humanism means being degraded to mere men.

Man is, on the one hand, a truncated being, and on the other, he is elevated to a supernaturalness. Human beings find themselves in the paradoxical situation that they are even unable to fulfill—relying on their own forces alone—the natural law that their intelligence presents to them. That is to say, they are in fact impotent *to be* just as they themselves know that they *must be*, and on the other hand, they *must be* much more than what they *are*; and they can be so on account of the fact that they have been made consort to divine nature. In both cases, the Christian paradox eliminates any possibility of humanism. This is why the Model and the Master of Christians is not a simple mortal, but rather the Son of God.

Humanism represents—and here lies its greatest virulence—the exclusion of the idea of redemption. True humanism attempts to redeem Man by itself. Yet Man cannot save himself. Self-redemption is the topical dream of modern Man. He finds himself thirsty for repair, he has recognized his own nullity, but he does not tolerate the intrusion of a Redeemer. Humanism is Man's titanic effort to save himself. Yet "a creature cannot save the creature," as St. Athanasius, Father of the Church, would say.[12] Moreover: not only can Man not save himself, Christians cannot save themselves either. This is what Christian humanism forgets.

The attempt to "baptize" humanism is, in a certain way, more dangerous, as it turns Christ's redemption into an enterprise that is merely superficial and extrinsic to Man, not only its principles, but also in its effects. Christian humanism cannot recognize the depth of redemption or the transformation occurring in human beings; rather it is forced to consider it a simple ersatz action of God due to the whim of his love. It is then that Man begins to feel "condemned" to be free and dragged to a supernatural destiny that he does not willingly accept. The humanist man is his own center; he has no internal space for God. The God of Christian humanism can only be an extrinsic God. If God were immanent to Man and transformed him into God, humanism would be wiped out. For humanism, only Man is immanent to himself.

---

[12] *Epistula ad Adelphium* 8 (*PG* 26.1082).

This is also the point when not only the problem of Man's collaboration with God's grace begins, as if this were about two more or less homogeneous factors, but also when problems causing an extrapolation of human reason into fields that transcend it are unduly posed, as reason considers all things according to its own standards. A typical example of this would be the debate about possibilities in God, a debate that is no longer "byzantine" but rather humanistic: Could He have created Man differently? Would God have incarnated if Man had not sinned? Would one drop of blood have been enough for redemption? Or perhaps, would one sole bloodless act have been enough? When the *morphe* in anthropo-morphism loses its "sym-bolic" (putting-together) character and turns into a simple "form," these and similar problems arise whose weak point lies precisely in the humanist supposition from which they stem.

For humanism, the supernatural is a mere supplement for Man. Christian humanism is a mere supernatural appendage that is added to Man. If God, and not Man, is the measure of man; if human beings can do nothing in the factual order in which they find themselves and very little in the natural order; if Man's end is not himself, and so on, then there is no possible humanism and any attempt to baptize humanism proves to be internally contradictory because, ultimately, what we would need to do would be to suprahumanize Man.[13]

Christianity cannot accept everything human *as human*, as is *essential* to humanism. Christian humanism would perhaps be acceptable in a purely natural state. But this has never existed. If we begin from the concept of Christian Man, this implies a series of suprahuman values that transcend all humanism, since it is not *as* human that these values are acceptable, but rather *as* divine. If we begin from the real factual man, humanism is also not sustainable, since Man's *vulnerata* (wounded) nature requires that he must renounce some inferior values in order to reach superior ones. Original sin is the coup de grâce to all humanism. *Omnis homo mendax.*[14] Man is a fallen being, and consequently there is no possible humanism. Whosoever does not hate even his own soul . . .

Let no one say that Christ as man founds Christian humanism. In Christ, humanity is not the end, the basis, the hypostasis, the person. Christ is truly man, but there is no human person in Him. The latter does not exist: its role is subsumed by the Divine Person. Christ is not a humanist. He has not come to fulfill his will, but rather to fulfill that of the Father who has sent Him.

In sum, humanism aims at making Man naturally human, but Christianity has come to make him divine.

---

[13] But this is something that humanism does not seem to want or to understand. See its characteristic language: "Pero no por eso el hombre asō elevado deja de ser hombre en su peculiar naturaleza, a saber, sustancia compuesta de alma y cuerpo y sujeto permanente de esta elevación, mientras que los dones divinos que lo transforman no son más que accidentes." L. Legaz y Lacambra, "Humanismo y Derecho," in *Scritti di sociologia e politica in onore di Luigi Sturzo*, vol. 2 (Bologna: Zanichelli, 1953), 379 (see, on the other hand, the theology of the beatific vision).

[14] Ps 115:11, also mentioned by St. Paul, Rom 3:4.

Metaphysic-Theological

We would have preferred to say that humanism does not find any *meta-theological* justification either, but the introduction of this word would require a digression that has no place here. What we wish to say is that the implicit assumption of humanism that is at the root of its incompatibility with Christianity consists in the alleged autonomy of human beings. The latter, in point of fact, are not autonomous in respect of God, not only as regards their actions or the moral field, but in the actual entrails of their being. Elsewhere we have tried to explain that the ontonomy of created beings cannot be mistaken with a monist heteronomy, and that it cannot be identified with a dualist autonomy either, as if created beings were something in themselves and outside of God.[15] In fact, God and the world are not "two"—two *what*? (this *what* would be superior to God in extension or in intention, and with this, God would cease to be the supreme being)—although they are also not "one." Monolithic monism makes all distinctions impossible and it shatters all life, both religious and philosophical. But let us apply these ideas to our specific case.

Humanism seems to recognize in Man a certain autonomy independent of God: Man as the starting point—even if it is to result in God—Man as foundation—even if it is later recognized that he is also founded—Man as a model and measure—even if it is said that his being this way is received—Man, in short, as a separate being—and not only different—from God. This is why the problems of freedom, of the relationship between civil and religious society, between the "profane" sciences and theology, between man and his fellow men, and so on, all have a special nuance in any humanism. God's role is limited to being a more or less important factor—and it is reduced to zero in atheist humanism—but anyway one factor among others. And even when He is awarded a certain superior dignity, He does not possess that absoluteness that characterizes all the positions that are integrally religious. The reason is obvious: humanism has been a reaction—sometimes healthy—against a heteronomous attitude that ignored the values of an intrinsically ontic hierarchy of reality (ontonomy).

It would be a great misunderstanding if these pages were seen as a plea to restore a heteronomous mentality of the past. Our purpose concurs with the intention of most of the so-called Christian humanists. The only remark we wish to make is that the point of departure should be different and that the Christianization of humanism transforms it in such a way that it ceases to be humanism and becomes theandrism.

The reaction has often been healthy, but we believe it has not been theological enough. Because of this, because it has disregarded the dogma of the Trinity (the only one that can maintain the constitutive tension of the contingent being between being and nonbeing without falling into a dissolving monism or into a separatist dualism), contemporary humanism has overstepped its boundaries, and even the

---

[15] See R. Panikkar, "Le concept d'ontonomie," in *Actes du XI Congrès International de Philosophie* (Louvain: Nauwelaerts, 1953), 3:182–88.

humanism that is so-called Christian has forgotten that all alleged human autonomy is nothing more than an illusion. Man, considered meta-theologically, is not even an "I" as the *ultimate* subject of operations and of being, but rather a "you"—called and created by God—who perceives himself psychologically as an I. God is the only "I." His full and total "You" is the Logos. That is why we *are* insofar as we participate in Christ, Only Begotten Son of the Father, Firstborn of all the creatures and through whom all things have been created.

Humanism has imposed on itself as a sacrosanct mission the defense of the human being against interferences on the part of society, technology, other men, and even God and the Church, considered—erroneously, though sometimes understandably—as powers that are alien to Man and that arbitrarily limit his freedom and reduce his dignity. Only an adequate theological consideration of the essence of God and the nature of the Church can undo the mistake in which more than one humanism has fallen in its fight for a noble cause and against obvious heteronomous abuses.

In other words, humanism represents either the maximum valuation of human nature, that is, Man's autonomy, and so it cannot be Christian; or it will discover the person in the human being and will constitute itself in a personalist humanism. But in the latter case, either it will consider the person as an aspiration for Being, as a relationship to Being that can only be understood and valued from its destiny, from its terminus of arrival and not from its point of departure—that is to say, from God and from the divinization of the human being but not from the factual situation of the present. In this case it is obvious not only that humanism is transcended but also that it ceases to be humanism; or the human person is considered as an aspiration for itself (not for God, as in the first case), and then humanism fails, destroys itself, and attempts to save itself by one way or another accepting this, its constitutive failure. Be that as it may, the truth is that in this case such a humanism can in no way call itself Christian. In brief, personalism either ceases to be humanism or it ceases to be compatible with Christianity.

Theoretically speaking, an anthropology that considers the human person as an aspiration for Being could still consequently be called humanist if it interpreted such an aspiration as a dynamism immanent to the human person itself, without any existing transcendence outside Man that stimulates and fulfills the very aspiration of human beings to transcend themselves. It is obvious that such a "modernist," or perhaps "existentialist," humanism would not be Christian either; but, furthermore, this position is not, strictly speaking, different from that which we have called *immanent personalism*, which considers the person as an aspiration to itself since it recognizes nothing outside of it. Briefly: if there is a God, humanism cannot justify itself because there is no sphere in which Man is either ultimate or definitive.

We do not want to introduce the issue of personalism, despite its obvious connection, yet we cannot help but mention in passing that humanism tends toward an individualist interpretation of personalism. The person is recognized as the maximum value on earth, the dignity of the person is a supreme value that no collective or common good is sufficient to devalue or extinguish. This is true, yet we still have to emphasize that the value and dignity of the person consists in something that, even if it is not collective, is also not individual. Without going into further disquisitions, let us suggest the authentic Christian sense by turning to the liturgy. In it—and because of it—Man acquires his perfection; in it and because of it, Christ's redemption is applied to us; in it and because of it, Man fulfills the action through which he constitutes himself truly and fully man: adoration and love for a God who is inaccessible any other way, reception and assimilation of a God who is not given to us any other way.

So, in the liturgy understood in the sense described, as *the Church in act*, man is certainly a person, with personal connections to God—so personal that they are realized by means of the Son of God and of Man—but he is not a simple individual who seeks his salvation or his happiness or his perfection, as he is also not an indifferent member of a group whose only value lies in the totality; rather he is a Christian, that is to say, a son of God and of man at once, a unique and unrepeatable member of the people of God, of the saintly Church, of the Bride of the *Pantocrator*, a fellow creature of God and of men, a son and a brother, a person, in one word, who can be neither isolated nor anonymized, nor singularized nor diluted. He is a person who fulfills his end by elevating the world and men, his brothers, and even carrying with himself the entire material creation, and so forth. In short, it seems to us that humanism, no matter how Christian it wishes to be, cannot account for or express, or offer a basis for, the understanding of this set of fundamental Christian truths that humanist culture had significantly left in the dark.

The Lesson of History

Sed sufficientia nostra ex Deo est.

2 Co 3:5

There have been three great humanisms in Western history: the classical one, the Renaissance one, and the current one. And none of them were intrinsically Christian.

The Greeks and the Latins could be humanists because they were not yet Christians and had not yet to decide in favor of the cosmic law of the cross that had not yet been promulgated, though it reigned over the world. Hence the fascination that Greece has exercised on all people who, lacking a living faith, have found themselves within a Christian environment: they would simply like to be "men," yet they are "condemned" to be something more. And nevertheless, there was in classical humanism a secret desire to overcome this world and an unconscious desire for transcendence.[16] Hellenic humanism could be theoretically perfect, but it was existentially truncated and irreparably sad. Neither the Socratic concept of Man nor the Platonic one is real. The wise man is not, without fail, a good man. Recognizing goodness does not imply

---

[16] "Man can live not insofar as he is (simply) man, but insofar as the Divine dwells in him," as Aristotle said in *Nicomachean Ethics* 10.7 (1177b).

it is followed. On this earth, truth and goodness are divorced much too frequently. Despite Plato's theocentric efforts,[17] the real Greek man is that of tragedy. Wanting to be fully and truly man, he succumbs before his own fate. Classical humanism is not possible because no humanism is sustainable. Man was born for God and to let himself be deified by transcending his humanity. Man is an unstable being, and when he wishes to maintain balance by means of his own strengths, he precipitates into the abyss of the tragic. "The Gods always help those who work for their own downfall," says Aeschylus. It is the lesson of Greek and Roman antiquity. Greek tragedy is the destruction of Hellenic humanism from within. It is neither in vain nor by chance that Greek culture fell into the hands of Eastern "mystery cults" and finally joined Christianity.

*

The case of the Renaissance is also instructive. Today we cannot deny that the essential sense of classical antiquity was just as well known in the Middle Ages as it was in the Renaissance. What distinguishes these epochs is not the knowledge of Man or the curiosity for antiquity, but rather the typically humanist, anthropocentric attitude of the historical trend that prevailed in the *Cinquecento*, which was given the name of Renaissance. This is why, even though the Middle Ages and the wrongly termed Renaissance admit the same truths, they present a completely different spirit. The medieval theocentric atmosphere turns anthropocentric; therefore, the same affirmations sound so different. The anti-Christian side of the Renaissance is its humanist side.

The aforementioned urge to strategically admit a Christian humanism is what has led some to defend the existence of a medieval humanism, and this has ended up demonstrating that Renaissance humanism did not consist in the cultivation of antiquity or in that of art or literature, since all of this already existed in the Middle Ages, but rather in the anthropocentric aspect awarded to human activities.[18]

The Renaissance was cowardly. It became aware of the Christian demands of the nascent epoch and became scared; it did not dare face its Christian destiny and preferred to return to Greece for protection, in order not to have to decide, as if Man had not experienced a radical change after Christ.[19] The success of the Lutheran

---

[17] "God is for us, first of all, the just measure of all things, much more than any man could ever be." *Nomoi* I.4 (716 D). This text was quoted by Pius XII in his speech of July 14, 1950.

[18] It is understandable that the church, in the fifteenth and sixteenth centuries did not know how to "accuellir et modérer à la fois l'humanisme et la Renaissance des arts" (Y. Congar, *Vrai et fausse réforme dans l'Eglise* [Paris: Cerf, 1950], 331).

[19] See, among others, the following fundamental works in order to understand the Middle Ages and its relationship to the Renaissance: M. D. Chenu, *La Théologie au XIIIème siècle* (Paris: Vrin, 1957); Chenu, *La Théologie comme science au XIIIe siècle* (Paris: Vrin, 1957); J. Leclerq, *L'Amour des lettres et le desir de Dieu* (Paris: Cerf, 1957); E. Gilson, *L'humanisme de Saint Thomas d'Aquin*, Proceedings of the Fifth International Conference

movement was partly due to the fact that it presented itself as a profoundly Christian solution against the compromise that had already spread from a Christian humanism. And the historical paradox lies in the fact that, by virtue of an internal dialectic, Protestantism—which was antihumanist at the start—was later "humanized." The underestimation of Man was compensated by the exaltation of the individual.

*

Finally, modern humanism is the last bastion of a culture that wants to save itself and is beating a hasty retreat. Just as the eighteenth century wanted to find a natural religion as that religious background common to all men so that there would exist a basis of shared comprehension, without realizing that one cannot minimize truth, so also, analogously, modern humanism is the "all-rounder" and the lowest common denominator for the most varied tendencies. It is an anemic unity that is devoid of content, subject to the fluctuations of the prevailing wind.[20] This is why there are atheist, materialist, pantheistic, idealist, existentialist, Marxist, Protestant, and Catholic humanists.

*

This is the great attraction and also the great temptation of humanism in our times: it apparently offers a common base for dialogue, a platform on which everyone may agree. It is always the same: if nature is the base, then Christ can no longer be so. And man can only truly find himself in Christ. Anything else is to fall short, and from the point of view of Christian sincerity, it comes very close to being a lie. Christ did not say: Be a man and *also* be a Christian. Rather he preached that the only way to be what God wants us to be, what we have been called to be, is by completely transforming what we initially are in order to resurrect to a new life, a new man, not waiting until the next world for this to happen and leaving this world to the jurisdiction of Christian humanism, but rather from this moment on, from the moment that by grace we participate in His very nature.

Let us record two instances of considerable importance in the life of Christendom that can be attributed to the humanist influence of the past centuries. "Modern" anthropomorphic piety that moves away from the liturgy, that creates "particular" religious observances for itself and that adopts the forms of an inflated anthropomorphism, is largely due to the humanist climate of the past centuries. Let no one say

---

of Philosophy, Naples, 1925, 984ff.; Gilson, "Le Moyen-Âge et le naturalisme antique," in *Archives d'histoire doctrinale et littéraire du Moyen-Âge*, 7 (1932): 5–38; Gilson, *L'Esprit de la philosophie médiévale* (Paris: Vrin, 1932); Gilson, *Héloïse et Abélard. Études sur le Moyen-Âge et l'Humanisme* (Paris: Vrin, 1938).

[20] The "universal scientific humanism" of Julian Huxley as the philosophy of UNESCO (when he was general director) is a typical example of searching for those words that are more or less universally accepted, even if everyone fills them with different content.

that all popular piety is anthropomorphic because that would be to confuse matters. Popular medieval piety was concrete and it was bonded to the earth; it was, if you wish, anthropo-symbolic, but not anthropomorphic. For the Middle Ages, what was human was σύμβολον and not μορψή. Its piety was bonded to the earth, but the earth was nothing but a footstool for the Creator's feet[21] and a stepping-stone for climbing to the afterlife.

The second example would be the fact that the majority of the post-Renaissance Church's missionary efforts simultaneously become civilizing zeal and humanist endeavor. Hence the close collaboration between political powers and the Christian message in missionary lands.[22]

That humanism does not lie at the base of the major accomplishments of European history is a thesis that we are merely allowed to suggest, but which we believe to be of a certain importance for the cultural interpretation of our own era.[23] In this we can perhaps distinguish it from modern Western culture, which appears to want to ignore antagonisms that require radical decisions. Humanism is a master of conciliation, not because of charity or prudence, but rather because of its spirit of compromise. The origin of Christian humanism[24] only serves to emphasize its characteristic of apostasy.

*

God, Man, and world are the three maximum existing realities—ignoring the angelic universe—and their conjugation gives place to the three historical humanisms mentioned. For Greece, Man was certainly a part of the world, one more among the many things of the universe, and his reason was one small part of the whole; however, this man rebels against the restraint of the universe and the tyranny of the Gods. This is why Hellenic humanism has such a fascinating heroic nature; it is Man's struggle to conquer his place in the world of Being, and even when Man succumbs in his attempt, he knows how to die beautifully and heroically. *Homo res sacra homini*, says Seneca. This is natural and tragic humanism.

The Christian conception was able to maintain the authentic hierarchy: Man is superior to the universe, he is its king; but he is completely subordinate to God. Moreover, he is inserted into divinity, as subordination could entail some sort of *right*, and not even a relationship of justice is possible in God toward Man.[25] The Renaissance was shocked in the face of the medieval pride that made Man the king of

---

[21] Is 66:1; Ac 7:49.

[22] Please read carefully what John XXIII says about "new forms of colonialism," in his encyclical *Mater et Magistra* (May 15, 1961) in order to understand the difference.

[23] See merely as examples: C. Dawson, *Progress and Religion* (London: Sheed & Ward, 1938); F. Heer, *Europäische Geitesgeschichte* (Stuttgart: Kohlhammer, 1953).

[24] See J. Maritain, *Humanisme integral* (Paris: Aubier, 1936).

[25] The *suum cuique* does not have a subject on which to lean. See the elegant Thomist commentary of J. Pieper, *Über die Gerechtigkeit* (Munich: Kösel, 1953).

Creation and the earth the center of the universe. But it was a hypocritical scandal. God and the world *were* before Man, ultimately, because Man himself postulated this. It was not by virtue of a revelation that Man accepted this submission, but rather because his very own spirit required it so. He positions himself in the last place, just as it is common courtesy for he who quotes to quote himself last. Renaissance Man is anyway the judge of all reality; he judges God and the universe. This is apostate and inconsistent humanism.

Finally, the latent dialectic of Renaissance humanism leads to present-day humanism, which is nothing but the consistent development of the Renaissance. This is why an epoch is now closing. Man, as judge of all reality, is tiring of the modest and inauthentic role the Renaissance gave him, and he is drawing the ultimate conclusions of his metaphysical autonomy. His technological accomplishments at dominating material nature confirm this, and subsequently he becomes the top figure in this reality. God becomes an increasingly superfluous hypothesis, and the material world loses consistency when it is diluted in the enormous human construction of physicomathematics. When society feels the need to proclaim the *rights of man* it is because it has lost its divine foundation and it must substitute it by means of an extrinsic promulgation. This is the beginning of atheistic humanism.

Cartesian rationalism leads to Kant, whose "thing-in-itself" is swept away by subsequent idealism. Hegelian *reason* turns into Feuerbach's and Comte's *humanity*. And Marx's humanist position logically emerges from there.

If we admit the existence of a Christian humanism next to other humanisms, then what is Christian would be nothing more than a mere accident of earthly life. It would, if you wish, be the only correct description for humanism, but accidental nonetheless. *Humanism* would be what is fundamental, and *Christian* would turn into a simple adjective.

Our Western culture, as we said, has lost living faith in God, and because we cannot live without faith, it has proclaimed faith in Man. And in order to make faith in God return, Christians have accepted this faith in Man. But faith cannot be a metaphysical point of departure. One cannot discover the substantial root of Man without first finding God, the same way that one cannot penetrate the metaphysical nature of things while ignoring their connection to the ultimate Cause.[26]

We have taken Man too seriously (and for this very reason—paradoxically—we are degrading him), absolutizing a series of values that are constitutively relative and a series of situations that are essentially temporary. Man, making himself, transforming himself through time, becoming, without yet being, *not-yet-being*, has a provisional nature. Man is not the end of Man, contrary to what Marx, exponent of this mentality, says. Man's function on this earth has been overvalued, more or less spiritually considered, as if it were the end of human beings.[27] When European

---

[26] See R. Panikkar, *El concepto de naturaleza* (Madrid: C.S.I.C., 1951), 273ff. Appears in volume XII of *Opera Omnia*.

[27] See Lk 21:34. This *cura*, concern, is what comes up in the existentialist *Sorge*.

culture lost faith in heaven (*paradiso*), it tried to substitute it for confidence in an earthly *paradise*. And, in general, the European embodiment of Christianity—which is essentially supernatural—has been degenerating into humanism—which is constitutively naturalist.

Christian Humanism

Opus ei non erat ut quis testimonium perhiberet de homine.

Jn 2:25

Some will say, all right, "Christianity is not *formally* a humanism,"[28] but this does not imply that a Christian humanism cannot exist, understanding by this a kind of humanist attitude—consequently, on the same plane as other humanisms—but open to the supernatural, and not only compatible with Christianity, but in a certain way as its very point of departure. Just as philosophy cannot be identified with theology, and nevertheless, many thinkers who have faith recognize the existence of a true Christian philosophy, similarly there is a Christian humanism, and to wish to fight it means going against the anthropological roots of Christianity itself.

We do not wish to take part in a discussion about Christian philosophy or to express our reserves. We will merely say that either "Christian humanism" is not a humanism like the rest—that is to say, it uses the same name with a different content, without explicitly warning of this fact—or it is not Christian in the sense in which Christianity understands and interprets itself.

In fact, any other humanism that is not the Christian one considers being anthropocentric one of its essential attributes as well as proceeding to Man's perfection without supra- or infrahuman interferences—unless they are postulated by Man's own nature. A Christian humanism cannot accept such postulates. If it did, it would no longer be Christian.

The counterresponse touches on a crucial point of Christianity and especially of the Christian culture of our times. It is in fact adduced, in order to weaken the previous argument, the celebrated Thomist axiom that Grace does not destroy but presupposes and perfects nature. With this, Christian humanism would belong to the order of a nature that is not destroyed by grace and that lies at its very base. Christian humanism would consequently be the natural human base on which the rest of Christian doctrine could be built.

This is not the place to carry out an in-depth analysis of the alleged axiom. Let us adduce, in a no less axiomatic form, a series of propositions that must be familiar to any Christian. Grace certainly *does not destroy* nature; but this does not mean that it does not destroy the constructions that have been built upon it, taking it as a sufficiently firm base to direct Man's improvement; and this is what humanism

---

[28] O. N. Derisi, "Cristianismo."

claims to do. Grace does not destroy human nature, but it *transforms* it in such a way that pure nature no longer really *exists*, and consequently a principle of operations that is independent or stands next to the supernatural—which is certainly not a new substance or another one either, but rather the "information" of nature by a superior principle and its consequent transformation—is not given in a Christian environment. In this sense, grace *supposes* nature, that is, as the former influences the latter and transforms it, but not as the former is *dependent* on the latter, a thesis that is little less than inseparable from so-called Christian humanism, since a humanism without a certain humanistic autonomy would not be humanism. Humanism would wish to pave the ways to grace; it would wish to offer an adequate base as if grace were not eminently free and supernatural and were not supremely independent of nature's demands. Finally, grace certainly *perfects* nature, not as a complement to Man's natural improvement, but rather as a radical transformation that is adequately expressed by authentic *conversion*, which does not consist in the rectification of some more or less important points but rather in death and the consequent resurrection. If Man were merely man, as we have already said before, Christian death would annihilate him. Because Man is something more than man, he is capable of resurrecting and becoming a new creature. If humanism, which is essentially natural, converted, what would resurrect would no longer be any kind of humanism, but rather something different, which, following Christian tradition, we have called *theandrism*.

In sum, humanism is natural, Christianity is supernatural; and between one and the other there is no other passage than the death and resurrection carried out by the work of grace, without merit or demand on the part of nature. If Christian humanism wishes to continue being humanism, we believe it pertains entirely to the natural order, and with this, in a Christian atmosphere, it declares itself to be impotent to contribute to the improvement of Christians.

Let us repeat this in an equally inopportune manner: Christian humanism tries hard to look for a common base between a merely natural conception of things and an exclusively supernatural one. We also wish to repeat that we share the reaction against a monodimensional supernaturalism, but we must add that between a sincerely natural *ultimate* conception and an authentically supernatural *ultimate* conception there is nothing in common, after all, because ultimateness can only be one. A natural conception of Man—not only insofar as it is closed, but also insofar as it is fundamental and basic, that is, ultimate—is not only incomplete, it is also false; any consideration that takes human nature as the ultimate object of operations fundamentally contradicts Christianity for which redemption has universal effects; Christ is the light that illuminates every man who comes to this world, human nature is either fallen or risen, and so on. Only when we do not descend to the last consequences or to the first principles can we speak of a common base; but then it is no longer a "base," but rather a simple abstraction of a more complete reality that cannot and must not be hidden.

One could say that human nature is valid both for Christianity as well as for humanism and that Christian humanism is based on this human nature that is recognized by Christians and non-Christians alike, thus becoming the necessary bridge, or rather, the path of the intellect toward Christianity.

Our answer is the following: *first*, such a concept of human is not completely independent of the anthropology that one follows, and this anthropology is different for a believer than for one who is not. In fact, different philosophies define human nature differently. For a Christian, the concept of nature is perfectly defined not only from below but also from above insofar as it is distinguished from the supernatural. Any effect of the supernatural on Man, any effect of original sin that a nonbeliever could detect, all of this will be included in *his* concept of nature, as he neither believes nor admits anything supernatural—besides the fact that, of course, diverse metaphysical assumptions approach the problem from a radically different perspective. Such a human nature, the alleged common basis for dialogue, then ends up being somewhat problematic.

Second, even if we admit to a common concept of human nature, the incompatibility between Christianity and humanism would not be overcome, since, unless humanism is identified with naturalism—in which case it is no longer compatible with Christianity—no humanism, and much less a Christian one, is satisfied with a simple phenomenological analysis of what human nature may be. Rather it builds a conception of Man and of things on this concept with the goal of channeling and directing Man's own perfecting. One could say that Christian humanism is an open humanism and that the perfecting of Man to which it aspires pertains to the merely natural sphere. In reply, we reiterate that neither its openness nor its naturalness weakens the previous argument, unless one assumes—as we have criticized that Christian humanism does—that the supernatural order is only a prolongation and a supplement of the natural order instead of being its transformation from its very foundation for an elevation not claimable by nature. Because of this, even if they agree on a common concept of nature, any construction that one wishes to build upon this concept either recognizes the Christian principles from its very beginning or whatever is constructed upon a "natural" nature becomes incompatible with Christianity. And humanism is not exactly a mere technical construction on a natural base; let us say something like a medical science that can build a whole therapy on a merely natural conception of Man. Besides the fact that from the viewpoint of integral medicine there would be much to say against such an independence of any factor superior to Man's mere rational animal nature, the fact is that humanism's aspirations are greater than that of being a mere natural human art. Christ is also a sign of contradiction here: we must choose between Christianity and humanism. The decision in favor of the cross is not an antihumanism, but neither is it "the work of the flesh nor of the blood nor of Man's will."[29] Christianity is not a humanism, but it is much less an antihumanism.

Perhaps Christianity, thus, does not destroy humanism; rather it supposes and perfects it, just as grace does much the same thing with nature. But Christian

---

[29] Jn 1:13.

thinkers will recognize, in the first place, what we have said about the axiom, and in the second place, they may perhaps agree with us in saying that just as the good nucleus of nature becomes sublimated and elevated by the supernatural, humanism, including the good one, that is, the Christian one, is overcome and sublimated by Christianity. None of the values that the good humanism wanted to defend perish in the Christian transformation; however, the new creature reborn in Christ can no longer be properly called *humanism*, but rather *theandrism*. In the same way that if a good Parsee converts to Christianity he ceases to be a Parsee in a certain sense, even if he preserves everything that is good and valid about his Zoroastrianism, converted humanism is not something inhuman and it collects and sublimates all of the values of humanism, but it cannot, strictly speaking, be called *humanism*. Not only does a true conversion transform us, but baptism confers a new name on us. Why this attachment to the old and resistance toward He who has come to make all things new?

Another, and very different, thing is what in fact many of those who defend Christian humanism do: they simply study philosophical anthropology in depth under the more or less direct inspiration and direction of faith. Their work has been and continues to be of inestimable value. This text does not intend to paralyze any positive attempt and even less to judge anybody. Its only desire is to clarify a set of problems. If some wish to call this theological anthropology "Christian humanism," no problem, provided they avoid misunderstandings and block the false paths that have been indicated.

Christian Theandrism

Quiescite ergo ab homine, cujus spiritus in naribus ejus est.[30]

Is 2:22

It is obvious that Christian humanism has excellent intentions, and excellent are its specific affirmations unconnected to the general perception of humanism. But its doctrine does not seem to us to be intrinsically compatible with Christianity.

Let us explain. As humanism is not a defined philosophical attitude, it cannot be formally and strictly anathematized.[31] It is not logic, but rather Christian sense that fights against it. Humanism may be coated in a series of propositions that are all orthodox in isolation, and yet its mood, its suggestive capacity, the tendencies that it triggers, the assumptions that it implies psychologically—not always logically—and so on, all have an a-Christian flavor and a naturalist accent that make it incompatible with an authentically supernatural life. A crucified God does not get on well with an autonomous humanism.

---

[30] "Beware of man, in whose nostrils there is nothing more than [a thin] breath [so, why should he matter?]."

[31] Nevertheless, all of chapter III of the Vatican Council I constitution *Dei Filium* is a global condemnation of humanism.

Humanism is also implicated in the loss of the *sense of mystery*, which we must urgently reconquer in order to invigorate the Christian mentality of our era. Christians live immersed in the Mystery, with a mystical sense that the humanist posture automatically destroys.[32]

The decline of the meaning of sin in modern society, which is a source of lament for current Christian thinkers, is also directly related to the spirit of humanism. For humanism, sin is, at most, a weakness, a mistake, a transgression, a disorder in the sum of the different reasons that propel us to action. But even if all this is not completely false, the true nature of the *mysterium iniquitatis* is forgotten, but that is the only thing that can give an answer to the anxiety of humanist believers—who cannot help but think that God has exaggerated somewhat by punishing sin with hell, and that the Passion of Christ comes to mean something like the insanity of love of a God who is excessively passionate, in order to thus "encourage" poor men to be a little more generous with their demands. We repeat that a lot of this may be true, but it is obvious that it does not correspond to the true Christian position and that Catholic theology has never been satisfied with such arguments, despite the humanist cultural onslaught.

Humanism also gives a deforming naturalist veneer to the magnificent current reaction in favor of a more human and natural Christian life. It is not necessary to spurn what is human in order to be Christian. Furthermore, without human virtues one cannot be a good Christian; in order to be one, one must be a true man. But the humanist atmosphere sometimes makes us forget the truths that complement the aforementioned statements, that is, that grace is not formally dependent upon nature; that the latter is not a cause, not even an occasion, for the former; that human virtues, in general, are not possible without a supernatural cause and that, as such, they are worth nothing for the salvation of Man. A clear example is the reaction that gave rise to humanism, and it is definitely worthwhile to dedicate another paragraph to it.

There was a time—which perhaps has not completely died out—when a Christian life seemed possible by cultivating so-called supernatural virtues, even the three Christian virtues,[33] fully independently of the natural ones. Theoretically, the "holier-than-thou" has always been considered a degeneration of the Christian spirit, but this sociological type was too frequent for us not to think about a monodimensional supernaturalness, which made it possible in a certain way: the heteronomous Christian attitude that looks to heaven without looking to the earth, believing it loves God but without serving one's fellow men, and so on.

Christian humanism reacted against all this with reason, and it achieved a certain success. Well, the opposite reaction of conferring primacy to the natural dimension and the heretical attitude of attributing to it a function of causality with regard to

---

[32] "Humanisme et Mystère s'opposent inconciliablement," logically affirms Odo Casel, *Le Mystère du Culte dans le Christianisme* (French translation; Paris: Cerf, 1946), 14 (original edition: *Das christliche Kultmysterium* (Regensburg: Pustet, 1932).

[33] Faith, hope, love; see 1 Co. 13:13.

the supernatural—both being actual dangers for humanism—perhaps contributed to making the cure worse than the disease: if supernatural heteronomy represents a degeneration and an error, natural autonomy is worth nothing in Christian terms, and is ineffective for the kingdom of God, even during our terrestrial pilgrimage. The true Christian *ontonomous* attitude recognizes the internal hierarchy of values and discovers something very dear to the humanist position, but that humanism alone is incapable of fulfilling. It discovers, in fact, Christian theandrism, namely that after the incarnation there are no disincarnate supernatural virtues; it is not ontologically possible to be a good Christian and a bad man; the authentically Christian love of God not only *leads* to love of our fellow men, but that it *is* a sole and only love; the real cultivation of natural virtues and even of theological ones carries with it the culture of all human values on earth. Moreover, Christian theandrism also affirms that the mover driving a man of goodwill to cultivate what we have agreed to call human virtues is something more than his simple nature, because the dynamism of grace acts in him, too, and Christ not only attracts toward himself the few privileged people who know and explicitly love him, rather he is the light that illuminates every man who comes into this world.

Humanism cannot even be used as a basis for the supernatural order, since the latter does not continue or complement nature, but rather impregnates it in its very entrails and turns it into the supernatural. Furthermore, there is only one way of fully being man, which is by being Christian, so that, in a certain sense, one must first be Christian in order to be a complete man. And we must not forget that, here on earth, Man is a transient being.

Not least of the evils of so-called Christian humanism is that, under the pretext of equanimity and justice, it places the natural and the supernatural on the same plane, turning them into two independent focal points of human activity and consequently losing any view in perspective and all axiological hierarchy. Because of this, it is understandable that humanism has a tendency to grant evil and error the same rights as goodness and truth, and that it advocates a heterodox compromise that is very different from Christian tolerance.

And this is another of humanism's pernicious effects: having reduced Christian morality to simple natural law. Men's creeds are very different; religions and philosophical systems are also disparate. The only thing that men apparently agree upon is a morality contained in human nature. Christian humanism will consequently defend that the only way of keeping this morality and of fulfilling its requirements, despite all kinds of temptations, is through Christianity. It is not incorrect but it has imperceptibly degenerated Christ's revelation until it is presented as a mere honorable naturalism, and reduced Christian morality, essentially supernatural and a transforming force for Man, as rational ethics. To the humanist *vivere secundum naturam* we can contrapose the Christian *secundum te vivere*.[34] And this would

---

[34] See the liturgical prayer "... ut qui sine te esse non possumus, *secundum te* vivere veleamus" (*Dom.* VIII *post Pentec.*).

not be so drastic if these rational ethics turned out to be stable and all naturalist considerations of the human being were true, even if incomplete.

Finally, let us add another consideration that tends to prove the forced anthropocentric accent of all humanism, including the Christian one. It does not seem to be possible for the latter to maintain an attitude that the Christian centuries free of humanist influence always held to be normal. We are referring to an attitude that, just to give it a name, we could call *spiritual theocentrism*; that is to say, that attitude whereby the following affirmations are experienced and accepted: Man can effectively and truly transcend himself and live a life in which his human nature is not his principle of operations; divinization is not only theoretically possible, but rather it is practically Man's "normal" state; I can spontaneously be more interested in others than in myself; God is more concerned about my sanctification than I am myself, therefore He is the decisive factor in such a process; the ultimate end of Man on earth does not lie so much in conquering, achieving, reaching his goal as in letting himself be conquered, letting himself be led, not putting any obstacles to God's action over us (humanism is essentially "masculine," while the Christian position is eminently "feminine").

The humanist demands rational obedience, an intelligent sacrifice, an efficient life, while the Christian posture that we describe, without denying this first part, accentuates that what is important is obedience, sacrifice, the dedication of life, because it instinctively possesses confidence not in Man (that implies a reflex mistrust of others), but in something superior to Man, ultimately in God, and a God immanent to the very structure of things. Humanism is certainly less naïve, but it has lost its innocence; real Christianity has lost this naiveté, but it has recovered innocence. In other words, for Christian humanism, heroism is possible, but it is something extraordinary; mysticism is possible, but it pertains to a regime of exception.

This is the same reason why humanism carries with it the absolute primacy of culture, and with this it closes the door on the greater demands of the kingdom of God, which do not always coincide with the maximum development of cultural norms. Culture is nothing more than the natural correlate of Man's elevation. Well, the so-called Christian humanism affirms that Man must collaborate with God in his process of perfecting, and this is fulfilled on the supernatural plane by grace and on the natural one by culture. But after original sin there is no pacific harmony, and the tragedy of historical Man lies in the fact that he must sacrifice the values of culture whenever human circumstances make these incompatible with evangelic demands. But Christian humanism is not equipped to deal with such demands that contradict its own principles. God has not left humanity on its own or to fulfill its own destiny; rather He intervenes directly from the outside, modifying the statutes of a possible humanism, transforming Man and society.

It is not by chance that history attests to the fact that all humanisms have always intended to be substitutes for religion. Humanism can be considered a sort of human-made religion on a human scale. Nothing that every religion possesses, including the Christian one—except when we want to humanize it—that is, the mysterious, the numinous, the revelation, God's free initiative, supramundanity and supranaturality and especially the gratuity that always makes Man's religious attitude be like waiting . . . none of this fits into humanism, which wants to measure everything, and even when it admits something superior to Man, it does so as something incommensurable, never as something infinite and much less as a mystery. Man is a religious animal, humanism might tell us, at most; but this humanistic religiosity often acts as a vaccine against an authentic religious attitude, characterized by the complete surrender to the Divinity, in the face of which Man can lay claim to no rights.

Furthermore, the humanist atmosphere suffocates any theological evaluation of reality, even of human reality. The main themes of Catholic mysticism—for example, the Trinitarian conception of Christian life, our divinization and participation in the Triune God, and so on—are problems that are strange and foreign to humanism. Briefly, theology, in its full meaning, as a constitutively theocentric science, is incompatible with humanism.

In a certain sense, insofar as only the Christian is fully man and even more than man, the only authentic humanism would be a Christian one. Yet this is not properly humanism, but rather theandrism. Humanism after the redemption can no longer be sustained. Humanism seeks in Man that which can only be found in God.

There is no need for a terminological discussion; but why must we still call "humanism" a doctrine that essentially defends that Man is not enough for himself, that nature is fallen, that reason must submit to faith and will to revelation? What does humanism have to do with a conception of life that proclaims that the poor and those who cry, suffer, and are persecuted are blessed? What does humanism mean in a thesis that defends that Man must deny himself and take up his cross, that affirms the need to transform oneself, to metamorphose into God until achieving unity with Him? It seems then that Christian humanism is ashamed and reluctant in the face of the maximum fact of Christianity on earth: the death of Christ naked on a cross, condemned by the legitimate civil and religious authorities.

"Be yourself," says humanism. "Be God," says Christianity. Affirm yourself, says the one; deny yourself, repeats the other. Discover your values, trust yourself, these are humanist maxims. Discover your transcendent destiny, trust in God, these are Christian maxims. Certainly, so-called Christian humanism will do whatever possible to accept humanist formulations and afterward give them Christian content. This is the Christian paradox, which as a dialogue with a non-Christian world certainly has its value, but which too easily assumes that the only and obvious point of departure is a naturalist one. The paradox will say, true affirmation of oneself leads to the recognition of our need to deny ourselves; perfect confidence in oneself is what leads us not to trust ourselves; the great discovery of our personal values drives us to humility and hatred toward ourselves. Everything can be understood in a perfectly Christian way. What we are criticizing here is the point of departure and the non-Christian perspective of this proposal.

Everything is reduced to the axiological value that is deemed more important. Who abdicates more: She who does not marry Mr. So-and-so because she truly becomes the bride of Jesus Christ or she who is not the wife of Jesus Christ because she has married Mr. So-and-so? Who is more authentically free—to remain within the paradox—he who *can* do as he likes (because he has the material power, that is to say, money, to do so) or he who *wants* to do what he can do? The atmosphere of Christian humanism, to provide other examples, is the atmosphere of a heaven in which God is in charge of "entertaining" us and awarding us because we have been good and we are deserving; of a hell in which God is pleased to punish. The true conversion of the mind to see Christian realities from a genuinely Christian point of view is alien to Christian humanism.

Because of Christian humanism, many Christian theses take on a color that, at the very least, darkens their deepest and truest Christian meaning. Christian humanism likes to say that the goal of Man is his perfection, and his mission that of giving God glory, and his end, the vision of divinity. We repeat that all these formulations are not false, but we would like to remind so-called Christian humanism that its interpretation is many times defective, since Man's end is not the end of man, it is not even the end that his nature requires or deserves because of grace, but rather the end of his Creator. The *finis operis* is subordinated to the *finis operantis*. The end of man does not lie in Man himself, but in God. God is the end of Man, but not God as an object for Man; rather God Himself, who has wanted to associate or join Man to himself. It is not the "glory" that we give Him that is definitive, but rather the union with Him. Likewise, the vision of God is not so much something active with regard to a God turned into an object, as is being seen, being known by Him, and along with Him, to see, to live, to "be" fullness.[35] Now is not the time to descend into greater detail or further entertain ourselves in describing what we wish to say.

In addition to the aforementioned distortion, Christian humanism wants us to face problems that, in truth, emerge from false premises. When a certain humanist mind-set is shocked because the Church does not more vigorously condemn the atomic bomb, racial discrimination, colonialism, the exploitation of the proletariat, or other similar cases that—rightfully—outrage and concern those who are thirsty for justice in this world, it frequently does not bear in mind not only that many of these problems are ambivalent and complex and that a simplistic judgment cannot be made when it comes to praxis, but also that the horizon in which the problems are usually posed is that of a human justice whose mission is not the direct responsibility of the Church. This life is transitory; there is no definitive establishment here, nor is any solution perfect. This does not mean—we tremendously dislike having to say this, as it is so patent—that either the Church, and even less Christians, can remain indifferent and with their arms crossed in the face of human injustice of whatever type, and especially in the face of that which touches the specific and singular human person.

Finally, a great deal of the climate of fear, insecurity, and anxiety that reigns in some places is also connected to humanism, without excluding so-called Christian

---

[35] See R. Panikkar, "Die existenzielle Phänomenologie der Wahrheit," 33ff.

humanism. Let us put forth a somewhat delicate example, delicate because our intent is not in any way to defend the atomic bomb or to become an accomplice to men's bellicose enterprises. We wish, as we have said, to describe a cultural atmosphere and make it apparent that it does not correspond to a genuinely Christian position. It is obviously true that the atomic bomb is a horrific weapon that puts a colossal destructive power in the hands of men, and it is obvious that its moral justification cannot easily be defended. We also have to stress, strongly and clearly, the undeniable Christian background of various movements in favor of peace and nuclear disarmament.

Nevertheless, there are a few considerations here that are not usually included in the mentioned attitude because they do not come from a humanist context: Is there any reason, besides a merely quantitative one, that forces us to condemn the atomic bomb more than the machine gun, the cannon, or the, let us say, classic bomb? Have we considered that the psychosis of insecurity that is created when describing the possible catastrophes that a nuclear attack can produce is exactly the same as the one that men from other cultures can have felt in the face of epidemics, wars, and meteorological catastrophes with the only phenomenological difference that "primitive Man" could turn to religious means to placate "God" while "modern Man" finds himself impotent to placate "Man"? But there is more still—and it is here that we must not be misunderstood: the authentic Christian position, in spite of fighting against the atomic bomb, as it fights against epidemics, floods, and wars, in spite of struggling against pain and all negative values, does not exaggerate their negativity nor does it lose its sense of proportion that is given to it by faith. Whether mankind's average age is thirty or sixty years, whether men die one way or another, this, ultimately, is not the most important thing.

There is no Christian who does not admit that the supernatural world is superior to the natural one, that the true kingdom of God is within us, that eschatology is an essential Christian dimension, that we must not fear death, and so on; but the humanist atmosphere has excessively disconnected these and similar theses concerning Man's practical and concrete life on earth, falling into the dangerous dichotomy of considering him citizen of heaven *and* of earth, vassal of the Church *and* of the state, natural Man *and* elevated Man, with a supernatural destiny *and* with *another* natural and terrestrial one, and so forth. All of this wishes to express something true, but humanism has done little less than level the two planes, and it interprets the copulative "and" like the conjunction of two homogeneous values, although in case of a conflict, Christian humanism would, more or less happily, recognize that it must lean toward the first element of the pair in question.

The real situation is quite diverse. In the first place, phenomenologically one cannot deny that heartbreaking and humanly tragic conflict has always been Man's condition on earth: There has never been an era of justice; never has humanity been free of all types of dangers that hover above it. The humanist myth of a possible human perfection on this earth from a merely natural point of view is a utopia. And yet human life has a meaning and an eminently positive value because its profound sense is not the restoration of a lost paradise, but rather the conquest of another kingdom that, although already present in this eon, does not properly belong to it. Whether what threatens humanity is a nuclear bomb or a flood does not much alter the human situation, certainly desperate, for those who do not believe that both the course of rivers as well as men's conduct and decisions are in the hands of One who has even the hairs on our heads counted, but it is normal for those who have discovered the real meaning of human existence. Today's humanists would like the Church to repeat the same thing that they judge to be a crass error in the Church's medieval history: that it indiscriminately condemns all those who do not think like it. And because they believe that the Church should do this and it does not, then they accuse it of being in collusion with the powerful on earth or of having lost its evangelic ferment.

Christian humanism, no. Human Christianity, yes; *quoniam oportet iustum esse et humanum* (Ws 12:19). And this is what the Christians who call themselves humanists want to say and to defend: positive evaluation of everything that is human, acceptance of everything that is natural, full incarnation of the created being in terrestrial reality; but not as human, natural, and created, rather as raw material for a true subsuming of humanism into an authentic Christianity. God and not Man is the measure of man. And the model is Christ. Ultimately, medieval anthropomorphism is closer to the truth than modern humanism is.

Furthermore, we must aspire to an integration of all human values into a Christian synthesis that unifies the human being. Redemption must reach Man's last fibers; baptism must descend from the head to the last corner of our personality. It is not about eliminating human values with a heterodox puritanism, also created by God, but rather about overcoming them and unifying them into the superior synthesis of Christianity. We must be fully and audaciously men in order to be able to be Christian; but not as a previous, independent condition, rather as the first effect of our supernatural elevation. In order to fulfill the divine paradigm of *Man* we must allow ourselves to be impregnated by supernatural grace.

Christianity is also not a *hominism*. Let us be clear. There has been a certain Christian position that believed it could not be humanist because it considered humanism an excess, because it believed that in order to be Christian it was necessary to carry out a series of fundamental human renunciations. This is the well-known ascetic position, which smacks of Manichaeism and Jansenism. We are defending the opposite position here. We are not rejecting humanism because being fully man is evil or dangerous, but rather because our Christian reality transcends that which is merely human. Christian humanism is not possible because even here on earth Christians are more than men and they must lead divine lives. There is no need to renounce any human values, but it is necessary to overcome them. Humanism is unacceptable simply because Christian demands are greater. Christianity is a transhumanism, a theandrism and not an infrahumanism.[36]

---

[36] See 1 Co 15:47.

We have the hope that today's Christianity is coming of age. Until now, even if synthesis was possible individually, socially we had not attained sufficient maturity for the Christian to be so in its fullness without needing to renounce any worldly, social values, especially family, politics, art, technique, and so on that complement and perfect human beings in this world. On the other hand, our Christian generation *is starting* not to fear this world or Man. And all of this without losing sight of the functional and relative character of human values. Today's man very easily forgets his contingency and his creaturability. He just needed humanism to fully justify the human tendency to take root on this earth and to forget his true homeland.[37]

Christ certainly made himself similar to us,[38] but so that we may become similar to God. The Verb does not incarnate so that we may be proud of being flesh, but rather so that we may thirst for Him so much that we elevate ourselves to God. Man's perfection does not lie in being a perfect *man*, but rather in fulfilling, now in truth, *in Christ*, the maximum dream that Adam did not achieve in Paradise because of lack of patience and hope: to become not *like* God, but rather God himself, forming a unity with the Son,[39] God of God and Light of Light.

Maledictus homo qui confidit in homine; beatus autem qui confidit et sperat in Te![40] The *Ecce Homo* whom Pilate showed to the Jews was a "man of sorrows,"[41] but also the Son of God. The incarnation of God is the overcoming of humanism.

In sum, we have declared ourselves against the humanism that calls itself Christian because: (1) it seems to us to be a concession of the spirit of a culture that is not Christian and that entails a set of non-Christian assumptions that later backfire on it; (2) its Christian acceptance is only possible by distorting humanism, on the one hand, and Christianity, on the other; (3) it limits Christianity to a form that, in the best scenario, will only be a possible form, and it makes it synonymous to one determined cultural form.

Nos stulti propter Christum.[42]

---

[37] See my *Patriotismo y cristiandad* (Madrid: Rialp, 1961).

[38] Ph 2:7.

[39] Jn 17:23 etc.

[40] Jr 17:5, 7.

[41] Is 53:3.

[42] 1 Co 4:10.

7

"De Deo Abscondito"[1]

Vere tu es Deus absconditus!

Is 45:15

In Europe, there is so much talk about crisis, the West's spiritual agony, the decline of Christianity, the "twilight of civilization,"[2] that this hypochondria is slowly taking over the rare, realistically optimistic cultural centers that still remain on the planet.

Undoubtedly, the cliché that we find ourselves in a crucial moment is no less true just because it is so often repeated. What can in fact be debated is the orientation and the interpretation of this crossroads in the history of thought—and of life—in the West.[3]

Christian Judgment of Modern Society

From the Christian point of view, it seems necessary to carry out an unyielding critique of the current situation, to later find a remedy, and finally to give an encouraging vision of the future, since any observer will more or less consciously realize that Christian optimism is little less than a dogma. But this solution usually has a flaw: It is not deduced from the premises; it seems more like something that has been added to keep up Christian appearances.

In the first place, we must point out that from a Christian point of view it is not necessary to defend an immediately positive solution, and there is certainly no shortage of thinkers with an apocalyptic vision[4]—indeed, the eschatological dimension is constitutive of Christianity. But, in the second and for us, now, foremost

---

[1] Published in *Arbor*, no. 25 (1948): 1–26.

[2] See the title of a brief treatise by Jacques Maritain, *Le crépuscule de la civilization* (Montreal: Éditions de l'Arbre, 1941).

[3] This chapter was born as a collateral study for an inopportunely announced weighty volume entitled *Cristianismo y Cristiandad*, in which the general problem mentioned here was studied.

[4] The journal *Dieu vivant* (1945, no. 1) opens with the following affirmation: "The journal *Dieu vivant* starts publication in a period that recalls the darkest pages in the Book of Revelation for the violence and ampleness of cataclysms as well as the atmosphere of spiritual death choking the world."

place, it is often the case that optimism is not founded on its own true base. There is a compelling antagonism between what Christians believe the world should be and what it truly is. The superficial overcoming of that antagonism gives rise to the alluded danger of an artificial optimism that is disconnected from reality.

Somewhere in the sacred texts it says that the thoughts of men are not the thoughts of God, nor are our paths His paths,[5] and many theoretical disquisitions about the current state of Christianity prove this point all too well.[6] Nobody can assign the role of genuine interpreter of God's designs to himself, yet nothing forbids us from dealing with the problem from a broader angle than a purely rationalistic one.

From the rational point of view, evil is serious and the remedy difficult, since it is not very plausible to expect that reason can hastily backtrack the path it has traveled. If we pose the problem from a purely speculative point of view, the situation is truly terrifying; evil is rationalized, and by doing this, we make it absolute. "Pessimism is—certainly—the best auxiliary of rationalism."[7]

But the vital resources of humanity, of *decadent* Christianity itself, are very different from those we would expect from mere rational speculation. We cannot forget that Christianization can only be the work of grace and that the "wind blows where it pleases."[8] And, as usual, what must be preached—and practiced— is penitence[9] and charity,[10] as the Precursor[11] and Christ[12] himself did, without preconceived plans or spiritual or intellectual strategies behind our testimony. Christ's example is obvious.[13]

Yet we do not wish to deal with a vital and pragmatic approach right now—for this we need not to diverge too much, but rather to act as an instrument of God in the task of establishing His kingdom—or with a merely rational digression either, but rather with a theological reflection, that is, the consideration of human intelligence illuminated by faith, not only in its principles, but especially in its axiological evaluations. And it is then that a series of aspects, that from an exclusively natural point of view remain completely unintelligible, appear with somewhat more clarity. And only then is Christian optimism truthfully founded.

---

[5] Is 55:8–9.

[6] Let us recall the commotion that was raised around the sociopolitical ideas of Maritain, as an orthodox example.

[7] A. Bremond, *Rationalisme et Religion* (Paris: Beauchesne, 1935), 2.

[8] Jn 3:8.

[9] Ez 18:21, 30.

[10] Jn 13:34.

[11] Lk 3:3.

[12] Mk 1:15.

[13] Christ certainly founds the church, but the foundation that He gives it is the living rock of Peter and not a code of laws. He founds his church but He does not organize it. Christ dies for all human beings, but it does not seem that He concerned himself to make us know it. The "public" life of the Lord does not transcend a simple parochial episode by much and it follows along the same lines as his "hidden" life.

If a Christian problem is posed, it is not enough to approach it—and even less possible to solve it—in an exclusively natural climate; we must introduce the Christocentric vision of things in its totality. Only thus can we move toward the true solution.

The Eclipse of God

There is a supernatural dimension of things and of events only visible to a mind illuminated by faith. In our case, this is not so much about a consideration of human facts *sub specie aeternitatis* as a delving deeper into these *in regno temporalitatis*, to reveal, simply, their full dimension, just as our vision, using two eyes, turns a figure that appears flat into a real, three-dimensional body.

But this third dimension only makes sense as such, that is, as depth, and never alone and isolated in a naïve, one-dimensional supernaturalism. This authentic side that things possess is truly beyond the scope of superficial rationalist consideration. This is why it is a hard test of faith and a fierce temptation against hope that is presented to the Catholic intellectual when he judges the current situation of humanity, no matter what his particular opinion may be, always subject to coefficients of error and inaccuracy. One must see—believe—what is invisible and have—hope—what one does not yet possess. The problem is general and, consequently, previous to the specific solutions that are defended. What we are discussing here is more the approach than the particular conclusions.

For a Christian, the current situation of humanity can be formulated as an experience of the *eclipse of God*. It is, if you like, the same concern that the form of the problem of evil took in other eras, and that among the common people of lacerated postwar Europe also adopts the same form under the guise of pain. How is so much evil, so much pain, possible in the world? Others are worried about inefficacy, about the apparent failure of Christianity in the world. "Why have we not been able to achieve what the communists realized?" they ask themselves, for example, with sincere, if somewhat myopic, zeal.[14]

It is not necessary to carry out a very profound assessment of current institutions to become convinced of the fact that, along with dreadful instability, they present an intrinsic disorder that is eroding them. Ultimately, it is this *disorder* that poses difficulties, not exactly to the theoretical problem of God's existence, but rather to that of His effective reign in the world. If God *exists*, He does not seem to be *reigning* as God over this earth. The fact that Western humanity has forgotten Him is not

---

[14] Ultimately, this is the dilemma that the non-Christian East poses for Europe: either Christianity supports the current state of the Old Continent [N.B.: the memories of WWII were still fresh when Panikkar wrote this]—and then it is monstrous—or it has not been able to tame European man after fifteen centuries—and then it is useless and inefficient. Properly, the fact is that Europe was Christian and it later collectively prevaricated, following the tragic human capacity to deviate from goodness.

the most serious thing; rather what poses a great problem for the intellectual and an unconscious aporia for the rest of Christians is that God has allowed Himself to be forgotten by a large portion of humanity.

We must not suppose that the boisterous triumphs of a pilgrimage, a Eucharistic congress, or a Catholic movie contradict the panorama we have outlined. To set all this against the aforementioned eclipse would mean not having grasped its meaning and confusing the eclipse of God with atheism.

We are not saying that for the modern mentality God does not exist, but rather that He does not reveal Himself—that is, people do not experience Him—as God, as total God, living and true. There have probably been few times when humanity has searched for God more desperately or more sincerely than now, and its very thirst for the Absolute and the Transcendent constitutes the ultimate basis of many of its aberrations. It adores the "splinters," the divine traces that it finds in things, but it does not know how to gather the fragments[15] and backtrack to the love of God, One and Trine.

Furthermore, this search of the absolute *in* the relative as well as a strong external and superficial religious color, a certain official religiosity,[16] to put it in political terms, or the abuse of the graces, if we turn to ascetic nomenclature, are not the only things that contribute to hiding God's true visage.[17] Let us not forget that God vanishes when even the least of His attributes is denied. The first religious crisis of today's child, especially on our side of the world, is produced when he observes the inconsistency between the faith preached by adults and their conduct. The most difficult obstacle the children who are preparing for First Communion must overcome is not the difficulty of believing that God is in the Eucharist—their divinely infused faith is palpable—but the eclipse of God in the minds and lives of the older generations. And even more precisely, what baffles and perturbs them is not exactly that God does not manifest Himself, but rather that people do not treat Him as such.

The God of a large part of today's Christian masses is reduced to a powerful and influential acquaintance to whom we turn to ask a favor or a recommendation when we find ourselves in trouble. His power may perhaps have encompassed creating the world, but He has stopped worrying or maybe He has grown weary of lovingly and providentially taking care of humanity. In both of these extreme cases, it is not the true God; some of his attributes can be recognized, but the personal God—and much more the authentic God, One and Trine—has become eclipsed from humanity. Let us not forget that a fetishism, concealed under the name of the true God, is possible.

---

[15] See Jn 6:12.

[16] The meaning that this word is given here is very easy to distinguish from the concept of "public worship," truly due to God.

[17] Let us also not fall into the illusion of seeing the world through Spain or of objecting that in Spain such an eclipse of God does not exist. The situation may perhaps be different, but the eclipse is the same.

If God exists, if the Church is the repository of truth and of true life, what the Christian intellectual asks himself is: How is this eclipse of God and his power, this general unhinging, possible?

Humanity, Christianity itself, believes today more than ever that God—in whom, in the end, it more or less vaguely believes—is hidden, has become eclipsed. Christianity suffers from this disappearance of God, and ultimately it complains of being abandoned by its God, just as the Israelites so often grumbled about YHWH having taken them out of Egypt.[18] Modern lamentations are more resigned, perhaps less conscious, but also more hypocritical.

Not only are we missing order and guidance, but even Christians lack an undisputed and specific goal in their lives; they suffer due to the absence of orientation. Entire groups cry out for precise and practical orders, yet these orders do not come; apparently, they do not exist. Everything leads us to think that God has hidden, that Christians have been left to their own devices.

The existence of sincere and generous attempts on the part of Christians to live fully as such, and at the same time, the scarce fruits of such attempts, are perhaps characteristic of the current time. Let us recall the attempts of Catholic groups in the social field and their apparent ineffectiveness with regard to solving the problem of the proletariat, which they have been struggling with for almost a century.

It seems as if God has left them, as if He has hidden, and therefore the only authentic Christian posture is that of recognizing that the children of this world are more prudent than the children of the light;[19] and that, having God abandoned the world to the disputes of men,[20] He is handing over the "miserable and perishable" earthly life in this "vale of tears" to evildoers, in order to adequately compensate them for the little good that they do, and that He reserves "that life up there which is the real life"[21] for those who are truly His—"those whom the world hates."[22]

But that there is a reverse to this eschatological picture, and that it is just as Christian as the obverse, is something that has been much too loudly repeated in our times for Christians to now be satisfied with taking refuge in a superhuman hereafter and simply consider themselves defeated in the struggle for the world, as if it were not true that possession of the earth was promised precisely to them.[23]

Christians have been told that they are not enemies of this world,[24] that they must remain in it,[25] that they must be leaven in the middle of the dough,[26] that their

---

[18] See, for example, Ex 14:11, etc.
[19] Lk 16:8.
[20] Qo 3:11 (*Vulgate*).
[21] St. Teresa of Avila, *Maxims*.
[22] Jn 15:19.
[23] Mt 5:4.
[24] See Jn 12:47.
[25] See Jn 17:15, 18.
[26] See Mt 13:33.

God is the God of the armies,[27] Lord of life and death;[28] they have been repeatedly told that they must not ignore any human value,[29] that God has faith in their work, in their apostolate, in the good results based on their natural virtues, with the means commonly used by all people.

Nevertheless, the facts are there, threatening all of those theories with ruin. It does not seem as if Christians experience Isaiah's words—*"for God is with us"*[30]—and that, therefore, the triumph of the good is ensured. In truth, Christians feel humiliated because they are the minority, because they lack means, they feel displaced at times, alone and solitary at other times. Christianity today relives the great drama of Job, the patriarch.

Today's Christians do not have that messianic consciousness that united the people of Israel, that consciousness of a mission and, above all, that assurance that God was with them, so that, when they were good, God blessed their enterprises, and when things did not work out for them, it was because God wanted to punish them for their prevarications.

David was king, and everyone obeyed and feared him, because the "Lord of the Armies was with him."[31] Nowadays, Christians, in their struggles in this world, do not feel that this same God protects them. They will, in any event, feel close to Jesus, "gentle and humble in heart,"[32] but without his complementary experience that, if necessary, they can pray to the Father to send them "more than twelve legions of angels"[33] to crush their enemies. Neither do they have the sense of church and the eschatological spirit of primitive Christianity that helped those early Christians endure the harshest tests, the toughest humiliations, without their faith wavering, since they realized that God asked them to be like the grain of wheat born to fall to the ground and die.[34] They have also lost the naïve—and determined—faith of the Middle Ages, of knowing they belonged to Christendom, those who had been chosen on this earth and were superior to the rest, onto whom God poured the graces of redemption more fully.

The Christendom of modern society lost its sense of this, but individually or in small communities—it is at this time that most religious communities with specific *concrete* ends emerge—it preserved its faith in God and in being those chosen by the Lord, the small flock[35] that in its life of apostolate—a new concept of Catholic action begins then—has a mission to fulfill in the world.

---

[27] See Jr 11:20.
[28] See Rom 6:9.
[29] See Mt 5:17ff.
[30] Is 8:10.
[31] 1 Ch 11:9.
[32] Mt 11:29.
[33] Mt 26:53.
[34] Jn 12:24.
[35] Lk 12:32.

But even this sense has mostly disappeared from the general legacy of today's Christians. They do not consider themselves to be the most valuable part of humanity, nor do they judge themselves superior to the rest of men, not even in a supernatural sense, as leaven, salt, small flock, but they simply have faith with no ulterior longing because of this, with no hope in the living God. Their God has hidden, has left them. It is true that we have been told that the two world wars were divine punishments; but secondary causes are all too easy to see; political turns of events are seen from too close to leave room to think about the First Cause. God is with the strongest battalion. *Good* Christians fight one against the other. God does not become involved in human affairs.[36]

Yes, the Christian masses still go on pilgrimages and with faith—Lourdes, Lisieux, Fátima, El Pilar, and so on—but the Divinity's actions are here limited to healing the sick, consoling the afflicted, "preaching the gospel to the poor,"[37] while the world follows its own rhythms, problems, preoccupations, attaching no importance to such "trifles." God, the God of armies, the Creator, the Omnipotent, does not reveal Himself. He is hidden.

There are certainly Christian organizations, media, societies, and others—even universities—but they all complain of limited means and lack of funds, compared to secular or state associations. They try to make themselves heard, but their racket cannot compare to that made by the other side; and, naturally, it is not the deafening racket of the Israelites, triumphant because their God is with them.[38] The God of the Christians seems to have become eclipsed.

There are certainly saints in our own time as well, but they do not generally seem to show much solidarity with humanity, or even with Christendom—for which they indisputably sacrifice themselves. Rather they join God and, in the best scenario, they attempt to gather—or gather themselves around—a small nucleus that follows them. Their God does not seem like the God of all mortals. Perhaps they sacrifice themselves for all sinners in their inner lives, but their action occurs as if they only had a limited number of concerns. They do not raise their arms, like Moses, to restrain God's ire; they do not come out at crossroads and paths as the men of God still did in the Middle Ages. They have erected an internal castle in their souls and they do not leave it very often, lest the world contaminate them, perhaps. Their God is also hidden in the bottom of their soul.

In turn, society also expects that those who are full of God do not manifest this externally and that they behave coldly and *correctly*. The modern world is insensitive to Greek *enthusiasmos* and Christian *carisma*. The manifestation of the divine is not tolerated. If God exists, His place is at the bottom of consciousness, hidden within the rhythms of everyday life, which prefers to handle itself without Him.

---

[36] See Lk 12:13–14.
[37] See Lk 4:18.
[38] Jos 6:20.

The social phenomenon of the entire nineteenth century, which bears the name *secularism*, has been very thoroughly studied in all of its manifestations. It is the maximum exponent of *God's exile* from current civilization. God exists, all right, but let Him not be our king![39] This does not automatically translate into a manifestation of atheism and, sometimes, not even into the absence of Christianity, but rather simply into a fear of the splendor of God's manifestation. The Christian people, just like the Jews in the desert, prefer that Moses be the one to deal directly with YHWH.[40] No theophanies are admitted.

The forces of evil also contribute to this state of affairs. Throughout antiquity and the Middle Ages, the Divinity manifested itself indirectly, allowing for public interventions of the demonic. Many people were frequently possessed—so many, in fact, that the Church was forced to create within its hierarchy a specific position equipped with a very special charisma.[41] Consequently, people remembered God whenever they saw the Devil. Now, on the contrary, diabolic possessions are not very frequent. If any do occur, they are catalogued as hysteria, neurosis, psychopathological reactions, and so on. The demonic now also participates in hiding God.

There is no doubt that as today's scientists delve deeper into the problems of the particular sciences, they always run into the need for a God in the end, and perhaps in this sense it is fitting to shout from the crow's nest, in happy seaworthy spirit, "God ahoy!"[42]

Not from a theoretical, but rather a practical, vital viewpoint, the cliff where the Divinity dwells is certainly in sight, and it is even the pole toward which the prows of most of human activities are headed; but this thirst for God is accompanied by ignorance of Him. The cliff is in sight, but God has not come out of the cave where, apparently, He is hiding.[43] Perhaps when Man disembarks—or when he is ship-wrecked—on this island of the divine and he can roam it barefooted, without any artificial vessel, he may discover the *hidden path* that leads directly to God Himself.

The religious anguish and unease haunting the intellectuals of our days proves that they have not yet found God's true face. From the fighting top of our society, on our way to God, we cannot yet hear the words, "God ahoy!" but we can hope that His Hertzian wave has been grasped and that we are headed toward Him whom we still do not see: "God within hearing!"

What is in sight is not *God*, but rather *Man* in his inner emptiness and in his desire for God. Let us be clear: We are not saying that God is not implicit in all of our knowledge, as in all our volitions, since by delving into any being, we reach God as its foundation, as philosophy once recognized.[44] What we affirm is that the

---

[39] See Lk 19:14.

[40] Ex 20:19.

[41] [Editorial note: That of exorcists.]

[42] J. Ortega y Gasset, *Obras completas*, vol. 2, *El Espectador* (*1916–1934*) (Madrid: Revista de Occidente, 1946), 605.

[43] See St. John of the Cross, *Spiritual Canticle* §37.

[44] "All knowing beings implicitly know God in anything they know" (Thomas Aquinas,

experience of present-day society, as such, is not that of God, but rather that of the anxiety of not having God, of angst for His eclipse, so complete that "humanism," which eclipses God as an opaque body does with the sun, does not allow us to even glimpse if what is "behind" really is God or nothingness.

God as a Hidden Being

God's eclipse is, thus, a cultural fact of our time. In the face of this, one can adopt a twofold posture: assign the blame to Man or attribute the mistake to God. The latter is equivalent to turning the eclipse into an absolute absence of God and to adopting the antidivine—and antinatural—position of wanting to change the Immutable, of trying to correct God. But the first position, along with a guilt complex, carries with it an indelible tint of pessimism: it is Man's fault that things are like this, they are not happening as they should, there is a disturbing disorder anchored in the depths of society because society does not find God, but rather a substitute for Him that lacks many essential divine traits. We worship a God we do not know, as St. Paul once pointed out to the Athenians.[45]

However—and here comes the deepest root of an authentically Christian optimism—this is not completely accurate, without being absolutely false either. There is a third position in the face of the proposed dilemma, which consists in simply saying that everything is neither all mistake nor all blame, since God's withdrawal has two different facets: one is God's *eclipse*, the other, His *discretion*.

It is Man, or better yet, it is the opaque mass of Man's sin that interposes between God and the creature, giving rise to God's eclipse from the created world. Human prevarication carries God's disappearance with it because Man himself has culpably blocked the path to the *Light from Light*.

But it is neither the mystery of sin nor the blind obstinacy of the sinner that we are interested in highlighting here, rather exactly the other facet of God's shadow—even if both factors play a combined role in the current situation, making it difficult to elucidate in each specific case how much corresponds to blame and how much to normality. God has hidden, not only because of Man, but because He is a being who dwells in the unknown and sees all that is done in secret.[46] We cannot, then, properly say that God hides, but rather that it seems to us that He does not manifest himself enough. Furthermore, God's most profound facet with regard to Man, the purest manifestation of His hidden nature, is precisely ineffability, incognoscibility, even, if you wish, *Vere tu es Deus absconditus!*[47]

A new manifestation—a new proof, and this one more serious—of God's eclipse is the ignorance, not simply nominal, but deep and vital, of a series of old

---

Sum. theol. I, q.12, a.11, ad 3).

   [45] Ac 17:23.
   [46] Mt 6:18.
   [47] Is 45:15.

and classic Christian theses that today sound almost completely new, perhaps not in the specialized minds of theologians, but certainly in the Christian environment, even the learned one. One of these theses is God's ineffability.

It is one thing that, in the face of the dangers of the agnosticism of the nineteenth century and of its lucubrations about the Absolute, the Transcendent, the Incognoscible, and so on, the theoretical and effective ability of our mind to know the existence of God and even His main attributes[48] was underlined, and another that the classic and "kingly street" of all apophatic theology be forgotten or even spurned.[49]

Not only has the mystical direction of Christian thought, from the beginning, been claiming that "after reaching the goal of our knowledge of God, we know Him as a person unknown,"[50] but even the purest Aristotelian trend has repeatedly affirmed that "we cannot know what God is, but only what God *is not*,"[51] and that "Man reaches the highest point of his knowledge about God when he knows that he knows Him not."[52] And this is not only due to mere human inability: it has a deeper reason. God possesses an intimate life that constitutes his purest essence, which no created being can reach. Therefore, if this facet of God's is absolutely transcendent, not only can it not change our conception of God, but it cannot in any way affect our relationship to Him.

Yet Man, in his factual historical situation, is, strictly speaking, more than human nature and more than mere creature. He has been elevated to the divine order and been called to participate in God's intimate vital movement, in the fecund intratrinitarian life itself. For this reason, the contact between historical Man and the Divinity possesses a special depth that only becomes clear thanks to the revelation. We are trying here to find the first sociological resonance of this fact. This is about discovering in the collective sphere something that is an undisputed reality in the individual field. The mystics know much about God's seclusion, about the silent hiding place at the *bottom* of the very soul immersed in the dark night.[53] This dimension of God—it is not only a mystical purification—is so real that it also plays an important role in the lives of peoples.

At bottom, it is the mystery of Christ.

The highpoint of the revelation of Isaiah is the Messiah, but a Messiah who is God and man, hidden God and sorrowful man. The prophet's man of sorrows is at the same time God hidden.[54] Israel was looking for its savior, and Isaiah already

---

[48]   See Vatican Council I, sess. III, chap. 4 (*Denz.*, 1795ff.).

[49]   I insist that "negative theology" neither displaces nor makes "positive" theology unnecessary. They are not two antinomic (Eastern European Churches) or even opposite (Nicholas of Cusa) paths; rather they complement each other (St. Thomas Aquinas).

[50]   Dionysius the Areopagite, *De mystica theologia*, I.

[51]   Thomas Aquinas, *Sum. theol.* I, q.3, proem.

[52]   Thomas Aquinas, *De potentia* q.7, a.5, ad 14.

[53]   "Where have you hidden, / Beloved, and abandoned me in my groaning?" begins one of the greatest mystical poems of universal literature: St. John of the Cross, "Spiritual Canticle."

[54]   Is 53:3.

advances his description: It is the Christ, who will call himself Son of Man, who is God concealed, but Lord of Israel.[55]

In Christ, his own divinity is hidden; it cannot be seen—nobody has ever seen God[56]—we must believe in it. Without faith it is impossible to convince oneself that Jesus is the Son of God, and not because of a lack of objective power in the corroborating arguments that refer to the Lord, but rather because of the subjective feeling of incompatibility between the divinity and the humanity of the Messiah, who suffers and grows weary and cries; that is something Man cannot overcome without an enlightenment of reason by faith itself.[57] This incompatibility, which ultimately is the aberration of the cross, "scandal for the Jews and foolishness for the Greeks,"[58] is only overcome if the most profound dimension of the Divinity as *Deus absconditus* is recognized.

It is ignorance of this characteristic, which the greatest of all the prophets of Israel tried hard to teach the Jews, that impeded them from recognizing the divinity of Jesus. They could not accept that he who was truly man[59] was also God, that their Savior was the son of a carpenter.[60]

In short, all of the apostles' problems derived from this same fact,[61] and all the rationalist critique that defends the gradual development of the messianic consciousness of Christ is equally founded on the ignorance of this intrinsic divine discretion.

In the fullness of time, God revealed his Son,[62] but his Son, who is God, is also Man. This is the high point of revelation: Jesus, the Christ, real God and real man, perfect God and perfect man.[63]

If Christ, therefore, is the center of history and he who gives it its ultimate meaning and direction, and on the other hand, Christ is God, this and nothing else will be the concept of God that counts for everything. In this sense, Pascal—who so profoundly experienced this antinomy—was right when he affirmed that the God who must be known and who solves all of the antinomies of history is the living God of Abraham, of Isaac, and of Jacob, and not the God of the philosophers.[64]

This synthesis of Christ as God and Man has been somewhat lost in our Christian consciousness. It is really difficult to maintain the union with Christ, Man, and God alive and taut. And the history of Christian spirituality sufficiently proves the oscillating movements through which Christianity has passed, which preferentially consider either Jesus Christ's divine aspect or his human one. Nowadays we

---

[55] Is 45:15.
[56] Jn 1:18.
[57] Vatican Council I, sess. III, chap. 4 (*Denz.*, 1796).
[58] 1 Co 1:24.
[59] Jn 19:5.
[60] Mt 13:55.
[61] See Jn 14:22, and the answer by Jesus, referring to *interiority*.
[62] Gal 4:4.
[63] *Symbol. Athan.*, see *Denz.*, 40.
[64] See Pascal's famous *Memorial*, November 23, 1654.

still believe in Christ, but we forget his divine personality a little. It seems as if the more frequent Holy Communion or the people's devotion that concentrates the fervor of believers on particular aspects of His Humanity had strengthened this approach, not "too human," but too little divine. Ultimately, our intelligence casts the first stone. Already in the first centuries, Prefect Culcianus, in judgment against Phileas, presented the fact that Christ *est Deus crucifixus*[65] as a difficulty against the Christian faith: How can a crucified God exist? And, surely, this is the great problem of Pauline—Christian—*stultitia*,[66] which triumphs over natural wisdom, *ut non evacuetur crux Christi*,[67] so that Christ's cross does not become inane.

One of the deepest Christological problems has a direct link to this dimension of divine humility. *Cur Deus homo?* (Why a God becoming Man?), states the disconcerting question in traditional language. The issue, as most present-day Christians solve it, is a new proof of God's eclipse: "Why? In order to save Man, to redeem him, to fulfill divine justice," they answer. But one serious difficulty remains. God cannot perform any task that is undeserving of Him, better still, that does not have His own glory as an end and that is not an authentic glorification of his Being. Well, at first glance—unless God is a *Deus absconditus*—it does not seem that the abasement of becoming man, and a man condemned to the gallows by other men, is a glorification of Divinity. There must then be a positive value that the incarnation fulfills and that is truly worthy of God.

Divine Discretion

Yet, ignoring all of these latent problems that surround the very essence of Christianity, our minds are not satisfied with this confession of pure supernaturalness, and they aspire to find the reason for this disrepute of the natural and to penetrate somewhat more into the *mystery of the cross*. Salvation is certainly the work of grace, and there is a supernatural sphere which is the truly valuable one; but the latter is not completely disconnected from the natural sphere, nor does it eliminate the function of intelligence, nor does it ultimately destroy any human value, even if it does overcome these and polarize many of them. There is a logic and an intellectual life that neither grace nor the cross destroy, even if their axiological judgments are profoundly modified.

Simply put, God remains hidden because this withdrawal is *more* perfect, contrary to how it may seem at first sight. Christ does not manifest his divinity because God's humility, this divine interiority, fulfills and embodies a greater value than the external apotheosis of a fearsome and feared God. This is the same reason why an authentic wise man prefers his knowledge and work to vociferous self-advertising. Our evaluation is sometimes so superficial that in our own naiveté we believe that

---

[65] Cited by R. Knopf, *Augeswählte Märtyreracten* (Tübingen: Mohr, 1901), 104.

[66] See, for example, 1 Co 3:18.

[67] 1 Co 1:17.

God does not promote Himself enough and that we would have planned things better, so that men would have had no alternative but to believe, without having their freedom limited in any way. It sometimes seems as if God had made an initial calculating error with his creation, as if he had failed with a world that has ended up rebelling and that has required a deicide so as to be raised again, and even so without much apparent fruit, as the Redeemer does not seem to be doing much better either. Human thoughts that do not coincide with those of God! Human apologetics that do not follow divine method!

But there is still more. Ultimately, we are right. The problem is that we express ourselves incorrectly. God does not mutilate his manifestations, God does not lock himself up to remain unknown, Christ does not remain inactive. But "behold, the kingdom of God is within you";[68] yes, the inner world is *objectively* (paradox notwithstanding) more valuable than the exterior one, and a single spiritual thought carries more weight than the entire material world;[69] a single supernatural action has a greater dignity and ontological substance than the entire world of an exclusively natural culture.[70] This is the pure Catholic doctrine.[71]

The illusion of quantity is another way of inducing error. Whoever lets themselves be easily discouraged by amounts will not realize that the realm of quality lies infinitely above that of quantity. In other words, the *glory* that a *saintly* soul can give to God—understanding both these expressions in their strict ontological sense—and the proper goal of creation and of the creature are both fulfilled "more" by the elevation of a single created being to being God and to participating in His intratrinitarian effusion itself than by the more or less vegetative life of the masses.

This argument should not be understood as disdainful of the masses in the face of a chosen minority, since all people share the *same* divine destiny, and the selected minority must be at the service of the majority. Let this therefore be interpreted as an affirmation of dignity—better yet, of the ontic weight of Christians and, consequently, of the personal responsibility that weighs on all Christians and forces them to be among the righteous few who are needed to save the world.[72] And this not because of some more or less whimsical decree of God's, but simply because the goodness of the righteous few surpasses by far the evil the rest of mortals may commit.

Furthermore, it is not a matter of consoling oneself by saying that, after all, things are not as bad as they seem because there is even more goodness, but rather about discovering that the superior ontological and axiological value of interiority and of the righteous not only neutralizes exteriority and sin, but it also assimilates

---

[68] Lk 17:21.

[69] "The whole world is not worth one thought of man, as this is only due to God" (St. John of the Cross, *Puntos de amor* 37).

[70] This is what Pascal saw so very clearly: "All the bodies together and all the understanding together and all their productions are not worth the smallest gesture of charity, because charity is of an infinitely higher order" (*Pensées* [ed. Hanet], 269).

[71] Thomas Aquinas, *Sum. theol.* I-II, q.113, a.9, ad 2.

[72] See Gn 18:20ff., esp. v. 32.

and redeems them, *similarly* to how in our intrinsically hierarchized universe, Man assumes the material world up to the vision of God (resurrection of the flesh), or, *similarly* also to how the Eucharistic Supper is medicine for immortality[73] and truly makes us divine.[74]

The Christian is strongly interested in universal history, but in the same way that the vision of history as a mere succession of wars and battles has already been surpassed, the idea of history as a small political or cultural oligarchy must also be surpassed.

We are not denying, then, that it is not human to suffer because of this discretion of God; rather we are affirming the need to know how to surpass this pain, which clings too much to a "shallow" vision of events. Moreover, the experience of the apparent carelessness with which God asserts his rights is not only human but it also constitutes the genuine starting point for a supernatural vision of history.

The ancients already lived and suffered this experience, both in its pressing and specific facet—see the apparent abandonment in which God left Job, that is to say, the problem of evil and of pain—as well as in its more philosophical and social aspect: "Why this uproar among the nations, this impotent muttering of the peoples?"[75]

The abandonment of God or the proofs that He may send are not what worries the believer, but rather the social aspect of the problem. He suffers more because of God's disrepute than for his own humiliation. Why, if Christ is the King of nations, is he not recognized as such? Why do the peoples, as such, not worship him as their Lord? Or is his reign perhaps fictitious, lacking in strength and effectiveness? Perhaps the external failure of Calvary is the destiny of all of Christendom. But then, how is redemption universal, how is Christ the Son of the living God, terrible and vengeful, whom nobody has yet mocked?[76] "Let him come down from the cross now, and we will believe in him."[77] It is the same situation also nowadays. Like today's Christians, the Jews also asked for a sign to believe in the Messiah. And they were given no other sign than the death and descent to the bosom of the earth:[78] interiority. "If this is what you are doing, you should *reveal yourself* to the world," Jesus's own kin said to him.[79] And the Evangelist already comments, "Not even his brothers had faith in him."[80] The first two temptations in the desert asked Jesus for pure exhibitionism.[81]

But once again, the answer is personal and collective, at the same time external and, above all, internal, phenomenal—historical, if you wish—and, even more, onto-

---

[73] See Ignatius Antioch, *Epist. ad Eph.* 20.2.
[74] See Jn 6:53ff., etc.
[75] Ps 2:1.
[76] Gal 6:7.
[77] Mt 27:42.
[78] Mt 16:4.
[79] Jn 7:4.
[80] Jn 7:5.
[81] See Mt 4:3ff.

logical: He who is enthroned in the heavens laughs at the nations and their princes.[82] This encourages the believer to ask Him for the nations as his own inheritance (to be then returned to God), so that he may rule over them with an iron scepter,[83] as He is His son,[84] and therefore, lord of the world.

Let us never forget that there is a majestic dominion that differs from a plebian tyranny, that lordship does not mean despotic dominion or exhibition of one's own forces. The real lord governs without appearing to do so, just as certain people truly dominate when they make as if they were obeying. God can speak even by being quiet and continue to be Lord even after having taken the form of a slave.[85]

*

There are evident examples of God's discretion. Not only does the fact of incarnation itself, its circumstances and Jesus's thirty years of hidden life, make the value of interiority manifest, but so do all details about God's behavior—in his earthly, Eucharistic, and mystical life. Jesus hides when they try to make him king;[86] he recommends secret prayer[87] and silent fasting,[88] so that only "the Father who sees all that is done in secret" will reward us.[89] Not to mention his Eucharistic presence or his mystical life in souls. But what we are interested in here is the social and historical aspect of this divine behavior.

There are some affirmations made by the prophets[90] and corroborated by Jesus,[91] which at once entail remarkable exegetical difficulty and are the maximum exponent of God's withdrawal.[92] It seems as though God likes withdrawing from profane gazes so much that he explains only to his followers what to the rest of people he expresses in parables, so that "they may look but not perceive, listen but not understand."[93] Whatever the exegetical explanation may be,[94] we cannot deny a divine tendency toward hiding, toward fleeing from too much exteriority and penetrating in the

---

[82] Ps 2:4.

[83] Ps 2:8–9.

[84] Ps 2:7.

[85] Ph 2:7.

[86] Jn 6:15.

[87] Mt 6:1–6.

[88] Mt 6:16–18.

[89] Mt 6:4.

[90] Is 6:10.

[91] Mt 13:14.

[92] See the dense Pauline text: 2 Co 4:3–4.

[93] Lk 8:10.

[94] I will only record Theophylactus's charitable and intelligent version: "Christ hides from them so as not to be too prejudicial to them, in case they despised his mysteries after learning them. In fact, those who understand them and then despise them will undergo a harder punishment" (quoted in Thomas Aquinas, *Catena Aurea*, in Lk 8).

inner reign, like a thief,[95] in the night[96] and without observation,[97] at the least likely hour.[98] Not only does God not force anyone, rather he compels people to carefully look for Him and demands a pure heart to be understood.[99]

Another example of this divine discretion, intimately connected to the previous one, is the case of prophecies. God foretells with the necessary opaqueness in order not to wound human freedom and so that what he wants to say will not be completely understood—the prophet preaches a hidden God—and he launches his prophecies with indispensable clarity so that, a posteriori, his predictions may be confirmed.

Indeed, could it not be that God hides Himself a little in our epoch, as he has already done in others and continues to do in the consciences of many of his best servants, so that people become a little more concerned for their neighbors and the search for God takes place through the second dimension of the only commandment? The Lord already told Isaiah something along these lines.[100] For "I desire mercy, not sacrifice."[101]

Needless to say, even if God is a hidden Being, he is not the God of darkness, but of light. It is precisely light that possesses discretion and not darkness; in fact, shadows only appear with light, and are stronger according to the potency of the luminous spotlight. Light is invisible if it does not have bodies onto which to fall; darkness, on the other hand, is dark. *Tu, Lumen de Lumine, vere es Deus absconditus!*[102]

Christian Optimism

And here is where authentic Christian optimism is founded, without needing to turn to transcendent theories or immanent solutions.

God is truly hidden to external eyes, because there is an inner realm in which He lives and reigns. This inner realm is not only eschatological and transcendent, but it is inside us personally and collectively, that is to say, it is immersed in the world and it constitutes its soul and motor, as it were. In the same way that the uneducated man only believes in material forces and does not realize that he, more than anyone else, is a product of his environment and slave to the ideas he has received, the man without faith does not know that there is an inner realm, more valuable, more effective, and even more real than the worlds of culture and of exclusively rational

---

[95] Rev 3:3.

[96] Mt 25:6; 1 Th 5:2.

[97] Lk 17:20.

[98] Mt 25:13; Mk 13:35.

[99] Jn 3:20.

[100] Is 58:1–9.

[101] Mt 9:13; 12:7; cf. Hos 6:6; etc.

[102] "You really are a hidden God, O Light from Light!" See Meister Eckhart's deep reflection: "*The light shines in the darkness* [Jn 1:5] because the Principle keeps universally hidden, but He shines and reveals Himself in the Principled [the Son] insofar as the latter is His Word" (*Expositio sancti Evangelii secundum Iohannem* 75).

thought. It would be a shame if this entire aporia emerged just because God does not reign on earth the way a man who was given the power of God would reign! Let no one yield this fruit of a petulant anthropomorphism! God is not a man with more power, perfection, and a few attributes that we are lacking, but rather simply and ineffably, God. The *analogy* of the created being with God is not a *univocity* with less degrees of being, that is, with a merely quantitative difference; rather it is a qualitative difference, even more, a substantial difference of *being*.

The efforts to found Christian optimism could be summarized by the following solutions:

(a) Transcendent solution. Only the other life is worthwhile, only souls are worthwhile. The important thing is salvation—that people, even at the last minute, are reconciled with God. A greater religiosity in the world would be desirable, but ultimately this is secondary, and Christianity must only worry about finding a happy end for souls. It is not too important that technology, civilization, and culture follow a different path, provided they allow for a minimal freedom so that *individuals*, after having lived this life, are saved in the next one.

This is a Christian reaction forged within the same molds as liberalism; it is, if you wish, liberal Christian optimism—full of inaccuracies, but not lacking common sense in many of its details.

If judged from the point of view of religious all-inclusiveness, the world is going from bad to worse since Man has been drawing away from God in his daily life; but this vision is fruit of a narrow perspective. Religion is not everything; it does not even exhaust the object-God. "God is also a secular issue,"[103] according to this position. If religion exercises its functions next to the baby's cradle and at the deathbed of the dying man, it has fulfilled its role, leaving the world free to follow its secular laws; then it still has enough reason to be optimistic. If, in short, the other life is the authentic and valuable one, as long as it is something assured, even at the expense of renouncing strident utopian demands, it suffices for Christian and bourgeois optimism.[104]

(b) Immanent solution. The world is not so black as it is painted. Along with all this negative scenario that makes so much racket, there is a positive scenario that, without being noisy, is superior to the bad one. Natural goodness is widespread even among those people who have lost faith and who are perhaps subjectively justified. Pessimism is a unilateral and tendentious description of the world situation. Goodness surpasses evil by far. Europe may not be perfect, but we cannot understand it without Christianity; and if it is compared with other, non-Christian civilizations, we can easily see its superiority. Man's life on earth is a tapestry facing God: only He sees it as is, while we become frightened because what we see is the back, because we are contemplating the scene from behind the curtain.

---

[103] Ortega y Gasset, *Dios a la vista* in *Obras completas*, Vol. 2, *El Espectador* (1916–34), p. 605.

[104] I will forgo the critique of the different solutions, and especially of this first one.

(c) Progressive solution. Things are going really badly now, but *soon* the day will come when they go well, and we can already predict the fruits. At that time we will be "one sole flock and one sole shepherd."[105] This solution puts its trust in small groups or in a particular type of devotion or a movement. It is the παρουσία that is already approaching, despite the jerks of the dying Evil. Prayer can help us make this day come sooner. This is the optimism of the heroic posture.

(d) Realistic solution. This is the one we would like to suggest. It obviously gathers much from the three previous solutions, but it does not remain with a vision of the hereafter, spurning the present world (*a*), nor does it become blinded in the face of the evil and disorder that really exist (*b*), nor does it raise its hopes for a παρουσία whose seeds are problematic (*c*). And yet it accepts all that is positive and balanced from these three positions: (*a*), the eternal is superior to the temporal and immeasurable with it; (*b*) it is, however, present in the *now*; and (*c*), it lets itself, nonetheless, be fulfilled via a historical dynamism and a real, free effort.

The realistic solution simply bases optimism on truth. It does not mutilate reality nor does it adopt unilateral polarizations that are only heroic in appearance. It is a young and mature optimism, simultaneously human and superhuman, rational and theological.

Both pessimism and optimism essentially look to the future, but more than asking for an intervention or an active organization for the sake of it, they simply give two different evaluations of the same facts—axiological evaluations, nevertheless, which are the fruit of a previous personal attitude. Only he who sees himself as able to influence the future can feel optimistic. This is why authentic Christian optimism cannot be possessed until one personally experiences that Pauline saying that "everything cooperates for the good" of the good.[106] But, in turn, this saying is only in force for those who are instruments of God on earth, personally and freely.

The Task of the Current Man

This is the task that presents itself to modern Man: to recognize the absolute hidden character of God and to interpret it correctly in an integral vision of the world, from which the supernatural dimension is not excluded. Only thus will he be able to solve without anxiety the personal and urgent aporias posed before our daily existence.

Although it may seem tautological, we must not look for God where He is not. Not because He is not present everywhere, but because the places where we look for Him are not a place, but rather a caricature of Man: we look for Him in a part of His being, in the truncated man, separated from the most authentically human spirit, that is a supernaturally free gift. If God has hidden, it is because Man has

---

[105] Jn 10:16.
[106] See Rom 8:28.

withdrawn, he has minimized himself, he has disregarded his faith, but the God his reason discovers for him is not enough.

It is a position of struggle. For the time being, we must go in search of God with faith and confidence. It is not that God has become eclipsed, but rather that Man has grown smaller and become content with being less than Man. This is why in the search, on the march in pursuit of God, Man's encounter with himself is being revealed. The twilight (God) does not take place because the sun is setting, but because the earth (Man) is turning on itself.

We must once again inoculate faith in God and in Christian solutions—which must sometimes be invented—reliving the daring and positive spirit of the earthly Christian community that calls itself the militant Church. Is God good for anything? Yes, for a trifle like saving not only our individual souls but also our bodies, including all things, and the entire universe. The incongruence of our times lies in the fact that things appear to make sense completely divorced from God. The darkness caused by the culpable eclipse of God—different from his own discretion—prevents us from seeing the real foundations of things, and we believe ourselves to be in possession of their ultimate meaning when a certain consistency presents itself, just like small children who believe that puppets are alive only because they do not see the strings.

Modern angst already takes care to dissipate this illusion. Now it is about turning to faith so that faith may show us the true reality that our sinful existence cannot glimpse with its natural vision. Evangelical μετάνοια once again consists, strictly speaking, in a *purification of the mind*, so that the latter, eliminating the darkness responsible for the eclipse, penetrates through the "ray of darkness"[107] into the invisible Light of Divinity.[108]

Vere tu es Deus absconditus: Hidden like the true essence of things, which is hidden inside them; like authentic reality, which does not show itself at first glance; like truth—ἀλήθεια—which is a concealed nucleus that must be unveiled; like the kingdom of heaven itself, which is similar to a hidden treasure,[109] yet a treasure that lies in our hands.[110] God's *epiphany* is the manifestation of the "mystery hidden for generations and centuries."[111] But what is revealed to us is the "humanity and kindness"[112] of Him whose face is hidden.[113] "It is you in the hiding place (*guhā*), God it is You!"[114]

---

[107] St. John of the Cross, *Noche oscura*, bk. II, chap. 5. St. John attributes this expression to Dionysius the Aeropagite.

[108] See Dionysius the Aeropagite, *Epistolae* V (*PG* 3.1073).

[109] Mt 13:44.

[110] 2 Co 4:7.

[111] Col 1:26.

[112] Tt 3:4 (according to the *Vulgate*).

[113] Is 53:3 (according to the *Vulgate*).

[114] *Jaiminiya-upaniṣad-brāhmaṇa* III.20.1. See also 1 Kgs 8:12, and *Śvetāśvatara-upaniṣad* I.1.3: God is hidden in his own attributes (qualities, *guṇas*).

8

CHRISTENDOM AND THE CROSS[1]

A Theological-Historical Investigation

Per quem mihi mundus crucifixus est, et ego mundo.

Gal 6:14

The Christian Tension in the World

The church has an existential and integrally human mission, that is to say, a supernatural mission and, therefore, one that differs from that of civil society, which only covers one aspect of Man's life on earth. In our epoch, in which institutions subside and values that seemed definitive disappear, the Church has been accused of being partly responsible for this social breakdown. This is true, but on a much more profound plane. The church is not directly involved with these types of civil affairs. "My friend, who appointed me your judge?" Jesus replied to the man in the crowd who wanted him to exercise his divine authority to settle a problem regarding an inheritance.[2] The church has not come to take from Caesar what is Caesar's,[3] but rather to make Caesar a Christian. This is why the kingdom of God—and the church is here for its coming—is within[4] and even above[5] us. But it is not yet of this world;[6] or more precisely, while the universe moves on, it does not yet identify with the church.

This does not mean that we should confine the church to the "sanctuary of consciousness" and make it withdraw from life, but rather that we recognize its integral mission—which, therefore, is above all that is partial, though obviously it influences the latter and consequently holds the right to intervene in the political field when, according to its superior criteria, it considers it convenient for Man's sole and supernatural end.[7]

---

[1] Published in *Arbor*, no. 84 (1952).
[2] Lk 12:13–14.
[3] Mt 22:21.
[4] Lk 17:21.
[5] Jn 16:16ff.
[6] Jn 17:16.
[7] See a more thorough examination of this issue in my announced *Cristianismo y Cristiandad*, in which the demands that *eternal* Christianity poses to *today's* Christianity are studied.

That said, if the church does not primarily have a civil mission, her children, Christians, do. If the church, as a supernatural organism of Man's divine life is, as such, transcendental to cultural situations, today's Christians are responsible for our era. Christians *are* the church, but they are not *the* church; they are members of the Mystical Body of Christ, but not all of the Body. Each Christian forms part of the church, but the church does not end with him or her. Christians never cease to be citizens, even if they are much more than mere citizens. This is why they find themselves immersed in all human affairs in their own right and they are naturally and supernaturally, that is to say, existentially, interested in this world that they form a part of and that they must—priestly—take on in order to lift it to God.

The church shapes Man; it transforms him, elevates him, purifies him, and turns him into a Christian; afterward it is Man who takes action as a Christian—since one will never be able to cease being so; as *part* of the church that one is, but not as *the* entire church as such. These actions that Christians perform in the midst of the world, as citizens of this earth—which they have received as their inheritance–[8] and at their own risk and personal responsibility, are what crystallizes in the Christian social regime that has been termed Christendom.

That said, the function that these "crusaders" (literally: "crossed," marked by the cross), Christians, exercise in the world, in the edification of Christendom, is also integrated under the sign of the cross.[9] The Christian—we know—is personally subject to the law of the cross, and their personal triumph entails immolation of their own being. But the triumph of Christendom, socially and collectively, and therefore the political mission of the Christian, also takes place via the cross.

This public task confers on Christians the enormous tension that defines them. On the one hand, their kingdom does not belong here;[10] the children of darkness seem more prudent than the children of light;[11] the life of Christians is a constant mortification[12] and a denial of this world,[13] which they cannot model themselves on.[14] Those who find consolation in this world are cursed.[15] But, on the other hand, Christians must not remove themselves from the world,[16] nor despise those who live in it,[17] nor give up control of society to non-Christians,[18] while they remain cloistered within a comfortable and criminal abstentionism. But how, then, must they harmonize the seemingly twofold jurisdiction to which they are subject? How

---

[8] Ps 2:8.

[9] When medieval Christendom was forced to affirm itself in the face of Muslim power, it called its men *crusaders* though they often did not behave as such, but rather as *warriors*.

[10] Jn 18:36.

[11] Lk 16:8.

[12] 2 Co 4:10.

[13] Jas 1:27.

[14] Rom 12:2.

[15] Lk 6:24.

[16] Jn 17:15.

[17] Pr 14:21.

[18] Jn 17:18.

can Christians integrate their faith and their social activities? What must their inner and exterior norms be in civil life?

It is not easy to achieve the required synthesis. While some accentuate the aspect of fleeing from their time, others exaggerate worldliness and, by wanting to Christianize the relative values of this world, they end up absolutizing them—and herein lies the danger. The tension between these two poles is not exclusive to our days. It is indeed as ancient as Christianity, and even as man himself, who has always been subjected to the attraction of the hereafter and—also always—been captivated by the fascination of the here and now. From the Tower of Babel, which expected to rise to heaven *from* the earth;[19] from the constant hope of the apostles for a messianic kingdom of Israel, even after Jesus had died and risen again;[20] to many of our current dreams for a new Christendom, human thoughts and desires have been affected by the same concerns.[21] Ultimately, this is about our more or less conscious search for a substitute for the cross. But life lies in it alone.[22]

But the cross does not solely represent the transcendent aspect. Nowhere does it say that the messianic kingdom will not be established one day. Christ did not deny its arrival, he merely limited himself to saying that it was not for us to "know times or dates that the Father has decided by his own authority."[23] Furthermore, our lives are not alien to the kingdom of Christ on earth. He is King of nations.[24] "Social reign of Jesus Christ" affirms a formula sanctioned by custom.[25]

The cross, however, *is* cross, immolation, sacrifice, and here on earth, pain and suffering. Many Christians who gladly accept the personal cross rebel against the kingdom of the cross in society. They possess the indispensable faith to accept the cross in their own lives, but because they have not penetrated the glorious and profound sense of the cross, they cannot tolerate that it be spoken about in the public life of humanity or of the church; to them this seems like an insult against God. They forget that Christians, with their cross, are a spectacle to both angels and men.[26]

What happens to us instinctively—when our faith is weak—is similar to what happens to good mothers who love their children spontaneously and indiscriminately: they try to keep them from paying their tribute to pain and perhaps they only succeed in postponing it and, therefore, increasing its intensity. We would like Christ to reign in the world in a "more effective" manner, we say; "more sparklingly

---

[19] Gn 11:4.

[20] Ac 1:6.

[21] See R. Panikkar, prologue to Gustave Thibon, *El pan de cada dōa*, 4th ed. (Madrid: Rialp, 1962).

[22] "In cruce salus, in cruce vita!" Thomas à Kempis, *The Imitation of Christ* II.12.1.

[23] Ac 1:7.

[24] See Is 9:6–7; Dan 7:13–14; Lk 1:32–33; Jn 18:37; 1 Co 15:25; Rev 1:5; etc.

[25] "Now, if we order that Christ the King be worshipped by all the Catholics in the world, we will thus provide for the needs of present time, bringing a most efficacious remedy to the plague which is infesting human society," says Pius XI in his encyclical on the royalty of Christ, *Quas Primas*, December 11, 1925 (*Acta Apostolicae Sedis*, XVII.593ff.).

[26] 1 Co 4:9.

and pompously," we think at bottom. We become shocked, in a more or less hypo-critical way and with a stentorian voice, because the small flock of the Gospel[27] is always so minute—and sometimes even so paltry. Our thirst for greatness is often not Christian. Like the disciples, we secretly aspire to a spectacular reign.[28] We would like, along with Christ, to dominate the world in our own way. We are reluctant to fully accept the cross. We are willing to die for ourselves, but *obviously* provided that the cause triumphs. We accept being victims, martyrs; we understand that our path is the cross, but we cannot tolerate that Christ may *externally* lose the battle here on earth. This is the great temptation of the cross for "good" Christians, "political Catholicism," as if Christendom were simply the political party of the "right." But "blessed is anyone who is not scandalized by me."[29]

Christians, say, feel they must demonstrate to the world—as if they were depen-dent on the judgment of the world and not on divine criteria—that the truth is with them, that their God is the creator of the entire universe, that being Christian is not a human dishonor, and that Christians do not render Man useless for any of his functions on earth. Christ has jurisdiction not only over Christians but rather over all of humanity.

Forced, however, by the power of facts and evangelical demands—therein lie the paradoxical Beatitudes—we must admit that reality does not conform to our dreams, and then we separate church and Christendom and load the entire intrinsic tragedy of the cross onto the former. Yes, the church, as Christ's bride,[30] bride of the sacrificed Lamb[31]—*sponsus sanguinis*—[32] will always suffer persecution on this earth[33] and will be misunderstood and abused, on occasion even by its own members.[34] The visible church will suffer and endure battles to the death against the forces of evil. These will not overpower it,[35] but they will win many battles and the Antichrist will be present until the end of time.[36] Furthermore, were the last days not shortened, nobody on earth would be saved.[37] Apparently, the church will emerge defeated, like its Master.[38]

Now then, we say—and it is true—that the church cannot identify with the Christian world. But we have been all too careful to make this distinction meticu-lously, and we cannot bear the Christian world having to suffer the humiliation of

---

[27] Lk 12:32.
[28] See Mk 10:35ff.
[29] Mt 11:6; Lk 7:23.
[30] Rev 21:2.
[31] See Rev 5:6; 21:9.
[32] See Ex 4:25.
[33] See 2 Tim 3:12; Lk 17:1.
[34] See the strong—and heart-rending—words of St. Paul to the Christians who ignore the law of the cross (1 Co 4:10ff.).
[35] Mt 16:18.
[36] Mk 13:22.
[37] Mk 13:20.
[38] Mt 27:39ff.

hearing itself called obscurantist, enemy of progress, despiser of culture, inhuman, and so on. We wish, in any case, to spare it the law of the cross. And then the ruthless critique against current Christian life emerges, and the latter is branded as narrow and dull because it has become separated from the world; it has shut itself up in its own redoubts, which grow smaller and weaker with each passing day. All of humanity is headed toward God, and we cannot suffer that the "chosen part" is not heading this movement and consecrating all the progresses Man achieves to Him. For this, many preach, we have to return to the world and adapt to it.

Many of the statements here affirmed are true, but they originate in an environment that often lacks an authentic Christian spirit, a profound sense of the cross, that is the touchstone of Christianity. Some compromises are betrayals. There is a serious danger of reacting "simply so that they will not be persecuted for the cross of Christ,"[39] forgetting the intense tension of the Christian response to the world. Christ is the solution for the world, but by means of his redemption on the cross; He is the only way, but this path of salvation is a *Via Crucis*.[40]

Nobody doubts that Lamennais's intentions were good, as were those of Lacordaire, Montalembert, Dupanloup, and that of the political movement Le Sillon—to give specific examples from the recent past and not refer to current instances: but perhaps the anti-Christian critique wounded them too deeply. They took it too seriously. Let us not forget what Christ had been told: "If you are the Son of God, descend from the cross!"[41] And he did not descend from the cross precisely *because* he was the Son of God. Any other man with the ability to do so would have come down. Christ climbed onto the cross once for all, and no matter how much our proud reason proves to be shocked by this and yells at Him to come down, he does not. He did not want to descend from the cross to prove his divinity. The mystery of the cross is inaccessible to Christian reason itself.

This obviously does not justify adopting the opposite position—which is both selfish and criminal—of disregard for the world and of a calamitous gentrification in one's own truth, which then becomes captive and adulterated. Christians must embark on the construction of the earthly city armed with the cross. This is the only possible way of building Christendom.

The Primacy of the Cross

One of the objectives of the construction of Christendom is the attainment of an earthly social order in which Man finds the way of accomplishing his ultimate eternal and supernatural end by fulfilling his civil and earthly ends. This is the task of Christendom: to be humanity's leaven and producer of the value of the cross in

---

[39] Gal 6:12.

[40] "All of Christ's life was cross and martyrdom" (Thomas à Kempis, *Imitation of Christ*, II.12.3).

[41] Mt 27:40.

its most external social and public aspect.

This is its essential attribute, since beside it lie other contingent and temporal characteristics proper to the different specific incarnations of the *ideal* of *Christendom*. It is obvious that the concrete social expression of Christianity must be very different in our times from that which existed in the first Christian centuries or in the Middle Ages. Nevertheless, there must be some essential trait that allows us to call all Christian social orders *Christendom*, no matter how different their historical wrapping.

This distinctive criterion possesses an internal and an external aspect. From the external point of view, any social order that, as such, acknowledges *the universal and primary function of the church* and, consequently, of the supernatural order will be Christendom. We could call *Christendom* any social order that ultimately—and one way or another—depends on Man's supernatural order and goal. Christendom is not a dogmatic, closed-off system, or a political theocracy, or a social clericalism. The only thing it requires is an authentic and sincere Christian social consciousness that recognizes Man's sole existential end and, therefore, the religious mission of the church in society.

This external and necessary characteristic entails a seed of tragedy inherent to Christendom, since it makes hypocrisy possible—and even facilitates it—despite the fact that it is its very antithesis. The hypocrite is one who obeys socially—even with sincerity in some cases—the letter of the law but is internally void of the spirit that produced those very same social manifestations. The existence of Christendom itself, as an external social Christian order, creates the perfect climate for hypocrisy.

This is why the external feature needs to be completed with an intrinsic facet which, as such, reaches deeper into the essence of Christendom—though it is more difficult to be checked as a criterion. And that is none other than the primacy of the cross.

For society to *say* that it wants to be catholic is not enough. Christendom must make an intrinsically Christian social order possible. Note well: an *intrinsically* Christian *social* order, that is, one that is not only compatible with Christian doctrine, but also imbued with its very spirit—but this does not mean a *perfectly* Christian *metaphysical* order. Christendom is not a utopia; rather it is a human and historical reality that is compatible with Man's misery, evil, and even mediocrity,[42] as well as with the imperfection of social structures themselves.[43]

---

[42] We must highlight this realistic quality of Christendom in face of Puritan idealisms that mistake the purity of the Church with a world on the way to becoming Christian. See, for example, Giovanni Papini's exclamations: "The authentic truth is that no true Christians exist. And it is impossible to *go back* to the Gospel, because it has never been reached before. . . . Christianity is the most virgin and newest thing on earth; it is more than modern, because it has never begun" (*La Scala di Giacobbe* [Florence: Vallecchi, 1932]). Though it may seem paradoxical, this longing for pure essences is a remnant of rationalism. Reality is not pure rationality.

[43] While a staunch atheist communism or a liberal capitalism is incompatible with a

But we are also not saying that this is an easy ideal. Christendom exists insofar as the cross occupies the central—internal—place in social order. And this is where the great human resistance—also put up by Christians—to the establishment of an authentic Christianity comes in. The cross is what conditions the essence—and even the very existence—of Christendom. This is what we will try to see.

We need much more faith in order to recognize and implant the primacy of the cross in Christendom than in individual lives. Christians are asked to have total and absolute faith in Christ. Without Him they can do nothing.[44] Christendom must also have trust in the strength of the Lord as the only one able to build the earthly city.[45] This intrinsic confidence is also much needed in our times. We are very far from boasting about our weakness so that it may be substituted by the strength of Christ.[46] It is true that secondary causes really are *causes*, but we cannot forget that they really are *secondary*.

At times, we become disenchanted with the deeds of Christians because we have been misled beforehand into thinking that their action in the world should merely be natural; we simply forget that victory is obtained through the cross.

In addition, the primacy of the cross has another facet, somewhat forgotten by humanity. Not only is it true that the supernatural is the most important thing and that natural culture must be at the service of Man's highest end, but the natural cannot be upheld without the cross of Christ, ultimately because pure nature does not exist. Such a nature has been "wounded" and cannot remain within the right order by its own devices. An exclusively humanist culture—better yet, natural—is also impossible without the aid of the supernatural cross.[47] Humanism, like Man's purely natural self-sufficiency, is a utopic myth.[48]

Strictly speaking, there is no such thing as a pure nature or a disembodied supernature, but rather there is only authentic and real existence on the universal path to Redemption.

Restoration of Values

"Social reign of Jesus Christ," we have heard; but Christ only reigns from the cross. There is no possible escape or middle of the road of any kind. Either the Beatitudes are a utopia, and the Sermon on the Mount a code for citizens of another world, or there is a supernatural law that is valid on earth whose breach has led humanity to these recent suicide attempts. And this is the law of the cross.

---

regime of Christendom, this is not the case with an open socialism or a mitigated capitalism, despite the undeniable flaws of both systems.

[44] Jn 15:5.

[45] See Ps 126 [127]:1–2.

[46] See 2 Co 12:9.

[47] See the chapter "*Extra Ecclesiam Nulla Salus.*"

[48] See the chapter "Overcoming Humanism."

Compromises and adaptations have been tried throughout time in search of a solution that does not sound so harsh to human ears.[49] But the demands of the Gospel still stand, and the time has come to try to apply them in society with all of their strength and purity. This does not exclude prudence, moderation, or common sense, but must these virtues that govern our activity always be accompanied by laziness, a spirit of compromise, and cowardice?

For this is the fact that we will not found or develop here, and we will merely record it: the social order that Christendom aims at establishing is not a mere prolongation or a simple perfectioning of the human social order in the natural sphere; rather, it is essentially and intrinsically different.

In fact, a society's order is conditioned by its end, since order is nothing but the adequate regulation of the means that lead to an end. But Man's end and, consequently, that of society have been modified by Christianity; the *common good* will no longer be the same. Or rather, Christianity discovers—reveals—Man's *only* supernatural end, and it provides the normal means to reach it. The Christian regime—and we must have the courage to affirm this—modifies even the most insignificant laws of the city from their roots. It modifies them, sometimes distorts them, even if in general it does not revoke them in their judicial formulation. The right Christian order is not a simple complement or a small correction of the natural human order; rather it is simply different. In the same way that what is good for an animal body is different from what is good for Man's body, due to the fact that the latter exists in union with a spirit, the irruption of the supernatural order not only expands Man's aspirations in the order of the ends, but it intrinsically changes them.[50] *Splendida vitia* (admirable errors) is what St. Augustine—exaggerating a little—calls the natural virtues of pagans.[51]

This does not mean that the order of grace contradicts that of nature. But we must bear in mind that if grace perfects nature, and in this sense presupposes it, it also truly modifies it, and therefore Man's ends likewise vary, as do the means to achieve them.

The order introduced by Christendom will certainly, once implanted, prove itself to be the most perfect order for humans—not, however, with reference to the ideal man that reason creates, but rather to the real man, who is very superior insofar as he is elevated to a supernatural order, and simultaneously very inferior insofar as the stigma of sin—original and personal—weighs down upon him. That is to say, only faith will sustain a Christian order, even if its effectiveness and viability are only proven a posteriori.

---

[49] See Jn 6:60.

[50] This is the ultimate meaning of the well-known Augustinian saying about the infidels: "They *do* run, but not in the [right] path; and the more they run, the more they go astray, as they deviate from the path" (*Sermones* 141, c. 4, num. 4).

[51] We must not, however, unilaterally exaggerate the supernatural to the point of condemning human nature itself. See the proposition by Bayo, then condemned by the Church: "All the works of the infidels are sinful, and the virtues praised by philosophers are vices" (*Denz.*, 1025). See the authentic Augustinian point of view in *Contra Iulianum Pelagianum* IV.3.19.

That said, it is understandable that a God who dies on a cross does not establish a different order than that proclaimed by the Sermon on the Mount; not as the resentment—I repeat—of a crucified God, but rather as an expression of the ultimate—historical—structure of the contingent being and, consequently, of humanity.

From the natural point of view, the common good that civil society pursues is its end, and as such we cannot help but consider it absolute; and with this, when a series of good values turns into absolute values, they become an obstacle for the *new* end that grace introduces within human society itself. This is why the cross, as immolation of all to God, brings about an overturning in the values of human communal life.

In general, when we speak of the Christian axiological revolution, we are exclusively thinking about its effects on the individual. It is said that Christians must follow Christ and imitate Him in his death and abandonment on the cross, yet we want to prevent this from being also the destiny of Christendom at all costs. We forget that if Christians are pilgrims and strangers on this earth, all of humanity also finds itself on pilgrimage, and that the overturning of values introduced by Christ also has direct repercussions on the very substance of society.

Society, as such, also depends on God and on Christ, and it must also be religious and Christian; it must carry out its function of worshipping God and of being able to offer itself in immolation to the Divinity. We have often wanted to separate humanity from Man's supernatural destiny, and then humanity appears as the mere recipient in which each individuality shapes its own destiny; but human society is a supra-individual reality, humanity is a unit, and Christ equally its Lord and Head.

Strictly speaking, the term "overturning" is not completely adequate, as it suggests a specific original order that was subsequently modified. Christ did not come to capsize any values; rather he came to reveal and restore the authentic hierarchy between them, whose consciousness—and whose reality—men had lost. Let us not forget that, as a matter of fact, the real end of divine action *ad extra* is supernatural order.

We had the illusion of our race being immortal, since we were not so individually. There still is the echo of the tempter's hiss in humanity's ears: "You *will be* like gods,"[52] and we had imagined that humanity would gradually become deified.[53] This is explicitly the case of Marxism, exploiting the religious desire of a secular culture: humanity as the future—and end—of Man himself.

Humanity's destiny, its authentic apotheosis, is neither undefined progress nor one determined perfection, nor universal well-being, but rather the preparation of παρουσία, the attainment of the necessary maturity for the second coming of

---

[52] Gn 3:5.

[53] The temptation of the devil was subtle because it was aimed at the greatest ambition of the created being—to become deified—but it did not by any means attain the promised reality: true deification. Christ did not say that we would be *like* Gods, but that we would *be* Gods (see Ps 81:6)—and even more, *God* in his union and communion with the Father. See Jn 6:56–57.

the Son of Man. Humanity walks toward the fullness of the Body of Christ. When
the number of chosen ones is complete, then it will be the end. And it seems as if
accelerating His coming by increasing the number of those who are saved was a little
in our own hands. It is the threefold personal, social, and eschatological dimension
of the *Adveniat Regnum tuum*!

This does not mean—I repeat—that Christendom must withdraw into an interior
world. Its field of action is precisely the earthly city, and the above-mentioned overturning of values is not, as we have just said, a collapse of a natural order, but rather
the restoration of an integral order. In many cases this is about nothing more than
a methodological variation—that is, the introduction of a new way, the way of the
cross, in order to achieve these very same goods. Thus, for example, the Beatitudes
as a code of the new law do not say that tears, hunger, thirst, persecution, and so on
are positive values as such, but rather reveal that, while recognizing the value of joy,
feeling full, peace, and so forth in this real world, the way to achieve them passes
through total and absolute immolation of ourselves.

This is what Christendom must learn. Certainly "power is at full strength in
weakness";[54] not because weakness is better than strength—this would be a thorough distortion of values—but because *astheneia* helps and completes virtue itself.
Strictly speaking, then, it is about an authentic integration of values. In the eyes of
God, nothing is lost and everything finds a meaning. It is true that human wisdom
is foolishness in the eyes of God,[55] but the fool is commanded to become wise.[56]

Christendom, therefore, is at once strong and weak, triumphant and defeated.
Tanquam nihil habentes, et omnia possidentes![57]

Christendom's Discretion

The first dimension of the cross in Christendom is the sacrifice of its external
triumph. It is true that Christendom truly triumphs because of the cross, but it is a
silent triumph and a discreet influence, maybe without external effect.

Christ has forecast it: scandals will necessarily take place[58]—the cross itself is
the biggest scandal;[59] you—plural—will be universally hated;[60] but hold your head
high when these things begin to take place.[61] It does not matter. For now, let the
wheat and the darnel grow together, and it is currently good not to separate them.[62]

---

[54] 2 Co 12:9.
[55] 1 Co 3:19.
[56] 1 Co 3:18.
[57] 2 Co 6:10.
[58] Mt 17:7.
[59] Gal 5:11.
[60] Mk 13:13.
[61] Lk 21:28.
[62] Mt 13:30.

The time will come when there will be one sole flock and one sole shepherd.[63] In the meantime, the kingdom of God suffers from violence,[64] and you must pray at all times[65] for its coming.[66]

What does all this mean? If we pay attention, it is a calling to discretion and interiority. God is a hidden Being, and His kingdom is among us.[67] What good will it be for a man if he gains the whole world, yet forfeits his soul?[68] God is discreet, and Christendom must also be so.[69] But this does not prevent Christians from also feeling they are *heirs* of this earth that God has given them,[70] and that they therefore attempt to be in possession of it, in accordance with the mandate received.[71]

And, in fact, Christendom sacrifices its own human prestige to God, but it does not give up guiding humanity's destinies. In the same way that Christians personally influence and have a weight in the world, even when their own personal destinies may have an external appearance of failure and inferiority; in the same way that, ultimately, once he was outrageously killed by men, Christ drew people to himself,[72] so analogously Christendom, and even more so the church—although *in fieri* and in gestation—influences and governs the destinies of peoples, despite its apparent insignificance and often thanks to the very oppositions and persecutions. *Graecia capta ferum victorem capit!*

Christendom will never, or almost never, have an external apotheosis, and nevertheless it will directly or indirectly govern the destinies of the peoples, steering them toward the Light. Similarly as to how politicians are simple executors of ideas initiated by others and assimilated by them, so the social structures that dominate Humanity are also channels of ideas that are either for or against the ascendant movement of peoples toward God, guided by Christendom. There is no possible middle course.[73]

It is not necessary to delve very deeply into the history of the past twenty centuries to realize that the vast majority of the positive values that humanity, including the unfaithful part of it, has acquired come either directly or indirectly from Christians, many times through the oppositions suffered by Christendom. We can recognize the invisible trace of the gospel even within the nucleus of truth in the false doctrines. Let us recall socialism and communism, for example, not to mention humanity's great conquests: the abolition of slavery, the recognition of human dignity, of personal freedom, the role of women, and so on.

---

[63] Jn 10:16.
[64] Mt 11,12.
[65] Lk 21:36.
[66] Lk 11:2.
[67] Lk 17:21.
[68] Mt 16:26.
[69] See above, chapter 7, "*De Deo abscondito*."
[70] Ps 2:8–9.
[71] Gn 1:28.
[72] Jn 12:32.
[73] Mt 12:30.

Christendom is the bearer of great human values, even if sometimes it does not itself put them into practice. By means of its immolation to God and its apparent ineffectiveness—through the cross, therefore—Christendom is still the primary power on earth. Sometimes we must just be a little patient. "Everything now covered up will be uncovered."[74] *Crux docet!*[75]

A little bit of leaven will always be what makes the dough rise. And Christendom has been called salt of the earth,[76] light,[77] yeast.[78] *Paucis humanum vivit genus* (humankind survives thanks to few people), the ancients already used to say.

Cultural Sacrifice

But there is more. Silent success and discreet influence only constitute the first aspects of the law of the cross of Christendom. There is more, and herein lies the greatest test for Christians who strive for a better social order: the primacy of the cross is really cross, that is, authentic sacrifice.

Well, this immolation is glorious and triumphant, though no less difficult or painful because of it.

If we were to make use of profane paradigms that are only sensible to the phenomenal world, if we were to follow the anthropocentric line of humanism, we would say that Christendom's intrinsic constitution condemns it to failure, just as the failure of Golgotha was where its Master ended up. We would then say that Christendom represents the frustrated and utopian attempt to model this world on an unreachable and harmful ideal. The idea of Christendom then appears as a motive of discord, a sign of contradiction, an inconvenient emetic that paralyzes humanity's greatest efforts to easily and comfortably settle on this earth, since thinking too much about the other world is an obstacle to knowing how to live in this one. "Since we are to live just few, wretched days on earth, worrying about anything is pointless"; this is what Christians seem to be preaching. Christendom then appears to be a regime hostile to the world that paralyzes the earthly boldness of the sons of men. Its social ideal of resignation and detachment would be the opium of the masses and the main obstacle to progress and civilization.

---

[74] Lk 12:2.

[75] An exciting example of Christianity's expansive power is constituted by the history of Hindu spirituality in the nineteenth century. Ramakrishna, Vivekananda, Ram Mohan Roy, Keshab Chandra Sen, Debendranath Tagore, et al., literally bump into Christ, and the shock is so strong that it intrinsically transforms the interpretation of their multimillenial religiosity, and it would have—possibly—led them to Christianity if they had run into a sufficiently great Christian personality who had been prepared to dialogue with them. . . . But the majority of Christians from 150 years ago were worthy representatives of *microdoxy*.

[76] Mt 5:13.

[77] Mt 5:14.

[78] Mt 13:33.

It is understandable that, at first glance, the law of the cross appears inhuman and unacceptable. It is no wonder that it was folly in the eyes of the Gentiles.[79]

If this earth were the greatest good in existence and *comfort* were Man's end, then we could establish some kind of dialogue with the aforementioned point of view. But, even in that case, it would be possible to successfully defend the Christian thesis, since the cross not only reigns in the supernatural sphere, but also in the natural one, as we have said. Chateaubriand, for example, would know how to do this very well.

But the real situation is very different, and consequently the approach to the problem itself is another one altogether. The entire world, even the infrahuman one, has received the cosmic effect of redemption and has been influenced by it.[80] Humanity, specifically, has received a new end, a superior destiny that intrinsically modifies natural structures.[81]

Christianity is something more than a humanism, and the cross is something more than the heart and end of a natural culture. The cross on earth is internally heart-rending. Christians are not ordinary people who, *in addition*, await and believe in another life as a complement to this one; rather, baptism has modified the most profound aspects of their being. They are "new creations."[82]

Were we to remember that Man is *viator* and humanity is in constant pilgrimage, in pilgrimage toward the Absolute, it would no longer be so surprising that God has assigned Christendom the role of spoilsport in the bacchanals that men instinctively organize in order to inhabit this "bad inn."[83] This is not wholly true, but it is also not false if we approach the issue from a naturalist perspective.[84]

Yet the correct approach is quite different. If the end of humanity is not found on this earth, we must learn to overcome and transcend this earth. We are not preaching contempt for what is human, but rather a certain disdain for the earthly as a way of overcoming it, of elegantly transiting through it; not as an onerous but necessary mortification, but rather as a glorious and honorable sacrifice that liberates us from the humiliating subjection to what is perishable and mortal.

---

[79] 1 Co 1:23. This is why Julian the Apostate, who understood Christianity so diabolically well, mocked Christians because of their cult to the cross: "You worship," he said to them, "the log of a cross, you make this sign on your foreheads and put it on the doors of your houses. . . ." Quoted by Cyril of Alexandria, *Contra Julianum* I.6.

[80] See Ep 1:22; Heb 2:8, etc.

[81] To be precise, this manner of speaking is still much too rationalist since, properly, that which is Christian is that which is primary as, ultimately, *that which is existential is that which is Christian*. But it is not necessary to develop this originally and radically Christian proposal right now.

[82] 2 Co 5:17.

[83] St. Teresa of Avila.

[84] See Christ's reaction, human and divine at once, crying over Jerusalem and predicting its ruin (Mt 24:1ff.).

And herein lies the sacrificial function of Christendom: to live *in* this world, but to use it and dominate it *for* the highest end to which men have been called. Culture is not an end in itself, and neither is civilization.

Christendom cannot scorn any good, however earthly it may seem, precisely because through these goods it fulfills its transcendent and divine function. And herein lies the entire issue: it is *through* earthly values, passing among them, using them like instruments, sacrificing them to God, in a word, that Christendom attains its end and fulfills its mission. This is the true law of the cross.

This does not represent the death of civil society, but rather the exact opposite. We said immolation, not assassination. The cross is the first value of society itself, and if it is fulfilled, the rest will be given to us in addition, not as a magnanimous present from an arbitrary[85] God, but rather as the mature fruit of the existential nature of things themselves. This is the radical relativity of human axiology to which we alluded earlier.

Man always needs to overcome and defeat his environment, and in order to embody any value he needs first to overcome it. In order to exist, human society—like Man—needs there to be constant struggle and tension; otherwise, it degenerates. This is the true meaning of the *struggle for life*. Christendom is responsible for maintaining the transcendent fire that keeps the tension in human life and prevents it from degenerating into simple animal existence. The cross also keeps this difference in potential active, so that divine current may flow between men.

Technology that is too perfect, which solves everything for Man, dulls the senses. It has been called "precarious *ersatz* of the preternatural gifts of the paradisiacal creature."[86] Technology is not there to substitute spirit, but rather to help it. The world knows too much about greenhouse cultivation, and—unfortunately—so do Christians. When those scented wild roses from which we extract the essence of rose are cultivated in a greenhouse, the number of petals certainly increases from five to thirty, and even up to one hundred in some cases; but this happens at the expense of the degeneration of the stamen, their male organ. These roses are sterile, and at the same time they have lost a great deal of their scent. In general, any vegetable species—and nonvegetable ones as well—that is grown in captivity becomes sterile.

Culture is not an absolute good. The Christian longing for culture is radically different from the cultural thirst of those who see in it the salvation of the human race. This is why the immolation of culture can seem blasphemous to non-Christians.

Any Christian fulfillment must be ascetic. All social functioning finds itself imbued with a radical relativity that demands asceticism in order to overcome the

---

[85] Literally: voluntarist, with reference to a medieval—and also later—theological doctrine. [n.d.t.]

[86] H. Delfos Mandrioni in his prologue to the Spanish edition of G. Papini, *La Scala di Giacobbe.*

inherent imperfection of any human situation. Christian asceticism extends to Christendom itself. If Christendom is to help men achieve their goals, reaching God, it will have to try to free men from their own constructions; it will not promise men heaven on earth, and yet it will try to make our terrestrial stay as perfect as possible. Christendom will push men to transcend themselves, and it will offer them the best possible springboard for this. Christendom is essentially the preacher of the heavenly city and, as such, it must comply with the essential law of the Precursor: *Illum oportet crescere, me autem minui.*[87]

Christendom, by means of this immolation of its own values, by means of sacrificing that which is visible—politics, technology, culture, and so on—for the sake of that which is invisible—goodness, virtue, grace, and so on—will teach Man—and will try to make him act accordingly—that his value does not lie in what he can *do*, but rather in his simple and naked *substance*, in his deified *being*, from which his different deified activities will emerge like mature fruits. In short, it will teach him that his earthly existence itself makes no sense outside of Christ. And only thus does Man attain his true freedom, raising himself above his environment and affirming his personal value.

But this immolation is heroic. It is true that it can be recalled, with the aid of the faith, that God has promised a hundredfold reward to those who would consecrate themselves to Him,[88] but complete surrender is not any easier because of this. Christendom, which is a passionate supporter of human values, must know how to position these in their place and not let itself be dominated by them. And this is true in literature, art, politics . . . , in any human manifestation.

But grace is necessary for this task. Humanity alone cannot resist the attacks of the Prince of Darkness. Christendom has an active role to play in the cosmic struggle against the Antichrist. This is why it cannot be understood without its intimate connection with the church through the personal union of Christians, who are the natural workers of Christendom and children of the church. Christendom itself is an integral part of the church.

Christianity has come to proclaim the insufficiency of this world, not because it is evil, but because it is not yet divine, and the mission of Christendom is to make us live this insufficiency so as to project us to the supernatural hereafter by means of its own immolation, in order to uncover Man's divine nucleus. And this is its intrinsic law, in such a way that by means of this service it attains its maximum perfection.

Christians must sacrifice themselves in order to become men, and Christendom must be willing to perform Abraham's sacrifice in order to subsist. Whoever does not forsake everything, whoever who does not take up his cross, cannot be a disciple of Christ.[89] These are the demands of the cross.

---

[87] Jn 3:30.
[88] Mt 19:29.
[89] Mt 10:38.

The Establishment of the Cross

Because the cross is a divine value, Christendom will suffer enormously when it introduces it among men. Christendom will always be imperfect for two reasons: the unworthiness of its members and the unfeasibility of being fully established on this earth.

Nothing human is ever finished—perfect—or absolute. Much has been said about the unworthiness of Christians. There is always room for criticism. And there will always be dissatisfied and puritanical Christians who cannot adjust themselves to the provisional nature of earthly life, and therefore of all its solutions, who do not have the audacity and the humility to be imperfect, and who cross their arms and wait for an optimal and transparent utopian situation in order to start working together, forgetting that the wheat and the darnel will not be separated until the end of time.[90]

But the imperfection that weighs the most on Christendom is not that of its own members, but rather the objective one of its own constructions. Christendom is called to structure a city in the world, but whose right to citizenship *cannot* be fully recognized on earth. If the kingdom of Jesus were of this world, his servants would already have fought to establish it and prevent him from being surrendered to his enemies, but his kingdom does not belong here.[91] And yet, it is here that it must begin to be fulfilled. So it is not exactly the human element—that which is "too human"—that most makes Christendom suffer, but its very transcendent mission constitutes its pain and Calvary: the divine—the "too divine"—only miscible with the earthly in small proportions and at great temperatures.

"With this sign you will prevail!" They say[92] this was revealed to the first man who made it possible for the regime of Christendom to be established on earth. Yes, it is a victory that Christ has come to bring to the world,[93] but a victory from the cross, *in hoc signo*, has been promised to Christendom: to triumph by dying. *Crucis victoria!* This is the reason why martyrdom has perennial value within the Christian social order. This is also why there are "eunuchs" for the sake of the kingdom of God.[94]

Poor and yet making many people rich;[95] when we are cursed, we answer with a blessing. . . .[96] If, on the one hand—from the point of view of the world—Christendom appears to be perishing, on the other—from the point of view of God—it rules and dominates history.

The establishment of the cross is not only heroic but also supernatural. Convincing humanity—and making it act accordingly—of the fact that its existence on earth

---

[90] Mt 13:30.
[91] Jn 18:36.
[92] Eusebius, *Vita Constantini* I.28.
[93] See Jn 12:31; 16:33, etc.
[94] Mt 19:12.
[95] 2 Co 6:10.
[96] 1 Co 4:12.

makes no sense beyond Christ—as the mission of Christendom can be summarized—can only be done by being directly connected with the church, from which Christians, the builders of Christendom, receive the supernatural grace necessary to fight against the forces of evil and of its prince.

Christendom is on the warpath. Man's life on earth is like military life.[97] The fact of sin cannot be forgotten. Humanity, without Christ, finds itself under the power of the *prince of this world*.[98] Christendom collaborates in completing the redemption of the human race by establishing the most favorable social base under any historical and geographical conditions for the penetration of evangelic *kērygma*.

This is why Christians must prepare to penetrate the earthly order, not so as to exercise tyranny over the world, but rather to serve it and channel it toward the achievement of its highest ends. The world has been left for men to dispute,[99] but Christians are just as much men as other men, and even more so than the rest.[100] This is why they must, once and for all and obeying divine commandment,[101] hurl themselves into the arena of life, leaving aside all lazy noninterventionists and hypocritical Puritanists and dirty themselves in the difficult and ungrateful, though noble and beautiful, fight for this earthly world in which we all have our deepest roots. Christians must know once and for all that they can judge on everything, without being judged by anybody.[102] But this ἀνάκρισις—examination, interrogation—does not mean that they can judge their fellow men, all of whom, without exception, are their brothers.[103]

Christendom bears on its shoulders a cosmic struggle in which God and the whole of creation take part. And what is fascinating in this battle, even more than the victory, is the *freedom* that God respects in this dispute. It is true that there are serious eschatological prophecies by St. John, St. Paul, and Christ himself in which the end of the world does not appear to be too promising for Christendom—this is how He purifies and supernaturalizes its function on earth—but it is no less true that these same prophecies are full of mysteries and that, like all prophecies, they are undecipherable before their fulfillment, as otherwise the assurance of human liberty, which is precisely what gives them their value, would be in peril. And this is where Christendom must act with the true freedom of the children of God, for whom "nothing is impossible."[104] The history of the world is not governed by some

---

[97] Jb 7:1 (*Vulgate*).

[98] Jn 14:30; See also Jn 12:31; 16:11.

[99] Qo 3:11 (*Vulgate*).

[100] There is an Arabian proverb that states that the world is God's, but that He has rented it out to the most courageous. Of course, Christian courage is not bellicose violence or a "holy war," or an armed crusade, but rather resistance in faith (1 Pet 5:9) and the absence of human fears (Mt 10:28).

[101] Gn 1:28.

[102] See 1 Co 2:13–15.

[103] See Jas 4:11.

[104] See Gn 18:14 and Lk 1:37. It is interesting to notice that this saying, in the Old and

fatal rigid laws; humanity is not subject to any fatalism; the "good" are not in an inferior situation to the evil, since this earth is no longer the seat of the Prince of Darkness, as he has already been judged and defeated by the King of this world and the other one.[105]

Christendom cannot take refuge in the hereafter, abandoning this earth that it has inherited precisely in order to cultivate it.[106] The eschatological vision purifies its intentions, but it does not paralyze its strength. The world is in our hands, in the hands of the children of God. And we must configure it according to Christ's commandments.

The God of the New Testament is just as alive as YHWH. And if in the history of the people of Israel we can read that God—always fulfillling his pact—changes His behavior according to the behavior of the Jews, why should He not be able to change the course of history if Christians win His battles, armed with the faith that makes them invulnerable?

The idea may seem daring: to modify the plans of Providence. But if men's sins have repeatedly made God's plans vary at certain times, why can't the virtue of Christians also modify these plans? Ten upright men would have saved Sodom through the petition of one patriarch.[107] The destruction of Nineveh and its exact date—forty days—was prophesied, and the penitence of the entire city placated divine justice.[108] Everything seems to indicate that Isaiah predicted what the idyllic messianic kingdom *would have been* had Israel accepted the message of the Messiah.[109] Why, then, could not the virtue of Christendom delete the terrible sentences of Christian eschatology, just as the noncorrespondence of the Jews modified God's plans over and over? It has also been prophesied that Israel will return to the fold[110] and that there will be only one flock, only one shepherd.[111] It is a new vicissitude of the Mystery of the cross. Perhaps Christ never felt as tragically and majestically free as when he was in Gethsemane, when he sacrificed his human will to God: *Non sicut ego volo, sed sicut tu.*[112]

The whole of history is at the service of Christendom. Christendom must dominate the course of history by virtue of the natural and supernatural personality of Christians. Human freedom is a cosmic force that controls the universe's destiny and its return to God.

If Christians are lords of the earth, Christendom must also possess this lordship over what is created, which makes it able to sacrifice all that is earthly to God, in

then in the New Testament, appears in reference to the births of Isaac and Jesus.

[105] Jn 16:11.
[106] Gn 2:15.
[107] See Gn 18:32.
[108] Jon 3:1–10.
[109] Is 11:1–9. See also Is 2:2–5.
[110] Rom 11:25–26.
[111] Jn 10:16.
[112] Mt 26:39.

order to turn its civic life into a *sacrificium laudis*. This is the human weight of the cross. This Christian lordship makes the greater weight and the greater responsibility of the destinies of the world fall on Christendom. The Communion of Saints is a reality; it is the definitive crystallization of the community of all humankind.

Humanity is a family. Folk wisdom says that the upright pay for the sinners. And this, on top of being true, is just—in the first place, because only the upright have something to pay, and in the second place, because being able to take on the weight of the rest of the people is precisely one of the prerogatives of their virtue. Because they are upright, they are able to live this superior life that allows them to make amends and offer themselves in holocaust, to save not only themselves but also carry along many others. It is the privilege of the man who has reached fullness. And this is true both in a social and a personal sense.

Neither expiation nor vicarious satisfaction would make sense in an animal, for example, and a merely rational nature would not be able to accomplish them.[113] Only Christians are susceptible to this superior form of vitality. God loves a cheerful giver.[114] Christians who complain of their state and long for the fleshpots of Egypt[115] are transgressors. He who lives his dignity like a load, he who does not see greater honor in greater service, he who complains that evil is forbidden, has not yet transcended the animal dimension of his being, has not yet understood that there is more happiness in giving than in receiving[116] and that he must donate that which he has received freely.[117] And what does Man have that has not been given to him?[118] So, this is the destiny of Christendom. If Christians are the salt of the earth, Christendom must be the light of the world.[119] The kingdom of Christ is an eternal and universal kingdom, of truth and life, of sanctity and grace, of justice, love, and peace.

The Task of Christendom

The task of Christendom seems paradoxical: to embark on the structuring of a Christian culture in its broadest sense and immediately thereafter immolate it in order to attain a higher end; to use the earthly city like a scaffolding to scale the celestial city; to construct a human order and then burn it in holocaust for a divine order. Strictly speaking, the paradox is only apparent because these orders are not

---

[113] "It is not on human scale to carry the cross, to love the cross" (T. Kempis, *De Imitatione Christi* II.12.4).

[114] 2 Co 9:7.

[115] See Nb 11:5.

[116] Ac 20:35.

[117] Mt 10:8. See also Mt 25:18ff.

[118] 1 Co 4:7.

[119] Mt 5:13–14. See the Christian feeling of superiority that St. Augustine shows in spite of the persecutions that Jesus's followers will be subjected to: "Only those who lie on the ground can be trampled on; but those whose hearts are firmly in heaven do not lie on the ground, even if they have many bodily sufferings on earth" (*De sermone Domini in monte* I.6).

separated here on earth. Furthermore, only Christendom can build an earthly city that is solid and stable, reinforced as it is with the internal structure of everlasting life, as the celestial city is already here on earth, informing its external sheathing, with which, at each temporal moment—this is important—it forms an existential unity. This, then, is not about an insincere service to this world or about an earthly presence with ulterior motives. It is about the highest service rendered to this world so that it may also fulfill its mission; it is about the discovery of the innermost goal of *terrestriality* itself.

Upon *any* Christian culture—as there is no Christian culture par excellence— there weighs a twofold fate: one of truly being *culture*—that is to say, crystallized work, accumulated energy, stable order of earthly society—and another of being authentically *Christian*, that is, of leading Man toward his ultimate end—Christ— transcending itself so that Man may end up in his authentic fatherland. Here lies the self-immolation of Christian culture; it must help Man overcome this earth and become a medium to attain the other life.

But this does not mean that it would then be best to turn the earthly city into some sort of uncomfortable and provisional waiting room—in the first place because this would be to contravene the explicit commandments of God and the implicit ones of our own nature, which continues to be genuinely human, and in the second place because the other life is gained precisely by using and experiencing and delving into this one to the fullest. Whoever has will be given more.[120]

The entire world is the work of God, and this is why it is beautiful and it is pleasant to remain within it—and this is also why it can turn into a temptation; but Man has been destined for another, and better, mansion. We must not scorn this earth, but neither should we overvalue it. It is not the supreme value. This is the great temptation of Tabor Mount, which Christendom must continuously defeat: the apostles want to settle there, but Jesus tells them to rise.[121] We must make humanity walk and not let it build permanent homes on this earth.[122] And this is the cross. It is also significant that the topic of the glorious conversation Christ held with Moses and Elijah was about the coming crucifixion.

Christian culture must make humanity walk toward its transcendental goal. As long as it is walking there is no danger. Christendom reminds men that they are pilgrims. Christian culture is essentially on a pilgrimage. All paths lead to God, as long as they are that: paths, and not stagnant puddles or egocentric concerns moving in a ring. One thing is as good as another, as long as it allows us to go to God. This is the foundation of that "indifference," full of nobility and of love, of Christian asceticism that must prevail in Christendom. This is why everything is good for the upright[123] and why Christendom is optimistic.[124] All human values play a role; they are steps to

---

[120] Mt 13:12; 21:29.

[121] Lk 9:28ff.

[122] See Heb 13:14.

[123] See Is 3:10.

[124] See Rom 8:28.

rise up to God. But steps must be walked on, that is what they are there for; we must go up them, we must abandon them.... "You must let yourself be crucified together with the Crucified."[125]

The main idea behind Christendom lies in recognizing its relative nature. The world and all its constructions are relative, and therefore they only have a functional importance. At the same time, Christendom must possess enough humility to dedicate itself to the cultivation of these relative values. The world is to the Christian what his body is to his soul: not an enemy to defeat, but rather one "next step" to overcome, and ultimately they form a profound unity, since overcoming the body does not mean to abandon it, but to resurrect it.

Culture, then, will be a true liberation, a strengthening of human powers and not an oppression; it will help us overcome material or merely earthly preoccupations, and it will prevent us from becoming attached to this earth, thus leading us to the very doors of the supernatural. Technology will be at the service of Man; machines will substitute Man's mechanical and material tasks, not with a view to greater production, but rather so that he may dedicate himself to more spiritual tasks. The end and the meaning of culture is not to establish *comfort* on this earth, but rather to elevate Man—in a function that is parallel and analogical to that of grace, and in intimate collaboration with it—over his material needs and to improve his spiritual powers, urging and channelling the thirst for the Divine within him.

And this is what Christendom must be constantly reminding the sons of Adam, who quickly forget that they are only pilgrims on this earth. Despite the enormous tragedies through which the world has recently passed, humanity does not seem to have learned to look up yet or to understand that it is foolish—and impossible, in fact—to want to establish itself definitively on this planet. The reaction of the non-Christian masses after the Second World War has been to have the most fun possible in order to make up for the previous years of privations and calamities. And at times they have turned to dizziness in order to avoid the scandal and pain of the cross.

We have wanted to go beyond a conception of history as a mere heterogeneous description of wars and more wars. Nonetheless, a realistic vision of the facts must recognize the central role played by the struggles between men in the life of humanity. And sometimes we criticize God for allowing so much destruction and evil. Apart from the fact that wars are caused by *Man's* evilness, they possess an enormous cathartic function insofar as they make us experience the provisional nature of this life and of all earthly values. This consciousness has had an enormous influence in the latest European generation; in general, the possibility of being violently pulled out of the environment in which one peaceably lives, the personal experience of war, has been a constant historical factor. This is another way that the law of the cross can be experienced. The value of a man then concentrates in his substance, not in his actions, his external power, or his physical strength, but rather exclusively in his spirit, the only thing that can voluntarily and fruitfully accept the immolation of

---

[125] Pseudo-Macarius, *Homilies* XII.4 (PG 34.560).

Man and his resurrection to a new life, defeating all external, individual, and social catastrophes.

Today's Man has stopped believing in humanity, as well as in progress and even in culture, and he wants to take refuge in God; he has experienced the instability of everything human too intensely. But he still does not understand that because God has created all things from nothing, any being who wishes to return to Him must first turn himself into nothing, that is to say, immolate himself in a holocaust of adoration of the Divinity. Humanity has not yet understood the law of the cross. Deep down, it has experienced that all human values are relative and, therefore, are pushing toward a countervalue; it has personally experienced that strength leads to hardness, solitude to incomprehension and stubbornness, society to herd instinct, and so on; but it has not yet understood that the only possibility of integration on earth—and in heaven—resides in the power of the cross. Only a goodness that immolates itself is not shallow and cloying; only a power that knows how to offer itself up does not turn hard; only loneliness that is offered in holocaust to God is fruitful and comprehensive.

Christendom must awaken the hope of the true fatherland within men. This world is an advent. All of its values make sense as long as they do not break the essentially expectant nature of men on earth—a waiting that sometimes becomes a distressing preoccupation in face of the nebulous and the enigmatic because it is devoid of hope. The task of Christendom is to fill this constitutive wait of humanity's with hope. *Et nos similes hominibus expectantibus dominum suum quando revertatur a nuptiis.*[126]

This is the cross of Christendom. It must proclaim that Jesus Christ is King[127] and that without Him society makes no sense at all; but it will always also be true that "anyone who makes himself king is defying Caesar."[128] And this contradiction hurts and shatters, even though it also fortifies and strengthens. Blessed are those who are persecuted.[129] And persecution is inevitable.[130] Because before being King, Christ is Priest and Victim.

The cross is the only perennial value in the midst of the fluctuations of cultures and the different human points of view. With the criterion of the cross, Christendom must judge over all events and over the different civilizations. Only the cross provides enough distance and at the same time the right perspective to pass judgment on all of history: *Stat Crux dum volvitur orbis* (the cross stands as the world turns) as the silent Carthusian monks meditate in their cells.

In this way, Christendom fulfills humanity's sacrifice of praise to the Creator, and—in the descent—it is able to sublimate and drain human values to the fullest extent, and thus attain the greatest possible happiness on earth. But everything relies

---

[126] Lk 12:36.
[127] Jn 18:37.
[128] Jn 19:12.
[129] Mt 5:10.
[130] St. Paul, 2 Tim 3:12, explicitly affirms it.

on faith—and the best faith is a *ray of darkness*[131]—and Christendom must maintain this faith on its own against men who imagine themselves to be Gods and against many Christians who insist on being so before their time.

The cross is a reality that may not be of this world, but it is definitely in it, and Christendom must implant it in society. The entire paradox lies here: in the irruption of a new, unexpected, and inaccessible order. This world is strewn with transcendent values, and the cross is the first of these. Hence the complexity of human life.

That said, Christendom does no more than share a little of the Great cross of the church, guarded by Christ himself. Christendom is not possible without Christians. And "the world hated them, because they belong to the world."[132] This is why it cries out with humbleness but with a great strength: *Maran atha!*[133] *Veni, Domine Jesu!*[134] God and Lord, why have you forsaken me?[135] And this is the *Mystery of the cross.*[136] *Ecce enim, propter lignum venit gaudium in universo mundo!*[137]

"Yes, I will come soon!"[138]

---

[131] See St. John of the Cross, *The Dark Night* II.5, following the Areopagite; cf., for example, *Epistulae* I (PG 3.1065).

[132] Jn 17:14.

[133] 1 Co 16:22.

[134] "*Come*, O Lord Jesus!" (Rev 22:20), or, as a Copt papyrus from the fifth century says as a variant of the *Didache* X.6, having its full application in the liturgy: "The Lord *has* come. Amen."

[135] Mt 27:46.

[136] See already the cry of Is 63:19.

[137] "And lo!, because of the wood [of the cross], joy came to the whole world!" (Good Friday liturgy).

[138] Rev 22:20.

9

THE EUCHARIST AND THE
RESURRECTION OF THE FLESH[1]

ὁ τρώγων μου τὴν σάρκα καὶ πίνων μου τὸ αἷμα
ἔχει ζωὴν αἰώνιον, κἀγὼ ἀναστήσω αὐτὸν τῇ
ἐσχάτῃ ἡμέρᾳ

Jn 6:54

Introduction

In Christo nova creatura.

2 Co 5:17

The Christian Mystery is one: it is Christ, whose very *being* constitutes the revelation of the Trinitarian God[2] and of the ultimate meaning of created reality.[3] In Christ all of reality, created and uncreated, is recapitulated. He is the ultimate, absolute, ontic synthesis, for "in him all Fullness (πλήρωμα) dwells."[4] So, from the point of view of the man who is still on pilgrimage, from the perspective of the real history of creation, the Eucharist is the height of divine revelation, since it is Christ himself in his definitive state as the Head, yet here on this earth, influencing space and time in order to carry out his mission, which glorifies all of creation.

Nevertheless, in order to be able to glimpse the brilliance of the Christian Mystery itself, faith must inform our intellect.[5] And for this, we must overcome the merely rational categories of our thought.

A concrete example that simply illuminates the relationship between two Christian mysteries will offer us an outline of this Christocentric way of thinking toward which theologians of all times have always tended.

---

[1] Paper for the International Eucharistic Congress of Barcelona, May 1952.

[2] See Jn 14:9.

[3] Col 1:16–17.

[4] Col 1:19.

[5] "Si non credideritis, non intelligetis" [Without faith, you will not undertand], says Is 7:9, according to the version diffused and commented by Patristic and Scholastic thinkers (the *Vulgate* reads, "non permanebitis" [you will have no steadiness]).

157

The authentic theology of the Eucharist is not so much about explaining the enigma of Eucharistic presence and the manner of sacramental transformation—transubstantiation, and so on; rather it makes more of an effort to present the meaning of the Eucharistic mystery itself and its significance in our lives and in the totality of the cosmos. That is to say, instead of considering the Christian mysteries from a previous philosophical conception and trying to understand them from this, theology attempts to carry out the opposite process, namely, to reach an intelligible synthesis from the data that have been revealed to us.

In this sense, the last step in the theology of the Eucharist, in connection with and from the Trinitarian issue itself, lies in the mystery of our identification with Christ.[6] So, our own resurrection consists in this incorporation—"conglutination," as the first scholastic thinkers called it[7]—in the glorious Body of the total Christ. This is the fulfillment that we want briefly to elucidate.

Because of the brevity of the space available to us, we can only offer a schematic summary and use concise, dense, and "telegraphic" language.

The Eucharist in the Divine Economy of Salvation

Et verbum caro factum est.

Jn 1:14

The Word became flesh, and not only inside Mary, as it is still becoming flesh and living among us by virtue of the unique action of the Mother of God. This expression must be interpreted in its full theocentric meaning, and for this we must overcome the illusion of *ego-chronic* thinking. I am neither the measure of time nor its center (Elizabeth I of England does not belong to the *past* because she was before *me*, neither does Elizabeth II belong to the future because she will be crowned in a few months in my future). Furthermore, we must learn how to think about transcending time in order to be able to position ourselves in the divine perspective to which faith impels us.

From this point of view, then, it is not that there was God, on the one hand, and flesh, the entire creation, on the other—nothing exists outside God—and that *afterward* a uniting bond appeared between them: the Logos incarnated. Or, if you prefer, it is not that the Word became flesh, in the sense that the flesh received a visit from the Logos as if it were the first time, but rather that the flesh became the Word; that is, for the first time the flesh emerged as the flesh of the Son of God, in the absolute order as well as in the temporal one.[8] More precisely, "in the beginning

---

[6] See Jn 17:23.

[7] Wolphelm de Brauweiler, *Vita* (PL 154.414).

[8] "When we say that God became man, we do not mean a change occurring in God but only in human nature" (Thomas Aquinas, *Sum. theol.* III, q.16, a.6, ad 2).

was the Word,"[9] and this Word through whom all things came into being[10] "became flesh,"[11] became creation, and with this the flesh emerged, the universe was created.[12] Christ is the only begotten Son of the Father[13] and the Firstborn of all creation.[14] He is the beginning,[15] the real beginning of all creation and of time itself.[16]

For our temporal, human calculation, first there was creation, then incarnation, and finally the Eucharist. For God, immutable and eternal, for whom there is no variation or time, things do not happen like this; rather they *are* in their fullness, which will later be gradually conquered by hope, *in regno temporalitatis.*

In this temporal development of the kingdom of God on earth, the Eucharist is the beginning of the ἀνακεφαλαίωσις;[17] it is the *inchoatio status patriae totius mundi, peracta in capite, perficienda in membris* (beginning of the final state of the universe, already fulfilled in the Head [Christ], and to be fulfilled in the limbs). The Word, made flesh, has come to save all flesh.[18] The Eucharist is the anticipation of glory.[19] Because of the Eucharist we live the same Trinitarian life as God. Just as Christ lives for the Father, so whoever eats Him will live for Him, through Him.[20] Because of the Eucharist the realization of the new heaven and the new earth has already begun.[21] This is why this world is transition, it is Passover, and its food and viaticum is the Eucharist.

Christ Eucharist is the Head of his mystical Body, which gradually incorporates us into Him, in order to become the full sacrament of divinized Creation.[22] It is the sacrament of the church[23] and the sacrament of unity, and of men among themselves,[24] with Christ[25] and with God.[26] Therefore, within divine economy, the Eucharist is the specific form through which God works to realize and realizes the divinization of the universe.

---

[9] Jn 1:1.
[10] Jn 1:3.
[11] Jn 1:14.
[12] See Col 1:16.
[13] Jn 1:18.
[14] Col 1:15.
[15] Jn 8:25 (*Vulgate*).
[16] See Rev 21:6; Jn 8:58.
[17] See Ep 1:10.
[18] "Et videbit onmis caro salutare Dei nostri" [All flesh will see our God's salvation], (Is 40:5), according to the classical Latin version commented by tradition and introduced into the liturgy.
[19] See Jn 6:57–58.
[20] Jn 6:57.
[21] See Is 45:17; 66:22; 2 Pet 3:13; Rev 21:1.
[22] 1 Co 15:28.
[23] See Ep 1:22–23.
[24] 1 Co 10:17.
[25] Jn 6:57.
[26] Jn 6:58.

The Resurrection of the Flesh in the Divine Economy

Haec est autem voluntas eius, qui misit me, Patris: ut omne, quod dedit mihi, non perdam ex eo, sed resuscitem illud in novissimo die.

Jn 6:39

Christ has come to earth to fulfill his Father's will.[27] And this will to save all men,[28] including the wicked,[29] consists precisely in raising us to the new life.[30] The Resurrection of the Flesh, this mystery[31] which St. Paul describes to us in the individual[32] and in the cosmic[33] orders, represents the final and, consequently, the definitive stage of creation. It manifests the definitive structure that the creature will possess when there is no longer any time,[34] upon reaching the fullness of Christ himself[35] and the restoration—ἀποκατάστασις—of all things.[36] It entails the gathering of the fragments of the being,[37] scattered in creation, which were not yet connected to the Spirit.[38] The resurrection of a spiritual body[39] makes us overcome the flesh[40] and truly be ourselves at the same time; that is to say, incarnated spirits, irreducibly human beings. From the dogma of the resurrection we can develop an integral anthropology that takes into account not only the existential end of the human being but also his basic ontic unity, characteristic of a being who is his spirit.

This is the ultimate and profound reason as to why we will be raised in our own body[41] and "eiusdem carnis quam nunc gesto" (with the same flesh I now have)[42]—as my being is inseparable from my true body,[43] in the same way that my body is not such if it is not united to my soul, forming a unit. The immortality that Christian consciousness, and even an existentially human consciousness, faces is not the indestructibility of a quintessential principle of our being—the soul—but rather the perpetuity of our complete I, of our true being with our authentic body. Death

---

[27] Jn 6:38. See also Jn 4:34; 5:30; Mt 6:10; 26:42; Lk 22:42; Heb 10:9; etc.

[28] See Ez 18:23, 32; 33:11; 2 Pet 3:9.

[29] See Mt 18:14, etc.

[30] See Jn 6:39.

[31] 1 Co 15:51.

[32] See 2 Co 4:9ff.

[33] See Rom 8:19ff.

[34] Rev 10:6.

[35] Ep 4:13.

[36] Ac 3:21.

[37] See Jn 6:21.

[38] 2 Co 5:5.

[39] 1 Co 15:44.

[40] Rom 8:9.

[41] See *Symbol. Athanas., Denz.*, 40 and also *Denz.*, 207, 287, 499, 464, etc.

[42] Leo IX, *Symbol fidei, Denz.*, 347. See also *Denz.*, 427.

[43] Thomas Aquinas, *C. Gentes* II.81.

violates us, it appears as a punishment,[44] as an anguish,[45] as the wage paid for sin,[46] and as Man's last enemy.[47] "And you will die in your sin."[48] Death is death because of sin, and resurrection is resurrection to life.[49]

Man's real body, his definitive body, is the resurrected, incorruptible, glorious, powerful, and spiritual body.[50] It is not a ghost, as a "ghost has no flesh and bones,"[51] but a real body that forms an essential, integral, and inseparable part of the type of corporal spirits, or spiritual bodies, that human beings are.

The resurrection that has been promised to us is not that of our body, but that of our *being*; it is the elevation of our complete being to the order of the Divinity itself. Resurrection is not an accidental addition to the glory or reprobation of the soul; rather it is the real and necessary destiny of our supernaturalized being.[52]

Even so, all these affirmations are connected to a series of theses about the problems surrounding the notion of separated souls, the essence of material beings and time, and the resurrection of the dead in the perspective of God, for whom time does not exist—which we cannot expand on here. Perhaps current theological investigation has not yet clarified enough the grounds for an adequate elucidation of this last dogma of Christian life.[53]

The Eucharist and Resurrection

Qui manducat hunc panem vivet in aeternum.

Jn 6:58

If all of the Christian mysteries have a profound connection, in this case the link has a peculiar nuance, insofar as the Eucharist produces and effectively realizes the resurrection of the flesh. This is why the Eucharist, according to Scholastic terminology, is necessary in order to save oneself, that is, in order to resurrect to divine

---

[44] Gn 3:3.

[45] See Mk 14:34.

[46] Rom 6:23. See also 5:12.

[47] 1 Co 15:28.

[48] Jn 8:21.

[49] See Jn 5:29.

[50] See 1 Co 15:42–44.

[51] Lk 24:39.

[52] See St. Thomas's unequivocal affirmation: "I reply by saying that the necessity of resurrection lies in the possibility for man to achieve the ultimate end for which he was made, and this cannot take place either during his life on earth or in the life of the separated soul [from the body, after death]. . . . Otherwise, man would have been created in vain, if he could not achieve the end for which he was made." *Sum. theol.* Suppl., q.79, a.2.

[53] See, for example, R. Guardini, *Die letzten Dinge* (Würzburg: Werkbund, 1940), and M. Schmaus, *Von den letzten Dingen* (Regensburg-Münster, 1948).

life, not only with the need of precepts but also of means:[54] "Nisi manducaveritis carnem Filii hominis, et biberitis eius sanguinem, non habebitis vitam in vobis."[55] It does not necessarily mean the sacramental communion—this was Fr. Antonio Rosmini's mistake[56]—but this does not prevent the Eucharist from being, anyway, what achieves the resurrection of each and every one of the beings that are to be resurrected.

The testimonies from the Holy Scriptures are obvious. There is no need to provide detailed exegesis in order to see that after the multiplication of the bread and the fish, Jesus's entire Eucharistic sermon expresses the following main idea: "I will give you bread which is life, which will keep you from death and will raise you on the last day of your life."[57] Furthermore, Jesus explicitly states that the Eucharist *produces* immortality, that it causes eternal life. The words of the Lord are peremptory. The ancient Jews ate the manna and they died. On the other hand, whoever eats the bread of life will not die, rather they will live eternally. This bread is his flesh, which He will give for the life of the world.[58]

The transformation begins right here on earth, where Christians have been raised with Christ.[59] And this catharsis of our being through the Eucharist apparently constitutes the ultimate motive in Paul's explanation of illness and sin in Christians.[60]

It is also needless to recall that the Eucharist is the sacrament by virtue of which we become children of God: "But to those who did accept him—ἔλαβον—he gave power to become children of God."[61] This reception fully takes place when we answer to his "take—λάβετε—and eat, this is my body."[62] In order to fulfill our incorporation in Him, Jesus remained in the Eucharist.

Patristic beliefs also follow this train of thought.[63] The Eucharist is the "drug of Resurrection"—φάρμακον ἀθανασίας, literally: drug of immortality[64]—as "it is not possible for our body to become immortal except by entering into participation with incorruptibility by means of communion with that which is immortal."[65] In fact,

---

[54] See, for example, R. Garrigou-LaGrange, *De Eucharistia* (Turin: Marietti, 1946), 27ff.

[55] Jn 6:54.

[56] See *Denz.*, 1922.

[57] See Jn 6:26–59.

[58] Jn 6:48–52.

[59] See Col 3:1.

[60] See 1 Co 11:30.

[61] Jn 1:12.

[62] Mt 26:26.

[63] See, for example, Irenaeus, *Adv. Haer.* IV.18.5 and similarly V.2.2, 3.

[64] Ignatius Antioch, *Epist. ad Eph.* 20.2.

[65] Gregory of Nyssa, *Oratio catechetica* 37; the entire text refers to the Eucharist. This same thought is expressed with even greater metaphysical power, if that is possible, by St. Cyril of Alexandria, *In Iohan.* 10.2: "What is corruptible by its nature cannot be enlivened except by bodily uniting itself to the body of Him who is Life by His nature, that is, the Only Begotten [Son of God]."

"Through this body I am no longer earth, or ash, nor am I captive any longer, but rather I am free; thanks to Him, I wait for the heavens and the goods I will receive there: immortal life, the same condition as the angels, the reunion with Christ."[66]

"Those who have not received faith in Christ, those who have not participated in Christ, will not live again on the day of the resurrection."[67] "Fiant (fideles) Corpus Christi, si volunt vivere de Spiritu Christi. De Spiritu Christi non vivit nisi Corpus Christi" (Let the faithful become the Body of Christ, if they wish to live by the Spirit of Christ. In fact, only the Body of Christ lives by the Spirit of Christ), says St. Augustine[68] in his habitual lapidary tone. The Scholastic tradition of the Early and Late Middle Ages developed this thought marvelously.[69] And this is the same thing that the Council of Trent[70] says, echoing the words of St. Thomas, later incorporated into the Liturgy.[71]

This thesis does not contradict, rather it complements and specifies, the famous statement that the resurrection of Christ is the last, efficient, and exemplary cause of our own.[72] It is obvious that if Christ had not resurrected, not only would our faith be inane,[73] but our own resurrection would also be impossible, as it is none other than a configuration of our body according to his.[74] He is the "primitiae dormientum"[75] and "primogenitus mortuorum."[76] But this risen Christ is the one who has given himself to us in the Eucharist in order to carry out his own resurrection in us.[77] "Christ ascended with his perfect body, and left us the sacrament of his Body."[78]

The Eucharist, as true sacrament, is "signum efficax," and consequently it not only symbolizes our union with Christ, but it also produces it. And this union with Jesus is what resurrects us to the new life. "This is the hour when the dead hear the voice of the Son of God and those who hear it shall live."[79]

---

[66] John Chrysostom, *Homilies on First Corinthians* 24.4.

[67] Cyril of Alexandria, *Commentary on John* VI.52. The entire context indicates that it is about our participation in Christ through the Eucharist.

[68] *Tractates on the Gospel of John* 26.13.

[69] See two documented works written at the same time (1939 and 1940), without any reciprocal influence: F. Holböck, *Der eucharistische und der mystische Leib Christi* (Rome, 1941), and H. de Lubac, *Corpus Mysticum* (Paris: Aubier, 1944), which exempt us from producing further testimonies.

[70] "He wanted this to be the pledge of our future glory and perpetual happiness." Sess. XIII, ch. 2, *Denz.*, 875.

[71] ". . . et futurae gloriae nobis pignus datur." *Ex Officio Smi. Sti.*

[72] See Thomas Aquinas, *Sum. theol.* III, q.56, a.1 and 2; and Suppl., q.76, a.1.

[73] 1 Co 15:14, 17.

[74] Ph 3:21.

[75] 1 Co 15:20.

[76] Rev 1:5.

[77] Jn 5:22.

[78] Gerardus de Cambrai (PL, 142.1280), quoted by H. de Lubac, *Corpus Mysticum,* 89.

[79] Jn 5:25.

The Eucharist, according to a long Patristic[80] and Scholastic[81] tradition, is the continuation of the mystery of the incarnation in space and time. Moreover, it is not only a continuation, but a manifestation of the mystery of the resurrection in the same spatiotemporal categories of our human history. He has promised not to leave us orphans,[82] and he has kept his promise. He has left us his Spirit[83] and his Body.[84]

Similarly, this confirms the traditional idea that we are made members of the Body of Christ through baptism. The Eucharist is the culmination of the baptism, and in it, the Eucharist is received *in voto*, since in a certain way the baptism is a spiritual reception of the Eucharist.[85] This is the only way we can explain the traditional doctrine of both sacraments. Christian thought does not let itself be imprisoned in the narrow net of a merely logical dialectic.

The Eucharistic vision of the resurrection would then present the following outline. "God has predestined us to conform to the image of his Son."[86] But this image is the one that Christ himself gradually configures within us, for which he demands that we die to ourselves,[87] that we hate our own soul,[88] that the man of old disappears so that the new one may rise.[89] Our old man has died and has been crucified, and with him "the body of sin"[90] has been destroyed in order to "put on a new self which will progress toward true knowledge the more it is renewed in the image of its Creator."[91]

And this is what the resurrection consists in. We have risen with Christ.[92] When He appears, our lives will also appear with Him in glory.[93]

Well, this process begins already on earth. Our entire Christian life is nothing more than this constant mortification,[94] so that by dying every day,[95] when our last day comes,[96] He may resurrect us to his own Life.[97]

---

[80] See M. J. Scheeben, *Gesammelte Schriften*, Vol. 2, *Die Mysterien des Christentums* (Freiburg im Breisgau: Herder, 1941).

[81] See Holböck, *Der eucharistische*, 210.

[82] Jn 14:18.

[83] Jn 14:16–17.

[84] Jn 6:27; Mt 26:26.

[85] See M. de la Taille, *Mysterium fidei* (Paris: Beauchesne, 1921), 557ff.; E. Springer, "Über das in der Taufe eingeschlossene Votum der Eucharistie," *Theologisch-praktische Quartalschrift* 74 (1921): 525–40.

[86] Rom 8:29.

[87] Jn 12:24.

[88] Jn 12:25.

[89] Ep 4:22–24.

[90] "τὸ σῶμα τηζ ἀμαρτίαζ." Rom 6:6.

[91] Col 3:10.

[92] Col 3:1; Ep 2:6.

[93] Col 3:4.

[94] See Col 3:5.

[95] 1 Co 15:31.

[96] Jn 6:39.

[97] Jn 6:58.

This is why we have a spiritual body that progressively develops on this earth and that is the one that will resurrect and gradually replace the earthly and animal body.[98] "The first man"—notice that St. Paul does not say "the first body," as we are an individual unity—"being made of earth, is earthly by nature; the second man is from heaven. The earthly man is the pattern for the earthly people, the heavenly man for heavenly ones. And as we have borne—ἐφορέσαμεν—the likeness of the earthly man, so we shall bear—φορέσωμεν—the likeness of the heavenly one."[99] We must not forget that we are already now walking "in novitate vitae,"[100] and that we serve him "in novitate spiritus,"[101] since Christ is already living within us,[102] after we have been buried with Him through baptism.[103] "Flesh and blood cannot inherit the kingdom of God; what is perishable cannot inherit what is imperishable."[104]

This gradual transformation of our being is carried out by the Eucharist. Through the *Body* of Christ[105] we have become dead to the old Law and so we participate in him who, after having risen from the dead, makes us resurrect, too, so as to yield fruits to God. *Through* the Eucharist and *in* it is our incorporation into Christ fulfilled. *Through* the Eucharist, insofar as Christ is the one who has remained on earth—sacrifice and Sacrament—and who carries out our gradual divinization by becoming *one* with us.[106] *In* the Eucharist, insofar as our personal progress in perfection is not detached from the Body of Christ, but rather it consists precisely in the fact that we increasingly incorporate ourselves into this Body.[107]

This incorporation, that is to say, this coming to form part of the Body of Christ itself, is precisely to acquire immortality gradually and to impregnate our body with His own Spirit. Or, in other words, the progressive spiritualization of the body means the conquest of our unity or, more simply, of our being.[108] We do not desire to change or to cease to be what we are, but rather to be this in the most effective and real way.[109] Resurrection is nothing less than the complete expansion of our being; certainly not of our nature, but of our real existence.

The Eucharist is not only the efficient cause of the resurrection, but it also provides us a model of "risen life" full of great lessons for our Christian existence; but now is not the time to deal with this.

---

[98] 1 Co 15:46.

[99] 1 Co 15:47–49.

[100] Rom 6:4.

[101] Rom 7:6.

[102] Gal 2:20.

[103] Rom 6:4.

[104] 1 Co 15:50.

[105] Rom 7:4.

[106] See Jn 15:4ff.

[107] Let us note the change of direction in humanist piety: the Eucharist, nourishment *for me*. This is true, but the Christocentric direction is no less true, but rather more central: I go to Him and I incorporate myself into Him.

[108] 2 Co 4:16.

[109] 2 Co 5:4.

After the outline we have sketched, the consequences for a conscious Eucharistic life are within our reach. Communion is the collaboration of Christ and Man for the glorification, the resurrection, of the latter. Communion is the communal task between Jesus and Man for the construction of the true and complete Body of Christ. This is how the Eucharist appears as a real necessity of means.[110]

But there is more. The Eucharist, as pledge and prelude of the resurrection of the flesh, reveals to us the hidden sacral nature of the entire world, which has been called, through Man, to join God. Through Communion, Man not only fulfills his incorporation into Christ, but he also collaborates ontically toward the resurrection of the world.

God does not leave his works imperfect. He has not left creation unfinished, nor has he abandoned it to question its own structures indefinitely. Rather He has called all of it to Himself so that one day the entire universe may penetrate *with* Christ *in* God.[111]

The main factor of this task, while we are still forced to work in the time[112] between the two comings of the *Pantokratôr*, is Jesus Eucharist, whose ultimate mission is the establishment of cosmic and divine peace, of achieving one sole flock,[113] so that, when all things are subject to the Son, God may, in the end, be all in all.[114]

---

[110] "In the Body of the Church, the Eucharist has the same place as the heart in man's body," says a beautiful medieval text. Petrus Cellensis (PL 202.1136), quoted by Holböck, *Der eucharistische*, 212.

[111] See Col 3:3.

[112] Jn 5:17.

[113] Jn 10:16.

[114] 1 Co 15:28.

10

THE MASS AS *CONSECRATIO TEMPORIS*

Tempiternity[1]

The Mass and Time

According to Catholic doctrine, the temporal multiplication of the sacrifice of Christ in the Mass does not pluralize it. Time appears as an accident that does not diminish the substance or the identity of Christ's salvific act. On the other hand, we cannot reduce the temporal multiplication of the sacrifice, in the Mass, to a simple commemoration that is external and foreign to Christ's sacrifice either.[2] *Today's* Mass is not *another* sacrifice, but neither is it a simple repetition that does not add anything, or a mere commemoration without any objective and real value.[3] The Mass's *today* does not multiply the sacrifice, rather it is during that *nunc*[4] that the sacrifice is fulfilled, that it represents itself and it emerges in the present, thus becoming powerful and efficient in a very special way within the current temporal coordinates. The Mass is the sacrifice of the Savior in the *nunc* in which the sacrifice-sacrament is fulfilled. Here, as in the rest of theology's and metaphysics' ultimate problems, identity and diversity are two conjugated categories, different but inseparable.[5]

From this point of view, the problem of time appears as a fundamental theological issue, as every ultimate problem does.[6] The object of this paper is one aspect of this question.

---

[1] Original text: *La Misa como "consecratio temporis." La tempiternidad*, in *Sanctum Sacrificium* (Zaragoza, 1961), 75–93. Translated from Spanish by Carla Ros.

[2] See *Denz-Schön*, 950.

[3] See J. A. Jungmann, *Der Gottesdienst der Kirche* (Innsbruck: Tyrolia, 1955), 152.

[4] "Now."

[5] Let us recall the fundamental Trinitarian, Christological, and metaphysical problems. *Coincidentia oppositorum* also belongs here. See within Hinduism, the issue of *Īśvara*, who "is not limited by time" (*Yoga-sūtra* I.26), equal to and different from Brahman. See my article, "Der Īśvara des Vedānta und der Christus der Trinität: ein philosophisches Problem," in *Antaios* 2, no. 5 (1961): 446–55.

[6] The bibliography about time that we would like to recommend would be endless. The following references should suffice (as well as those indicated in other footnotes): G. Quispel, "Zeit und Geschichte im antiken Christentum," in *Eranos Jahrbuch* 20 (1951); C. H. Ratschow, "Anmerkungen zur theologischen Auffassung des Zeitproblems," in *Zeitschrift*

This is not the time to take part in the already multisecular discussion, which is now almost exacerbated, on the relationship between the Mass and the sacrifice of the cross.[7] We will, however, allow ourselves one simple observation: we believe that a considerable part of the current controversy would collapse if, instead of wanting to harmonize theological data with a determined concept (Newtonian, secularized, "modern," perhaps Aristotelian,[8] etc.) of time, we turned once again to its genuine religious sense, which history shows us and theology proves to us.[9] But the purpose of this paper is more modest. It consists in clarifying the meaning of that *hodie*[10] of the Mass, to some extent.

---

für Theologie und Kirche 51 (1954): 360–87; O. Cullmann, *Christus und die Zeit* (Zollikon: Evangeliscer, 1946); P. Mus, "La notion de temps réversible dans la mythologie bouddhique," in *Annuaire de l'École Pratique des Hautes Études* (Paris, 1938–39), 5–38; H. Conrad-Martius, *Die Zeit* (Munich: Kösel, 1954); O. Clement, *Transfigurer le temps* (Neuchâtel: Delachaux & Niestlé, 1959); G. Dumézil, "Temps et mythes," in *Recherches philosophiques* 5 (1935–36): 235–51; R. O. Johann, "Charity and Time," in *Cross Currents* 9, no. 2 (1959): 140–49; H. I. Marrou, *L'ambivalence du temps de l'histoire chez saint Augustin* (Montreal: Institut d'Études Médiévales, 1950).

    [7] See, as an example, the summaries offered by Ch. Journet, *La Messe* (Bruges: Desclée de Brouwer, 1957); A. Piolanti, *Il mistero eucaristico* (Florence: Libera Editrice Fiorentina, 1955). See the already classic works by O. Casel, *Das christliche Kultmysterium* (Regensburg: Pustet, 1932); *Mysterium des Kommenden* (Paderborn: Bonifacius, 1952); as well as G. Söhngen, *Der Wesensaufbau des Mysteriums* (Bonn: Hanstein, 1938); B. Neunheuser, "Mysteriengegenwart," in *Archiv für Liturgiewissenschaft* 3 (1953): 104–22; J. Betz, *Die Eucharistie in der Zeit der griechischen Väter*, vol. I/1 (Feiburg im Breisgau: Herder, 1955); E. Mersch, *La Théologie du Corps Mystique*, 2 vol. (Paris: Desclée de Brouwer, 1949); P. Poschmann, "Das sakramentale Opfer," *Catholica* 11, no. 1 (1956): 36–50; K. Rahner, "Die vielen Messen und das eine Opfer," *Zeitschrift für katholische Theologie* 71 (1949): 257–317; J. Auer, "Das eucharistische Opfer," *Münchener Theologische Zeitschrift* 11, no. 2 (1960): 97–105.

    [8] See, e.g., J. Dubois, "Trois interprétations classiques de la définition aristotélicienne du temps," *Revue thomiste* 61, no. 3 (1961): 399–429; R. Labrie, "Note sur la définition aristo-télicienne du temps," *Laval Théologique et philosophique* 1 (1954). The controversy between C. De Konick and M. L. Guerard des Lauriers, "Nature de l'instant," in *Revue thomiste* 61, no. 1 (1961): 80–87, is also very instructive.

    [9] See M. Eliade, "Le temps et l'éternité dans la pensée indienne," *Eranos Jahrbuch* 20 (1951); G. van der Leeuw, *Urzeit und Endzeit, Eranos Jahrbuch* 17 (1949); A. K. Cooma-raswamy, *Time and Eternity* (Ascona: Artibus Asiae, 1947); W. T. Stace, *Time and Eternity* (Princeton, NJ: Princeton University Press, 1952); L. Lavelle, *Du temps et de l'éternité* (Paris: Aubier, 1945); F. Beemelmans, *Zeit und Ewigkeit nach Thomas von Aquino* (Münster: Aschen-dorff, 1915); J. Guitton, *Les temps et l'éternité chez Plotin et Saint Augustin* (Paris: Boivin, 1933); F. H. Brabant, *Time and Eternity in Christian Thought* (London: Longmans, 1937) ; L. Boros, "Les catégories et la temporalité chez Saint Augustin," *Archives de Philosophie* 21 (1958): 323–85.

    [10] Today.

Tempiternity

Past, Present, and Future

It is not necessary to recall that *quoties huius hostiae commemoratio celebratur, opus nostrae redemptionis exercetur,*[11] nor that the Mass, as sacrifice and sacrament, fulfills the task of uniting the past with the future and of being the ontological temporal bridge between the first and the second coming of the Lord.[12] Christ came in the final days,[13] and His action is fulfilled when the completion of time has come.[14] He is the end of time and its completion.[15] Nor do we need to insist in that our incorporation in Christ and the redeeming function of the Lord throughout time and space is realized in the Mass and by the Mass.[16]

We would like to underscore all these theses under the general perspective of the *consecratio mundi* (consecration of the world) in its most concrete aspect of transformation of the temporal structure of the cosmos, that is, as *consecratio temporis* (consecration of time). In other words, the journey from this temporal world to the new earth and the new heaven happens through Christ's action in time, which is progressively fulfilled by means of the Mass; better yet, the Mass is nothing but this efficient sacrifice and this active presence of Christ throughout time.[17]

The Mass extends its effectiveness, throughout time, to the present, past, and future things (*praeteritis, praesentibus, et futuris*), but its action is not limited to terrestrial time; its effects extend up to the kingdom of the dead and those who rest in Christ (*in Christo quiescentibus*). Thus, the time of the Mass is neither simply cosmological time nor is it merely historical time. Its temporal reality extends even further beyond.

All of this should be understood very seriously and literally. Today's liturgical renovation would be useless and we would not do justice to the luminous encyclical of Pius XII on this issue[18] if we believed that by overcoming the ceremonial and aestheticyzing concept of liturgy we are through with all of it. The current thesis

---

[11] "Each time we celebrate the memory of this sacrifice, the work of our redemption is carried out," from the Catholic liturgy of the Ninth Sunday after Pentecost. [Editorial note: Such quotations, throughout the essay, will obviously refer to the liturgical texts before the reformation of Vatican Council II.]

[12] See places and authorities in M. Schmaus, *Der Kult als Erfüllung echten Menschentums,* in the collective work *Der Kult und der heutige Mensch* (Munich: M. Hueber, 1961), IV.2.§ 233.

[13] See Heb 1:2; Mk 1:15; Lk 4:21; etc.

[14] See Gal 4:4.

[15] See Schmaus, *Der Kult,* § 293.

[16] See, besides the aforementioned works, L. Bouyer, *Life and Liturgy* (London: Sheed & Ward, 1956); *Le Mystère Pascal* (Paris: Cerf, 1950); and C. Vagaggini, *Il senso teologico della liturgia* (Rome: Paoline, 1957).

[17] See Schmaus, *Der Kult,* § 338ff.

[18] *Mediator Dei* (November 20, 1947).

within theology that the Church's raison d'être lies in liturgy keeps all of its validity. Of course this cult is not mere ritual but rather the human being's collaboration with the (unique, though triple *quoad nos*[19]) *opus divinum* of the creation, redemption, and glorification of the cosmos.

The royal priesthood[20] of all those who participate of the single priesthood of Christ by virtue of their ontological initiation to the sacramental order by means of the baptism—which entitles us to actively participate in the cult that the Mediator between Creation and the Father offers to God—is in a direct relationship with the order of problems that provide the framework for this study, even if we must now limit ourselves to the description of the concept of *tempiternity*.

Per Omnia Saecula Saeculorum

The most fundamental difference among all possible and imaginable differences is the one between God and the creatures.[21] One of the ways of expressing this difference is by referring to divine *eternity*[22] and the *temporicity* of the creature. This *temporicity* can, in turn, be divided according to the beings' modes of existence—the modes of existence that depend on the nature of those beings themselves.[23] According to the class of beings we consider, we will have a specific mode of existing and persisting in existence.[24] Temporicity could, thus, be divided into *eviternity*,[25] *temporality*, and (physical) *time*, whether we consider the duration in existence of angels, human beings, or the physical beings of our universe. (It is obvious that we could distinguish yet another temporicity proper to animals, though for reasons of simplification we will presently do without this.)

What we are concerned about is another dimension of the problem, which has been somewhat forgotten due to the predominantly humanistic and "philosophical" point of view from which human time has been studied. The nature of human temporality, in fact—its relationship to historicity, its peculiar way of storing the past and tending toward the future, and so forth—has been widely studied in our day. And yet, at least for the believer, it is still true that, even though temporality as

---

[19]   From our viewpoint, in a human perspective.

[20]   1 Pet 2:9.

[21]   See *Denz.*, 432.

[22]   *Aeternitas non est aliud quam ipse Deus* [Eternity is nothing else than God himself] (Thomas Aquinas, *Sum. theol.* I, q.10, a.2, ad 3).

[23]   See my *Ontonomōa de la Ciencia* (Madrid: Gredos, 1961).

[24]   See other Thomist texts in *Sum. theol.* I, q.10, a.1–6.

[25]   We provide a lesser-known description of eviternity by St. Thomas, so that its distinction from tempiternity may become more obvious: "*Aevum* properly indicates something *ancient*, which did not start existing recently; something *unchangeable*, as it does not measure motion but the unchangeable being [i.e., the angel]; something being measured *all by all*, that makes it different from time—in fact, the whole of time does not measure all according to all, but it measures the different parts of motion according to its own different parts" (in *Dionysii De divinis nominibus*, lect. 3).

the specific form of human duration ends here on this earth, human beings persist beyond this temporality and continue to exist even when there is no more time.[26] This is where the concept of tempiternity and the reality to which it refers are inserted.

What Christian terminology calls everlasting life—that is, the existence of the created being beyond death and, specifically, its union with God in heaven—cannot simply be called eternity nor eternal existence without falling into an indiscriminate identification with God—since eternity is a divine attribute and, as such, incommunicable.[27] Only God is eternal.[28] At most, Man would possess an "immortal time," says one of the apocryphal books.[29]

In order to describe tempiternity by way of approximation, we will first attempt to delimit it from beneath by comparing it to the concept of temporality, and then from above by distinguishing it from eternity itself.[30]

a. Temporality essentially entails present, past, and future, while tempiternity would rather represent—in an initial approach—the crystallization of the last moment of the temporal future, with all the richness of previous times but without further temporal cracks or distensions. The former presupposes change and transit from potency to act; the latter excludes all change and any active potentiality, that is to say, any potentiality that is not already actualized in act. It does not exclude a particular growth and a sui generis development, not meant as an acquisition of something that it did not have "before" or of a dormant potentiality, but as an unprecedented outburst and as an elimination of any repetition. This is due to the fact that being, in its fullness, is not a kind of static block, but rather life and novelty, without this entailing that we can speak of renovation or of change, as we would lack any terms of reference, both temporal and ontological. Tempiternity is as little mutable as it is immutable; it is beyond these categories.[31]

---

[26] See Rev 10:6.

[27] "This is why eternity is something sublime, it is the same thing as God, according to our reasoning mind" (Plotinus, *Enneads* II.7.5).

[28] Boethius's formula: "The flowing instant makes time, the still instant makes eternity" (*De Consolatione Philosophiae* V.6), which has had such fortune, along with his famous definition of eternity ("the all-simultaneous and perfect possession of unending life"), must be carefully understood and properly interpreted. See St. Maxim the Confessor, according to whom the "aeon (*aiôn*) is *immobile* time, while time is the aeon measured by movement" (*Ambiguorum Liber* [PG 91.1164]).

[29] 4 Ez 7:49.

[30] In the suggestive parlance of Meister Eckhart: "If I take a bit of Time, it will not belong to today nor to yesterday. But if I take the Now, it includes all time in itself. The Now in which God created the world—this very Now is as near as yesterday" (*Sermon* 10 in J. Quint (ed.), *Deutsche Predigten und Traktate* (Munich: Hanser, 1955), 195).

[31] Immutability must be understood in an exclusively negative sense as lack of movement—and this is how the Scholastics applied it to God—but it would be a mistake to understand it positively and then give ontological priority to the static over the dynamic. See my *Ontonomōa de la Ciencia*.

Temporality is the form of existence of a being that is in the making; tempiternity is that of a being that is already made. Tempiternity is the temporicity of a being that has already "be-come"; that *is* in its fullest sense; that has filled—to put it one way—all of the (potential) gaps of its being and has fulfilled all of the wishes (hopes) of its own becoming. Its being is total, ful-filled, ab-solute, it has reached its completion, Being, and its being is God.[32]

b. However, tempiternity is different from divine eternity. Tempiternal existence is a deified existence that has be-*come* God. God, on the other hand, has not *be*-come God. Eternity *has not had* a past, as tempiternity has. It is not the form of existence of a being who has be-come; rather it is the fullness of Being that neither has a past nor can have had one. God does not become. That which becomes is the creature, even if—as there is no other end to a real becoming—it becomes God (by virtue of the divine fecundity that allows such a union with God and full divine participation, without His absolute sovereignty decreasing because of this). It is commonly held that human beings, having had a *principium* (a principle as well as a beginning), have no end, while God has neither beginning nor end.[33]

The tempiternal being is a deified being; it is God, but God through participation, through grace, if you will; its being has become a theandric being equal to God, infinitely identical to God, but infinitely different as well (analogously as to how divine Persons are infinitely equal being infinitely different). Only within the Trinitarian and Christological Mystery can the peculiarity—and dignity—of tempiternal existence be glimpsed. Only the incorporation in Christ and our identification with Him, at once God and Man, is the key to tempiternity.[34]

The tempiternal being is not potential, though he has been. This "has been," however, does not mean a mere gravitation of the past in the present, as is the case with temporality: in the first place, because there is no longer a present as a point of intersection between a past and a future; and in the second place, because the surfacing of the past in the present (of the "been" in the "is") is not a simple presence as one more element to build the temporal being, but rather, it has been assimilated in such a way that it has lost all its individuality and temporality in order to form a single being without multiplicity of parts. The temporal being "has been," while in tempiternity there is no "having been," there is just "being." Divinization is not a varnish that superficially covers our contingency, in the same way that justification is not a mere juridical fiction, but a real transformation. The difference with

---

[32] The following Thomist expressions are well-known: *In Deo non potest esse aliquid quod non sit Deus* [In God there can be nothing that is not God], *De potentia* q.2, a.4, ad 7; *Et sic creatura in Deo est ipsa essentia divina* [Therefore creatures, insofar as they are in God, are the same as His essence], *De potentia* q.3, a.16, ad 24; *Quidquid est in Deo, Deus est* [Anything being in God is God], *De potentia* q.9, a.9, ad 6. See Augustine, *De Trinitate* V.2.

[33] See Thomas Aquinas, *Sum. theol.* I, q.10, a.5.

[34] See the clear parallelism that Christ establishes between our identity and Him, and between His identity and the Father's: Jn 6:57–58; 17:21–23, etc. See the complete Trinitarian reference in Jn 17:26.

God remains, nonetheless, equally complete. Although the creature, the "work" of Christ,[35] becomes God, *before* it *was not*; while for God the "before" and the "was" make absolutely no sense.

An observer blind to the difference between eternity and tempiternity would necessarily be a monist.[36] Hence the importance of the reality expressed by this concept. On the other hand, wanting to lower the category of being-deified, fearing—so to speak—our own identification with God, can cause an unsustainable dualism that ultimately results in atheism or in a materialist monism. The scar of tempiternity, the aftermath of *not* having been (because of coming from nothing) and of *having been* (because of coming from time) constitutes the most outstanding characteristic of our creaturability, phenomenologically speaking.[37]

After having delimited tempiternity from both extremes, let us proceed to describe it very briefly in itself.

Philosophy as *opus rationis* cannot help but to examine things *from beneath*, that is to say, from this earth, with the light from our cognitive faculties, in themselves wandering and provisional.[38] Theology as *intellectus fidei* allows us to glimpse things *from above*, that is to say, not from the platform of what things *are* now, but as functions of what they *will be* in their fullness.[39]

The problem of time provides us with an instructive example of all this issue.

Temporality, that is, human time on earth, appears to us as the tri-tension of human existence throughout what we call the time line; that is, the tri-tension of our ek-sistence is extended throughout the past, present, and future.[40] We are not yet "all of a piece," as it were; we have not reached that unity of life to which Man constitutively aspires. The temporal being, strictly speaking, is not (yet) a *being*, but rather a *not-yet-being* that sticks to its existence so as to be projected (in hope) toward its *will be*. This is why true mystical ecstasy is an experience of the end.[41]

The consistency and unity of the human being, however, is greater than that of the physical world. The main feature of temporality, unlike physical time, is a certain unity between the three temporal dimensions, which makes Man one (-self), and allows him to travel through his own temporal pilgrimage without fading into a mere punctiform succession of states of consciousness. We go on *being*, carrying around

---

[35] See Jn 1:3; Ep 2:10.

[36] Spinoza's expression is well-known: *Sentimus experimurque nos aeternos esse* [We perceive and experience that we are eternal].

[37] See my "Le concept d'ontonomie," in *Actes du XI Congres International de Philosophie*, Brussels, 1953, 3:182ff.

[38] See 1 Co 13:9–12.

[39] See Panikkar, "Le concept d'ontonomie."

[40] See the Aristotelian intuition that it is impossible that there be time without the existence of the soul: *Phys.* IV.14 (223–26).

[41] "For not what thou art, nor what thou hast been, doth God regard with his merciful eyes; but what thou wouldst be" (*The Cloud of Unknowing*, 75). Ultimately, so to speak, being is the end of a loving, divine gaze.

our past and projecting ourselves toward the future. Man's last instant contains the charge of his entire past; it sums it up in a certain way, and thus Man *is* what he has *be-come* in this last temporal instant.

True metaphysics is always eschatological. But because of faith, we know that there is more to this. Between the last temporal instant and the "contiguous" tempiternal existence there is the event of death and resurrection. The human being's temporality in heaven is not the linear integral temporality of sublunary temporal moments, but rather it represents a leap, a resurrection to a new (supernatural) sphere of Man that had already begun throughout his "specular and enigmatic"[42] pilgrimage in the body, even if it had not yet appeared.[43] Tempiternity is the fullness of human temporality, but in a much more superior sense than that of a simple integration of lived moments. Strictly speaking, we have already gone beyond the limit and left all of time behind.

Man is truly Man when he becomes that which he is called to become, that is, God.[44] Human existence reaches its fullness when, having overcome the temporal pilgrimage, it exists without any dis-tension. Tempiternity, in one sense, is no longer temporal; there is neither succession nor potentiality in it; there is no increase and no change; it does not belong to time but to the order of divinity.[45] Only the mystic is able to mutter something about this definitive state of being,[46] but, thanks to faith, we know it exists, and theology, in fact, has attempted to study and describe it. The theology of the beatific vision gives us the *morphontology* of the tempiternal being.[47]

When God is all in all,[48] when everything is brought together under Christ in God[49] and when life to us is no longer "ours" but Christ living in us[50] and our life is hidden with Christ in God;[51] when we are truly God[52] and not only *like* Gods according to Adam's hasty and impatient desire;[53] when time is no longer,[54] and no more sun or stars,[55] but nevertheless a new heaven and a new earth,[56] and we are

---

[42] See 2 Co 5:6.

[43] See 1 Jn 3:2.

[44] See Ps 82:6; Jn 10:34ff.

[45] "In Him, creatures are not in their essence but as in their cause through the similitude of ideas, which, insofar are they are in God, are not creatures," says St. Thomas, pointing out the divine order of tempiternity (*Scriptum super Sententiis* III, d.11, q.1, a.4 expos.).

[46] See, e.g., Blessed Henry Suso's beautiful description of the "out of time" operation in his *Büchlein der ewigen Wahrheit* [A Small Book on Eternal Truth], chs. 5 and 7.

[47] See R. Panikkar, "Die existenzielle Phänomenologie der Wahrheit," in *Philosophisches Jahrbuch der Görresgesellschaft* 64 (1956): 27–54.

[48] See 1 Co 15:28.

[49] See Ep 1:10.

[50] See Ph 1:21; Gal 2:20.

[51] See Col 3:3.

[52] See Jn 10:35.

[53] See Gn 3:5.

[54] See Rev 10:6.

[55] See Rev 22:5.

[56] See 2 Pet 3:13; Is 65:17.

perfected in unity;[57] when creation is no longer creature, but daughter, because its creaturability, like death,[58] has been defeated and absorbed by the perfect filiation[59] of the Son, who has incorporated us in Himself[60] (the You of the Father[61]) . . . then our humility, our *humus*, will still remain, because our tempiternity, cortically—to put in one way—equal to divine eternity, will make us realize that our entire being is a simple reflection, pure grace, a donation that is perfect—and deserving—of the Father of all light,[62] who has accepted the perfect sacrifice of his Son, who was one day able to utter in time, although with tempiternal effectiveness: *Consummatum est*.[63] Tempiternity is our destiny. In the meantime, we must acquire it by joining the sacrifice of the sole High Priest who has conquered it for us.[64]

The first consequence of importance for us is that true human structure is not so much of the order of temporality, one day called to disappear, as it is of tempiternity. From the point of view of tempiternity, the first correction of perspective concerns *egochronism*, that is, the flux of time being considered on the basis of its reference to my personal present moment (the death of Napoleon belongs to the past, and that of Elizabeth II of England to the future, only in reference to *my* own present time), instead of finding an internal and constitutive criterion for the flow of time. This criterion is Christ, by whom the eons themselves were made.[65] And God is His King.[66] But this is not the place to further develop these ideas.

The second consequence for us is limited to recognizing the relationship that already exists as of this life between temporality and tempiternity. This introduces us fully into the role of the *consecratio temporis* in the Mass. This temporal consecration is also related to what the history of religions calls *sacred time*[67]—sacred time which does not follow the rhythm of nature, which is equidistant from all sacred actions, which belongs to primordial time, and which therefore transcends temporality without being dependent of the tri-tension of the past, present, and future.

A considerable amount of Catholic affirmations about the Mass are little less than obvious considered from this perspective.[68]

---

[57] See Jn 17:23.

[58] See 1 Co 15:54–56.

[59] See Mt 3:17; 15:33; 17:5; Mk 1:11; Lk 1:32; Jn 6:40; 11:27; 1 Jn 3:1; 5:15; 2 Pet 1:17; etc.

[60] See Gal 4:6–7; Col 1:13; etc.

[61] See Jn 17:1; Lk 3:22; etc.

[62] See Jas 1:17.

[63] Jn 19:30.

[64] See 1 Co 6:20; 1 Pet 1:18; Heb 5:1ff.

[65] See Heb 1:2; 1 Co 10:11; etc.

[66] See 1 Tim 1:17; Rev 15:3.

[67] See M. Eliade, *Das Heilige und das Profane* (Hamburg: Hamburg, 1957); W. F. Otto, *Theophania* (Hamburg: Rowhohlt, 1956); L. Kerényi, *Umgang mit Göttlichem* (Göttingen: Vandenhoeck & Ruprecht, 1961); J. Cazeneuve, *Les rites et la condition humaine* (Paris: PUF, 1957), etc.

[68] See, to be read cautiously and with good judgment, C. G. Jung, "Das *Wandlungssymbol*

Consecratio Temporis

"Each Time"

If the existence of Christ were an *exclusively* historical existence, his presence in the sacrifice and sacrament of the Mass could not be *fully* real, but rather only commemorative on the part of Man, and divine (that is to say, presence insofar as God, but not insofar as Man) on the part of Christ. The physical-real presence of a historical personage is tied to a determined time and a space, and they cannot simply be transcended. Historical figures are "present" in the minds and hearts of later generations, perhaps also because of their particular influence and works, but they are no longer psychosomatically present in the *same* way that they were among their own contemporaries.

However, Christ's presence in the Mass is not of this type; instead it is integrally real, and this is possible because His existence, as is proper of a theandric being, is both historical and transhistorical, and His temporicity is tempiternity. (This is an important point in the ecumenical encounter of Christianity with other religions.)[69] Christianity's often underlined temporal nature does not only refer to the historicity of the incarnation, the passion, and the resurrection of Christ, but also to the Mass and the sui generis reality of the temporicity revealed by Christianity.

Christianity takes time seriously, thus the fundamental difference between tempiternity and that hypothetical and unreal existence of things in the divine mind "before" their creation. This is a *chronomorphism* that becomes evident when one speaks of what God "thinks" of things "before" these are. This "before" makes no sense, nor does it refer to God or to the thing before it is. The *regressus* (return) of the world to God is a real process; beings truly be-come insofar as they reach Being. Salvation is not the mere recognition of something that already *is*, but rather it is the real conquest of something that *becomes*.[70] The *quotiescumque* ("each time") of the Mass is connected to this process of salvation of the world because, in the concrete, real economy of our eon, the path to salvation is carried out through redemption, and redemption is attained by Christ on the cross, and it is perpetuated (that is, it is gradually fulfilled) through space and time by means of the Mass.[71]

That which the Mass we celebrate *here, today* brings to the sole sacrifice is precisely that particular portion of space and time that, through that very Mass, is incorpo-

---

in der Messe," *Eranos Jahrbuch* 8 (1940/1941); A. Watts, *Myth and Ritual in Christianity* (London: Thames and Hudson, 1953).

[69] See R. Panikkar, "La demitologizzazione nell'incontro tra Cristianesimo e Induismo," in E. Castelli (ed.), *Il problema della demitizzazione* (Rome: Istituto di studi filosofici, 1961), 243–66.

[70] This is a fundamental point of divergence with a certain conception of salvation in Buddhism and Hinduism. See, for a good introduction to the underlying issues, L. Silburn, *Instant et Cause. Le discontinu dans la pensée philosophique de l'Inde* (Paris: Vrin, 1955).

[71] See the incontrovertible text of 1 Co 10:16.

rated into the redeemed universe—a space replete of cosmos and time, loaded with events, and not mere formal shells devoid of content. The salvific act of the Lord, in what it has of the temporal, transcends mere temporicity and settles in the line of tempiternity. This is the reason why it can have a contemporaneous relationship with any temporal point of the universe. The presence of Christ in the Mass is not a miracle that suspends the laws proper to His being; rather it is the manifestation, the epiphany, of His way of being, which is precisely that to which we have also been called. Christ does not even suspend the laws of our being, which remain the same. It is one among so many examples of the divine "discretion."[72]

In short, Christ is present in the Mass not to make a simple apparition, but to associate us and the whole world to His own theandric destiny. The Mass is, for this reason, sacrifice and sacrament indivisibly, because it fulfills this double movement of Man to God (sacrifice) and of God to Man (sacrament) in order to carry out that "admirable barter,"[73] exchange between Man and God that takes place through Christ in the Mass: *Eius divinitatis esse consortes, qui humanitatis nostrae fieri dignatus est particeps.*[74]

"Each Time We Participate in This Altar"

There is no doubt that the Mass is carried out *in* time, just as the sacrifice of Jesus on the cross was carried out *in* time. And yet, both events transcend time and are placed in the line of intersection between temporality and tempiternity, analogously to death. There is a reason why sacrifice entails the death of the victim, and the sacrifice of the cross, as fullness of all sacrifices, far from being an exception, carries along the death of Christ. The sacrifice not only unfolds in time, but it is that which realizes and unfolds time itself.[75]

Christian faith believes that the sacrifice of Christ is the indispensable means of salvation. The Eucharist is the "drug of immortality,"[76] and nobody can be saved without eating the flesh of the Son of Man,[77] that is to say, without participating in the altar of the Mass. So, salvation means participation in divine nature itself. This participation takes place in the *altar* of the sacrifice. (Even though baptism already bestows sanctifying grace, we know that all the sacraments are genetically and theologically tied to the Eucharist.)[78]

---

[72] See "*De Deo Abscondido,*" in part 1 of this volume.

[73] See the Catholic liturgy of Christmas and the Eighteenth Sunday after Pentecost.

[74] "He wanted us to share in His divinity, He who deigned to partake in our humanity," from the Offertory of the Mass.

[75] See R. Panikkar, *Kultmysterium in Hinduismus und Christentum* (Freiburg-Munich: Alber, 1964).

[76] See "The Eucharist and the Resurrection," above.

[77] See Jn 6:54ff.

[78] See texts and explanations, for example, in H. De Lubac, *Méditation sur l'Église* (Paris: Aubier, 1954); M. J. Scheeben, *Gesammelte Schriften*, vol. 2, *Die Mysterien des Christentums*.

A great majority of religions consider the altar the center of the world, the point of beginning and culmination of time, the place that reaches heaven and the only bridge between Transcendence and this world. The altar of the Mass eminently fulfills everything that all other religions have surmised. The altar of the sacrifice of Christ is trans-spatial as well as transtemporal.[79] *In sublime altare tuum*, "To Your sublime altar," it is said in the Canon[80] of the Mass. The Mass, while remaining anchored in temporality, is the bridge that joins one shore to the other. The Mass and the sacrifice of the cross are one and the same (liturgical) act because this action, as such, is not a mere temporal act, rather it is pregnant with tempiternity.

By virtue of the Mass, Man transcends time[81] and begins to accomplish the leap of historical temporality to celestial tempiternity.[82] Neither conscious participation in the Mass nor sacramental Communion[83] are necessary for the transformation that occurs *in* and *through* the Mass to be applied to an individual or to a particular community. One way or another, either personally or vicariously, human beings must participate in that which takes place on the altar of the sacrifice if they are to reach the fullness of being to which they have been called.

From the point of view that concerns us, the transformation we have referred to could be described by developing and commenting on certain points that we can merely indicate here.

The act of sacrifice and sacrament of the altar is not limited, as is well known, to "producing" the presence of Christ for the faithful to adore, so that the Lord may descend unto them and sanctify them. The matter that is placed on the altar is the entire cosmos, and the liturgical performer is Christ himself, the Only Son of the Father[84] and the Firstborn among many brothers,[85] who, as Head of the Mystical Body[86] and in collaboration with His Body, offers the whole creation so that it may ascend with a pleasing smell[87] and reach sempiternal life.

Through Him, the double movement of sacrifice and sacrament gathers the fragments[88] of time and space, the leftover pieces of this cosmos that need to be redeemed, that is to say, pardoned and elevated, in order to be able to return to the house of the Father[89] and be transformed into a part of the Mystical Body. The

---

[79] See Rev 8:3; 9:13; Is 6:6; etc.

[80] [Editorial note: The official prayer, and more specifically the priest's prayer, when he consecrates the Body and Blood of Christ.]

[81] *Ut ergo tu sis, transcende tempus* [In order to *be*, transcend time], Augustine, *In Iohan.* 38.10.

[82] *Et de munere temporali fiat nobis remedium sempiternum* [May this temporal offering turn into an eternal remedy for us] (from the Canon of the Mass).

[83] See *Denz.*, 1922.

[84] See Jn 1:14, 18; 3:16; 3:218; 1 Jn 4:9.

[85] See Rom 8:29; Col 1:15, 18; Rev 1:5.

[86] See Ep 5:22–23; Col 1:18; etc.

[87] See Ph 4:18.

[88] See Jn 6:12.

[89] See Jn 14:2; Lk 15:18; etc.

Mass consecrates time, that is, it redeems it;[90] from a profane and damned one, it turns it into sacred and saintly. Human temporality, which was, and still is, under the sign of death and destruction as a consequence of sin,[91] gradually transforms into celestial tempiternity.[92] The Eucharist really bestows immortality.[93] Between the Eucharist and the Church, the continuation of Christ on earth,[94] there is a constitutive relationship.[95]

The coexistence of both temporal dimensions here on earth constitutes an underlying theme of mystical experiences of all times. Whoever, at one time or another, has had the consciousness of having penetrated into celestial tempiternity cannot stop "feeling" that this form of existence is true existence and that, as such, it cannot disappear, even when the immediate experience has already vanished.[96] Mystics live as if in two spheres, or rather, they have the feeling of living in a sphere, the *real* one, that is different from the one in which phenomenal events take place; it is as if they have a double experience of temporicity.[97] Not only does time remain still during their contemplation, but, during the passing of cosmological time, they maintain a certain consciousness that, together with that flow, there is a form of being that is the true form of being, and that holds an increasingly frailer relationship with temporal pilgrimage.[98] The purity of the soul consists in that "there clings to the soul no creaturely affection, no *temporality* or effective perception."[99]

The increasingly greater participation of Man in the Mass gradually turns his temporality into tempiternity. The *consecratio temporis* of the Mass consists in the transformation of the profane and damned time of a fallen creation into a sacred and supernatural existence. The participation in the temporal structure of the Mass grants us a tempiternal remedy. Those who participate of the altar receive a celestial blessing and they are filled with grace.[100] The ultimate meaning of history lies in that,

---

[90]   See Ep 5:16.

[91]   See Rom 6:23.

[92]   *Inchoatio vitae aeternae* [the first phase of eternal life]: so a traditional formula defines grace.

[93]   It is known that, at least for the Mediterranean world, immortality and divinization were synonymous. See A. J. Festugière, *La révélation d'Hermès Trismégiste*, I–IV (Paris: Gabalda, 1944–54). See also Wi 15:3.

[94]   See Leo XIII, *Mirae caritatis* (May 28, 1902).

[95]   See the voice of tradition in F. Holböck, *Der eucharistische und der mystische Leib Christi* and *Corpus Mysticum*.

[96]   See the vast reflections in Hinduism on the possibility of the *jīvanmukta*, that is, the soul that is completely liberated and united with God here on earth while it is simultaneously still united to the mortal body. Both quietism and Christian orthodox mysticism have broadly dealt with this problem under one form or another.

[97]   See Heb 6:5.

[98]   On the importance of this "preventive annihilation of time" (H. U. von Balthasar, *Therese von Lisieux* [Cologne: Hegner, 1950], 194) for Hinduism, see in brief M. Eliade, *Le Yoga* (Paris: Payot, 1954).

[99]   St. John of the Cross, *Ascent to Mount Carmel* III.3.4.

[100]   See the Canon of the Mass.

in it, human beings—in and by means of the Mass—collaborate in the passage, in the Passover, from *world* to Church.[101]

This consecration of time is obviously not a magical act that, by virtue of a simple physical causality, produces the forced unleashing of a spiritual and supernatural automatism; but neither is it (as some *microdoxic* interpretations could sometimes make us suspect) a simple act of particular devotion that "rewards" whoever "assists" in it with "graces" and leaves everybody else untouched.

The consecration of time entails the sanctification of everything that takes place "within" it. It means the transformation of history from profane into sacred, into a history of salvation. It entails the redemption of the temporal structures of this sublunary world,[102] accelerating the return of those that were inauthentic (mere appearances) to nothing, or conferring them their true and tempiternal being, if they were authentic.[103]

All of this does not automatically occur, but by virtue of that sacramental *opus operatum* which is the *opus operantis Christi*[104] performing in himself the *hic et nunc* of the sacramental action. But this *Christus* is not a Jesus of Nazareth separated from his Body, but rather the Head and members collaborating in the *meum ac vestrum sacrificium*[105] of the sacred action.

Here, as well as in other spheres, the Christian solution follows a fair *middle path* between liberal individualism and collectivist anonymity.[106] The consecration

---

[101] See R. Panikkar, "Christian Meaning of Human Values," *The King's Rally* 33, no. 4 (1956): 25ff.

[102] See G. Lazzati, "La *consecratio mundi*, essenzialmente opera dei laici," *Studium* 12 (1959): 794ff.

[103] Allow us to present a few somewhat forgotten quotes by St. Thomas, and whose application to what has been said can be easily deduced without any further comments: "Creature is a shadow insofar as it comes out of nothing" (*De Veritate* q.18, a.2, ad 5; cf. also *De Caritate* I, ad 11). "What has its being from another, considered in itself, is non-being" (*De Potentia* q.3, a.3, ad 4; cf. q.5, a.1, co.). "God cannot be the cause of the tendency to non-being; *this* the creature has on its own, insofar as it comes from nothing" (*Sum. theol.* I, q.104, a.3, ad 1; see also *C. gentes* II, 30). "Even that which in things is stable would fall back into nothingness (since it comes from nothingness) if the hand of the Divine Ruler did not keep it" (*Sum. theol.* I, q.103, a.1, ad 2). The expression by the Florentine Council, according to which God "made creatures good, since they come from the Supreme Good, but changeable, since they have been created out of nothing" (*Denz.*, 706), is found in almost the exact same words in St. Augustine, *De Natura Boni* X. For this and other quotes, see my *El concepto de naturaleza*, 149ff. Christ's action reaches the ontological depths of being, and salvation is truly transporting us to the other shore, that of divinity.

[104] [Editorial note: A "work valid *per se*" insofar as "carried out by Christ" himself through the priest.]

[105] [Editorial note: "My and your (= of you all) sacrifice," as Catholic priests say during the Mass.]

[106] *Pro nostra et totius mundi salute*, says the offering of the Chalice: "For the salvation of us and of the entire world."

of time does not mean either the exclusive sanctification of the private individual who participates directly in the sacrifice, or the automatic salvation of the human community without any inward participation. In this *middle path* is where we find inserted the prodigious dignity—and responsibility—of the Christian believer, who is the priest of humanity and of the entire cosmos, and whose function and mission are that of saving and redeeming all creatures.

Both the economy of salvation of the Old Testament as well as that of the New show us the communal nature of salvation.[107] It has perhaps been less noticed that, next to this communal nature, the economy of the Church era is that of "vicarious" satisfaction and salvation—but we must not understand this under a sociological angle or from a merely individualist viewpoint, but rather under the ontological perspective stemming from the very fact of redemption. Namely, Christ has died for all of us,[108] His redemption is universal.[109] And yet, this does not exempt anyone from participation—each one of us in our own appropriate measure—in the Lord's redeeming action.

The function of Christians on earth does not lie as much on saving themselves (something they cannot do alone, incidentally) as rather in collaborating with Christ[110] in the redemption of the universe. Their mission is not as much to "convert" people according to a human plan and make them sociologically confess Christ's divinity. Their task is not as much to struggle for an exclusively horizontal future, working for an external, problematic and hypothetical triumph of a Christendom (are we to say that *in the meanwhile*, the Church does not fulfill its mission, Christ has failed, and creation does not achieve its goal?). Their task, I was saying, is not as much "conversion" understood in this sense, as redemption, the "co-redemption" of the universe, *hic et nunc*.[111] And *this* redemption is in fact fulfilled, *this* is in fact the faith that overcomes the world.[112] Losing the vertical meaning of history and projecting the triumph of the Church onto a horizontal future would mean an infiltration of a naturalist, if not Marxist, mentality.[113]

---

[107]   See, e.g., L. Bouyer, *La Bible et l'Évangile* (Paris: Cerf, 1953); C. Vagaggini, *Il senso teologico,* 211ff, etc.

[108]   See 1 Jn 2:2; Rom 3:25; 9:30; Gal 4:5, and their interpretation by the Council of Trent (*Denz.,* 794). See also the *propter nos homines* [for us human beings (and our salvation)]," in the Symbol of faith; as well as the Councils of Nicea (*Denz.,* 54) and Constantinople (*Denz.,* 86).

[109]   The Church condemned the Jansenist proposition: "Pagans, Jews, heretics, and the like do not receive any [positive] influence from Christ" (*Denz.,* 1295). On the contrary: "As there is, has been, will be no Man whose nature has not been taken on by him [Christ], so there is, has been, will be no Man for whom he did not undergo his Passion" (*Denz.,* 319).

[110]   See 1 Co 3:9.

[111]   See the basic importance of the present tense in the entire Gospel, especially John, in reporting Jesus's affirmations, including, "Anyone who believes in the Son *has* eternal life" (Jn 3:36); "Your faith *has* saved you"; "*Today* you will be with me in paradise" (Lk 23:43); etc.

[112]   See 1 Jn 5:4.

[113]   See all of eschatology, essential to Christianity.

It is there that the *consecratio temporis* acquires an importance of the first order for Christian life. Christians are conscious that in the Mass they participate truly and effectively with Christ in the redemption of the world: *Pro nostra et totius mundi salute.*[114] Our mission lies in participating truly and actively in the only sacrifice that bestows tempiternal life because it makes us penetrate into God's eternal life.[115]

---

[114] "For the salvation of us and of the entire world," from the Offertory.

[115] *Ut mihi et illis proficiat ad salutem in vitam aeternam* [so that it may benefit me and them in view of the eternal life], Offertory. See also *Accipientibus nobis in vitam aeternam* [that we will receive for eternal life], Canon.

SECTION II
TRADITION

11

CHRISTIAN SELF-CONSCIOUSNESS AND WORLD RELIGIONS*

The Issue[1]

It has become commonplace to say that Man cannot live any longer in isolation and that therefore religions, if they are going to be relevant to contemporary humankind, cannot live, nor indeed can even survive, behind the several religious curtains that along the ages they have built, and which perhaps they *had* to build, for their very existence. The relation of religions with one another is therefore one of the most important religious and human issues. In a word, *ecumenical ecumenism*[2] is one of the most central issues for Man's life on earth, since religion shapes Man's culture, and today no religion is self-sufficient any longer. Religions have to dialogue in order to reestablish a truly human culture.

The issue is important and vital for Christianity for two main reasons: one de jure, the other de facto—that is, deriving respectively from the nature of thing

---

* Original version: "Christianity and World Religions," in M. P. John et al., *Christianity* (Patiala: Punjabi University, 1969), 78–127.

[1] This essay was originally written as a chapter for a book on Christianity which, together with other volumes, aimed at presenting the basic beliefs of several religions. See "Christianity and World Religions," in M. P. John et al., *Christianity* (Patiala: Punjabi University, 1969), 78–127 (Guru Nanak Quincentenary Celebration, Patiala, 1969). It is encouraging to notice that the things I wrote many years ago are becoming part of the common heritage of Christian consciousness. See, e.g., C. Thomas (ed.), *Attitudes toward Other Religions: Some Christian Interpretations* (London: SCM Press, 1969); R. E. Whitson, *The Coming Convergence and the World Religions* (New York: Newman Press, 1971); D. G. Dawe and J. B. Carman (eds.), *Christian Faith in a Religiously Plural World* (Maryknoll, NY: Orbis Books, 1978); Th. Empravil, *The Emerging Theology of Religions* (Rewa, India: Vincentian Publications, 1980); P. Knitter, *No Other Name? A Critical Survey of Christian Attitudes toward World Religions* (Maryknoll, NY: Orbis Books, 1985); H. Coward, *Pluralism: Challenge to World Religions* (Maryknoll, NY: Orbis Books, 1985); M. M. Thomas, *Risking Christ for Christ's Sake. Toward an Ecumenical Theology of Pluralism* (Geneva: WCC Publications, 1987).

[2] If *ecumenism* aims at establishing a worldwide Christian community without a priori condemning the different Christian confessions, *ecumenical ecumenism* aims at the religious harmony within the human family without any minimalist reductionism to an abstract religiousness, lifeless and devoid of human traditions.

itself and from its current situation. The first is the particular claim of Christianity to be a universal religion, with a message of salvation for every man. Thus, whereas another, quieter, and more passive religion may intend to guide its own flock and inspire its own people, Christianity (as some other universal religions do) recognizes no frontiers, either geographical or historical, and therefore confronts the other existing religions by virtue of its very self-understanding.

The second point is the historical situation of the world today: Christian churches are established all over the world, and Christians, not only individually, but also collectively, are present practically everywhere. The historical flux of our times is shifting from the West toward other parts of the world, and the West is incomprehensible if the Christian factor is not taken into account.

The issue then reads as follows: What, according to Christianity, is the relation between itself and other religions of the world? A very brief and condensed answer to this question is the aim of this dissertation.

I immediately make it clear that I will offer nothing more than a faithful chronicle of the current Christian situation, together with an interpretation of it that may make sense to our contemporaries, whether they belong to the Christian tradition or not.

De Jure: The Criteria

Our first task is to find the criteria we will have to use in order to answer the question. Since Christianity is no monolithic doctrinal block, we can find, throughout its history, a whole gamut of opinions. Therefore, we cannot be satisfied with a couple of authoritative statements, for we may find almost any number of assertions regarding the question, nor with the merely personal opinions of a single author. Since the time of Peter, James, and Paul, the first apostles,[3] there has always been, throughout the twenty centuries of Christian life, a tension between inclusiveness and exclusiveness, that is, between the achievement of self-identity by affirmation (of oneself) or by negation (of the other).

If we consider religions as living realities, and approach them not only as onlookers from outside but as believers from within, being also equipped with the most unbiased criticism, we will agree that neither a purely mystical view from within, nor a solely positivist one from outside, is going to furnish us with the criteria we are looking for. Religion may spring from an internal inspiration which we may call by various names, but it cannot be disconnected from its practice and realization through the ages. Just because someone, in his personal experience, may have realized the highest unity with God and with all men within the womb of a particular religion, one is not entitled to say, without further qualifications, that this religion preaches the unity and equality of all religions. Similarly, just because another may have personally experienced or witnessed in history examples of exclusiveness and/ or superiority, one is not entitled to draw the conclusion that a particular religion

---

[3] See Ac 15, etc.

simply condemns all other religions. We have to take religions in all their existential complexity.

I think that the criteria for a fitting answer may come from a study about

- The basic principles of a given religion
- The history of religion
- The theological interpretation of both theory and praxis

Taking just Christianity into consideration, we can sum it up with three words: Scripture, history, and theology.

According to the Christian doctrine, the so-called sources of revelation are two: *Scripture*, not only considered as the inspired written words about Christ but also as a true account of his sayings and actions, and *tradition*, not only considered as doctrinal hermeneutics, but as a vital and existential crystallization of that same revelation. If for the sake of clarity I am presenting *three* criteria, this does not imply that I am departing from the common Christian belief.

My basic principles in fact are drawn from both Scripture and tradition. What I called history and theology represent, respectively, the factual and theoretical interpretation of tradition itself. We will have to consider separately the three criteria as briefly and concisely as possible.

De Facto: The Situation

The encounter of religions and, more particularly, the relationship between Christianity and world religions is nowadays going through a unique opportunity. Never before have religions been in touch with one another to such an extent as now, never have they been involved in such a shared crisis as today, never have they viewed such planetary horizons, and never before has there appeared such a criticism as is now challenging the traditional religious forms to rethink their understanding of Man and reality.

If the situation is new, not a repetition of a previous one, the solution will also have to be new, and not a mere copy of old answers. The *principle of continuity*, fundamental for any living tradition, will have to be respected, but it must not be opposed to the *principle of renewal and growth*. If religions have to be alive, they cannot escape the law of growth, which implies not only a positive but also a negative metabolism, that is, not only an assimilation of new elements, but also a rejection of old ones. No serious attempt at tackling the problem today can be satisfied with parroting ancient and outworn answers—valid during their own times, to be sure, but no longer sufficient in the present-day situation.

The difficulty is greater than it may look at first sight. Let us imagine that I succeed in putting forward some new solution to the problem, from a Christian point of view, and also that my hypothesis is convincing. Who is going to decide whether mine is a Christian solution, and not just another individual opinion? Who is going to draw the boundaries of orthodoxy? According to Christian doctrine, only the church will be allowed to decide. But again, *who* is the church, and on what grounds is this church going to decide, if the problem is new, as well as the solution being promoted? Authority, particularly so in the case of the church, can only act as a qualified interpreter of tradition, not acting according to its own whims.

In short, only the life of the community, its history, and the further developments of Christian consciousness have the competence to decide whether that particular solution belongs to the mainstream of Christian tradition, or whether it has remained outside, that is, it is a heresy, a sect, or simply a partial opinion. On the other hand, without that particular hypothesis, the common consciousness might not have developed into *consensus*. The so-called *sensus ecclesiae*, the mind of the church, is also involved in the historical process. The whole church, here on earth, is on pilgrimage.

Being aware of this, I will try to be traditional in what I am going to say, leaving aside particular opinions, but expressing personal convictions nonetheless. Even while allowing room for criticism, I believe that the ideas expressed here are all perfectly Christian. Any criticism, in case, should lead the reader to the conviction that a deeply Christian pluralism is possible.

The Data

Scripture[4]

The Old Testament

There is a positive evolution in the Hebrew Bible, as to its judgment on other religions.[5] They are generally acknowledged and recognized as valid,[6] though unfit for the people of Israel,[7] and, to put it bluntly, not up to the mark.[8] The God of Israel is superior to all other Gods, and unique.[9] He alone is the Lord; He alone reigns over all other divinities.[10] The other Gods, in fact, are not even Gods.[11]

---

[4] The citations from the Bible will not be exhaustive, nor even, sometimes, univocal. They are not meant as "evidences" but simply as examples of the *milieu* in which the Judeo-Christian community lived.

[5] See, e.g., Y. Kaufmann, *The Religion of Israel* (Chicago: University of Chicago Press, 1960), 7–149; W. Eichrodt, *Theologie des Alten Testaments*, vol. 1, *Gott und Volk* (Stuttgart: Klotz, 1962); G. von Rad, *Theologie des Alten Testaments*, vols. 1 and 2 (Munich: Kaiser, 1962).

[6] See Jg 11:24.

[7] See 1 Sam 26:19.

[8] Is 44:9–20; see also other deities being recognized in the Old Testament, e.g., in Jg 10:6; 8:33; 9:46; 11:24; 1 Sam 7:4.

[9] See Ex 20:3; Dt 6:4; 7:6; Ps 82:1.

[10] See Is 49:6.

[11] See the collective work edited by L. Finkelstein, *The Jews: Their History, Culture, and*

This very fact leads, however dialectically, to a recognition that YHWH is also God for other peoples; as a consequence, the originally particular God of the tribes of Israel becomes the universal God, caring for all men, though entrusting Israel with a particular mission[12] and responsibility—a burden rather than a privilege, as the later tradition will underscore.

The Christian Canon

The Sayings of Christ

Christ's utterances shed an ambiguous light on this question. On the one hand, it seems as if Jesus were only concerned with the people of Israel. He declines to step beyond their boundaries, and he treats non-Jews with an attitude of assumed superiority, as many of his other fellow Jews did. In fact, he did not seem to care much about the outside world, and except for a couple of incursions into the areas just adjoining Israel, he did not pay much attention to other peoples or to other religions.[13] In the dated dispute between Samaritans and Jews, in spite of his lofty words that "there comes a time in which God will be worshipped in spirit and in truth," he emphatically states that right is on the side of the Jews.[14]

On the other hand, while opposing established Judaism, as for instance when he keeps on choosing the Sabbath as the day on which to perform his miracles,[15] and misses no opportunity to chastise the scribes and Pharisees,[16] he seems to be majestically above the limits of the religiousness of his fellow Jews. He stresses, again and again, that he has other sheep that the apostles do not know;[17] that he who is not against them is on their side;[18] that the Son of Man is judge of all nations and peoples;[19] that whatever is done to the littlest ones is done to him;[20] that he was before Abraham;[21] and he asks his followers to be like his Father who makes His sun rise on good and bad alike, and sends the rain on both the righteous and the unrighteous.[22] He commands his disciples to go to all the nations[23] and declares that his kingdom

---

Religion, 2 vols., 3rd ed. (New York: Harper—The Jewish Publication Society of America, 1960) for references.

[12] The major theme of Israel as a chosen people. See among other passages: Ex 19:5; Lv 20:24; Dt 4:7–8; 10:15; 14:2; 26:18; Is 51:4–5.

[13] The silence of the Gospels is here also revealing.

[14] Jn 4:22.

[15] See, e.g., Mk 2:23, etc.

[16] Mt 23, *passim.*

[17] Jn 10:16.

[18] Lk 9:50, etc.

[19] Mt 28:18, etc.

[20] See Mt 25:40. His brethren are all who suffer and are in need.

[21] See Jn 8:58.

[22] See Mt 5:45. The text asks us to care for all, though the others may be negatively judged.

[23] Mk 16:15.

is not of this world.[24] He seemed not to care for the destruction of the temple, and this fact was recalled during his condemnation to death.[25] Worship in spirit and in truth is not tied down to time and place,[26] and so on.

The Acts of Christ

Christ's actions present the same ambivalence as his words. On the one hand, he seems to consider himself within the fold of Judaism and claims to be nothing but a Jew. He acts as a Jew, fulfills the Law,[27] and even accepts the baptism of John.[28] He claims Jewish orthodoxy and solemnly swears so in his final trial before the Sanhedrin.[29] He has not come to abolish the Law and the Prophets.[30] YHWH is his Father,[31] and he does not seem to have acted in such a way as to proclaim a universal religion.[32] In fact, he does not seem to have acted so as to found *any* religion at all. He stresses his ties with Moses, and considers the Jewish commandments as the way of salvation for the Jews. He acts as a reformer of Israel against rigid traditionalism, is in favor of an inner participation, and so on.

On the other hand, his actions exhibit a superiority that could not but be irritating to the orthodox Jews. He speaks of a "small flock," to whom he promises his assistance and even his presence, so that that they can become salt to and light for the world. He proclaims in a most unambiguous way that, though this or that was said by the ancients, he on the contrary says another, different, and nobler thing; and the common people rejoice because he speaks as somebody acting on *his own* authority. His culminating actions in the Upper Room, before the Sanhedrin, and on Golgotha are performed with the consciousness of a cosmic and universal meaning. He promises to be with his disciples until the end of time, and makes quite plain that he is offering his life for the salvation of the whole world.

Moreover, he is food, food indeed for the life of the whole world: those who eat him will have eternal life. He identifies himself with his believers, so as to build a unity, as it happens with the branches of the vine. Without him, nothing is possible: he has in fact overcome the world and dispelled any fear from those who believe in him. They will perform even greater works than he himself did;[33] for his prayer will sustain them, and the Holy Spirit, a Spirit of Truth, will be sent by him to all who acknowledge him, and so on. Thus, nobody goes to the Father if not through him;

---

[24] Even if some sayings in the Gospel of John are not of Jesus, they express the faith of the apostolic church and thus belong also here.

[25] Mt 26:61; Mk 14:58.

[26] Jn 4:21.

[27] See Jn 8:46, etc.

[28] Mt 3:13.

[29] Jn 18:20–23.

[30] Mt 5:17.

[31] Jn 8:54.

[32] Mt 15:24.

[33] Jn 8:54.

those who see him see the Father; he is the Way, the Truth, and the Life; he *is*, and he is the principle that speaks to men.[34]

What They Say about Christ

In whatever ways the ideas on Christ—as put forward by the writers of the New Testament—originated, the fact remains that from the very beginning he was considered the manifestation of the cosmic or preexistent Christ, Firstborn of all creation, only begotten Son of the Father, the One in whom the whole universe has its consistency,[35] Judge of both living and dead, the Light that illumines every man coming into this world,[36] the One from whom everything has come and to whom everything returns, the Beginning and End of everything, expression of the invisible God, image of the Father, splendor of the Divinity,[37] in whom all the treasures of the Godhead are hidden,[38] so that in him the Divinity dwells bodily.[39] All things are destined to be submitted to him, before he submits himself—along with the whole creation—to the Father.[40] There is no other name in which there is salvation.[41] He is the only and unique Mediator. God has raised him so as to give humankind a Savior. Jesus is the Savior.

History

This survey of Christian Scripture has necessarily been cursory, but even after more thorough research, we are fairly certain that the image of Christ would not have been very different from what we have been delineating, for the impression upon the first generations of Christians was undoubtedly this: Christ is the *Pantocratōr*, the ruler of the universe,[42] "the Lord."[43]

Now this idea, which will prove crucial for our question, has undergone a series of interpretations that explain the different approaches that have been adopted

---

[34] Jn 8:24–25, as it was translated by the *Vulgate* [editor's note: v. 25 is currently rendered in a different way].

[35] Col 1:17.

[36] Jn 1:9.

[37] See Heb 1:3.

[38] See Col 2:3.

[39] Col 2:9.

[40] 1 Co 15:28.

[41] Ac 4:12.

[42] See 2 Co 4:18; Rev 1:8; 11:17; 15:3; 16:7; 19:6; 21:22, etc., although the scriptural texts refer directly to God, the Father of Jesus Christ. The expression is pre-Christian and applied to the Egyptian sun-god Mandulis as well as to Hermes, etc.

[43] See R. Guardini, *The Lord* (London: Longmans, 1956; translation of the German *Der Herr* [9th ed., Würzburg: Werkbund, 1951]), for a pastoral approach to the life of Jesus from this point of view; and the articles on *Kyrios* in Kittel's *Wörterbuch*, with abundant bibliography for a scientific study of the question.

toward the other religions. These interpretations crystallized in history. I will show here the different periods of this process, which will let us analyze the issue in a brief and condensed way. The advantage of such a comprehensive view is that it allows us to focus on the problem without at the same time falling into the trap of "seeing the forest instead of the trees."

Needless to say, if the devil can quote Scriptures for his own purpose, anybody can similarly use history to prove any thesis. Yet, I do not aim here at finding a few quotations here and there to substantiate one particular point of view, but at observing the course of the history of Christianity, and to discern the main and prevalent trend, coexisting of course with other streams and subcurrents, as happens in any living tradition. History thus turns into a theological category, into a "theological *locus*"—that is, a basic datum for Christian self-consciousness.

Periods

I will distinguish five periods, each of which puts a special emphasis on some aspect of Christian self-understanding.

Each of these periods shows a fundamental category as the expression of its basic concern. The key words are *witness, conversion, crusade, mission,* and *dialogue.* Each of these basic attitudes are the concrete result of an encounter between the peculiar historical circumstances of the time and the Christian consciousness during the last twenty centuries. None of these primordial attitudes should be seen as exclusive or absolute, as if they alone should represent the Christian position, not even in the periods in which they conveyed the mainstream of Christian consciousness. Taken in isolation, none of them can account for the whole of the Christian fact, nor, taken together, can they be prejudicial to the further historical and theological dynamism of Christian life.

From the Beginning to the Arian Controversy

The history of the first encounters of the newly born Christian faith with the religions of the neighboring countries has been for over a century a topic of deep reflection and thorough scholarly study. As a reaction to Harnack's thesis,[44] which tried to prove that Christianity has been utterly transformed by Hellenistic culture, starting from St. Paul, most modern studies, on the contrary, show that the fundamental pattern of Christianity remained Judaic, though nobody denies the speculative influence of Hellenic thought on Christian theology.[45]

---

[44] See A. von Harnack, *Die Mission und Ausbreitung des Christentums in den ersten drei Jahrhunderten* (Leipzig: Hinrichs, 1924; English edition: *The Expansion of Christianity in the First Three Centuries* [London: Williams and Norgate, 1904–1905]).

[45] See C. Tresmontant, *La Métaphysique du Christianisme et la naissance de la philosophie chrétienne* (Paris: Seuil, 1961) for an anthology of texts, although I do not agree with the thesis of the author. See also the essays by J. Daniélou, *Théologie du judéo-Christianisme* (Tournai: Desclée, 1958); *Message* évangélique *et culture* hellénistique (Tournai: Desclée, 1961; Italian: *Messaggio evangelico e cultura ellenistica* [Bologna: EDB, 2010]); *Les Origines du Christianisme Latin* (Paris: Cerf, 1978).

Usually, after the period of the writers of the Christian canon, scholars distinguish the so-called Apostolic Fathers, covering the latter half of the first century and the first half of the second (from the year 90 to 160 approximately), and the Apologists, who cover the period immediately following, and include the period of the great schools of Alexandria, Antioch, and others.[46]

The period of the Apostolic Fathers is concerned, on the whole, with establishing Christian principles without a direct dialogue or even concern for those who were not Christians.

The early Apologists, being themselves converted from the Greek religion and philosophically trained, were impelled to defend Christianity against the attacks of the outside world by such means as their Greek culture afforded.[47] For rather obvious sociological reasons, these writers often took a negative attitude toward the other form of religiousness, not so much on abstract and general grounds as because of the factual religious situation and practices of their contemporaries.[48]

Only in the third period would the properly called Church Fathers face the true confrontation.[49] Their two main ideas were the superiority of Christianity and its universality.[50] It is very interesting to note—and this idea should be better emphasized—that the consciousness of universality did not only "tame" that sense of superiority but also essentially modified it. In the minds of the Fathers, Christian faith is not simply superior, it is also universal. This, however, amounts to recognizing that, in one way or another, it is also present in the world outside, unless one maintains that there is only sin, darkness, and error outside Christianity.[51] In other words, if the Christian faith has a universal message, because it preaches a universal truth, it has to identify itself with truth, and thus to say that wherever is truth, there is also Christian faith.[52] It is not possible here to examine the issue in

---

[46] See the useful compilation by H. Krait, *Clavis Patrum Apostolicorum* (Munich: Kösel, 1963), for almost exhaustive references; and the two volumes published by G. W. H. Lampe, *A Patristic Greek Lexicon* (Oxford: Clarendon Press, 1961).

[47] See A. J. Festugière, *L'Idéal religieux des Grecs et l'Évangile* (Paris: Gabalda, 1932).

[48] It could all be summarized by the famous sentence of Tertullian: "What has Athens to do with Jerusalem!" (*De praescriptione haereticorum* 7). In the same passage he also affirms that, once we believe, we do not want to believe anything else, for we believe that there is nothing else to believe (ibid., PL 2.20).

[49] See K. Prümm, *Christentum als Neuheitserlebnis* (Freiburg, 1939); H. Rahner, *Griechische Mythen in christilicher Deuitung* (Basel: Herder, 1984, with an Introduction by A. Rosenberg).

[50] See "This partial philosophy is elementary, against the perfect science unveiled in Christ" (Clement of Alexandria, *Stromata* VI.8.68.1).

[51] See, e.g., "All other nations go astray and deceive themselves. Walking in darkness, they stagger one against another like drunken men. I do not hesitate to say that the world continues to exist only because of the prayers of supplication of the Christians" (Aristides of Athens, *Apologia* 16 [Quasten, *Patrology*, 1:194]).

[52] This even led to the theory that the Greek philosophers had been copying and borrowing from the Old Testament. See, e.g., Clement of Alexandria, *Stromata* I.17.87.2; I.22.150.1; V.5 *passim*; VI.2.27.5; Justin, *Apologia prima* 44; Origen, *Contra Celsum* VI.19.

detail. It suffices to give an overall view, showing the development of ideas rather than the historical evolution.

The leading, central idea of Christian faith regards the notion to be held about Jesus. According to whether Jesus is considered simply a man, or the Jewish Messiah, or the cosmic Logos, and so on, the relations between Christianity and the religions of the world will vary.

Now, it could be showed that the predominant idea of Jesus Christ up to the Council of Nicea in 325, and practically up to the Arian dispute,[53] conceived of him as a manifestation on earth of the preexistent Christ, identifying him—according to the different schools—with the Jewish God's eternal wisdom and/or the Spirit, while undoubtedly drawing upon the *Logos* of Plato or Philo.

As is generally the case, historical developments and the thinking process overlapped at least for one generation. I consider, therefore, this period to last, theologically, up to the fall of Rome under Alaric in 410 or the death of St. Augustine in 430.

Let us recall, in simplified terms, the theo-cosmological background of the Patristic period. There is God, or the One, or the Supreme Principle, He "who exists without a cause." This transcendent, ineffable Absolute, before the creation of the world, "produced" or "begot" either one or two "beings," which later Christian tradition would call the Son and the Spirit. This uncreated "being" (or beings) came into existence either in direct relationship with the creation of the world or even before (one-stage or two-stages theory), he knows all things,[54] and pervades everything; by him and for him all things were made. He is the *Pantocratōr*.[55]

According to the Church Fathers, in general, the Spirit or the *Logos* "was in the world,"[56] fills everything, is present in the midst of everything, penetrates everywhere, exists everywhere, fills the entire universe. In a word, this divine principle is immanent to the world, and transcendent as well, above time: it is the Timeless, the Invisible, who became visible to our eyes.

---

[53] The Arian dispute—which was triggered by the Christological ideas of Arius (256–336)—dominates the whole fourth century; its climax can be roughly located between the Council of Nicea in 325 and that of Constantinople in 381.

[54] "For before anything came into being, He had him as a counsellor, being His own mind and thought" (Theophilus of Antioch, *Ad Autolycum* II.22 [*PG* 6.1888]).

[55] See a Christological hymn by Melito of Sardis:
This is the first-born of God
who was begotten before the morning star
who made the light to rise
who made the day bright
who parted the darkness
who fixed the first mark for creation
who hung the earth in its place
who dried up the abyss
who spread out the firmament
who brought order to the world.

[56] See Jn 1:10.

One could go on listing authorities,[57] but what interests us here is the relevance of such a view for the issue under examination. The fact that Jesus is either identified with that immanent principle, whether it is called the preexistent Christ or the Spirit, or anyway seen in close relationship to it: begotten before all times,[58] born of the Spirit,[59] descended from heaven,[60] manifested in the fullness of time,[61] and so on, as well as the fact that Christians are called upon to witness the historical life and bodily resurrection of the Lord, produces in their consciousness a peculiar combination of concreteness and universality.

They feel that they are the bearers of a very concrete message (the deeds and sayings of a crucified young man, whom they called "rabbi" even though he was not) together with the wholly universal and general view of an all-pervading divine principle. Jesus is not another "person" from the Divine One, as theological language will afterward say in order to stress that in Jesus a fulfillment, a perfection, a new aspect of the universal belief is revealed, namely that the Divine—whose existence is taken for granted—has "appeared," "descended," been "incarnated," or "pitched his tent"[62] among us. Some Fathers dared say that all those who lived according to the *Logos* were Christians, even though they had been previously seen as atheists.[63]

The keynote here is that of *witnessing*.[64] "You will be my witnesses to the furthest ends of the earth," said Jesus to his disciples,[65] and they conceived their mission as the

---

[57] "Thus there is one God the Father, as we have shown, and one Christ Jesus our Lord, who comes by a universal dispensation and recapitulates all things in himself. But in all things Man also is comprised, a creature of God; therefore he recapitulates Man in himself. The invisible is become visible, the incomprehensible is become comprehensible, and the impassible passible; and the Logos is become Man, recapitulating all things in himself" Irenaeus, *Adversus haereses* III.16.6.

[58] See "[He] who did not receive his being in time, but was begotten of the Father before all ages in a manner eternal and incomprehensible" (Cyril of Jerusalem, *Catechesis* IV.7 [*PG* 33.461].

[59] See Mt 1:18–20; Lk 1.35.

[60] See "He who was the pre-existent, Controller of all things, at length descended to us from heaven" (Eusebius, *Laudes Constantini* XI.7 [in J. Quasten, *Patrology*, vol. 3, *The Golden Age of Greek Patristic Literature. From the Council of Nicaea to the Council of Chalcedon* Utrecht: Spectrum, 1960], 328).

[61] Gal 4:4.

[62] Jn 1:14, in the original Greek text.

[63] Justin, *1 Apologia* 46ff.

[64] This witnessing is in spite of themselves. See, e.g., the words by Lucian of Samosata, meant as an attack against the first Christians: "You see, these misguided creatures start with the general conviction that they are immortal for all time, which explains the contempt of death and voluntary self-devotion which are common among them; they are converted, and deny the Gods of Greece, and worship the crucified sage, and live after his laws. All this they take quite on trust, with the result that they despise all worldly goods alike, regarding them merely as common property" (in his *Works,* transl. by H. W. and F. G. Fowler [Oxford: Oxford University Press, 1905], 4:83).

[65] Lk 24:48; Ac 1:8.

duty of proclaiming Jesus of Nazareth as the manifestation of the Divine, embodied in a man, with power to forgive sins, to save humankind from damnation, and to give them eternal life.[66] But this Jesus, though a man, is also fully divine; he is nothing less than that preexisting, uncreated Being who has made himself manifest all over the world, who pervades everything and gives life to every living being. He himself was at the beginning of the world, in order to help in the creation of it, and He was widespread all over the universe.[67]

Thus the Christians, when witnessing to Christ, did not at all think that they were talking about something foreign and novel. On the contrary, they held the belief that they were proclaiming the expected good news of the promised Savior. The attitude of Paul, telling Athenians, "I am disclosing what you, unknowingly, were already worshipping,"[68] was the background of almost any Christian proclamation. The Christian message does not come to impose or even to preach a new "religion" (a concept that is rather new, and not to be found in the Christian canon), but to disclose something that was hidden in very many forms and ways.[69] Christ, in a way, belongs to all, because he is the revelation of "what is already there"—a revelation indeed, which, once known, is extremely demanding, for it asks for the recognition of its earthly manifestation and confronts us with the foolishness of the cross, upsetting all human wisdom. The first Christians would not dream of thinking that their faith was foreign to any religion or any human being. It is equally revolutionary for everybody, Jew or Greek, free citizen or slave, man or woman, and it is equally suitable for anyone, into whatever religion it is inserted.[70]

Once the Christian message was freed from the Jewish tutelage, it felt at home and, at the same time and to an equal extent, looked new and radical in any cultural and religious setting.[71]

---

[66] Mk 16:16, etc.

[67] Col 1:18.

[68] Ac 17:23.

[69] See Rom 1:16, etc.

[70] Cf. "Everywhere throughout the world the cross shines out, beyond the brightness of the sun. Among Kings and Generals and Rulers and Consuls, slaves and free private persons, wise and foolish, barbarians and all the various races of mankind, and whatsoever land the sun overlooks through this vast extent, His name is spread, and His worship" (John Chrysostom, *Contra Judaeos et Gentiles quod Christus sit Deus* [in Quasten, *Patrology*, 3:468]).

[71] To give an overall picture of Christian life during these first centuries it will be useful to quote some passages of the famous *Letter to Diognetus* 5–6: "For Christians cannot be distinguished from the rest of the human race by country or language or customs; they do not live in cities of their own; they do not use a peculiar form of speech; they do not follow an eccentric manner of life. They live in their own countries, but only as aliens. They have a share in everything as citizens, and endure everything as foreigners. Every foreign land is their fatherland, and yet for them every fatherland is a foreign land. To put it simply: what the soul is in the body, that Christians are in the world. The soul is dispersed through all the members of the body, and Christians are scattered through all the cities of the world."

If I were to express in contemporary words the thesis of this first period as to the relationship between Christianity and world religions, I would begin by saying that the Christian church did not perceive itself as one religion among others—not even as a "religion." In the Mediterranean world, in which Christianity spread, there were several religious traditions, some in obvious decay, others successfully blossoming. To all of them the Christian church announced the same message: the internal power (of Stoics), the hidden God (of mystics), the uncreated Wisdom and preexistent *Logos* (of Jews and others), the saving Mystery (of mystery cults), the power of the external icon and the might of the sacred formula (of popular religiousness), and even the authority of Caesar or any other authority (of the state religion) . . . *all* this comes from the Father of all lights[72] and is therefore connected with his Son and proclaims him. At the same time, those expressions have all been superseded by the fullness of the revelation in Jesus Christ. The Christian is simply the witness to this new and ultimate disclosure of the Divine. He has to be prepared to lay down his life for this truth as a response to the love of God, who has chosen him to shoulder the responsibility of such witnessing.

Christian consciousness in this period sees Jesus as the fulfillment of and, at the same time, the judgment on every religion.[73] No wonder the first Christians were often considered not only as atheists but as people of no religion, even as irreligious people.[74] This also explains why Christians adopted, with little misgiving, the religious practices of their environments when they did not look incompatible with their witness to the Lordship of Christ. They utilized everything they could as a way of expressing this Lordship, precisely because they found this attitude to be obvious and natural, consistent with the very nature of things. After all, was not Christ the *epiphany*, that is, the manifestation of that hidden Mystery at work everywhere? So, we find that in the liturgy, both the Jewish and any other pattern was followed, that the feasts were of non-Christian origin, that the iconographic models were all already

---

[72] Jas 1:17.

[73] "Not even in the past ages was the word without this same grace, which after the resurrection of our Lord Jesus Christ has spread everywhere and of which Scripture says, *Thy lightnings enlightened the world* [Ps 77:19]. Indeed the heaven and the earth, the sea and every creature that man can see or know, is for the service of mankind; and chiefly for this purpose, that the rational beings, when contemplating so many beautiful things, enjoying so many good gifts, receiving so many so many favors, must need learn to worship and love the Author of them all. The Spirit of God, *in whom we live and move and are* [Ac 17:28], fills the whole world. For, although salvation is far from sinners, yet nothing is devoid of His saving presence and power" (Prosper of Aquitania, *De vocatione omnium gentium* II.4 [*PL* 51:689–90]; *The Call of All Nations* II.4 [*Ancient Christian Writers* (1952), 14:95]).

[74] "That we are not atheist, seeing that we acknowledge one God, I have sufficiently demonstrated. Who, then, would not be astonished to hear that people who speak of God the Father, and of God the Son, and of the Holy Spirit, and declare both their power in union and their distinction in order, are called atheists?" Athenagoras of Athens, *Apologia* 10.

existing religious figures, and that their theology was simply a new interpretation of existing concepts, and so on.[75]

In other words, Christians felt themselves at home everywhere just because they were convinced of being both pilgrims and leaven. That is why they mixed freely with every kind of people and were present in all social levels, among peoples having very different religious origins, and never feeling as strangers or aliens among men. They stressed, following the Gospel, that they were *in* the world, not *of* the world;[76] but precisely because of this, they did not consider themselves outside the society in which they lived—and we know that society was then wholly permeated with religion.[77] To be a citizen implied a basic *communicatio in sacris*, a certain religious communion.[78] It has been said, not without reason, that Christian life flourished in Europe as long as "paganism" was a living reality. In fact, without a fundamental religiousness as a basic human attitude, the *kerygma*—that is, the Christian proclamation—remains barren.[79]

Precisely because of this intimate mingling and close collaboration, so many conflicts arose with the surrounding religions: neighborhood conflicts, as well as purification and criticism of their actual religious practices. The Patristic period unmistakably shows this tension. As Jesus was considered a new challenge and a new expression of every form of religiousness, it is obvious that Christians were bound to come into conflict with the conservative forces of every religious sect. No wonder, then, that the sharpest criticism against other forms of religiousness is also to be found in this period, from the very beginning.

---

[75] It is well known, for instance, that Christmas, Epiphany, the Ember-days, the Lord's Day (*Shabbat*), sacrifice, sacraments, etc., all have pre-Christian origins, and that the Jewish liturgy provided the pattern to the Christian one, Apollo was the model for the statutes of Christ, etc.

[76] See Jn 17; 11:14.

[77] See, e.g., "If somebody objects: He [Jesus] was crucified, but this is in common with [Hercules] the son of Zeus—as you call him—who suffered, as previously listed; since their fatal sufferings are narrated as not similar but different, so his unique passion should not seem to be any the worse—indeed I will, as I have undertaken, show, as the argument proceeds, that he was better, for he is shown to be better by his actions. If we declare that he was born of a virgin, you would consider this as something in common with Perseus. When we say that he raised the dead, we seem to be talking about things like those said to have been done by Asclepius" (Justin, *Apologia prima* 22).

[78] To forget this basic fact, in any society except the secularized one, had lethal consequences on the life, e.g., of Christian communities in Asia and Africa. As for India, see I. Puthanangady (ed.), *Sharing Worship. Communicatio in sacris* (Bangalore: National Biblical, Catechetical and Liturgical Center, 1988).

[79] This is forgotten by all those who think that Christianity was a block fallen "as is" from heaven. See T. Molnar, *The Pagan Temptation* (Grand Rapids, 1987).

From Arius to the Clash with Islam

The Arian controversy had a tremendous impact on the whole of Christian life. Not only was the Christian world astonished to find itself heavily infiltrated by Arianism, but the anti-Arian movement was forced to focus on fundamental aspects of Christian theology from a very specific perspective.[80] Out of fear of Arian interpretations, for instance, the formula of Christ as "Firstborn of all creatures"[81] was dropped from all confessions of faith, since Arius interpreted it as a proof that Christ also was a creature. Due to Arius also, and for the same reason, the double-stage theory concerning the generation of the *Logos* (see above) was practically abandoned. If the Logos had been begotten in a second moment, even in the very womb of the Godhead, this would seem to jeopardize His Divinity. Another victim of this controversy was the idea that the Logos was born "out of the will" of the Father, for the world had been created out of God's will, and the anti-Arian church had to stress the *difference* between Christ and creation.

All these apparently highly theoretical discussions had very practical and pastoral consequences. Christology began to be independent of the doctrine of the Trinity; Christ somehow became *the* God of Christians—to put it forcefully, though wrongly. His existence became independent, as it were, of the universal Divine Mystery. As Israel had started with a tribal God, now a tribal Christ was being conceived.[82]

The practical consequences for our problem are obvious. The followers of Christ were no longer primarily those who recognized in Jesus the epiphany of the preexistent and uncreated Divine Reality, but those who simply declared that Jesus was God, always of course with due theological safeguards, though these were almost forgotten in the popular and common approach. To be a Christian amounted to being converted to Christianity as a religion. *Conversion* is here the keynote.

Anyway, conversion is still seen not so much as a change of religion as a change of heart; it is not so much seen as a shifting from one religious group to another as

---

[80] See a brief summary of the Arian doctrine given by a contemporary author who played a central role in the Council of Nicea in 315, i.e., Alexander, bishop of Alexandria: "God was not always the Father; but there was a time when God was not the Father. The Word of God was not always, but was made from things that are not; for He who is God, fashioned the non-existing from the non-existing; wherefore there was a time when he was not. For the Son is a thing created; and a thing made; nor is He like to the Father in substance; nor is He the true and natural Word of the Father" (*Epistolae de ariana haeresi* II:3 [*PG* 18.574]), translation based on Quasten, *Patrology*, 3:16.

[81] Col 1:15.

[82] Currently, the great challenge implies that, as it happened with the Jewish God (probably at the times of prophet Isaiah), we succeed in passing from a tribal Christology to a universal, and therefore kenotic, Christ. See the doctorate thesis by R. W. Buckalew, *A Return of the Servant: Kenotic Christ and Religious Pluralism in the Thought of Raimundo Panikkar and Wilfred Cantwell Smith* (Union Theological Seminary in Virginia, 1987 [Ann Arbor: UMI, 1988]).

a new emphasis and the discovery of a hidden dimension of reality, a new birth;[83] in Christ we are a new creature.[84] Meanwhile, however, because of the events of the time, the Christian faith was becoming, *first*, an officially recognized religion; *second*, an official religion; and *third*, a religion of the officials. The period of the great mass conversions began. We should not misunderstand those movements, nor judge them according to our current views. For our purpose, suffice it to say that Christianity began to be seen as *the* religion, the fulfillment of religion, which is as good as saying the best religion.

The *conversio morum* was still championed by the monastic movements. Christianity was gaining political power, and power corrupts. The Christian needs a conversion in order to become a true follower of Jesus Christ. But Christ soon becomes a model for anything: the crown of thorns turns into a crown of glory, the cross accompanies the sword—and the sword the cross. The contemporary effort to integrate the whole of life under the claims of the Christian faith is well known. Christianity had to inspire and organize the whole of life. Laws were needed, and the inculcation of Christian principles into the different spheres of individual and social life was the great creative work of the times.[85]

The relationship of Christianity with other religions began to take on the character of the better religion vis-à-vis the imperfect, hence the false ones. Yet the dialogue continued, and the confrontation was fair.[86] Non-Christian people did not see Christianity as an enemy.[87]

From the Clash with Islam to the Discovery of America

It would take us too far to describe in detail the change of attitude and mind that occurred in Christendom when the encounter with Islam was entangled in a maze of political complications. Both powers were considering themselves, rightly or wrongly, as the defenders of a higher religious order, besides aiming at worldly

---

[83] Jn 3:5.

[84] See 2 Co 5:17; Gal 6:15.

[85] See a single example written by Orosius, disciple of Saint Augustine, about 417: "If the barbarians were sent to Roman soil for this sole end that the churches or the East and West should be filled with Huns, Suevi, Vandals, Burgundians, and diverse innumerable races of believers, we must praise and exalt the mercy of God since, though it were through our destruction, so many nations saw the truth revealed, and could certainly only discover it in this way." That quite strikingly matches the "reason" given by sixteenth-century Spaniards to justify the conquest and conversion of Indians. See the examples collected by Gustavo Gutiérrez in his *Dios o el oro en las Indias. Siglo XVI* (Lima: Instituto Bartolomé de Las Casas, 1989), 111, etc.

[86] See A. V. Seumois, *La Papauté et les missions au cours des six premiers siècles* (Paris/Louvian: Église Vivante, 1953), which gives the historical and theological references; G. Bardy, *La conversion au Christianisme durant les premiers siècles* (Paris: Aubier, 1949).

[87] See the monumental work, in seven volumes, by K. S. Latourette, *A History of the Expansion of Christianity* (New York: Harper, 1937–1945), for documents and references.

power or territorial expansion.[88] Religion and politics were now not only related but almost identified.[89]

The *crusade* is here the dominant keynote. The others are not simply non-Christians but "infidels," nonbelievers, with a connotation of *perfidy*, as the etymology of this word still betrays.

Yet the dialogue between Christians, Jews, and Muslims was not always stained with the fight for power. In medieval Spain, for instance, during several centuries these three religions conversed and even collaborated. It seems to be a fact that a turning point in the Christian theological understanding of religions occurred just when political struggles started to spoil Christian-Muslim relations.

The kingdom of God was also an earthly empire; it therefore needed an earthly power. The theology of what began to emerge as Christendom was an extraordinary bulwark, but it was a quasi-private affair for Christians only. The other religions were hardly considered; they were supposed to provide a field for the sword rather than for the cross.

Christianity here undergoes a fundamental crisis. It affirms its own identity by a process of contrast and rejection. It becomes the religion called upon to dominate the world together with the Empire—and to do so, undoubtedly, for the sake of justice, peace, understanding, and even salvation; but nevertheless, Christian theology, by and large, supports the *imperial* attitude of "Christian" monarchies.

The relationship between Christianity and other world religions in this period is quite one-sided. There is no other true religion besides Christianity. Only Christian faith saves you. At most, a "heathen" can be saved if he is under the "invincible ignorance" of the only one and true path shown by Jesus Christ. Only a good conscience in good faith, in circumstances in which it is absolutely impossible to acknowledge Christ, can perhaps, thanks to the infinite mercy of the Lord, save the non-Christian.

It is no use hiding or minimizing this attitude. We may add that it also has its greatness and even beauty: it represents an uncompromising attitude of loyalty toward God, a total self-giving for the sake of the kingdom, which sometimes implies violence, and demands our total docility and obedience, out of love and zeal for His glory.

---

[88] See, as a single example, the tone of the papacy of the time: "These pagans have made a vigorous onslaught on the Christian Empire: they have pillaged and laid waste the whole land with unheard-of cruelties up to the very gate of Constantinople. They have occupied these countries with tyrannical violence and massacred thousands and thousands of Christians like beasts. If, therefore, we have any love for God, if we are truly Christian people, the unhappy fate of this great Empire and the deaths of so many Christians must be for us all a great anxiety. Our Lord's example, who redeemed us, and the duty of Christian charity bid us not only to lament these misfortunes, but also, if it be necessary, to give ourselves in sacrifice for our brothers" (Gregory VII, *Bull to the Counts of Burgundy, St. Gilles and Savoy* [February 2, 1074]).

[89] J. Lecler, *Historie de la tolérance au siècle de la Reforme*, vols. I–II (Paris: Aubier, 1955); I.104 shows the sociological and psychological parallelism between the Muslim concept of holy war (*jihad*) and the Christian idea of crusade.

Is it not a law of nature that only a minimum of individuals pass from a lower to a higher stage? How much waste of matter and energy is needed in order to produce a small amount of organic matter! What an enormous display of organic matter in order to produce a little tiny thing called life, and how insignificant is still on earth the conscious or human "layer," which required so many millions of years and consumed so much energy before thought finally appeared! Could it not equally be that only a small minority reaches the supernatural realm? Salvation is not a birth right, it is grace. A hierarchical structure of the universe leads to monarchy in state and church, and to the salvation of the few.

The Christian is a militant. "Doesn't every man have to work hard on this earth?"[90] The Christian is a crusader. The superiors of the new religious orders are no longer called "abbots" (*abba*), "fathers," but "generals." All this, which becomes more and more manifest in the following eras, up to our own times, began in that period.

From the Discovery of America to the End of Modern Age

It was again a historical fact that awakened a new consciousness among Christians. When, at the end of the fifteenth century, Europeans discovered America, they found peoples with very elaborate religions, though some of them in a state of disintegration or decadence. At any rate, the situation was essentially reversed in comparison with Islam. Here Christians could no longer consider themselves as victims and justify their position by saying that they were defending their right to exist. They had to justify, not a crusade to reconquer the Holy Land or a war to defend themselves, but an outright conquest.

An offset of the crusade spirit is mission theology. *Mission* is here the leading keynote: the goal no longer being to conquer an empire, or to install Christendom and plant the church, no longer to kill bodies, but to delete evil from other religions and civilizations. Has not the church been a wonderful civilizing power? Does it not boast of having been the pioneer in the field of education, welfare, concern for others, and so many other human values? Wheat and tare are often intermingled, and it is not my task now to pass any judgment or to contest any of the good works that Christians may have undertaken in a spirit of evangelization.

During this period, all previous insights on other religions have certainly not disappeared from the theology of Christianity, but the dominant note is that of condemnation, without finding any place for the other religions in the Christian economy of salvation. An underlying current, a less negative one, can be also detected, but it is not the prevailing one.

Interestingly enough, this theology has two "moments." At first, everything that is not Christian is attacked, in the name of Christian faith, as the work of the devil, condemning all other religions as false and their followers as being on the road to hell, and so forth. In the second moment, in the name of the same Christian faith, the attacks are directed against Christendom itself, trying to make it collapse and

---

[90] Jb 7:1.

disintegrate. Now Christianity *also* is condemned as a work of the devil, and any religion is considered to be the result of human pride.

(Christian) faith is not religion: it is the primordial idea, then turned into politics by Luther, and into theology by Karl Barth.

From the End of the Modern Age to Our Times

Seldom can such unanimity be enjoyed as when we say that we have reached the end of the so-called Modern Age. The changes in our contemporary scene are radical in almost every sphere of life. No wonder that world religions are also in a hurry to revise their traditional positions. This is what has happened and is still happening within the various Christian churches as well as in theological schools.

The password today is *dialogue*, and dialogue requires not only an open mind, ready to both listen to others and learn from them, but also a readiness to be convinced and to engage in a common search for truth. In the minds of some, dialogue may still be a means of conversion or propagation of belief, but from the standpoint of theological thought, as well as those who are engaged in *real* dialogue, it is no longer—for the most part—a strategy, but a religious task in itself. That is, dialogue is in itself a religious action, a sacred act, a rite through which Man recognizes, first, his individual insufficiency, and second, his constitutive relatedness to his fellow beings in order to be fully himself.[91]

More and more often, in the life of the church today, we find such examples of dialogue and openness. The actions of the penultimate three popes[92] and the initiatives of the World Council of Churches, to give only two examples, should be sufficient to prove how deeply the situation and attitude have changed—from "perfidious infidels" to "beloved brothers."

It would merely be wishful thinking, or plain untruth, if we said that the current Christian consciousness has already developed a theology of religion capable of embracing and accounting for the religions of the world. At least the theological world is aware that such a theology does not exist. As I have tried to show elsewhere, what we have is *theologies* of religions, not a theology or, if we prefer, a philosophy of religions, capable of embracing from within the various facets of more than one religious tradition.[93]

The great problem for Christianity today is to find a middle way between an exclusiveness that needs to be rejected and a syncretism that would endanger the very nature of the Christian message. Very many efforts are being made in this direction,

---

[91] R. Panikkar, *The Intrareligious Dialogue* (New York: Paulist, 1978); revised and enlarged edition, 1999. Now in vol. VI, pt. 2 of this *Opera Omnia*.

[92] John XXIII, Paul VI, John Paul II.

[93] See an overview in L. Swidler (ed.), *Toward a Universal Theology of Religion* (Maryknoll, NY: Orbis Books, 1987); and my criticism to the claim to universality put forward by that very book: *The Invisible Harmony: A Universal Theory of Religion or a Cosmic Confidence in Reality?*, in Swidler, *Toward a Universal Theology*, 118–53.

but Christian consciousness at large is not yet open to such new winds.

A few, however, seem to be inclined toward a certain consensus among Christians. World religions cannot be considered simply wrong. They cannot be considered sufficient either, or complete; most theologians dealing with these matters might include Christianity in the statement. The question about the place of world religions in the Christian economy of salvation has definitely not found a unanimous answer in today's Christianity. The old ideas are considered insufficient by nearly everybody, but the effort to replace them with a different theological hypothesis is still too recent, too new, to permit us to speak of a consensus.[94]

Lessons of History

It should be emphasized that the five above-mentioned moments are neither dialectical nor strictly chronological, but rather *kairological*.[95] One moment does not exclude the other but complements and corrects it. These are all expressions of fundamental Christian attitudes, though they may sometimes have been one-sidedly overstressed and even wrongly interpreted. At any rate, we should not commit the methodological mistake of judging a past historical situation with present-day categories. There *can* be—to be sure—creative hermeneutics. The old concept of Christian mission, for example, can be reinterpreted not as antithetical to dialogue but as a mission of dialogue.[96]

Balancing the five above-mentioned elements and making them fit the current situation is a duty for contemporary Christian theology.

In spite of the simplified way in which we have rushed through history, we may be able to draw some leading ideas from the way Christians have envisaged their relations with other religions.

• The Christian message claims to be *universal* and thus is concerned with the existence of other religions.

• It seems that simple *coexistence*, in a sort of horizontal or democratic "let live and do not bother" attitude, is irreconcilable with the Christian truth.

• A positive, not a merely "negative," relation between Christianity and world religions has to be set. Meanwhile, the relationship of *substitution* has been practically

---

[94] See J. Hick and P. Knitter (eds.), *The Myth of Christian Uniqueness* (London: SCM, 1988).

[95] By this neologism, built out of the word *kairos* (a favorable, starting, right, real, and also eschatological time) over against *chronos* (period of time), I mean a perspective that sees history not as a mere report on a series of events but rather as a peculiar temporal disclosure of Man and the world. See J. Barr, *Biblical Words for Time* (London: SCM, 1962), according to which the Bible does not imply such dichotomy between *kairos* and *chronos*. I do not mean, anyway, to go into the well-known discussion about *kairos, chronos, aiôn*, etc.

[96] See the interesting contributions to the Sedos Research Seminar on the Future of Mission, published by M. Motter and J. Lang (eds.), *Mission in Dialogue* (Maryknoll, NY: Orbis Books, 1982).

abandoned, and one may wonder if it was ever a genuine Christian attitude. Christ had said that he did not come to destroy or abolish but to make perfect and fulfill.[97]

• The idea of *conquest* and therefore destruction of other religions would not find today any positive echo among the vast majority of Christians. The so-called method of the tabula rasa would be quite unacceptable today.[98]

• The word *conversion* today is certainly still current, though its concept has been interpreted in various ways down the ages. The predominant conception today would be that as found in the New Testament: a change of mind, a turning toward wholeness, a discovery of something better that was already in the interior of my being and that I bring to light by means of an external aid. World religions would accordingly be on their way to conversion, or facing the challenge of an ever-recurring conversion.

• This conversion should also apply to Christianity, so as to avoid any kind of self-complacency. Conversion, in this sense, would not mean a turning toward Christianity but toward that reality around which Christianity itself is also turning. I have elsewhere interpreted the evangelic *metanoia* not only as a conversion in the sense of changing one's mind but also as overcoming the mental level.[99]

• The central figure of Christ as Lord is still the apex of the whole Christian conception, but the understanding of Christ varies according to the degree in which this Christ is considered to be present in the different world religions.

• Another idea that history highlights is the *cross-fertilization* of religions. Christianity, like any other religion, has adapted itself to its surroundings, not only drawing inspiration from them, but also the materials on which to build its own life. Growth implies a positive metabolism, which should not be mistaken for the indigestion of eclecticism.

The present-day name for this is *dialogue.*

And not the least lesson of history is to remind us that it is not yet finished, that it is still on the move, with the last word not yet spoken. Everything is provisional for the time being. The interrelationship among the five kairological categories (and other fundamental attitudes that may possibly surface in the future) is not left to intellectuals or theologians, but belongs to the very realm of human life, to the destiny of history; it is the prophetic element of living religiousness.

In what follows I try to offer a certain elaboration on this question from a Christian point of view vis-à-vis the world religions. It is simply an essay, but it can be considered as an example of the trends of present-day theological reflection on the issue.

---

[97] Mt 5:17.

[98] See the Preface of A. C. M. Perbal to C. B. Papali, *Hinduismus* (Rome: Collegium Internationale OCD, 1960), 2:XI.

[99] I could recall the many conversations with *Abhiṣiktānanda* on this subject. See *La montée au fond du coeur* (Paris: OEIL, 1986). The last spiritual principle in the last song of Milarepa is, "Let go of concepts."

Theology

In order to introduce a certain orderliness, I distinguish three levels on which the dialogue may be carried on.

From a simply descriptive point of view, we may call them the Absolute, the instruments, and the relative—or, in other terms, the end, the means, and the factual situation. In still more traditional terminology, we can speak of the Mystery, the fundamental rite, and the concrete application of it.

Man is a pilgrim, or if we prefer, an unfulfilled creature. In order to attain his destiny, however we may envisage it, Man needs a certain awareness of his end and a certain willingness to move toward that end. In traditional Christian terms, these three moments refer to Christ, the church, and Christianity, or in more general terms, Mystery, sacraments, and religion. What is at stake here is not a discussion about the nature of the Ultimate, but an inquiry about its manifestation—in other words, an investigation about Man and his horizon.

One could equally well use terms of a not specifically Christian character, and point out that the three levels can be found in practically all religious traditions. I will, however, restrain myself from doing this, both for reasons of space and to avoid embarking on any comparative study, which is not the direct aim of this text.

The distinction looks important anyway. Many misunderstandings in the relation among religions can be avoided if we are aware of the level we are dealing with. The word "Christianity," in fact, is here misleading, as indeed are the labels being put on the other religious traditions. When we say "Christianity," we can refer to any one of the three levels—though its proper place is the third.

Christ Is the Mystery

The doxology in the Letter to the Romans, as well as the core of St. Paul's theology, does express it most clearly: "The Mystery hidden for eternal eons"[100] manifests itself in the "icon" of the invisible God, the Firstborn[101] of all creation and God's only begotten Son,[102] by whom everything was made and in whom everything subsists.[103] Such revelation of the Mystery was called, according to the culture of that time, "the Lord."

From the very beginning the first Christians, both by instinct and belief, used to call Jesus by the name of "Lord." The ambivalence of the word, irritating as it may be to some scholars preferring clear-cut concepts, is to be found in the Hebrew *adon* as well as in the Greek *kyrios* and in modern translations. This word expresses the *theandric* character of the subject to which the name is applied: God, king, husband, master, and so on. Paul, who never called Jesus by the very name of "God" (*ho theos*,

---

[100] Rom 16:25.
[101] Col 1:15.
[102] Jn 1:18.
[103] Col 1:17.

with definite article), did constantly call him "Lord," and he often used the latter term in such a way that it cannot be said with certainty if it was applied to God, to Jesus, or both.

In any case, the name—whatever conception we may have of it—stands for the Ultimate in its relation to Man. Since the beginning, *Adon[ay]* was one of the titles of YHWH, and the *Septuagint*, the Greek translation of the Old Testament, made it (*Kyrios*) even more popular. The Christian communities immediately applied it to Jesus, being fully aware that, by this, they were proclaiming his Divinity. In fact, the whole of Christian faith could be summarized by saying "Jesus is the Lord." But this sentence cannot, without qualifications, be stated in reverse—that is, the Christian faith does not say that "the Lord is Jesus," so as to exclude any power, manifestation, and reality of the Lord outside Jesus. From a Christian standpoint, Jesus is indeed the Lord in the sense that the ultimate Mystery of the world, by whatever name we may call it, has manifested itself in Christ (the risen Jesus).

The first level refers to what a *Hindū* calls *Śiva, Viṣṇu, ātman* or *mutkidata*; a Muslim, Allah; a Jew, *Ha-Shem* ("The Name," without pronouncing the *Tetragrammaton*); a Marxist, the future of humanity; a humanist, the truth; a philosopher, the absolute, nothingness, being, and the like. "This," which the traditional religious parlance calls "the Lord," refers to the supreme principle not so much as it is in itself, but as it manifests itself to us. Of course, *this* is neither a concept nor an essence, the doctrines of the various religions being in fact different. The names I have just mentioned as examples cannot be equated straightaway without distinctions and restrictions. Besides, a balance should be kept between the essential *quid* and the existential *quid*, and neither should be overstressed to the detriment of the other. The notions we have of reality also belong to reality, but they cannot be confused with reality as a whole, nor can they exhaust it. Neither reality is a pure product of the mind, nor is the mind a mere element of reality.

Neither an extreme realistic position nor an exclusive idealistic one will help to overcome the problem. The former oversimplifies the issue by assuming that there is a reality—the Lord, in this case—which is absolutely independent of ourselves. The latter impoverishes the richness of reality by dismissing all that the mind, in theory, cannot assimilate.

Therefore, if reality cannot be reduced to knowledge, however real that knowledge may be, reality will obviously be described by different and even opposite names and concepts. Reality, as transcending the power of our mind, cannot be exhausted within the limits of a single concept. It would amount to sheer "conceptolatry" to believe that a concept may be the perfect *medium quo* to embrace any reality, let alone the ultimate reality. Since the very beginning, this has been the pivotal principle of the Christian project.

It should be clear, however, that the concept "Lord," which in almost all religions has been developed within monarchical or feudal societies, must no longer be interpreted as the consecration of an outdated mind-set. Let us remember, in fact, that the Lord is the manifestation of God, the revelation of the Mystery, its personal side, rather than a specific term belonging to a hierarchical society, in which any authority has a divine origin.

According to Christian belief, at this level, the Lord is everywhere, pervading everything and transcending the whole universe; this Lord exercises his lordship in and through all possible agencies, especially the world religions. What is called "the Lord" stands—almost by definition—for anything that has any type of ultimate lordship over Man, whatever conception we may have of this "thing" and of its lordship.[104] Elsewhere[105] I have tried to work out the structure of a *theological argument*, presupposing an agreement already reached as to the *what* of our religious discourse: *what* we ultimately refer to, in order to affirm or negate something about *that*, which we conceive in one form or another. Otherwise, we would not deal with the same thing; we would simply talk at cross-purposes.

Christian belief says, further, that a sui generis manifestation of the Lord takes place in Jesus the Christ. The specificity of this Lordship constitutes the distinctive feature of Christianity. In a word, Christ, according to Christians, stands for the universal principle, the ultimate core of everything, the beginning and end of reality.

Church, the World Sacrament

Christian self-consciousness does not stop at the statement that Christ is the Lord. It adds—and this statement belongs to the second level—that there is on earth a peculiar, "mysteric" community that transmits the message of the Lord.

The very English word "church" expresses the ambivalence of the concept. On the one hand, it is etymologically derived from the late Greek word *kyriakon*, which means "the Lord's (house)." Yet "church" also claims to be the semantic translation of the classical Greek word *ekklêsia*, which had no sacred meaning, except when it translated two Hebrew words: *qahal* and *edah*. It meant an assembly of "full-privileged citizens" in Greek, and a religious assembly of believers in Hebrew. The ambivalence depends on its double meaning as "house" on the one hand and "assembly" on the other. Modern theology has not yet found a satisfactory conception of the church that can embrace these two fundamental, and apparently almost opposite, features: the church has a body and a soul, it has been suggested; it is visible and invisible, it is the body of Christ, but a Mystical Body, whose limbs may belong to realms unsuspected by many. The church is holy and at the same time sinful; it is the bride of Christ and at the same time a *casta meretrix*, and so on.[106]

---

[104] See R. Panikkar, *The Unknown Christ of Hinduism* (London: DLT, 1964), where I try to examine the possible correlation between an aspect of the Christian concept of Christ and the *Hindū* notion of Īśvara; vol. VII, *Opera Omnia*.

[105] See R. Panikkar, *El silencio de Dios* (Madrid: Guadiana, 1970); *The Silence of God, The Answer of the Buddha* (Maryknoll, NY: Orbis, 1989). A new version completely reviewed in *Il Silenzio del Buddha. Un a-teismo religioso* (Milan: Mondadori, 2006), and in vol. V of *Opera Omnia*.

[106] See, among others, H. U. von Balthasar, *Sponsa verbi* (Einsiedeln: Johannes, 1961);

It is not necessary here to develop a whole ecclesiology, but only to indicate certain features of this second level. The best description is maybe the one showing the church as the "sacrament" of the whole world, or (taking the term from the original Greek[107]) the *mystery* existing at the very core of the world—which, in the language of the New Testament, is called the kingdom of God. I am well aware of the difficulties in identifying the church with the kingdom, and that the expression is again ambivalent. I only maintain that there is a sacramental structure of reality, a historical ground common to all human beings, and a deep human dimension that is the truest core of any authentic existence. There is, in other words, an immanent level of triteness, of everyday common business; and another level of ultimate human concern, of authentic human life, and religious existence.

Now, Christian faith here again says two things in one single expression. On the one hand, it says that the church is the authentic world, that for which God created the universe, which existed from the very beginning, the transformed and deified cosmos, the kingdom that is within us, the invisible seed that grows even without ourselves being aware of it,[108] the gathering of all those who did good works, even if they were not aware[109] that those actions were religious (Christian); the already transformed dimension of every man, the cosmic mystery of the unity among all men of goodwill (and who lacks it?). On the other hand, it is the house, the concrete and visible organism (not necessarily organization) of the consciously believing Christians, the belief in that which the hierarchy of that very church declares to be trustworthy; a little flock, a handful of people with a priestly role of mediation and with one specific mission of witnessing—even up to death—that the second coming of the Lord is at hand. We have here undoubtedly two different notions of church.

It is not my task here to analyze this tension further on. It is enough to say that the question of the relations among world religions should be better explored in the light of this distinction of levels. When, for instance, it is affirmed, according to an ancient *dictum*, that "outside the church there is no salvation" or that "all good and true utterances, by whomsoever made, belong to Christians"; or when it is repeated that "whatever truth is inspired by the Holy Spirit" or that "the church admits, accepts, and welcomes everything having any positive value, from whatever culture," the first concept of church is implied. The statement does not affirm, properly speaking, that the church *is the place* of salvation, but that, wherever salvation takes place, *there* is the church. This conception of the church is not confined to Christianity as a religion; it has no other limits than the limits of the whole humanity on pilgrimage, following their own paths, and sincerely searching for light, truth, and goodness.

J. Leipoldt, *Von den Mysterien zur Kirche* (Hamburg: Reich, 1962); H. Rahner, *Symbole der Kirche* (Salzburg: Müller, 1964); from a different viewpoint, but very useful, see also A. Dulles, *Models of the Church* (Garden City, NY: Doubleday, 1974).

[107] The Greek word *mysterion* had been translated as *sacramentum* into Latin.
[108] See Mk 4:27.
[109] See Mt 25:37–44.

On the other hand, if the above statements are interpreted as conferring—upon the visible church—a sort of monopoly on everything positive, not only would this be a preposterous notion, but it could be clearly shown that the church itself has rejected authoritatively such a claim, condemning, for instance, the proposition that "outside the church there is no saving grace."

Yet the church does affirm itself to be a particular sign "raised up among the nations," the true "people of God," a visible community, a special and distinctive body united by love—a living, and therefore concrete and limited organism.

We have, then, two almost opposite notes of one and the same concept: universality and concreteness. This becomes clearer from the two given quotations.

The subject of the two statements—"Outside the church, no salvation," and "There is no grace outside the church" (the first having been approved, the second condemned)—cannot be the same; otherwise we would fall into the most flagrant contradiction. The church "outside which there is no salvation" can by no means be the visible one, for there *is* grace outside the church, and grace—by its very Christian definition—is the instrument of salvation. Nor can it be said that the (visible) church is the proper place of grace, if by "proper" one understands an exclusive property.

Here is, once again, the already mentioned tension between the concrete and the universal. "What is the place of the church in the heart of world religions?" This would be the Christian way of putting it. The same question could be put differently by asking how the world religious communities deal with salvation to their members. We have here an open question for a dialogue in depth.

The historical fact of the identification, in practice, of the visible Christian church with one particular culture and religion makes it difficult for the established church to enter into a dialogue with the other religions without abdicating, or getting rid of what I have elsewhere[110] called "the Mediterranean garb." The church recognizes its own universal nature by stressing that its core is the Eucharist, and that the sacramental Body of Christ builds up its Mystical Body, and vice versa. It underscores that the cross of the Lord and his resurrection are the center of the church.

To put it briefly, the notion of church is independent—both by its nature and its action—of any particular culture and, as such, it is compatible with any civilization.[111] The first principle may be called the *principle of transcendence.*

The church, however, cannot exist as disembodied, without shaping at least one culture; it needs culture as the expression of its being. I would add that the present-day culture in which the church is presented or "dressed" does not satisfy

---

[110] See R. Panikkar, "Deporre il manto mediterraneo. L'unica chance del cristianesimo: la sua cattolicità," in *Humanitas* 11 (1962).

[111] See some affirmations of the Roman hierarchy: "If in certain periods of time or in certain parts of the world this or that civilization or ethnic group or social layer of society has had a predominant influence upon the Church, this does not mean that the Church has become entangled in, or dependent upon any of those groups, nor even that she has become frozen at a certain moment of the human history, being therefore impervious to any further development" (Pius XII at the Consistory of June 20, 1951).

any longer the needs of the people; indeed, is not adequate to fulfill its mission outside the realm of Mediterranean culture—nor inside, it seems. This can be said to be the *principle of incarnation.*

The church does not identify itself with any culture, and no religion or civilization can be an adequate vehicle of that for which the church stands. There is always an inadequacy, a dissatisfaction, and not only a margin of imperfection but also of error, that is, in-authenticity, hurried conclusions, false injunctions, and so on and so forth. The church has to transform all of its structures. We could sum this up under the heading of the *principle of redemption.*

These three principles could give us a starting point for dealing with the urgent and delicate problem of the relation between church and religions. This is what was meant by the definition of the church as Sacrament of the world.

There is a mystery of the world: the cosmos has a sacramental structure. This is the church, according to Christian thought. I have pointed out the ambivalence of the word and of the concept of church. Christianity cannot dispense with the notion and reality of the church, but does not need to interpret it in an exclusive or restrictive way—and, in fact, it has never done so, in spite of certain "microdoxic" interpretations. The discussion remains open.

In a word, the church, the Mystery of the world, stands for the *historical principle:* the historical ground of humankind on pilgrimage on earth.

Christianity as Religion

It is important to recall that long before the word "Christianity" and the notion contained in it became popular, the concept of Christendom prevailed. It meant not only Christian doctrine but Christian life embodied, as it were, in the social order. It was considered as synonymous with the Mystical Body of Christ. It was not simply what today we would call "religion," but a whole lifestyle permeated by the principles of what we today call "Christianity." Christendom was the church, not in theory or in abstract, but in life and practice. This amounts to saying that religion does not necessarily refer only to a set of beliefs and practices of an almost artificial kind, but it can mean a way of life pervading the entire range of human experience—from universal, intellectual tenets down to concrete social manifestations. In a word, we cannot forget that, whatever origin a religion may have had, and whatever transcendence it may claim to possess, it is also a cultural and sociological setup with rules, cultural regulations, social demands, and the like.

This third level is, in point of fact, the level of religion as a cultural element, as a factor shaping cultural life with its laws (either customary or written), its rites and approach to the different events of life, and so on. The religious principle, or religious intuition, or inspiration, cannot but have a major influence on the life of people. What is generally called "religion" is just one aspect of this religious crystallization, in only one sector of human life.

Obviously, such a religious structure, inspired by the tenets of a particular religion, can claim to be valid only within the frame in which it has grown, or in which it has itself been shaped. The Christian laws on marriage, for instance, or the sacramental symbols of water, oil, bread, and wine, are expressions and manifestations of a certain religious worldview, but they do not constitute the core of the religious message, for they are tinged with the cosmological, anthropological, or simply social presumptions of a particular human group.

Now, again, the relationship is a delicate one, because here the concrete and limited stands for the universal and infinite. Both may and must be distinguished, but cannot and should not be separated. What is essentially connected and what is not, what is at a certain precise time and particular place the necessary vehicle and what is not, is a very delicate and risky operation to determine, though it is not for that reason to be avoided.

Does Christianity as a religion imply the present-day marriage laws, or the present-day forms of worship, while distinguishing itself from any other cultural and religious setup, or does it not? It cannot be decided a priori. If it can be shown that the so-called essence is maintained intact when changing a particular feature, then there could be no objection to that change. But if "the baby is to be thrown out with the bath water," then that feature will have to be defended as a fundamental tenet of that religion. The two above-mentioned examples are in themselves clear enough, and require no further explanations.

We are here dealing, ultimately, with the touchy problem of self-identity. Can any organized religion, for the sake of understanding and dialogue, give up that which constitutes its self-identification as a religion? Is Christianity ready for a de jure, and not only de facto, acknowledgment of other forms of worship, marriage laws, ethical codes, and so on—that is, for the recognition of other religious rites in their full right? Each problem has to be dealt with on its own, and one has to go back to the sources in order to see what type of relationship can exist between different religious bodies.

The dialogue that has been officially opened nowadays does very often carry with it the "burden" of an existing organism (which is at the same time an organization), an organism that can only preserve its identity by differentiating itself from other religious bodies. It is obvious, however, that the exigencies, at this level, are quite unlike those at the two previous levels.[112]

In a word, Christendom, as "the religion," is a *sociological* fact, analogous to any other similar sociological crystallization.

Some Conclusions

If the distinctions I suggested are correct, I may formulate three Christian statements regarding our problem:

---

[112] See, for instance, the debate on polygamy in African Christianity, or the new rethinking on marriage problems, from divorce to birth control, to abortion.

1. Christ is the Lord.
2. The Church is the organism of salvation.
3. Christendom is a religious structure that directs various aspects of human existence, aiming at salvation.

At the same time, these statements as *not* saying that

(a) The Lord is only [in] Jesus.
(b) The church is the visible Christian church.
(c) Christendom is the only valid religion (called Christianity).

From a philosophical point of view, one could express the Christian belief by saying that it claims to give a *concrete* expression to the universal truth. The *logos*, which can be interpreted in many ways (an image, the concept, the expression, the word, etc.) became flesh, incarnate, concrete, took shape and form in time and space, but it did not cease to be God, the Divine, the Transcendent. How to combine both is the philosophical kernel of Christian Mystery, and ultimately of any religious attitude.

To stress only one aspect is to do violence to the Christian claim. The specific element of Christian faith is that it believes itself able to hold the two poles together, without falling into contradiction. Here also, the best symbol—from more than one perspective—is the cross, the crossing of all the opposites, the Divine and the human, the universal and concrete, the eternal and the temporal, the cosmic and the historical . . . and the "folly of the cross" also consists in going on believing that such an embrace is possible, even though the price—once more—is the giving up of one's life on the cross. Is this not, in point of fact, a fundamentally religious, and even radically human attitude?

World Religions

Having stated the problem from a rather general point of view, we will now work out some principles of a Christian answer that may make sense for our times. We will have to avoid slipping into a confused and syncretistic opinion, misled by a sentimental ecumenism, as well as stubbornly defend the position, equally misled by a not less sentimental fidelity to tradition. The former attitude would lead us to an unproductive eclecticism, and the latter would push us toward a stifling "provincialism."

In any case, this theological pattern draws inspiration from the most traditional Christian principles, so that it looks perfectly justified to talk about the *place of world religions in the Christian economy of salvation.*

Below we will be quite succinct; we will use the traditional Christian parlance, but I insist on saying that we could as well use a nonmonotheist or even nontheist language, and come to analogous results nonetheless. It must be remembered that our goal is to speak in the present name of Christian self-consciousness, and to show that tradition can safely go on (this being a redundancy, incidentally) by opening itself to the world religions.

Three Christian Axioms

The Possibility of Salvation

God Wants All Men to Be Saved

This principle can be justified by starting both from the very concept of God and from Christian Scriptures.

If there is a God who creates every man, and destines him to attain that fullness of life that is generally called *salvation*, it seems to be an imperative of justice that every man is provided with the means to reach salvation. This is simply a corollary of the Christian understanding of Christ and his justice. I would say that precisely this is the theological bearing of the doctrine of monogenism: the fact that man has a common destiny (not only a single biological origin).

Christian Scriptures say, again and again, that God has a universal saving will; that He does not make distinction of persons;[113] that people from the East and the West will come to His kingdom,[114] an innumerable crowd not only made up of righteous believers but also harlots and publicans,[115] that is, sinners; and not all who call Him "Lord, Lord" will enter the kingdom,[116] since He scrutinizes the most intimate intentions, and only these latter are decisive. Moreover, since we cannot know intentions by ourselves, He told us not to judge anybody, nor call anything impure among the creatures, which all come from God.[117]

Or, in the words of the Vatican Council II (*Nostra Aetate*, 1), "One is the community of all people, one their origin, for God made the whole human race to live over the face of the earth. One also is their final goal, God. His providence, His manifestation of goodness, His saving design extend to all Men, until that time when the elect will be united in the Holy City, where the nations will walk in His light."

The Projects of Salvation Are the World Religions

This corollary is self-evident. If the will of God is not a whimsical caprice, it must supply the average man with the ability to attain human fullness. Now, world religions claim that *they* provide their followers with salvation, in whatever form this salvation may be conceived. No other agency in the world claims to save Man.

---

[113] See Rom 3:22, etc.
[114] Lk 13:29.
[115] See Mt 21:31.
[116] Mt 7:21.
[117] See Ac 10:15.

This is so certain that, if any system, ideology, or whatever thought pattern claims to bring salvation to Man, this, too, should be considered as a "religion" for those who, in good faith, follow it. Christian humanisms, and the various types of Marxism, materialism, and so on are in this sense all religions, offering a milieu in which human life fulfills itself according to its very nature.

It would be anthropologically unlikely, and ethically improper, to assume that salvation is normally conveyed to Man through a channel different from his own religion. This does not mean that people cannot change their religion, or that they are not obliged to strive for a constant reform and better life both for themselves and those around them, and thus to bring about an ever-recurring renewal of their religion. This, however, means, first of all, that it is unthinkable that the message of salvation may reach the immense majority of men outside the normal, ordinary ways. In that case, in fact, the message would prove unintelligible, and even suspect. For a great part of humankind, lacking individual consciousness to the extent that any individualistic decision, or even revelation, would be meaningless, it would be just a dream to think that the normal path of salvation may be discovered through individualistic efforts *against* the whole tradition that molded one's ways of thinking, judging, and living. Can, for example, the average citizen, within the technocratic system, skip the ways of thinking induced by mass media?

Moreover, it would be quite *awkward* to assume that, in order to reach the fullness of my being, I have to despise or throw away my personal tradition, to deny my own background and follow another religion that is known to me only from the outside and has no roots in my soul nor in my people. Christian doctrine is the first to ask its followers for this kind of wisdom.

In other words, the thesis that world religions are the normal and ordinary means of salvation for those who bona fide follow them is a logical corollary of the Christian position. However, it does not deny that there may be false or degenerate religious forms, or that there may be cases in which the individual, or even a community, must rebel against a manifestly unjust order, a basically wrong situation, or the like.

It goes without saying that no religion saves by its own power, but each simply provides the means to salvation, because only the grace of the Lord, that is, the Lord himself, saves—or however this may be expressed in other languages. What we say here is that religion is not magic, although it quite easily runs the risk of becoming such.

The Universality of Faith

There Is No Salvation without Faith

This principle also can be shown on the basis of a general philosophy of religion, and of Christian Scripture.

The history of religions substantiates, and the philosophy of religion explains, that salvation is not an automatic process, something like a happy end to any possible life. Whatever idea we may form about the contents of salvation, and how it can be reached, and even about what exactly it is, the general notion of salvation is that of the ultimate human condition, the goal of Man, his fullness, the total meaning of his life, be it called God, heaven, humanity, justice, annihilation, absurdity, or anything else. In one thing, religions—taken in the broad sense of the word, as suggested above—agree: salvation is the result of an act of faith, be it acceptance of a fate, a decision, a grace, a choice, or knowledge, experience, enlightenment, intuition, or liberation from ignorance.

Phenomenology of religions will speak of a rupture of plans, of passing from the natural to the supernatural order, of crossing the river, of being enlightened, of satori, salvation, and so on. Now, in order to attain this, faith is required—that is, the awareness, grace, thrust, impulse, realization, knowledge, instinct, sentiment, or whatever, "that" which makes us realize the goal of our life and puts us in a position to get it—to jump, as it were, from our factual condition to that other situation that is the destiny of human being. It goes without saying that this situation does not need to be interpreted as an afterlife or as an ontologically separated reality. Man is a pilgrim here on earth, not yet a finished being; faith is the ticket that takes him toward his final destination. In a word, faith—by definition—is that which brings salvation to Man. It is not salvation itself, but the door, or the key, through or by which we reach our final stage.[118]

Few convictions are more clearly expressed throughout the Christian Scriptures than this: faith is required for salvation. "Your faith has saved you" (which was said by Jesus with reference to miraculous healings) has been understood, since the very beginning, as the very condition for salvation. Only those who believe can be saved; "without faith, it is not possible to please God";[119] even "good works, without faith, are useless";[120] Man cannot reach his goal without faith, and so on. "Only faith can save" has almost become the central motto of Christianity, equally shared by Orthodox Churches, Catholics, and Protestants. This conviction lies at the base of the expansion of Christianity throughout the world.

Faith Is a Constitutive Human Dimension

There is a human tendency, confirmed by sociology, according to which something having a very great value is the privilege of very few. Good is rare, is dear. Thus it is a common belief, which can be found in practically all traditional religions, that the number of "the chosen" is a very small one. We find it in Hinduism, Buddhism, Islam, and others.

Our times have witnessed radical changes in both the cosmological and the anthropological fields. The instinctive trend today inclines toward believing that a

---

[118] See R. Panikkar, *Myth, Faith and Hermeneutics* (New York, 1979), 185–229, where *faith* is described as a constitutive human dimension of openness, the *act of faith* as the realization of such openness, and *belief* as the (mostly intellectual and public) articulation of faith in a given time and space. Now in vol. IX, pt. 1, of this *Opera Omnia*.

[119] Heb 11:6.

[120] See Rom 3:28, etc.

positive value does not need to be the monopoly of a few or the privilege of a group. This change directly affects our problem. Present-day humankind can hardly believe that a failure like hell, even if theoretically accepted as possible, may be the lot of the majority—or that liberation can be attained only after thousands of reincarnations.

However this may be, in its essence, faith is not a privilege for a few selected people, but a saving power and free gift of God (to put it in theistic terms), given as freely as one's very existence. Only when the rational nature of Man was overemphasized did we begin to forget that faith consists not so much in a correct answer in the realm of doctrines (orthodoxy) as in the integration and sincere searching in the realm of life (orthopraxis); that faith does not only lie in the intellect or will, but in the whole man. Faith, in short, means the existential openness of Man, his openness toward the *not yet*—toward the transcendent, I would add, if the word had not so many other connotations. Every man recognizes that he is a nonfinished—that is, a nonfinite—being, a being still in the making, still provisional; he is *not yet*, for he longs, desires, strives for an ever- transcendent goal, which many religions call God. Every man is a "man of faith" inasmuch as he is aware that he has still to fulfill his life. In Christian terms, one could venture the formulation that the "baptism of desire" is not the desire of baptism, but the baptism of all deepest desires. And what does Man desire, but longing for happiness?

This itinerant character of Man amounts to recognizing that he is not (yet) full, perfect, achieved, arrived, happy, complete, . . . God. It is faith that makes him aware that he is not God, and that he tends toward a *more* or *another*, under whatever form or name.

To this faith as a *dimension* belonging to Man's very constitution, Man responds by the *act* of faith.

Indeed, putting the *locus* of faith in the realm also of orthopraxis does not imply to abandon orthodoxy, nor does it make the correct answer to the existential quest less important. Far from it—the corollary to this axiom (that faith is absolutely necessary for salvation) only points out that faith is a general gift to Man, together with the gift of existence, that it is a constitutive human dimension, although it requires an act of faith, a response, that has to be given in "good faith."

This saving act of faith, as a starting point, is not denied to anyone. That would be injustice. The problem is that this act expresses itself within a belief, and human beliefs are so different from one another. So, can an authentic act of faith be channelled through a "wrong" belief? This is nowadays a basic theological question, and a philosophical one as well, as the very nature of truth is at stake here.

The Uniqueness of the Lord

Christ Is the only Mediator

If rightly understood, this idea also could be proved by means of pure philosophical thinking by stressing that if Man has one goal (whatever this may be), all the ways leading to this goal ultimately have to present an underlying oneness. I will not press this argument, however, for it is not essential to our purpose here. Suffice it to say that no Christian approach to this problem can dispense with the central tenet of Christianity: the "mediatorship" of Jesus, the Christ. He is the only mediator, the only Name;[121] nobody goes to the Father except through Him; He is the door,[122] the way and truth and life—in short, the Savior.

Christianity would simply disappear if it did not bear witness to the Lord in Jesus. He is the historical manifestation of the Lord, existing and acting since the beginning of the world.

There could perhaps be an interpretation of Christianity "without God," meaning the God of the Old Testament, but it would amount to sheer contradiction in terms to speak of a Christianity without Christ, or of Christ as Lord but without Jesus of Nazareth. This concreteness has been, in the past, the stumbling block preventing Christian dialogue with other religions, but we cannot—not even for the sake of dialogue—neglect the problem by neglecting Jesus, or overlooking the central Christian affirmation that Jesus is the revelation of the Mystery; in traditional terms, he is the Lord.

The Presence of Christ

These basic assumptions of Christian faith enable us to expound the following thesis: the Mystery that manifested itself in Christ is present, effective, albeit hidden and unknown, in the world religions as well.

This is not only a rational way to avoid the disastrous consequences of a literal and "fundamentalist" interpretation of this third axiom, but it is also, irrespective of the consequences, the theological conclusion of the same.

The philosophical difficulty in accepting this statement may lie in the fact that the principle of individuation is generally taken in a very narrow, if not materialistic, way. But what makes me *me* is not the matter of my body, nor the atoms of my bodily being, which after some years have all gone and been replaced by others; even less is it the contents of my consciousness, which also, after some years, generally change radically.

The principle of individuation, which makes me *me* and gives me a certain continuity through the changes, is something that belongs to another order. We may accept a philosophical theory of momentariness (and deny any *substratum*) or an underlying *ātman* or substance: in any case, we have to recognize that the principle of individuation lies much beyond the realm of manifestation, of appearance.

Similarly, when we say that the Mystery that revealed itself in Jesus is also present, effective, hidden, and unknown in any religion, we are not assuming that the atoms, or flesh, or thoughts of Jesus are present everywhere. We do not say that Jesus of Nazareth is the universal prototype, nor that He is everywhere, or that we should

---

[121] Ac 4:12.
[122] Jn 10:7.

introduce Him everywhere. We say that what makes Jesus *Christ* is not absent in any authentic religion, and any religion can discover in Christ a homeomorphic equivalent to its own innermost core, helping itself—in case—to deepen, improve, and fulfill its own basic insight.

If this is true, then the duty of the so-called Christian calling does not vanish, but shifts to a more ecumenical and deeper level.

It may be worth underscoring that the thesis has a general meaning, thus avoiding the possible misunderstanding of considering Christianity (as a religion) as an exception. We are here referring to the three different levels we mentioned above. "Christ" is the name Christians give Mystery; this name is something more than a nominalistic label. It includes—so to speak—aspects of that Mystery that had remained hidden so far, as St. Paul would put it.[123] That does not deny, however, that what we call Mystery also has other aspects, and is different from the more or less rough concepts of it held by this author or the other. Apophatism is not a theological, nor a philosophical luxury. Christian language maintains its validity, and from a certain standpoint, it can and must be seen as definitive, but it is not the only language.

This having been explained, I can succinctly develop my insight.

The Mystery is *present* everywhere. In any given situation, in any human being, in any encounter, in anything, there always is more than what meets the eye; there is always a mysterious presence, a superior instance, a higher reality. Nothing is exhausted by what can be seen at the level of appearance. The Mystery is present. The theological task is to detect this presence, and to worship and love it wherever it can be found. Moreover, this activity obviously requires collaboration with theologians of every religion.

I used the words "worship" and "love" on purpose, to remind modern Man, Christian or not, that accepting reality respectfully and loving everything that *is* are fundamental features of human existence, however different can and must be the ways in which they are interpreted. This very attitude gives the freedom and trust needed in order to cooperate, together with the other elements of reality, to the transformation of reality itself. Here's something that does not only belong to our "job" but to our "making": the making of ourselves by making the world, and transforming reality by transforming our being. This process clearly surfaces when we overcome our ego and stop identifying with it.

The Mystery is *effective* everywhere. His presence is not a merely passive one; it is an active presence. This supreme instance is not simply a spectator to our efforts, nor a "judge" who will intervene later, but an effective presence, an active factor in our lives and in the existence of everything.

It is not a matter of applying to magical powers or prescientific attitudes. Science is the first and most authoritative example, in our days, of the effectiveness of something that surpasses the scientific realm. The calling of the Christian is to cooperate with the Mystery and with men, and remove the obstacles from the work of the

---

[123] Rom 16:25.

Spirit, from the action of His grace, in Christian language—or, to put it another way, perform the good works of mercy, love, and service.

The Mystery is *hidden* in every religion. This power is not subject to the ordinary ways of verification. Reality is richer than ourselves and transcends our consciousness of it. Whole dimensions of reality are actually hidden; our being itself lies hidden in our possibilities, in our unknown values.

The Christian may, at this point, feel the need to lift up the veil. But if there were nothing hidden and nothing veiled, lifting the veil would have no meaning whatsoever. The Mystery can reveal itself only if it exists, if it is present, albeit hidden. The Christian does not believe in a foreign Lord or introduce a new God: he just reveals what was hidden since the beginning of the world.[124] It is almost unnecessary to add that the Christian is not the only instrument of divine revelation, and to remind that many others were performing miracles in the name of the Lord without the apostles knowing it; in fact, they were rebuked by Jesus when they tried to hold a certain monopoly.[125]

The Mystery is *unknown.* Reality, truth, value, and so on are not only latent and sleeping, as it were, in our interior, or in the depths of every being; they are also unknown. We are all too often unconscious of what we are: we simply *do not know*, in a way that does not even allow for a certain awareness of the Unknown. Sometimes we surmise the existence of something greater than ourselves, but other times we do not even suspect the existence or reality of that power. There are ignorances that only a revelation can overcome. In the end, the Lord was even unknown to those who had so long been walking with and talking to Him.[126] The Christian calling consists of proclaiming the good news in every circumstance, especially to every suffering person, keeping that indestructible optimism according to which everything will turn out well. The good news has to be not only good, joyful, and enjoyable (all this is implied in the word), but also new, something not yet known, and renewing itself everyday.

The four adjectives I have been using carry on the echo of the four famous adjectives of the Council of Chalcedon concerning the two natures of Christ, the divine and the human: inseparable, indivisible, unchanged, and unconfused.[127]

We end by saying that the experience of Mystery does not cease being a need for any consciously religious person, and that the things that have been here expressed in Christian terms could be expressed in some other religious terminology, or even by means of purely humanistic or secular concepts. There would be differences indeed, but fundamentally, all those expressions would point in the same direction.

---

[124] See Mt 13:35.
[125] Lk 9:55.
[126] See Lk 24:16.
[127] See *Denz.*, 148.

Religious Pluralism

The history of Christianity, focused under the perspective of our problem, could be summed up starting from an invariant that can be spotted in all ecumenical councils and other decisive moments in church history. We may say that it is always about the same problem, showing the same dynamism, finding the same solution, and all because of the same reason. A good case is the so-called Council of Jerusalem (Ac 15).

In a very condensed way, I would say that, each time, it was about

- *The same problem.* "Unless you are circumcised according to the custom of Moses, you cannot be saved."[128] And afterward: unless you are "circumcised" according to the philosophy of Plato, or Aristotle, or Thomas, or Luther, or Marx, or Heidegger, you cannot be saved, because you will not be able to express adequately the Christian Mystery, and so you will fall into heresy.

- *The same dynamism:* The growth of the church outside certain walls—the boundaries of Judaism in the first case, and geographical or political or cultural or philosophical barriers afterward. The church was at home within Judaism until its growth made it feel uncomfortable there. There were too many people coming from other horizons. The price for survival was to break its links with Judaism, up to a certain point. Later on, the "walls" are geographical or political or cultural or philosophical, but those bounds become unbearable, too, when too many people live *extra muros*, outside the walls, as belonging to different worlds.

- *The same solution.* On the one hand, a step forward, breaking out into a new ground, abandoning old positions: "We should not trouble those peoples who turn to God."[129] On the other hand, a compromise in order to save the continuity, a break in the speed in order to allow the rest of the community to follow as well, without being divided from the other end. The apostles decided to write them and say that that there was no need of circumcision, they should just "abstain from pollution of idols and from unchastity and from what is strangled and from blood."[130]

We could exemplify this by referring to any era in church history: Chalcedon, Constantinople, Trent, Geneva, the Vatican Councils, Uppsala, and so on. On the one hand, what is sought is liberation from the old ways of life and thinking, and so forth. On the other, a compromise is made and formulae are composed that, seen out of context, may seem unsatisfactory. Nobody is content with the solution if he sticks adamantly to his particular ideas. Perhaps only a man of faith can see the signs of the Spirit. On the one hand, most people today do not need to abominate the "heathens" in order to be orthodox Christians, but at the same time, not many are ready to drop their sense of superiority, and so on.

---

128 Ac 15:1.
129 Ac 15:19.
130 Ac 15:20.

• *The same reason*: The identification of faith, of Christian faith, with a particular cult, doctrine, philosophy, culture—or religion. "If you do not distinguish between essence and existence, you cannot be Christians." "If you do not affirm that God is the Being, you cannot understand the Father of Jesus Christ, and so cannot take part in the sacramental Mystery of salvation. . . ."

The problem can be solved once and forever, as long as history continues. What is needed is simply to try to find a fitting perspective to focus on the problem. Within present-day Christian consciousness, nobody will find anything objectionable in the fact that people following different—even incompatible—philosophical schools are nonetheless regarded as true and orthodox Christians. The appropriate word for this is *pluralism*.

There is in the present church ample room for philosophical as well as for theological and even cultural pluralism. The church has stressed, again and again, that it is not linked to any particular culture, but by and large, there has not so far been room for a true religious pluralism. Pluralism anyway is not just beginning to dawn. That so-called non-Christian religions may have a place in the Christian economy of salvation is still an unabsorbed idea, although it finds more and more acceptance. Honestly, the categories and the tools to handle the problem are not yet ready.

It is neither a question of ill will nor of shortsightedness, but as long as there are no proper tools to manage the problem, we run the risk of distorting the truth while trying to get an over-hurried synthesis. Patience is not only a personal virtue; it is also a historical imperative.

The character of this study forbids me to say anything by way of a definite conclusion. Only by way of summing up what seems to be the relationship between Christianity and the other world religions do I venture the following statements.

Christianity can be understood as *Christ*, and Christ as the Mystery. In this sense, Christianity claims to make manifest the Way, Truth, and Life to the world.

It can be equally understood as *church*, and, as such, it claims to be the visible element of that Mystery that saves the world. Its function is to serve and not to be served, to be leaven and salt for the world, without implying that the whole mass has to become leaven or all the food be converted into salt. Rather, the salt disappears and only enhances the taste and flavor of the different foods—the existing religious traditions, in our case. Moreover, nobody knows the boundaries of the church. The world religions are not ipso facto excommunicated.

Christianity can also be understood as *Christendom*, as the religious structure of ordinary life, which is an instrument to help Man in the pursuit of his goal—or in other words, as religion. As such, it is a religion besides the others, to be judged and evaluated on its own merits, and engaging with them in healthy emulation, in the new situation in which humankind finds itself today.

In this situation, traditional religions will seriously have to ask themselves what kind of radical conversion they are called upon to perform. Death has always been the condition for resurrection.

12

SALVATION IN CHRIST

Concreteness and Universality, the Supername*

Το ονομα το υπερ παν ονομα
The name above all names

Ph 2:9

Myth: Salvation[1]

The Text, the Context, and the Texture

In scarcely a single other epoch of history, and undoubtedly never on such a worldwide scale as today, has Man been so acutely confronted with the question of identity: What or who are we? It is one of the basic problems of every culture, lurking in every human consciousness: How can Man preserve his own identity without falling into solipsism or being drawn into an undifferentiated collectivity? How can a worldview be both concrete without being closed, and universal without being diffuse? How may I be loyal to my own tradition and yet open to another one, without being either dogmatic or vague? How may I follow my traditions and belong to my contemporary society, be both the child of my parents and the parent of my children, all in one, without schizophrenic fits or double standards? If we try to state the problem of self-identity for a contemporary Christian consciousness, we may ask: How is it possible to be a loyal Christian, owing allegiance to one particular religious tradition of the world, and a person abreast of the times, aware that the human family not only shares a common origin but also a common destiny, and thus an equal chance of reaching that goal? Or, to use the blunt terms of traditional Christian terminology: how can a "non-Christian" attain salvation?

We can also express the same idea in evolutionary terms, more acceptable to some ears. In the passage from "we consciousness" (i.e., from group consciousness,

* Inaugural Lecture at the Ecumenical Institute of Advanced Theological Study, Tantur, Jerusalem (Santa Barbara, CA, 1972), 1–81.

[1] A shortened version of this first part was delivered as a paper in the Consultation held at Dharmaram College, Bangalore, in September 1971, on "The Meaning of Christ."

in which there is no individual and thus no sense of *my* life or *my* death), from the state of innocence, if we prefer, to the individualized state, to the birth of the ego, where is the place for both the concrete and the universal? Where is the place for the mature human person, which is neither an abstract and abstracted individual nor a faceless and impersonal collectivity? Or in still more general terms, Does the *logos* necessarily dispel the myth? Are *logos* and myth incompatible? Is self-consciousness always consciousness of the ego, and never of the self?

The philosophical or hermeneutic approach to the problem may also serve to illustrate our query. We are fully aware today that no text can be properly understood outside its context. Each text leans on a context, that is, on a background out of which the text emerges and against which alone it has a meaning. The morphological difference between text and context is that the latter is not thematically understood, but only indirectly known when set against a new and wider context. In this case, the context has already become another text. The context is therefore double: an immediate context, which makes the text intelligible, and the ultimate context, which we would like to call the *texture*. The texture is taken to be universal; that is, it is taken for granted. The context is offered by the knowledge of the immediate intellectual environment of the text; the texture is provided by the actual range of human experience—qua human and not qua tribal. It is, in each case, the underlying myth that offers the basis for any understanding.

The relation between context and texture is a peculiar one. Once we are aware of the fact that the understanding of the text depends on the context, we also direct our attention to the context, but in order to know the context we need to view it against the background of a wider context, which becomes the texture when it claims to have universal validity.

What has happened in the cultural situation of our time is that people have become increasingly aware that they have to do not only with several texts but also with various contexts. Limiting ourselves to the Christian situation, we may say that the context that has hitherto given meaning to the Christian text has expanded in two different directions; out of the dynamism of this context, a degree of consciousness has emerged that some thinkers would like to call post-Christian. Furthermore, this context has also outgrown its own boundaries by allowing itself to be penetrated by alien forms of experience that are no longer merely marginal or complementary. Asian and African experiences are beginning—just beginning—to be part and parcel of Western/Christian experience, and vice versa. In short, the only possible horizon that can today provide a valid context for the understanding and evaluation of any text is the planetary horizon of a worldwide experience: the *human texture*.

For the sake of accuracy, we must add that this is by no means a formal novelty. It has always been claimed that the context of any text offers a universal range of experience for its understanding. This is what is meant by the claim to truth which is in-built in any text. The new factor today is the awareness that the old mountains and seas are no longer *finis terrae* and *non plus ultra*: they have become "provincial." The *oikoumenê* is no longer the Mediterranean Sea and its cultural colonies but the "four seas" of our planet. The novelty today is not just the discovery that there is another land beyond the mountains, but that those *terrae incognitae* are also populated with people who have their own horizons, and that only by meeting in the valley of peace (which at first is a no-man's land but can soon become the promised land) can human experience be brought into harmony and unity—a goal that does not mean, obviously, dullness and uniformity.

Nor is this all. We should not fall prey to an easy optimism.

The ways of becoming aware of a context are certainly not the same by which we understand a text. There are different types of intelligibility. A text becomes clear and intelligible when it is under-stood, that is, when it is situated *under* the *stand* of its proper context. This cannot be the case with the context, for this would constitute a *reductio* or a *processus in infinitum*. The context is simply taken for granted, and we are only aware of it in and through the understanding of the text; we do not understand a context as if it were a text. The context allows consciousness but not reflective consciousness. When knowing a context, I do so with reference to a wider horizon, which in turn becomes the actual context and changes the former context into a new text. Indeed, unless that wider horizon emerges, I cannot know the context. This means that the search for a wider context cannot be thematic or pragmatic. New horizons cannot be directly thought out or planned. The process is an existential common growth in which we all are involved with the whole of ourselves, including our thoughts and our reflection on the problem.[2]

Therefore, we cannot manipulate the horizon of our human experience, and, in fact, once the horizon of human experience has changed, the understanding of a text undergoes a change as well. Of one thing we may be sure: if we go on repeating the text without being aware that its context has altered, the text we repeat does not any longer convey that which it did convey to those who had another under-standing of it.[3] In our case, the context against which the universality of Christ's saving action was understood has changed so radically that, in order to understand that "text," we will have to adjust it in accordance with this change of context—that is, we will have to translate, to shift its message and, paradoxically enough, its very "meaning" so that the *meaning* may remain the same.[4]

The tantalizing question remains. Can we, in any possible way, understand the experience of the other man, his culture or his religion, in order to incorporate it into our personal horizon? Can we understand a text that has emerged out of another

---

[2] See the pertinent criticism of modern Thomistic philosophy by L. Dewart, *The Foundations of Belief* (New York: Herder and Herder, 1969), *passim*, but especially Appendix 2, 499–522; and *Religion: Language and Truth* (New York: Herder and Herder, 1970), Appendix, 145–69.

[3] We may refer here to Rudolf Bultmann and the whole problem of demythologization.

[4] "Meaning" refers here to Platonic or otherwise unchangeable essences, and *meaning* to the dynamic relationship between the understood "object" and the understanding "subject." See C. K. Ogden and I. A. Richards, *The Meaning of Meaning* (New York: Harcourt, Brace and Co., 1938).

context unless we share that context or a wider horizon that includes that context? In other words, have we the right to speak on behalf of the whole humankind, if our horizon is not that of the whole humanity? Have we the right to extrapolate without knowing the rules of extrapolation? Moreover, how shall we know the rules of extrapolation before we share the experience of the other? I may know that people are living behind the mountain in the background, but that does not mean that I know those people, or that I have a real message for them. It would be, perhaps, castles in the air or sheer commonplace.

All this makes up a cluster of problems underlying our question. We will not be able to tackle all of them here, but we need to be aware of them so as not to vitiate our specific field of inquiry from the outset.[5]

We will now revert to our more limited concern, which is one instance of the more general problem. How may our thinking be concrete and universal at one and the same time? Can there be *a* concrete way of salvation claiming at the same time to be *the* way of salvation?

Not only within Christian tradition but also within most other religious traditions of the world do we find two types of dialectically possible answers. We may call them the exclusive or discriminatory, and the inclusive or assimilatory one.[6]

Exclusivism

This type of answer preserves self-identity by exclusion, and affirms that, properly speaking, only those who belong to a particular group comply with the conditions required for salvation. Salvation is here seen as a privilege rather than as a right. It is not the right of birth, but the privilege of rebirth; it is not natural but super-natural; not a reward, but grace.

There is no injustice in assuming that not everybody is called to the same destiny, when this destiny is not seen as the goal of human existence as such, but as the culmination of a supernatural process. Moreover, rarity or scarcity seems to be the character of any great (extra-ordinary) value. In practice, in almost all traditions we can find a trend of thought maintaining that salvation—whatever it may be—is the lot of only the very few. Furthermore, even nature seems to show that its law implies a hierarchical structure maintained at the cost of a tremendous and lavish expense. Only a thin layer of matter is organic matter; of this organic matter, an even smaller portion has developed into living organisms, while among these latter the vegetable kingdom outnumbers the animal kingdom, and the latter is more extensive than the human species. Among men, those who reach *nirvāṇa*, heaven, realization, the end,

---

[5] This has been one of the main issues of my courses during the years 1967–1972 at Harvard University.

[6] See R. Panikkar, *Religione e Religioni* (*Opera Omnia* II), with presentation of Card (Brescia: König, Morcelliana, 1964), where the two corresponding psychological approaches are described.

salvation, are even fewer. A whole worldview underlies this conception. The "other," the outsider, the noninitiated, the uncivilized man, the barbarian, is not necessarily despised but undoubtedly belongs to another category: Christians/non-Christians, blacks/nonblacks, civilized/uncivilized, brahmans/nonbrahmans, proletarians/ nonproletarians, and so on. Self-identity is reached here by recognizing identity in confrontation with and contradistinction from the other, the nonidentical. Identity here corresponds to transcendence. God, in this line of thought, is transcendent precisely because He is identical to himself (or vice versa).

Inclusivism

This second type of answer preserves self-identity by including the others either within the particular group (anonymous Christians, baptism of desire, everybody is born a Muslim, etc.) or by recognizing a common sharing on a higher level (grace outside the church, bona fide worshippers, etc.). "Salvation" is here a common term that refers to the fulfillment of Man. Men attain it because, although religions may be different rivers, what really matters is the quantity and quality of water that the rivers carry. Religions, according to this view, even if they cannot be said to be the same (for they may represent higher and lower stages in human evolution, etc.), are nevertheless considered valid ways toward salvation insofar as they carry saving waters. Saved are not only those of one particular way, but all those who, though following their respective ways, share the same waters, because there exists an underlying unity, and the ways are, ultimately, mutually inclusive, up to a certain point. About the number of those reaching the goal, one can here hold either position—that is, that practically everybody reaches it or that hardly anyone fulfills the conditions for this personal achievement.

The plausibility of this mentality comes from its conviction that all men are ultimately equal and that they have the same destiny, and therefore equivalent means for reaching it. Self-identity is here reached by recognizing identity through participation in the other. Identity here corresponds to immanence. *Brahman*, in this line of thought, is immanent precisely because it is identical to itself (or vice versa).

Ultimately, the two approaches are conditioned, in great measure, by two types of thinking: by exclusion (relying mainly on the principle of noncontradiction) or by inclusion (relying mainly on the principle of identity): "A *is* that which is-not Non-A," and "A *is* that which is A."[7] These two different types, although one or the other may be more prominently present in one or another tradition, are not peculiar to any religion, and so we find theological schools defending either position in the several religious traditions of the world.

---

[7] See R. Panikkar, *Kultmysterium in Hinduismus und Christentum* (Freiburg im Breisgau: Karl Alber, 1964), 39–41.

The Universality of the Church

We turn now to the present-day Christian situation. The church has always lived under the tension created by the belief that it is, on the one hand, concrete, a little flock, incarnated, historical, and historically committed to the facts of history[8]—and, on the other hand, universal, "tailored" for the whole world, possessing within itself a constitutive thrust toward expansion, claiming to have a message for everybody and a right of existence among every people, race, and culture.[9] It is the tension between the church considered as a visible social organization and as a Mystical Body.[10] We could call these two notions the sociological and the theological notion, and remark that, in point of fact, they do not have the same "material" object.

Until now, the tension has been more or less minimized, or rather made dynamic, under the assumption that the values that the church represents are universal and valid for every human being qua human being.[11] The church sees herself as the embodiment of the universal message of salvation for humankind.[12]

This message was *substantially* identified with certain "universal values," understood in the light of the particular time and culture in which the church happened to live. It is true that the distinction between the natural and supernatural realms afforded a high degree of flexibility, so as not to impose structures or doctrines considered to be of the natural order only; but, even theoretically, that distinction only makes sense in a very particular context, and in practice there is no doubt that the church in its doctrines, practices, and even self-understanding is, by and large, a product of the Mediterranean world. Are we today so sure, for instance, that "idol worship" is, without distinctions, intrinsically evil? That polygamy is incompatible with Christianity? That bread and wine are indispensable for the sacrament of the Eucharist? That certain philosophical systems are intrinsically wrong? That the Roman *Sacrum Imperium* first, and a more general Christian *imperium* afterward, were of divine right, as well as the only universal and "civilized" forms of human government? Do not many today still think that democracy and science, for instance, are positive and universal values embodied in the Christian under-standing of Man and the world, just as they had been previously extolling Christendom and monarchy?

---

[8] See, as a single instance, H. Küng, *Kirche* (Freiburg im Breisgau: Herder, 1967), *passim*, esp. 158–60 and 408–25.

[9] See also, as an example, H. De Lubac, *Meditation sur l'Eglise* (Paris: Aubier, 1953), *passim*, but esp. 9–40; 107–37; 175–203.

[10] See *Denz.*, 350, 3166, 3685, and CIC, 1322 § 2, for instance.

[11] See the traditional doctrine *de virtutibus*, for example, with its three theological virtues and four cardinal virtues, etc., claiming to offer an all-embracing anthropology. But what about equally central and basic anthropologies like those of Daoism, Confucianism, etc.? (Not only *yin* and *yang*, but also *jen* and *yi* for instance, etc.)

[12] See *Lumen gentium*, I.1.

Religious Pluralism

Another attitude is gaining ground. It tries to go a step further and preaches more tolerance. The key word for this is *pluralism*. Most Christians today have reached the conviction that political, philosophical, theological, and—perhaps with greater reservations—even ethical and cultural pluralisms are justified within the church, and they think that Christian faith does not aim at turning those who accept it into Thomists, Calvinists, rightists, Democrats, Westerners, and the like. In spite of all cautions, provisos, and hairsplittings, we can be fairly sure in saying that pluralism has been recognized by most theologians and authorities in the Christian church.

Indeed, we should immediately add that the church has never considered itself to be monolithic. She has thought of herself as catholic—that is, perfect, complete, and therefore also universal.[13]

The church would say that it is not imposing a certain limited and particular structure, but proclaiming the liberation of Man from man-made chains and structures. But the question arises again in the moment we critically ask *what* is considered to be man-made, and *how* we should interpret such a supposedly universal message. Whereas some values may appear to be universal for a certain degree of consciousness, they may look different from other standpoints or other forms of consciousness. On what grounds can one speak of (let alone impose) a universality de jure, if there is no universality de facto?

We are now getting closer to our specific problem. In traditional terms, one may ask what the *minimum* is required for being a Christian—that is, the *minimum* required for salvation[14]—for the church does not want to impose anything that is not absolutely necessary.[15] Or, in our terms, what is the kind of concreteness compatible with the claim to universality? If salvation takes place in Christ, and this salvation is offered to all Men, how should we understand this Christ, who alone can give salvation?

It is here that we should introduce the notion of *religious pluralism*, not only cultural or theological pluralism. In Christian theological parlance, what is the place of world religions in the economy of salvation? There is, de facto, a plurality of religions. Is there any way of justifying de jure, not only tolerating, a pluralism of religions? Have not only theologies, philosophies, and cultures but also religions their pluralistic *raison d'être*? Or again, is there any middle way between a narrow-minded exclusivism, which verges on fanaticism, and an amorphous syncretism,

---

[13] It will be opportune to remember that the original meaning of καθολικα, being applied to the Church, besides stressing its difference from a single congregation, was not the Aristotelian καθ'ολου, i.e., "universal" (see *De interpretatione* 17a; *Metaphysics* 103a; etc.) but it rather implied the concept of perfection. The Church was primarily considered "catholic" not because of its universality, but because of its perfection or completeness.

[14] See Heb 11:6 and the traditional theological commentaries on it.

[15] See Ac 15:28, where the problem is originally and paradigmatically stated.

which verges on a disembodied and therefore inhuman attitude? Where is the passage, the transit, the *pascha* from plurality to pluralism?

One word should immediately be added about the nature of pluralism. Real pluralism does not mean that we recognize the equivalence of the different systems and equate them intellectually. Pluralism does not mean the discovery that there are several translations of one and the same thing. If this were the case, he who knows more than one language or the system that could speak a meta-language would have the upper hand, and that system would then be the real and true system, for it would embrace more than one worldview by possessing the clue of the different translations. This is no pluralism, because it implies a super-system that governs and dockets the different systems. There cannot be a pluralistic worldview, a pluralistic system. This would be a contradiction in terms, nor would it take seriously the claim of the different philosophical or religious traditions of the world to offer each one of them a universally valid view. If I claim to understand the other and even make room for him, though the other does not understand or even tolerate me, this is not pluralism but paternalism.[16]

Pluralism means that we accept a nonrecognition of the equivalence of the various worldviews, religions, ideologies, and systems. Pluralism cannot be used, by those who recognize it, against the "sectarians" who are not pluralistic. Pluralism means the existential acceptance of the others as others—that is, even without being able to understand or co-opt them. Pluralism is humble; it only knows that I or we may not possess the whole truth and does not pass judgment as to whether the other may also be right or, as it may turn out, wrong.

Pluralism belongs to the orders of confidence (that the other may also be right), of hope (that we may reach a higher and more comprehensive understanding), and of love (that embraces, makes room for and accepts what it does not know or understand). Pluralism is a modern word standing for the old and perhaps abused term *mysterion*.[17] In any case, pluralism is an emerging myth: it certainly does not belong to the order of *logos* but of myth.

Two words that sum up the current theological attitudes toward the problem of the universality of the church are *minimalism* and *maximilism*.

Minimalism

Given the difficulty and implausibility of thinking that the church in its present-day structure embodies a universal value, there is a trend among theologians of different tendencies to give up a direct claim to universalism and take refuge in being the "small

---

[16] *Mādhyamika*, neo-*vedānta*, and Christian liberalism could show examples from among their respective followers, just to mention three different traditions.

[17] See R. Panikkar, "*Pluralismus, Toleranz und Christenheit*", in H. Schomerus (ed.), *Pluralismus, Toleranz und Christenheit* (Nuremberg: Abendländische Akademie, 1961), 117–42 (*Opera Omnia* VI.1).

flock" and the "remnant" of the Lord, with a very limited and particular mission. The church, according to this trend, should give up its claim to convert the whole world, or to proclaim its message to the vast universe, so that it may really be humble, a servant, leaven, and the like. This mood claims to put an end to the Constantinian era, with all the vaunting pretensions of the church. We might also mention here the modern distinction between church and the kingdom of God, of which modern exegesis has shown the scriptural basis. The kingdom would then be what Jesus preached and would be really universal, whereas the church would only be a very particular community.

Maximalism

The other and opposite trend, equally evident today, considers the church as being—by nature—the place of human encounter, the place that, precisely because of its specific character (in traditional terms, its supernatural character), offers the actual platform for meeting, dialogue, understanding, and also disagreement. According to this view, the church, precisely because it represents a kingdom that is not of this world, is the agency capable of presenting a meeting ground where the most disparate tendencies may meet and come to grips with one another, and eventually fertilize each other, because each of them does function within that underlying human communion or community. This agency would still be called by some the *kyriakê*, that is, the church, the place, or property of the Lord—or the *ecclesia*—that is, the assembly, the congregation of the children of Man as well as the people of God.

This dilemma is clearly full of immediate consequences, as it betrays a double and opposite ecclesiology. If the church is "only a remnant," it is completely right when it resists any external influences and retains its compact organization, together with the Latin, Gregorian, or whatever values have given it a specific identity. If the church is the universal congregation, it is urgent and good to strip it of everything not corresponding to its universal vocation; the church must be disentangled from its present status quo in order to make it ready for an ever-new and renewed incarnation in the world.

"Extra Ecclesiam Nulla Salus"

In this connection, the discussion about the old saying, "Outside the Church there is no salvation," can be seen in its proper ecclesiological and theological perspective.[18] Either the church has nothing to do with salvation, and this would mean the total secularization of the church, which would turn into a nonreligious agency for

---

[18] See, among other modern documents, the four contributions of Küng, Fransen, Masson, and Panikkar at the Theological Congress during the Bombay International Eucharistic Congress in 1964; then published in J. Neuner (ed.), *Christian Revelation and World Religions* (London: Burns and Oates, 1967).

humanitarian purposes of all sorts; or there is no way of escaping the dilemma as to whether there is salvation only inside the church.

If we say that there *is* salvation outside the church, it will be added anyway that the church has nevertheless a unique role to perform, *a pars pro toto*; that, in the words of the Bible allegorically interpreted by Vatican I, it is a *signum levatum in nationes*,[19] or in the terms of Vatican II, a *sacramentum mundi*.[20] This amounts to saying that the church is supposed to have a universal role, even if this role is not understood as involving geographical expansion: *salus per ecclesiam*.

If, on the other hand, one maintains the principle that there is *no* salvation outside the church, it will be necessary to affirm that the church is not overlapping or identical with the visible church, for the assertion that *extra ecclesiam nulla ceditur gratia*[21] has been repeatedly rejected. Indeed, the church itself condemned as heretical the opinion according to which the grace, needed for salvation, cannot be found outside the church.

The only way of solving the dilemma is to reconsider the very concept of church, for undoubtedly it cannot be the same in both statements without falling into flagrant contradiction.[22] If outside the church there is grace, and grace is what is required for salvation, this amounts to saying that there is salvation outside the church. The "church" outside which there is grace (and therefore salvation) is the institutionalized or visible church. The "church" outside which there is no salvation is the *ontological* church, whose relationship with the *visible* one is a major ecclesiological problem.[23]

In order not only to avoid plain contradiction but also to be true to the traditional insight of the church as the ark of salvation, I would like to reverse the phrase and unambiguously affirm that the church is so constitutively the place of salvation that, wherever there is salvation, there is the church—the church being by definition the *locus*, the place, of salvation.[24]

We may now recall what we said about pluralism, and understand that to say that the church is the place where the ultimate human encounter can take place

---

[19] See *Denz.*, 3014, as to the Vatican Council I quoting Is 11:12.

[20] See *Lumen gentium*, I, Introduction.

[21] See *Denz.*, 2429, 3866–73.

[22] See R. Panikkar, "*Extra ecclesiam nulla salus.* Die innere Unzulänglichkeit einer nicht-christlichen Welt," in *Neues-Abendland* 10, no. 5 (May 1955): 259–66.

[23] For a recent condemnation of such a narrow interpretation of this principle, see the story of the "Boston Affair" told by C. G. Clarke, *The Loyolas and the Cabots: The Story of the Boston Heresy Case* (Boston: Ravengate Press, 1950).

[24] See the IV Proposition of Teilhard de Chardin, in his 1947 article reprinted in *L'Avenir de l'Homme*: *Oeuvres* (Paris: Seuil, 1959), 5:285: "Dans la genèse de l'organisme social humain, l'Église n'est pas un epi- ou para-phénomène; mais elle forme l'axe même (ou noyau) du rassemblement" [In the genesis of the social human organism, the Church is not an *epi*- or *para*-phenomenon, but it forms the very axis, or core, of the gathering]. Or, to quote an article by Cardinal J. Daniélou: "En ce sens, elle est le rassemblement de tous les sauvés depuis les origines de l'humanité jusqu'à la fin des temps" [In this sense, the Church is the gathering of all the saved ones, from the origins of humankind to the end of times], in *Le Monde*, July 23, 1971.

is to affirm that the church is the place of Mystery.[25] Any other limitation of the church would change it into a sect. The church is not the "society of the chosen ones" but the "congregation of the called."[26] The difficulty with the first alternative (the church is only a visible body) lies in defending universality, whereas the difficulty with the second (the church is a mystical body) is in maintaining concreteness. The relationship between the sociological and the theological church is an *outstanding* problem, but the two concepts are not incompatible. The fact that the church is visible does not imply that its limits are visible to everybody, or to anybody. Precisely because it is visible, the church presents the possibility of different limits of visibility. Whereas some do not see much beyond their churchyard, others encompass a wider horizon. To affirm, then, that the church boundaries touch the very limits of humankind (without saying that they coalesce) does not contradict the visibility of the church.

The Keys of the Kingdom

We may sum up the issue by saying that the problem of salvation and of universal salvation plays a central role both in the Christian "economy" and in most religious traditions of the world, even if salvation is not called by the same name or interpreted in the same way.

Moreover, the myth of salvation is an almost universal myth. There exists, in fact, an underlying conviction that Man is a pilgrim, that he is on pilgrimage (individually or collectively) toward a goal that may well be called the salvation of Man. But who has the keys to the kingdom?

Logos: Christ[27]

We will not study here the role of Christ in the universal economy of salvation—that is, how he may or may not be considered the universal savior, or what kind of knowledge of or link with him may be required in order to reach salvation. Neither will we study the many possible understandings of the term "salvation."

---

[25] See R. Panikkar, "Church and the World Religions," in *Religion and Society* (Bangalore, 1967), XIV-2: 59–63.

26 Besides some bibliography given below, see some modern essays favoring a certain type of universal salvation: C. S. Duthie, "Ultimate Triumph," *Scottish Journal of Theology* 14 (1961): 156–71; H. H. Farmer, *God and Men* (New York: Abingdon-Cokesbury Press, 1947); J. Feiner, "Particular and Universal Saving History," in *One, Holy Catholic and Apostolic Church* (ed. Vorgrimler) (London, 1968); N. F. S. Ferre, *The Christian Understanding of God* (New York: Harper, 1951); J. A. T. Robinson, *In the End, God* (London: Clarke, 1958); "Universalism: Is It Heretical?" *Scottish Journal of Theology* 2 (1949): 139–55. Against an indiscriminate universalism, and offering an alternative, cf. J. D. Bettis, "A Critique of the Doctrine of Universal Salvation," *Religious Studies* 6:4 (1970): 329–44.

[27] A shortened version of this second part was submitted as a paper for the International Theological Congress on Evangelization held in Nagpur (India) in October 1971.

We will limit ourselves to a critical essay on the meaning of the *name* of Christ as expressing that ever-hidden and nonetheless liberating Mystery that transcends all names.

Who Is Jesus?

John the Baptist, truly performing his role of forerunner, poses the right starting question: "Are you the one who is to come, or have we to wait for someone else?"[28] The answer of Jesus is in fact very precise, but many commentators, significantly enough, seem to find it somewhat vague. Jesus's answer may sound evasive if it is expected to be couched in terms of a static and individualistic conception of "himself," while on the contrary, it indicates a set of actions, giving concrete examples of a certain function he is performing. His answer is functional, not substantial. This very misunderstanding may be the reason why he immediately adds that "blessed is the man" who is not offended or scandalized by him. The *who* of Christ cannot be individualized by pinning him down to a "here" or a "there."[29] He is constantly ο ερχομενος, "the coming one," and even as the risen One he always is "not here."[30] "Go and tell John what you hear and see: the blind recover their sight, the lame walk, the lepers are made clean, the deaf hear, the dead are raised to life, the poor listen to the good news. And blessed is the man who does not trip upon me as a stumbling block."[31]

Jesus's answer, in point of fact, is the most appropriate to John the Baptist and us. To John, because he was expecting the "kingdom" of which the Messiah is only the "regent" in God's name; therefore, the focus should not be on one individual, but on a collective event for the people of Israel. To ourselves, in every age in history, because it liberates us from our very obsession with individuals and focuses our attention on the actions being performed, the mission and the things that are happening. "O unbelieving generation!"[32]

Nevertheless, the quest for the person is unavoidable. It was and is of no avail to say that Christ did not even want to be called "good,"[33] nor did he accept the common title of "father,"[34] or to recall that he acted as a servant,[35] "wore" the form of a slave,[36] and "made himself nothing."[37] The question persists, and from the very beginning the search for the *who* has stirred human consciousness.[38] "Are you the One?"

---

[28] Mt 11:3; Lk 8:19.
[29] Mt 24:23.
[30] Mt 28:6.
[31] Lk 7:22–23.
[32] Mk 9:19.
[33] Mk 9:9.
[34] Mt 23:9.
[35] See Jn 13:4ff.
[36] See Ph 2:7.
[37] Ibid.
[38] See incidentally *RV* X.121.1 and more explicitly *TB* II.2.10.2, etc., where God is simply

No Other Name

We know the traditional answer of "Peter, filled with the Holy Spirit,"[39] which incidentally seems to echo the word of the Lord regarding the *skandalon*:[40] "There is no salvation in anyone else (εν αλλω ουδενι), for there is no other name (ουδε γαρ ονομα εστιν ετερον) under heaven for men by which we may receive salvation."[41]

If we want to find a Christian answer, we cannot escape this affirmation. That salvation occurs in the *name* of the Lord is a recurrent proclamation in the New Testament: salvation is in the name of Jesus,[42] miracles are performed in his name,[43] devils are expelled in his name,[44] baptism is performed in his name,[45] the only prayer that is granted an answer is the prayer in his name,[46] and before the name of Jesus— and no one else—the three worlds will bow,[47] and so on.

From the point of view of a morphological analysis of cultures, one could easily show that sacred *names* usually play such roles, and that they can only be properly understood if the mythical power of names and their mythical contents are taken into account, so that to interpret those sacred names outside their context would distort their proper meaning. One could also add that, as soon as the mythical dimension of names shifts or loses importance, the name becomes either magical or a mere label.

These reflections also apply to our specific study and should convey a herme-neutic warning against the *kata-chronical* mistake of interpreting ancient concepts with contemporary tools of understanding. Here, however, we are not dealing with exegesis nor with any attempt to justify scriptural texts. We simply try to elucidate a truly acceptable position for our time, one taking the contemporary situation into consideration, keeping loyal to the Christian tradition, without betraying other streams of humankind's religious experience.

Christian Scripture and tradition cannot be more precise and emphatic: there is only one name in which there is salvation. Yet, it is easy to notice that the name here stands for the named; the name is not a mere nominalistic label, but the *real symbol* of the "thing" being named.[48] The whole question will therefore turn into the need to know *who* or *what* is this name. Obviously, it is not a sound, of which

---

named by the interrogative pronoun *Who?* See U. M. Vesci, "*Ka,* le nom de Dieu comme pronom interrogatif dans les *Vedas*" in E. Castelli (ed.), *L'analyze du langage théologique* (Paris: Aubier), 145–64.

[39] Ac 4:8.

[40] Ac 4:11; cf. Ps 118 [119]:22.

[41] Ac 4:12.

[42] See in Acts alone: 3:6, 16; 4:10ff.; 5:40; 8:12, 16; 9:14ff.; 10:43, 48; 15:25; 16:18; 19:5, 13; 22:16, etc.

[43] Ac 3:6; 4:10.

[44] Mk 9:38; 16:17; Lk 9:49; 10:17, etc.

[45] Ac 2:38.

[46] Jn 14:13; 15:16; 16:24, 26.

[47] Ph 2:10.

[48] See Rev 3:4, where ολιγα ονοματα (few names) obviously means few people.

there is no record available, just—at most—a guess. Nor is it a sign. No sign can save. A sign can, at most, be an intermediary, not a mediator.[49] Furthermore, it is not a label, for it would amount to the worst type of magic to claim that you have to know a label in order to be saved. It is a symbol—that is, the very "thing" as it manifests itself in the world of our experience. The symbol stands for the "thing": it is the thing as it stands, but this "standing" is its proper manifestation, so that the symbol reveals *what is there* by the very fact that it clothes and expresses it. Existence is never naked, as it were; it is always symbolical in the very act of existing, as the object and the subject, the form and the content. No "thing" can exist without a name. No "thing" exists *in vacuo*. That which exists is its own symbol. What is, then, this real name outside which there is no salvation? "Is there anything greater than the name?" asks an *Upaniṣad*.[50] And the answer is categorical: "The word, certainly, is greater than the name."[51]

Modern scholarship has been studying for at least three or four generations the so-called primitive thinking.[52] And it has rediscovered the old wisdom according to which names are not mere signs, but real symbols, epiphanies of things.[53]

This does not only apply to so-called primitive thinking, but to any name function.[54] Any name, even in the most sophisticated and nominalistic culture, is always part of the thing named; it is a name, and not a mere sound, precisely because it is understood as a *pars pro toto*. In other words, a name, in order to be such, needs a meaning; but as soon as a name has a meaning, it ceases to be a merely conventional nominalistic sign (even if it were so at the beginning), for it enters or springs from our minds so as to form part of the thing so named. The name in fact links together the "thing in itself"—whatever this may be—and my understanding of it, my concept.[55] The

---

[49] See the happy phrase of Ernst Cassirer in "Sprache und Mythos," reproduced in *Wesen und Wirkung des Symbolbegriffs* (Damstadt: Wissenschaftliche Buchgesellschaft, 1969), 78: "An allem Zeichen aber haftet der Fluch der Mittelbarkeit" [To any sign, however, the curse of mediateness sticks].

[50] *CU* VII.1.5.

[51] *CU* VII.2.1.

[52] Since Lucien Lévy-Bruhl's 1910 *Les fonctions mentales dans les sociétés inférieures* and Émile Durkheim's *Les formes élémentaires de la vie religieuse* (Paris: Alcan, 1912) up to Claude Lévi-Strauss's *La pensée sauvage* (Paris: Plon, 1962) (where it is no longer about the thought "of primitives" but "primitive thought"), we have gone a long way, and yet we are just beginning to surmise that we also have our own myths.

[53] See the epoch-making study by Hermann Usener, *Götternamen. Versuch einer Lehre von der religiösen Begriffsbildung* (Bonn: Cohen, 1896).

[54] See the deep intuition of *RV* X.71.1: "O Lord of the Holy Word! That was the first beginning of the Word, when the seers fell to naming each object," which describes the theandric function of name-giving. See also Gn 2:20 where Adam gives the names to all animals, and also Plato, *Cratylus* 400d–e, on the names of the Gods and our names for them.

[55] See the mediatory function of the Word (*Vac*) in the Cedic tradition.

name is infinite, as an *Upaniṣad* says.[56] Any name with meaning is not autonomous but has a proper *ontonomic* constitution. The name is neither merely subjective nor solely objective. Any real name is a symbol, and a symbol is precisely that which is "thrown" from the subject to the object and vice versa, remaining—"swinging"—in the middle,[57] but expressing all that needs to be expressed.[58]

The name outlives people, according to more than one tradition, the biblical tradition not excluded. The name has a special role to play in human immortality. Hence also the importance of God's real name, which many religious traditions carefully preserve as a secret[59] and which certain traditions forbid to utter, except in the worshipping vocative.[60]

We could again formulate the problem in purely philosophical terms. Any language is not only a collection of different sounds and signs but also represents a different conception of the world.

Any name belongs to a particular language, and in this language it has its proper meaning. To affirm that a certain name has a universal validity involves the affirmation that the particular worldview from which that name originates has a universal validity. This, in point of fact, was the underlying assumption on more than one occasion in the history of religions. In the present world's religious and human constellation, such an assumption seems untenable.

To affirm—in order to escape the just mentioned aporia of the universalization of names—that a particular name is not universal as such, but it is translatable, amounts to saying that the name in question is a common name and not a proper name, and this would make the "no other name" tenet meaningless. It implies, further, that we have the key for a translation by having access to the reality that is intended by the name. We would be able to do so by virtue of sources *apart* from the name in question: those sources would let us establish an equivalence.

How may we, therefore, meaningfully understand that "there is no other name by which we may attain salvation"?

---

[56] *BU* III.2.12: *anatum vai nama*. (See also *TB* II.8.8.4). Śaṅkara comments that the name is infinite because it is eternal, here echoing the *mīmāṃsā* tradition.

[57] "Symbol" comes from συν and βαλλω: to throw, to put, etc., but also to swing.

[58] A legend of the Maori reports that, when they arrived in New Zealand, they did not carry with them their old Gods but only their names, i.e., the prayers that gave them power over the Gods themselves (in Cassirer, "Sprache und Mythos," 115, quoting S. Brinton, *Religions of Primitive Peoples* [New York–London, 1907], 103).

[59] See B. Baeumer, "Le nom secret dans l'hindouisme," in E. Castelli (ed.), *L'analyze du langage théologique*, 135–44.

[60] See the Biblical and Qur'anic prohibitions about the making of images of God and the utterance of His name in vain. See also K. Kerenyi, "*Theos and mythos*" in E. Castelli (ed.), *Il problema della demitizzazione* (Padova: CEDAM, 1961), 35–44, for a study of Greek religion, in which the Divine is less esoteric, and mingles with the human more than in other traditions.

Which Name?

It is here that the real problem starts. "This people honors me with their lips, but their heart is far from me."[61] Calling the name alone will not do.[62] "Not those who say to me, *Lord, Lord,* will enter the kingdom of heaven!"[63] How can we pinpoint Jesus? Who is he? "Who do men say that the Son of Man is?"[64] Peter's answer was perfect, in his own context: "You are the Messiah, the Son of the living God."[65] However, this answer needs to be effectively translated, if it has to be understood (in the sense Christians understand it) as we take one step outside the Jewish world of St. Peter.[66] If a translation is not made, and if we do not belong to the Semitic cultural world, we may well understand that the Jews had a particular god, and they were expecting some savior, and now He has come, but we will not relate Him to ourselves nor will we be able to give any further or relevant meaning to that revelation. We will only understand it in its own particular terms, but without any internal participation, just as we may understand the meaning and even grasp the beauty of Uitzilopochtli, the protector of Tenochtitlan, the old capital city of Mexico. One cannot transplant a text outside its proper context without first finding the growing points of the other context, which alone will make the transplant viable and the translation authentic.

Let us give an example of such a translation. The elders of a certain tribe in Australia once received an explanation on the Christian sacrament of the Eucharist. As soon as they understood what it really meant, they translated it by saying that it was a dance.[67] Dance was, for them, an act in which Gods and men, as well as other spirits and creatures, took part; dance was the concrete expression of the union between the material and the spiritual, the body and the soul, nature and supernatural; dance was the sacrifice, the offering, and the victim together; dance was the cult act par excellence. Hence they did not know any other way of translating what the Christian Mass meant. Had they any other way to express what the Christians from other lands wanted to express? Is not a positive symbiosis the first step for understanding?

---

[61] Mt 15:8; Mk 7:6.

[62] See Lk 6:46.

[63] Mt 7:21.

[64] Mt 16:13.

[65] Mt 16:16.

[66] It is interesting to note that, in 1969, the Indian Theological Association dedicated its triennial session in Ranchi to the issue of a right translation of Peter's answer into the various Indian languages. If a literal translation is given, it will certainly fail to convey the original meaning: in fact, according to Indic tradition, almost anybody could be called "the son of the living God." See the remarks by K. Klostermaier, *Kristvidya: A Sketch of an Indian Christology* (Bangalore: CISRS, 1967), and R. Panikkar, "Confrontation between Hinduism and Christ," *New Blackfriars* 50, no. 584 (1969): 197–204.

[67] See E. Reclus, "Le primitif d'Australie", cited by Cassirer, *Wesen und Wirkung des Symbolbegriffs*, 109.

The historically trained Western mind has taken spatiotemporal coordinates as the central point of reference for answering the question about Jesus's identity, being well aware, however, that this answer does not suffice. If Jesus Christ were *only* what the tempo-spatial coordinates yield, no Christian could speak of the real presence of Christ in the sacraments, nor accept that whatever we do to the little ones, we do it to "him,"[68] nor that he is "yesterday, today, and for ever,"[69] much less admit that he was before Abraham.[70] The cosmic Christ of the letters of St. Paul and many other sayings of St. John, his Prologue, and so on, would be unintelligible. Indeed, if Christ were only *that*—that is, an entity belonging to the temporal and spatial order, which existed at a certain time in history and had a certain place in geography—the whole of Christian faith would collapse.[71] No Christian would say that the living Jesus of his or her faith is only a personage of the past; nor would they affirm, on the other hand, than when they receive Christ in the Eucharist, they eat the proteins of that Jesus of Nazareth who walked through Galilee twenty centuries ago.

Who, then, is Jesus? If our translation is only a literal one, it will not work as a real translation outside the boundaries of the Semitic world, and we will remain within the context of Mediterranean cultures.

What about those who were expecting no Messiah, for whom "He who comes"[72] has no meaning whatsoever? What about those who think that we *all* are children of the living God?[73] What about those in whose languages the very words of Peter's answer do not even exist, or they have a radically different meaning? Must they be "converted" to the ways of Judaism? Must they be circumcised in their minds, despite the fact that the Council of Jerusalem decided that circumcision, the most sacred token of fidelity to the covenant between YHWH and His people, was no longer needed?[74] In order to understand what Jesus is all about, let alone accept him, must one embrace the categorical thought-world of one particular culture?

It is here that we have to ask whether many of the assumptions, which Christians until now have taken for universal assumptions, are not peculiar to the Western world. Is there not a new consciousness now emerging that disturbs those who believe that the Christian *message* is truly universal and appropriate to all men? How can such a question be decided a priori? In other words, unpopular or disturbing though they may be, has one necessarily to be a Semite spiritually in order to be

---

[68] See Mt 10:40; 18:5; Mk 9:37; Lk 9:48; 10:16.

[69] Heb 13:8.

[70] Jn 8:58.

[71] See 1 Co 15:14.

[72] Mt 11:3.

[73] See a typical reaction in India: "It was more than I could believe that Jesus was the only incarnate son of God, and that only he who believed in him would have everlasting life. If God could have sons, all of us were His sons. If Jesus was like God, or God himself, then all Men were like God and could be God himself" (M. K. Gandhi, *An Autobiography of the Story of My Experiments with Truth* (Boston: Beacon Press, 1957), 136.

[74] Ac 15.

a Christian? Or more theologically, what are the place and function of the Bible in Christian faith?

If any speech about Jesus needs to be intelligible to one who lives outside the cultural area in which that language has been forged, it will have to be actually "translated," not only "transliterated." We may here remember that "the letter kills."[75] There is no possible intelligibility, much less the proclaiming of any message, if partners do not share the same context of experience. Otherwise, the worst kind of misunderstanding would occur: when the listener claims to understand, when in fact he does not even know that he does not understand.

We should not blur the issue by uncritically oversimplifying the fact that a Christian has "only" to accept the person of Jesus Christ, or to profess that He is the Son of God. This is, first of all, in point of fact, not true. In order to be a Christian today, one cannot but accept a score of ideas, share a set of statements, and follow a series of practices that only make sense within a particular culture. Being a Christian in the twentieth century is not the same as being a Christian in the first century, for there is not only a certain evolution in Christian dogma but also a real growth in the understanding of what being a Christian means—and, by that, a growth in Christians themselves. Second, even the bare affirmations stated above are far from being universal and acceptable or even understandable to all cultures. I repeat: Has one to accept and to follow the Semitic tradition if one wants to acknowledge Christ?

We should face up to the problem in all of its earnestness and with its far-reaching consequences. Although we cannot here deal with the whole issue, we will have to revert to our central question: *Who* is Jesus of Nazareth, the Messiah, the Son of the living God? Who is *he*?

The Principle of Individuation

One particular way of framing the understanding of Jesus's identity has had serious consequences in the history of Christian thought. We refer to the application of the so-called principle of individuation in order to find out the identity of Jesus.[76] The question, "Who is Jesus?" has then been understood as synonymous with, "What makes Jesus *Jesus*?"—what individualizes or distinguishes Him? When can we say that we "have" Him or "touch" Him? When can we say that He is really present? Or *what* or *who* is that "Jesus" whom we name when we pronounce that name?

The many attempts of the Western tradition[77] to solve this great,[78] most entangled,[79] and very thorny[80] question may be reduced to two types of answers:

---

[75] 2 Co 3:6; cf. Rom 2:29.

[76] See, for example, the whole discussion about the "historical Jesus" from the nineteenth century up to our days.

[77] For another tradition, cf. P. Horsch, "Le principe d'individuation dans la philosophie indienne," *Asiatische Studien* 10 (1956) and 11 (1957–1958).

[78] "*Magna quaestio*": Augustine in his *Epistula* XIV.4.

[79] "*Implicatissima*": Suárez in his *Disputationes Metaphysicae*.

[80] "Spinosissima": Leibniz in his *Confessio philosophi*.

the one finding the principle of individuation in the very being itself[81] or in some constitutive elements of it,[82] and the other finding it in some principle extrinsic to the being in question, such as space and time, which differentiate between things.[83] The famous "principle of indiscernibles" formulated by Leibniz[84] and taken up by modern logical analysis[85] could provide this criterion of distinction.

In fact, if the *principium identitatis indiscernibilium* is true—that is, if "two" indistinguishable things must indeed be considered as "one," as identical—then the principle of individuation is extrinsic to things. Whereas, if there can be—*de potentia Dei absoluta*, at least—*two* indiscernible things, it is because the principle of individuation is intrinsic to the thing itself.[86]

However we may consider the philosophical principle of individuation,[87] its application to our case is not without difficulties, for it presupposes a particular form of thinking.[88] What do we ask, in fact, when we apply the principle of individuation? We search, undoubtedly, the identity of a "thing"—Jesus, in this case—by looking for what the "thing" *is* in contradistinction to and differentiation from all other things. We assume that that which a thing *is*, is something exclusive and "individualizing"; we assume that what makes Jesus *Jesus* is something that is His "own," his "exclusivity," his private individuality.

Now, in the Western world, since Leucippus and Democritus, the individual, the indivisible, the ατομον, called "the each-one," το καθ'εκαστον, was the opposite of either the universal, το καθ'ολου, or the species, το ειδος.[89] In either case, however, we are dealing with the numerical individualization in a series, whether this latter be conceptual or factual. So, the word "individual" presents a dangerous ambivalence, not always clearly detected: the opposite of the *many* and the opposite of the *other.* This may be, incidentally, the reason for its shift in meaning, especially in English.[90]

---

[81] E.g., the *haecceitas* of Duns Scotus, or the *individuum seipsum individuat* of Leibniz.

[82] See most Scholastic theories originating from Aristotle's thought, e.g., the *materia signata quantitate* of Averroes and Thomas Aquinas.

[83] Schopenhauer could be adduced here as an example.

[84] *Monadologia* Q.9 (ed. Gerhardt); V.608, etc.

[85] See, for example, A. J. Ayer, "The Identity of Indiscernibles," in *Proceedings of the XI International Congress of Philosophy*, Brussels, 1953, 3:124–29; D. F. Pears, "The Identity of Indiscernibles," *Mind*, no. 64 (1955): 522–27.

[86] Kant, for instance, could not accept Leibniz's theory, since for him the appearances do not yet constitute the thing itself. See *Kritik der reinen Vernunft*, A.264, 320, etc.

[87] See J. Ferrater-Mora, *Diccionario de Filosofia* (Buenos Aires: Editorial Suramericana, 1965), *s.v.* "Individuacion" for a good summary. For the Thomistic views, cf. G. M. Manser, "Das thomistische Individuationsprinzip," *Divus Thomas* 12 (1934): 221–37, 279–300.

[88] St. Basil speaks of a "criterion of differentiation": λογος διαφορας (*Epist.* XXXVIII.3; *PG* 32.328C) and applies it to the Trinity, thus making it clear that it can differentiate but not individualize.

[89] See Aristotle, *Metaphysics* I.4 (985b).

[90] The word "individual," when applied to persons, often conveys a pejorative meaning in Latin languages, which is not the case in English, which commonly uses the word "individual" for "person."

Starting from the traditional and etymological definition of an individual,[91] we may say that a thing has *singularity* when it is indivisible in itself, is undivided, atomic (*in se indistinctum*); and that it has *individuality* when, besides, it is different from others (*ab aliis distinctum*). The two aspects should be carefully distinguished.[92] Singularity is a particular case of plurality.[93] There is no singularity, except against a plurality. To call "single" something that cannot have a plural is a contradiction in terms. Individuality, on the other hand, does not need to be quantitative, and stands for the internal constitution of those beings that have a certain possession of their own being.

From this point of view, one could distinguish a double principle of individuation: a *principle of singularity* that would rely on external factors to distinguish one thing from another; and a *principle of individuality* that would be grounded in the internal constitution of beings capable of self-identity.[94] The principle of the identity of indiscernibles would apply to singularity but not to individuality. Two "indiscernible" particles, crystals, molecules (if they happened to exist) would not be "two"; two indiscernible human beings (in case) would remain two.[95]

---

[91] See the traditional definition "individuum autem est, quod est in se indistinctum, ab aliis vero distinctum" [an individual is what is undivided in itself, but divided from others] (Thomas Aquinas, *Sum. theol.* I, q.29, a.4).

[92] See X. Zubiri, *Sobre la esencia* (Madrid: Sociedad de Estudios y Publicaciones, 1962), saying, "No hay individuación de la especie, sino especiacion del individuo" [there is no individuation of the species, but speciation of the individual; p. 166] and distinguishing between *singleness* and *individuality* (pp. 166ff.). Every individuality is single, but not every singleness is individual. The elementary particles in modern physics, for instance, would be single but have no individuality, whereas a living being would have at least an inchoative individuality, and Man would fully be an individual, according to this terminology.

[93] See Aristotle, *Categ.* II (1.b6-7).

[94] *De nominibus non est disputandum* and the terminology is sometimes just the opposite, like in the following beautiful passage: "Gaudet igitur unumquodque de sua singularitate, quae tanta in ipso est quod non est plurificabilis, sicut nec in Deo nec mundo nec angelis" [Everything enjoys its own singularity, which is so strong in itself that it cannot be plurified: not in God, and not in the world and angels, either] (Nicholas of Cusa, *De venatione sapientiae*).

[95] We have here to renounce any further elaboration of this old question, a little neglected in our individualistic times. See, for an initial study, Bernard Bosanquet, *The Value and Destiny of the Individual* (New York: Kraus, 1968); *The Principle of Individuality and Value* (New York: Kraus, 1968); W. Büchel, "Individualität und Wechselwirkung im Bereich des materiellen Seins," *Scholastik* 30, no. 1 (1956): 1–30; "Zur philosophischen Deutung des quantenmechanischen Indeterminismus," *Scholastik* 32, no. H. 2 (1952): 225–40; Karl Löwith, *Das Individuum in der Rolle des Mitmenschen* (Darmstadt: Wissenschaftliche Buchgesellschaft, 1962); Jan Lukasiewicz, "On the Principle of Contradiction in Aristotle," *Review of Metaphysics* 34, no. 3 (1971): 485–509; Rainer Schubert-Soldern, "Kann man heute noch von Individualität sprechen?," *Akten des XIV Internationalen Kongresses für Philosophie*, vol. 5, *Philosophische Anthropologie* (Vienna: Herder, 1970), 21–29; Schaumann, "Das Prinzip der Individualität bei Alexandre Vinet," *Theologische Studien und Kritiken*, 1902.

Now, two questions emerge. First, how is it with the case of Jesus? Second, must the question of identity necessarily take the form of singularity?

The Case of Jesus

The first question amounts to asking whether Jesus is an *individual* in the sense of asking for his *singularity* as a member of a species. Traditional theology had a very pertinent answer. Christ is not an individual in the sense in which historical personages are said to be such.[96] Christ has indeed a human nature, he is a man, but he is not a "human person." His "individuality" is a divine one.[97] He is a divine Person, the second Person of the Trinity, having taken on a human nature. The problem, however, remained lurking below the surface; although after Chalcedon it could be argued that Christ took upon Himself the human nature as a whole, He anyway did it by taking *a* human nature, the human nature *of* the man Jesus—whose human person did not even come into being, because that person was subsumed by the divine Person of the Logos.[98] In this context, Christ is man, but not *one* man, a single individual; he is a divine Person incarnated, a divine Person in hypostatic union with his human nature.[99] The divine *Logos* is revealed in Christ, and through Christ humankind gets in touch with the *Logos*, but Christ's presence for the believer is the *divine* presence. We are ultimately confronted with the issue of *uniqueness*, instead of the problem of *individuality*.

There is no need to stress the danger of docetism or disincarnationism, if such a doctrine is pushed too far. Do we really meet Jesus, if He is not a human person but "only" a divine Person with a human nature that is not individualized by its human (proper) personhood, but by a divine Person, and which is so transformed by His divine personality that any empirical evidence of His human nature is nearly deleted? It is difficult to affirm, according to this hypothesis, that Christ took on *a* human nature, for *a* human nature does not exist without *its own* personality.[100]

We cannot follow all the meanderings of Patristic and Scholastic theology, worked out in order to reply to the varying objections. We are here concerned only with the main tenet of the traditional solution, namely that the living Christ is the risen Christ, and that—as such—he has no singularity. "God raised him to life again,

---

[96] This would offer the appropriate context for the Adam-Christ theology. See "Just as all Men die in Adam, so will all Men be brought to life in Christ" (1 Co 15:22).

[97] "We can not even think a hypostasis without a nature," says Maxim the Confessor, *Opuscula theologica et polemica* (*PG* 91.264A).

[98] See P. Schoonenberg, *Ein Gott der Menschen* (Zürich: Benziger, Zürich, 1969), 92, where he says that Christ's unity is that of a person who is divine and human precisely *as* a person.

[99] *In humanitate Deus* (εν ανθρωποτητι θεος) is a typical expression of Cyril of Alexandria speaking of Christ; see *Homil. Pasch.*, XVII,2 (*PG* 77.776).

[100] Traditional Christian theology tried to solve this theo-anthropological problem by introducing the concept of hypostatic union.

setting him free from the pangs of death."[101] The principle of singularity does not apply to him, because he is not simply a numerical specimen of the species "human mortals." Christ's divinity is safeguarded, but his true humanity is in jeopardy.[102]

The opposite doctrinal trend—that is, the one stressing Jesus's humanness—when it tries to express the Christian understanding of Christ, it has to maintain with equal emphasis that the man Jesus has in Himself something peculiar, which, although it does not diminish His humanness, yet transcends it in such a way that it makes a sui generis relationship with Him possible. This uniqueness (given in the resurrection) is, in a way, the very negation of singularity and individuality, for—by definition—individuality is that which exclusively belongs to a particular being and not to another. I can share everything with another, except individuality.

What we are aiming at is the fact that Christ—as Christian faith sees Him, namely, as someone who is living, who is present in the sacraments and in our brothers, who transcends time and with whom you can enter into an intimate relationship—does not fall within the category of the *individual* in the philosophical and current sense of the word.[103]

The Identity of Christ

Second, we are led to the question of whether Christ's identity needs to be sought in terms of individuality. Why the desire to pin Him down, or at least to pinpoint Him? "Then, if anyone says to you: Look, here is the Messiah, or: There he is, do not believe them!"[104] He is not an individual who can be said to be here or there. Rather, "Like the lightning from the east, flashing toward the west, will be the coming of the Son of Man."[105]

This may be taken as a figure of speech or as a literal statement. But we cannot say what a *who* is (in our case, who Jesus is) without being ourselves both in the question and in the answer. An individual never answers the question of *who*, but only of *what*. When we ask *who* somebody is, we are not looking for his individu-

---

[101] Ac 2:24.

[102] See the postconciliar theology on the problem, after the vivid discussions (Galter, Diepen, Parente, etc.) regarding Christ's "I" in the decades before Vatican II. For a more recent bibliography: J. Ashton, "The Consciousness of Christ," *The Way* 10, nos. 1–2 (January and April 1970): 59–71, 147–57; R. Brown, *Jesus, God and Man* (London: Chapman, 1968); R. Guardini, *Die menschliche Wirklichkeit des Herrn* (Würzburg: Werkbund, 1958 [English trans., *The Humanity of Christ* (London, 1964)]); E. Gutwenger, "The Problem of Christ's Knowledge," *Concilium* 1, no. 2 (January 1966), 48–55; A. A. Ortega, "Cristo, su conscienda humana y su person divina," *Homenaje a Xavier Zubiri* (Madrid: Editorial Moneda y Crédito, 1970), 1:99–119; K. Rahner, "Dogmatische Erwägungen über das Wissen und Selbstbewusstsein Christi," in *Schriften zur Theologie* (Einsiedeln: Benziger, 1962), 5:222–45; P. de Rosa, *Christ and Original Sin* (London: Chapman, 1967), esp. 1–14, 23–72.

[103] See my introduction to the Spanish translation of J. Guitton, *La Virgen María* (Madrid: Rialp, 1952), 30–34. Also vol. I, book 2, *Opera Omnia*.

[104] Mt 24:23.

[105] Mt 24:27.

ality—that is, what he is exclusively "in himself," but the "you" he is to me or to somebody else.

We are not asking a question about a "thing in itself," but about a living person. Asking for a *who* means looking for a *you*.[106] Individuality is essentially that which does *not* answer the question of *who*. We cannot approach nor participate in individuality.[107] We are not really looking for a person if we are searching for individuality. No answer to the question *who* can have a meaning if it does not involve *me* as much as it involves *him* or *her*. For this very reason, a merely subjective, as well as a merely objective, approach will never satisfy us. Epistemological realism is as insufficient as its idealistic counterpart. The *who* that we seek in Jesus is the risen one, whom men crucified and whom God made both Lord and Anointed.[108]

We could begin with a simple philosophical reflection, aiming at the core of my *who*. Who am I? What makes me *me* is neither my body alone, or my thoughts or my will alone, nor what I am today or I was yesterday, neither an ever-escaping and ever-receding substance, nor a phenomenal bundle of empirical data. Nor will any concept or idea satisfy me as an expression of what I am. In the quest for the I, we are obliged to transcend every singularity and overcome any essentialistic and objectified approach. To find an object is certainly not to discover the living "I." What makes me *me* is not individuality but personality, not the private property of my "substance" but the connection of the accusative *me* with the nominative *I* that utters *it* (me), not singleness but communion, not incommunicability but relation. The search for the *I* always passes through a *you*, and it also implies a *he* or *she*.

The identity of Christ we are looking for is not what we may expect from any accurate historical information, or an analysis of His physical and psychological diagrams, not even what a philosophical scrutiny of His words and doctrines may reveal about *who* He is, but that type of identity that is found in the encounter with a person, that knowledge that springs up when we really know and love somebody—which is more than, and different from, the results of all examinations of objective data (assuming that such objective data exist).

Individual and Person

Whatever solution we may be inclined to follow, and without pretending to solve this ever-recurring problem of self-identity, we will now study the issue at a level in which several hypotheses may concur. Whether we accept a substantialistic view or

---

[106] Christian spirituality has always affirmed that the true human quest for God is, in point of fact, only the conscious answer and reaction to the divine search for Man. The *I* looking for his *you*: "You are my beloved Son" (Lk 3:22) were the words Christ heard during the event of his own initiation (and realization).

[107] *Individuum ineffabile atque incommunicabile*, says Christian Scholasticism, commenting on Aristotle. See, for example, Thomas Aquinas, *Sentencia libri De anima* II.12.375, on Aristotle, *De anima* II.5 (417b22).

[108] See Ac 2:36.

not, whether we follow an *ātman* or an *anātmavāda* theory, in both cases we may agree that there is a fundamental distinction between "individual" and "person."[109] We will refrain from elaborating a whole theory and will concentrate only on the distinction insofar as it applies to our case.[110]

Here we come upon one of the semantic plays in which human culture is so ironically rich. The Latin term *persona*, rendering the Greek πρόσωπον, referred to the mask that "personifies" the role of a human being on the stage of a theatre—as well as, later on, in the theatre of the world. The mask, the persona, does not individualize, but it personifies—that is, it frees us from our individuality and consequently allows us to play our role, overcoming individualistic inhibitions by involving us in the web of interrelations of human existence. Every human being has a different persona that allows him or her to perform the role for which he or she has been called into existence.[111] Every man is a "personified" image of God, his Creator, in the traditional Christian worldview.[112] You *are* what you *act*, what you perform, the role you play.[113] Starting from here, the *person* came to mean the deepest core of human being, one's personhood.[114] The mask was interiorized but also substantialized.

The identification between individual and person is a consequence of a complex process. On the one hand, it is the result of medieval nominalism grafted into the Cartesian system and mingled with other insights of the Protestant era in Europe. On the other hand, it is the fruit of an evolutionary growth from a more collective *we*-consciousness to a more personified awareness of the intricate web of relationship that constitutes the world.[115] This identification finds its climax in our technological times, which cannot deal with persons unless the person is given the status of an individual—and an isolated individual at that.

---

[109] We may note—without, however, insisting—that the notion of "corporate personality" is closer to the biblical understanding of Man than the modern notion of individuality.

[110] See Max Scheler, *Der Formalismus in der Ethik und die materiale Wertethik: Neuer Versuch der Grundlegung eines ethischen Personalismus* (Halle: Niemeyer, 1921).

[111] Since it would be clumsy to put each time "him/her" or "he/she" or "man/woman" when speaking of the human person, we will mostly use the masculine form with an androgynous meaning.

[112] For the Christian contribution, with numerous bibliographical references, see S. Alvarez Turienzo, "El Christianismo y la formación del concepto de persona," in *Homenaje a Xavier Zubiri*, 1:43–77.

[113] We recall the fundamental, classical distinction between constitutive *acts* of the human being and his accidental *doings*, in line with the *poiêsis* and *praxis* of Aristotle, the *agere* and *facere* of the Scholastics, etc.

[114] See from a neo-Thomistic point of view, A. Malet, *Personne et Amour dans la théologie trinitaire de St. Thomas d'Aquin* (Paris: Vrin, 1956); and also A. Kröger, *Mensch und Person: Moderne Personbegriffe in der katholischen Theologie* (Recklinghausen: Paulus, 1967).

[115] This would not justify us in considering the "individual soul" as *Grundvoraussetzung* of Christian belief, as, for instance, in E. Cassirer, *Individuum und Kosmos in der Philosophie der Renaissance* (Darmstadt: Wissenschaftliche Buchgesellschaft, 1963).

However this may be, we will now leave aside historical and cultural anthropological questions, as well as any metaphysical substantialistic or antisubstantialistic,
ātman- or *anātma-*conceptions, just maintaining that *Man is a person but not, properly
speaking, an individual.* The concept of individual is only an abstraction, for practical
purposes, from the more complex reality of the human being, and if substantialized,
it is the expression of a reified, lifeless, and naively realistic worldview.[116]

In modern civilization, the need for an individualized status is becoming—for
good or for ill—increasingly important, even for survival, but no individualization
touches the core of the human being. The purposes of individualization are limited
to problems of quantification, considering Man as a specimen of a species, as an
individual within a larger group. When we say "individual" in the modern world,
we ultimately think of just the opposite of what the philosophical word suggests.[117]
We say "individual" and we do not mean what is unique and personal, but all that
is quantifiable, one element of a multiplicity: mouth (to feed), body (to clothe),
citizen (to be given a job), soul (to save), and so on. We mean all that can be simply
considered as one instance among many.

The concept of person does not belong to this field. A person is not quantifiable.
Five individuals are, or may be, more valuable than three, and it might be justifiable
to sacrifice ten individuals in order to save a hundred. All this does not apply to
the person. My person does not end in my fingernails; my person is the center of a
network of relationships that may extend to the very limits of the world.[118] A person
cannot be seen or judged from inside; a person cannot be manipulated nor amassed
in a heap. It is not quantifiable, so therefore there would be no meaning whatsoever
in saying that one hundred persons are more important than ten. Each of them is
unique; in the language of logic, anything may be predicated of a person, but the
person cannot be the predicate of anything.[119] The person is not a predicate;[120] its

---

[116] See two modern witnesses: "Ce n'est pas en s'isolant... mais en s'associant *convenable-
ment* avec tous les autres que l'individu peut espérer atteindre à la plénitude de sa personne"
[Not by isolating himself... but by associating himself *fittingly* to all others can the individual attain the fulfilment of his person] (Teilhard de Chardin, *L'Avenir de l'Homme*, 5:248
[emphasis in original]). "The Christian does not confuse the person with the individual, and
does not consider his relation to the ground of Being as a purely subject-object relationship"
(Thomas Merton, *Mystics and Zen Masters* [New York: Farrar, Straus and Giroux, 1967], 214).

[117] See, e.g., "est de ratione individui, quod non possit in pluribus esse" [it belongs to
the concept of individual that it cannot be in more subjects], Thomas Aquinas, *Sum. theol.*
III, q.77, a.2.

[118] See Father Zossima's brother giving the Russian monk as his testament the insight
that "everyone is really responsible toward all Men, for all Men and for everything," in
Dostoevsky's *The Brothers Karamazov*, VI.1.

[119] See Aristotle, *Categ.* V (2a11) saying that the ουσια πρωτη (first substance) can have
predicates, but cannot be itself a predicate.

[120] See the famous "Sein ist offenbar kein reales Prädikat" [Being is clearly not a real
predicate] against the ontological argument, in Immanuel Kant, *Kritik der reinen Vernunft,*

entity resides in its entire being.[121] A person is a unique center of relationship, as a qualified knot in the fabric of the ontological threads composing the warp and woof of reality.

There has been, in modern times, a growing confusion between these two terms, due in part to the surfacing of individual consciousness, characteristic of Western modernity.[122] If the birth of consciousness can be said to be the *original sin* originating the birth of the species *Homo sapiens*,[123] the birth of individual consciousness represents the *cultural sin* of the West, although in both cases one could speak of *felix culpa*.[124] However this may have been, the fact is that in more traditional societies, personal consciousness was lodged, as it were, in the collectivity, so that the awareness of being a "knot in a net of relationships" (what we today call "a person") was somewhat blurred. Or rather, the knot was what *was* known as corporate personality: a fruit of the *collective conscious*. We should not underrate the importance of the growth of personal consciousness and its disentanglement from the web of more complex and amorphous human conglomerates, but this should not blind us to the fact that the person "disappears" if we freeze those centers of relationships and handle them as if they were independent knots, capable of separate manipulation.

I discover myself as a knot when I discover the threads that are concurring and being entwined in that knot. Without the weave I would be nothing, but the knot is something more than just the weave, even if this "more" is neither quantitative nor independent of the threads that make up the knot.

In point of fact, the term "person," properly speaking, does not allow a plural form, not only because each person is unique and therefore nonquantifiable, but also because a peculiar plural or rather polarity is internal to the very concept of person. Person in fact always implies society, relations with several centers or focuses, so that the very concept of an "individual and individualized person" would be a contradiction in terms. Properly speaking, neither the singular nor the plural applies to the person. An "I" is such only if there is a "you," and vice versa. There is no "I" without a "you," and there is no "you" without an "I." This is a vital circle. Besides, the I-you (and we-you) relationship is only such if there is a "he" or a "she" (and "they")—that

---

A598, B626. See also Averroes saying the same, centuries before, in his *Tahāfut-al-Tahāfut*, and the commentary on it by T. Izutsu, *The Concept and Reality of Existence* (Tokyo: Keio Institute of Cultural and Linguistic Studies, 1971), 81ff.

[121] See Leibniz's thesis: "omne individuum sua tota entitate individuatur" [every individual is individualized by the whole of its own identity]; this is true, properly speaking, only of the person.

[122] Existential anxiety, in Tillich's sense, is nothing but the consciousness of becoming more and more an (isolated) individual. It cannot be removed, of course, unless the individualistic root is deleted.

[123] See the works by R. C. Zaehner, *The Convergent Spirit*, then reprinted as *Matter and Spirit* (New York: Harper & Row, 1963); and *Evolution in Religion* (Oxford: Clarendon, 1971).

[124] See the chapter, "La superacion del humanismo," in my *Humanismo y Cruz* (Madrid: Rialp, 1963, 178–253). See *Opera Omnia* III.1.

is, a further pole of the person, offering the horizon, as it were, in which the I-you (we-you) relationship emerges and becomes meaningful and real. These relationships are not only psychological but ontological, or more simply, constitutive.[125]

Personal Identity

We may now approach the issue of personal identity, applying it immediately to our case. The theological formulation of it could be the following: "No one can say, *Jesus is Lord*, except in the Holy Spirit."[126] In other words, no one can really point at Jesus and refer to Him as a living person, except under the action of the Holy Spirit—that is, under the spell of love and the inspiration of an inner contact, a participation in an ontological network of relationships in which Jesus is disclosed not as a mere individual but as a person. This can only be done if one enters into a personal relationship with Him, if the discovery is really a personal encounter with a living *you* that conditions me (my "I")—as well as my "I" conditions him (his "I").[127] Here, personal relationship should not be imagined as an external, dialectical encounter between two "beings," but as their constitutive relation, which in that particular context was inchoative and abstract until the *you* surfaced in the relationship and made the *I* meaningful and real.[128]

What makes Jesus truly *Jesus* is His personal identity, and this personal identity can only be said to be real, and thus true, if we enter into a personal relationship with Him. Only then can one discover the living Christ of faith, who lives in the interior of oneself.[129]

We should not mistake *personal identity* for *personal identification*. The latter means the identification of a person by means of external marks—that is, all those

---

[125] Here again the problem transcends our limits, and the literature is overwhelming. See only as an example: K. Nishitani, "The Personal and the Impersonal in Religion," in *Eastern Buddhist* 3, no. 1 (June 1970): 1ff.; R. Taylor, "The *Anattā* Doctrine and Personal Identity," *Philosophy East and West* 19, no. 4 (October 1969): 359–66.

[126] 1 Co 12:3.

[127] This is implied in the Christian conception of the Mystical Body of Christ, together with the Christian idea of the growth of Christ not only in the heart of the believer, but also in history and reality. This leads to the *una persona* of St. Augustine and his definition of heaven: "et erit unus Christus amans seipsum" [there will be One Christ loving himself], *Epist. ad Parthos* (*PL* 35.2055). See also E. Mersch, *Le Christ, l'Homme et l'Univers* (Paris: Desclée de Brouwer, 1962).

[128] See the two theological studies by H. Mühlen, trying to recover the personal-centeredness of ecclesiology and pneumatology: *Una Mystica Persona. Die Kirche als das Mysterium der heilsgeschichtlichen Identität des Heiligen Geistes in Christus und den Christen: Eine Person in vielen Personen* (Paderborn: Schöningh, 1967); and *Der Heilige Geist als Person in der Trinität, bei der Inkarnation und im Gnadenbund: Ich-Du-Wir* (Münster: Aschendorff, 1967).

[129] See Rom 6:10; 14:7f.; Gal 2:20; Ph 1:21.

empirical features that, properly speaking, do not belong to the person. It is a juridical term, an expression used by the police to "identify" someone. It has little or nothing to do with the person. Personal identification belongs no more to the person than an ID card. It answers the "what" question. Personal identity, on the other hand, refers to the core of the human being, as present to oneself and to others; it means that by which the person is himself or herself. Personal identity answers the question "who," and it is expressed by the proper noun, the authentic "I" that is only real when involved in the network of personal relationships.

A personal identification of Christ would discover Him as an undoubtedly interesting and probably great man in history, but it would not entail any living relationship with Him whatsoever. The historian mistrusts the believer, in the same way the judge is suspicious toward someone who is serving as a witness for some close relative or intimate friend. The knowledge that emerges in this way cannot properly be called *personal* but only *historical.* Jesus will appear as a historically relevant figure of the past, with a still uncommon influence on the present, but the only point of reference will be His historical coordinates and His impact on the lives of people. Ultimately, this approach does not discover Jesus as a person but only as a historical personage. The risen Christ has here no place, and any kind of resultant belief must be catalogued as mere psychological conviction.

Personal identity, on the other hand, can only be discovered by entering into a living relationship with the person concerned. It enables one to answer the question about "who" because one discovers the *who* within oneself—that is, the *who* has become a *you*, or at least a *he* or *she*. In other words, only through faith, that is, only in the Spirit, can we have a personal relationship with Jesus and discover his personal identity.

This implies that the word "Jesus" has basically two different meanings: one as a historical category, and another as a personal category. The former is attained by means of historical identification, which permits us to speak of Jesus and the belief Christians have in and through Him. The latter is attained by means of personal identity and allows us to discover Him as a "part," or rather a "pole," of our personal being, as one of the many traits that make up our person. Personal identity regards the other as well as me, and only this internal discovery lets me take upon my lips the real and proper name of the other: the proper noun.

We are here dealing with the special case of Christ, but the distinction between personal identification and personal identity applies to any human person as well. There cannot be any personal relationship, love, even personal knowledge without the involvement and participation implied in personal identity. And to discover the personal identity is to enter into the mystery of the person. The concept of neighbor could perhaps be developed here. "Who is my neighbor?"[130] The answer does not just say "every man," but defines him as the one who is really close to me, the one

---

[130] Lk 10:29.

for whom I also am effectively a *who*, a *you*, a person. The neighbor thus possesses a constitutive relationship with me. Until people become neighbors to us, they are not yet really persons for us, nor are we for them, but only objects. Our humanness matches the quality, intensity, and closeness of our relationship with our fellow-beings; and the same could be said regarding God. We can only love God as our neighbor, and He can only become such to us inasmuch as He enters into personal identity with us; otherwise, He remains an object, an idea perhaps, but not a living reality. We begin by discovering God as a *He*; subsequently He becomes the *You*, and finally the *I*.

Reverting to our case, the Jesus of Christian believers is in fact the risen Lord, in whatever way we may like to interpret resurrection. In other words, He is not simply the historical Jesus but the risen One, a Jesus who enters *as person* into the very structure of our own personal existence. He cannot be discovered in the exclusively outer world of history, nor in the exclusively inner world of our own thoughts, feelings, or beliefs. Morphologically speaking, the figure of Christ is ambivalent and, in a way, theandric.

While recognizing this ambivalence, we can proceed to affirm that, among all the elements of Peter's answer—"You are the Messiah, the Son of the living God"[131]— the only universal element is the *you*, and the fundamental issue is not so much to elucidate intellectually the predicates in the sentence, but to discover existentially the subject, the real *you*, who is much more than a projection of my own *ego*. Now, this *you* cannot be pinpointed by any unequivocal means of identification, and it is not without reason that idolatry—that is, the "freezing" of the ineffable Supreme Being into a particular object of the senses or the mind—is said to be the greatest sin against the Spirit. The *you* grants identity, but no identification: "Why do you ask my name?"[132]

The Cosmological and Historical Context

One of the causes of the present-day disorientation about the figure of Jesus is the shift from the cosmological context to the historical one, that is, the cosmological myth being changed into the historical one.

Traditional Christology works within the context of a Trinitarian doctrine, inscribed in a particular cosmological worldview. In this worldview, Christ is considered to be the center of the whole universe, ontological as well as cosmological and personal. He is the Mediator[133]—not the intermediary, as later periods tended to

---

[131] Mt 16:16.

[132] Gn 32:30; cf. Is 9:6; Jg 13:18; Ps 8:2. See also Dionysius, *De divinis nominibus* I.6 (*PG* 3.596); Eckhart, *Expositio libri Genesis,* in *Lateinische Werke* (Stuttgart: Kohlhammer), 1:95ff., and the excellent commentary by W. Lossky, *Théologie négative et connaissance de Dieu chez Maître Eckhart* (Paris: Vrin, 1960), 13–96.

[133] See 1 Tim 11:5.

imagine him.[134] He takes the innumerable polarities of reality upon Himself, and in Him all opposites coincide.[135]

He is not only Man and God, or more exactly Son of Man[136] and Son of God,[137] but also alpha and omega,[138] beginning and end;[139] he is the only-begotten Son,[140] the Firstborn among the dead[141] and the living,[142] the immortal one[143] and the *eschaton*,[144] He who made everything[145] and He for whom everything has been made,[146] He who has not been "convinced of sin"[147] and who "became sin" for us,[148] the universal reconciler,[149] and so on.

Christ, in this conception, is the center of a cosmic *maṇḍala* from which the whole of reality emerges and into which it goes.[150] Everything that *is* comes and refers to this center. It could be said that every being is a *Christophany*.[151] The universe is ordered, organic, and centered. This center is, by definition, Christ.[152] We have here a Christocentric universe. God is here less conspicuous: He is behind the curtain, as it were. He is the Father,[153] the *fontalis plenitude*,[154] the *fons et origo totius divinitatis*,[155]

---

[134] See a good deal of European and Roman Catholic spirituality of the eighteenth and early nineteenth centuries.

[135] From Dyonisius, Bonaventure, and Nicholas of Cusa to Blondel and Teilhard de Chardin, one could trace an interesting theological line. See, e.g., E. Cousins, "The Coincidence of Opposites in the Christology of Saint Bonaventure," *Franciscan Studies* 28 (1968): 27–45.

[136] See Mt 8:20 and *passim*.

[137] See Mt 14:33 and *passim*; Jn 1:49, etc.

[138] See Rev 1:8; 21:6; 22:13.

[139] See Rev 1:17; 21:6; 22:13.

[140] See Jn 1:14.

[141] See Col 1:18.

[142] See Rom 8:29.

[143] Ac 2:24; Rev 1:18.

[144] See Rev 1:17; 2:8; 22:13.

[145] Jn 1:3; Col 1:16.

[146] See Col 1:16–17.

[147] See Jn 8:46, etc.

[148] See 2 Co 5:21.

[149] See Ep 1:10.

[150] See E. Cousins, "Mandala Symbolism in the Theology of Bonaventure," *University of Toronto Quarterly* 40, no. 3 (Spring 1971): 185–201.

[151] See R. Panikkar, "Le concept d'ontonomie," *Acte du XIe Congrès International de Philosophie*, Brussels, August 20–26, 1953 (Louvain: Nauwelaerts, 1953), 3:187.

[152] See Bonaventure describing Christ as the *medium metaphysicum, physicum, mathematicum, logicum, ethicum, politicum, theologicum* of reality (*In Hexaemeron* I.n.11–39, Quaracchi, ed., 5:331–35), quoted by Cousins, "Mandala Symbolism," 187.

[153] See the expression of St. Basil: "We confess *one* God [the Father], not in number, but in nature," in *Epist.* VIII.2 (*PG* 32.248C).

[154] See Bonaventure, *I Sent.*, d.27, p.1, a., un, q.2, ad 3. An expression then reused by more than one Council of Toledo (namely the VI, IX, and XVI); cf. *Denz.*, 490, 525, and 568.

[155] See Augustine, *De Trinitate* IV.20.29, where the expression "principium totius

the transcendent Origin, the Ultimate Cause and External Principle.[156] Christ, in function of his theandric nature of only-begotten Son of the Father and Firstborn of creation, is at the core of everything as well as the very power of God, His *Śakti*. Even the Thomistic tradition acknowledges that by the same act by which God begets the Son, He creates the world.[157] The words in the Latin version of Psalm 62—"Semel locutus est Deus, duo haec audivi"[158]—were interpreted by Christian tradition as, "God speaks out just once, but we hear it twice; eternally in the womb of the Trinity, and temporally in the creative explosion of Being."[159]

When this tradition speaks of Christ as the universal Savior, it is simply stating a qualified tautology (as all principles are). Christ is the Savior because He is the central point that gives cohesion and meaning to the entire universe.[160]

---

deitatis" occurs. See *Denz.*, 3326 for the utilization of the same sentence by Leo XIII in his 1897 encyclical *Divinum illud munus*.

[156] For an example of the horizon of these ideas, see *Propositions* 2 and 18 of the *Liber XXIV Philosophorum:* "Deus est sphaera infinita cuius centrum est ubique, circumferentia nusquam" [God is an infinite sphere whose center is everywhere, the circumference nowhere]; "Deus est sphaera, cuius tot sunt circumferentiae, quod sunt puncta" [God is a sphere having as many circumferences as points]. See also Bonaventure, *Itinerarium mentis in Deum* V.8 (Quaracchi, ed., V.310), quoting Allan De Lille, *Theologicae Regulae* 7 (*PL* 210, 627).

[157] See the astonishing and refreshing text: "Deus enim cognoscendo se, cognoscit omnem creaturam. Verbum igitur in mente conceptum est repraesentativum omnis eius quod actu intelligitur. Sed quia Deus uno actu et se et omnia intelligit, unicum Verbum eius est expressivum non solum Patris, sed etiam creaturarum" [By knowing himself, God knows every creature. So, the word conceived in one's mind represents everything that is conceived in act. But, since God by one act understands both himself and everything, his only Word not only expresses the Father but also the creatures], Thomas Aquinas, *Sum. theol.* I, q.34, a.3. See also, "Quia una actione generat Filium, qui est heres, lux de luce, et creat creaturam, quae est tenebra, creata, facta, non Filius nec heres luminis, illuminationis et creationis" [Because by one act He begets the Son, who is the heir, light from light, and He creates the creature, which is shadow, created, made, not the Son, nor the heir of light, enlightenment and creation], Eckhart, *Expos. in Ioan.* I.5.73.

See another example from the Christian tradition: "Der Vater wendet sein Auge auf sein eigenes Wesen, das seine Natur ist, und schaut sich selber. Und da Er sich selber schaut, da schaut Er alle Dinge auf einmal. Und da formt Er ein Wort und spricht sich selber in das Wort und alle Dinge, und das Wort spricht sich zurück in den Vater" [The Father turns his eyes to his own substance, i.e., his own nature, and sees himself. And by seeing himself, He sees all things together. He then forms one Word and—by that Word—He expresses himself and all things, and the Word expresses himself in the Father, in his turn], Henricus de Hanna (Hane der Karmelit), *Vom ungeschaffenen und vom geschaffenen Geist*, cited in *Vom inwendigen Reichtum* (Leipzig: Hegner, 1937), 81.

See also the recurrent Upaniṣadic sentence: *vato vaco nirvante* [whence words return], *TU* II.4.1; II.9.1.

[158] Ps 61 [62]:12.

[159] See Lossky, *Théologie negative*, 51–60, for a simple example, with ample references.

[160] See the medieval and postmedieval discussion, "utrum, si Adam non peccasset,

It would not be totally adequate to call this conception a merely cosmological one: the primacy here given to Christ is also personal and theological.[161] Christ is the central myth, giving cohesion and conferring order to the whole universe. The traditional model of the Mystical Body, in order to explain the place and function of Christ in the universe, could here offer immense, unexplored perspectives.[162] This universe has also a soul, a vital principle, an *anima mundi*.[163] This is the realm of the Spirit, which Christian tradition has identified with the Spirit of Christ.

In the contemporary scene, the emphasis has shifted to the historical realm. In our modern times, history plays the mythical role that the cosmological setting played in past times. Christ is no longer seen as the *Pantocratōr*,[164] nor therefore as the theophany κατ'εξοχην; He ceases to be the King of the universe, and becomes the center of history—of human history, of course. He does not need to be deified. It suffices to stress—in a particular, singular way—His humanity and the role He plays in making Man more human.[165] Every history is salvation history; entering into history amounts to accepting the Christian economy of salvation. Similar affirmations are very common in recent literature.[166] Christ plays here a secular role, and the gospel becomes the secular Bible.[167] Now the man Jesus invites us to get rid of all Trinitarian and especially Christological "screens" that mediate and deform His real presence.[168] In this context, He cannot be said to be the "center" of history, because, by and large, the circle as a figure of speech has lost appeal, but He

Verbum incarnatum fuisset" [whether the Word would become incarnate, in case Adam did not sin].

[161] See the bibliographical references given in L. M. Bello, "De universali Christi primatu atque regalitate," *Acta Ordinis Fratrum Minorum* 52 (1933): 293–311. For more recent bibliography and discussions, see J.-F. Bonnefoy, *La Primauté du Christ selon l'Écriture et la Tradition* (Rome: Herder, 1959), and for an exegesis of the capital text of Col 1:15—with abundant bibliography—see A. Hockel, *Christus der Erstgeborene* (Düsseldorf, Patmos, 1965). Or again, G. Maloney, *The Cosmic Christ from Paul to Teilhard* (New York: Sheed & Ward, 1968); L. M. Bombin, "El titulo 'Primogenito de toda la creación' en el himno de *Col.* I, 15–20," *Claretanium* 10 (1970): 5–78.

[162] See E. Mersch, *La théologie du Corps Mystique*, 2 vols. (Paris: Desclée, 1949) for a fruitful beginning.

[163] See T. Gregory, *Anima mundi* (Florence: Sansoni, 1955), and Mersch, *Le Christ*, 20ff., giving many examples, also within the Christian tradition, of the world considered as a living entity.

[164] See Rev 1:8; 4:8; 11:17; 15:3; 16:7, 14; 19:6, 15; 21:22.

[165] The innumerable studies on—and promoting—Christian humanism could offer a good example of what we are trying to say. See the above-mentioned chapter in my book, with ample bibliographical references.

[166] The names of O. Cullmann, W. Pannenberg, Y. Congar, et al., come immediately to mind.

[167] See the works by P. v. Buren, H. Cox, G. Vahanian, T. J. J. Altizer, etc.

[168] See M. Legaut, *Introduction à l'intelligence du passé et de l'avenir du christianisme* (Paris: Aubier, 1970).

is the new starting point and the furthermost end, the Omega point, the Absolute Future, and the like.[169]

Our point here is only to stress the continuity between the previous periods and the present times. The contents have certainly changed, but in each period Jesus plays a decisive role. The myths are different, but their structure remains the same.

The Spirit: Salvation in Christ

Is Christ Universal and Concrete?

We can now go back to our starting point. Is there any way of understanding Jesus Christ in a universal way, without watering down His concreteness? Is it possible to fully acknowledge Jesus without having to be spiritually a Semite? Is there any way of fully accepting the Bible as the sacred book of one religious tradition of humankind, without however reducing other traditions to mere "shadows" or simply preparations? Can we believe in Jesus without having to recognize Christendom as the only social structure conveying His message? In one word, is it possible to disentangle Jesus from the cultural and even religious garb with which He has been vested—not only the Hellenic or Western one, but also the Semitic and biblical one?[170] Does Jesus belong to the human race, or only to biblical and postbiblical history?[171]

There are, in fact, two different moments of one and the same problem: (a) to claim particularity and concreteness for the universal. This was the theological approach probably since the Patristic period. The question was centered on the *incarnation of God*; (b) to claim universality for the particular and concrete. This was probably the approach of the first church, and certainly the present-day one. The question becomes here the *divinization of Christ*.

Here we should insert an important reflection, namely the critical evaluation of the question itself, that is, the way of presenting the problem. The very query about universality and concreteness, in point of fact, springs from a perspective that is far from being universal. The concern for universality arises from a preeminently

---

[169] See A. C. Dyson, *Who Is Jesus Christ?* (London: SCM, 1969), as an example of Troeltsch's cry, "Alles ist geschichtlich geworden!" [Everything has become historical!].

[170] "And because the life of Jesus has significance and transcendency, I believe that he belongs, not only to Christianity, but to the entire world, to all races and people; it matters little under what flag, name, or doctrine they may work, profess a faith, or worship a God inherited from the ancestors," wrote Mahātma Gandhi in *Modern Review*, October 1964, 67. See the religious movement of K. Subba Rao in South India: a former Hindū schoolteacher preaching Christ but refusing to be baptized in any "church": "Have the very fanatics that destroyed you [Christ] in the name of Religion now made you an article of merchandise?" Cited in K. Baago, *The Movement around Subba Rao* (Bangalore: CISRS, 1968). See also the words of R. Garaudy quoted below.

[171] See R. Panikkar, *Die vielen Götter und der eine Herr* (Weilheim: O. W. Barth, 1963), 126–29 and *passim*.

theoretical thinking, whereas the primacy given to concreteness belongs to a rather mythical and empirical level. This means that, all too often, intellectuals do not feel the need for concreteness, and almost instinctively consider concreteness as a condescension, just needed for those who are intellectually or even spiritually "less developed." On the contrary, for the Man steeped in the concrete, the very problem of universality does not arise (not being a concrete problem itself), and he will feel like betraying his religiousness if he indulges in talks about universality.

Two Options

We can now examine the two hypotheses that are still susceptible to a Christian interpretation: *first*, Christ is Savior but not the only one, and *second*, Christ is the unique Savior.

We may repeat, once again, that by using the words "salvation" and "Savior" we do not mean any particular, definite sense. Anything helping Man to reach the final destination of his human condition, whatever this may be, suffices here for our purpose, which is not to study the nature of salvation but the meaning of the name of Jesus as Savior.

The first option begins to be favored by an increasing number of recent studies, as a reaction against the second, more traditional one. The first option appears to be more irenic and tolerant.

We would like to show, on the one hand, that the first option is only a less direct and more concealed way of formulating the second option; and, on the other hand, that the second one does not need to be interpreted in an exclusivistic and monopolistic way.

Further, we may succeed in showing that we have ultimately to do with the greatest issue on which human consciousness can reflect: the One and the many, the εν και πολλα of the Greeks,[172] the *ekam advitiyam* of the *Upaniṣads*,[173] the one or many Saviors of our query.

Nor is this all. We would like to suggest that the whole problem arises because of the reification of Christ, and the confusion of His *what* with His *who*—that is, His historical identification with His personal identity.

There Are Many Saviors

This first option will admit other Saviors and will have to explain the traditional Christian belief in Christ's universality by stressing three factors that may account for it. The first factor is (a) historical and cosmological; the second, (b) psycho-anthropological; and the third, (c) logico-epistemological.

This explanation will amount to showing that the statement, "Christ is the universal Savior," is a valid and true *text* only within a particular *context*, but not

---

[172] Plato, *Phileb.* 15D.
[173] *CU* VI.21.

outside it. We may reflect here on the change of horizon in our times, so as to explain the supposed claim to universality of the Christian Savior. It would all boil down to recognizing that the realm within which Christ's universality was conceived and affirmed no longer covers the whole horizon of human experience, so that we can recognize a certain legitimate claim to universality inasmuch as the context was assumed to be the universal *texture*. But we deny any actual universality, because the *world*, that is, the range of human experience, both subjective and objective, has radically changed since the times in which the Christian doctrine was formulated, and it can no longer be identified with the Christian context. It could be said that it is a process of demythologization, or rather remythologization, for it exchanges one myth for another.

(a) The historical-cosmological factor implies the fact that, until now, most people have lived in closed cultural, geographical, and historical environments. We say "the whole earth," and we basically mean our country or the countries we know; we say "history," "world," "culture," and "religion," and we do not make one step beyond the respective horizons of our experience. So far, Christians have mostly lived in the Mediterranean world and its colonies (of all types). No wonder their claim to universality was tied up with the horizon of their experience. They claimed universality without realizing their boundaries, and now they have to recognize that those boundaries are not the confines of the human horizon. Within Christian theology, one could find a number of examples taken from biblical exegesis. One could, for instance, say that, just as there is no need to affirm that darkness covered Patagonia when Christ died, for the "whole earth"[174] mentioned in the Gospel had other geographical limitations, likewise do the cultural limitations of Christ's action account for the "material" limitations of *this* universality, without invalidating His "formal" claim to universality within a given context.

(b) The psycho-anthropological factor derives from the inherent claim to universality inbuilt in any statement. "A is B" implies that any possible *a* belonging to A is really B. If Christians hold Christ to be the Savior of human beings qua human beings, they are implicitly holding Him to be the Savior of Man. They may recognize that de facto this is not the case, but they will tend to affirm that de jure, *in voto,* potentially, in one way or another, the "others" also are under the saving power of Christ.

We may get around this difficulty by recognizing that such a way of thinking "freezes" truth, objectifying it. Against an objective paradigm of beauty, goodness, or sympathy, no man can say that his wife is the most beautiful, no parents affirm that their children are the best, and no friend think that his or her friend is the most agreeable and sympathetic on earth. Yet one can easily realize that living values and relationships cannot be tackled as objectifiable ideas. Christ can be, thus, the best and most effective Savior once you discover Him and enter into a believing relationship with Him, like a mother can find her child the most charming little baby ever, but

---

[174] Lk 23:44.

the statement cannot "jump" over the living and loving relationship that is inbuilt in the truth of the statement itself. This should not be understood as reducing Christ to a merely subjective figure. To affirm that pure objectivation will not do does not mean that we will fall into the opposite extreme of a sheer subjectivistic position. This simply means that the object-subject dichotomy, in the epistemic identification, has to yield to the actual discovery of personal identity.

(c) The logico-epistemological factor is linked with a peculiar way of thinking of the Semitic mind. It is a way of thinking we have already alluded to: the primacy of the principle of noncontradiction in discovering the self-identity of a being. By using this method of intelligibility, the affirmation, "Christ is the Savior," is seen as equivalent with, "No other than Christ is Savior." The realization that the two sentences are not necessarily equivalent may provide the rationale for this first option (Christ not being the universal Savior). The Christian interpretation would then be that of accepting all positive Christian tenets, but without defending them with the negation of their contraries. The statement, "Christ is Savior," will accordingly be understood as saying exactly what it does, but without implying that there is no other Savior. Even if one affirmed that there is no other Savior, the sentence would be understood as, "There is no other Savior for him or her who proclaims or understands the Gospel."

This first option (there are many Saviors) amounts to saying that there is only a formal and empty concept of salvation, which is then "filled up," as it were, with the different existential and concrete "Saviors."

Therefore, the proper place of Christ depends on our understanding of Christ. What is the *He* that allegedly has a universal saving power? If He is only a geographical and historical reality, that is, only a spatio-temporal reality, it can be hardly said that "Jesus Christ is the universal saving power." If, on the other hand, it is recognized that Jesus promised to send his Spirit;[175] that it was good and convenient that he went away, otherwise the Spirit could not come;[176] that he had other disciples whom the apostles did not know;[177] that he was and is present in the "little ones" we love and help[178]—that, in a word, he is a transhistorical reality—then this understanding of Jesus can lead to the serene acceptance of many Saviors, all of them embodying that saving power that Christians call the Spirit of Jesus. The remaining, and serious, theological problems would then regard the relationship between Jesus of Nazareth and "His" Spirit.[179]

[175] See Jn 15:26, etc.
[176] See Jn 16:7.
[177] See Jn 10:16.
[178] See Mt 25:40.
[179] The astounding affirmations by Meher Baba—"I am the Christ," "I am infinite consciousness," "I am the Highest of the High," "Before me was Zoroaster, Kṛṣṇa, Rāma, Buddha, Jesus and Mohammed"—this and the all-pervading love he has infused to his disciples, for instance, constitute a serious problem that an unbiased theologian cannot simply dismiss as hallucinations or aberrations. See D. E. Stevens, ed., *Listen, Humanity*

Without pursuing this argument further, we would like to turn to the second alternative:

There Is Just One Savior

Christ is the universal Savior: this is, certainly, the most traditional Christian interpretation. It enshrines the core of Christian belief, even though it has often been interpreted in an uncritical and unacceptable way.

I will try to suggest a valid hermeneutic, without now examining other possible interpretations.

We have already seen that sentences such as, "Jesus is the unique Savior," and "in no other name there can be salvation," can only have an acceptable meaning if they do not refer to an *individual* but to a *person*, and this reference involves the speaker as much as the person referred to. In scriptural terms, "Nobody can say *Jesus is Lord*, unless in the Holy Spirit."[180] But the action of the Spirit is never an external one. The Spirit is the immanent divine principle, the inner divine force making room for human growth and allowing Man to reach transcendence.

Christ the Savior is, thus, not to be restricted to the merely historical figure of Jesus of Nazareth. Or, as we have already said, the *identity* of Jesus is not to be confused with his historical *identification*. To say, "Jesus Christ is Lord,"[181] may be considered as the epitome of the Christian confession of faith, but this sentence is not reversible without qualifications. This is so, to begin with, for obvious grammatical reasons: We destroy the subject if we convert it into a predicate, but also because to say, for example, "Buddha is Lord," may not necessarily contradict the Christian sentence. All depends on the *who* we refer to by so different names.

A Christian will say, "Jesus Christ *is* the Lord," but a non-Christian will understand that the Christian is saying, "The Lord is Jesus Christ." Some Buddhists will affirm, "Buddha is the Lord," whereas non-Buddhists will understand that they are saying, "The Lord is Buddha." Everyone who has not made a personal act of faith toward Jesus, Buddha, . . . will invert the sentence and understand, "The Lord is Jesus, Buddha, Man, history, . . ." And we come back to our starting point: the *what* (seen from an objectifying, external perspective) is not the *who*. But *who* is the Lord?

Here again the problem of language becomes of paramount importance, both theologically and philosophically, and linguistic analysis stops being a neo-positivistic tool to handle a central ontological problem.

(New York: Dodd, Mead and Co., 1967). This is only one example among innumerable ones, but this one raises the problem of identity-identification in a very poignant way—in spite of the weak philosophical and historical-religious expressions, as is very often the case when partners speak two different languages, or are on two different levels.

[180] 1 Co 12:3.
[181] Ph 2:11.

The Monopoly of Names

When a name, ceasing to be the carrier of a myth, becomes almost exclusively the sign of an idea, it tends to become the monopoly of the culture, or subculture, that has begotten that particular idea. When names like "grace" or "revelation," for instance, cease to be myths to which many people can refer without filling them up with precise conceptual contents, they become more technical expressions, of— say—particular Scholasticisms, and tend to be used only in that particular formal sense, so that any other use will be considered improper. Any Christian Scholastic theologian will feel uncomfortable (to follow up the example) if these two words are used outside the Christian context. He will maintain that to speak of "revelation" in other world religions is confusing, because it is about a different *concept* of revelation altogether. He will affirm that grace, the precisely meant supernatural and sanctifying grace, cannot habitually exist outside the realm of Christianity. On the natural plane, he will concede, there may be a certain "grace," but, in the supernatural order, Christian grace is the only existing one.[182]

We could equally give a more secular example, taking the word *history* in its modern Western understanding. If by *history* we understand the modern Western concept of historicity, most non-Semitic traditions, of course, have no "history," nor can we use this word to denote homologous notions in other cultures.[183]

In a word, names, within a closed cultural setting, tend to become proper nouns and to become the private property of the users of that culture.

It is just the opposite with the names in which the mythical, and not the *logos*-content, is prevalent. They are of general use and common property, even if the precise concepts expressed by those names may be at variance.

The name of God in a great part of today's world can provide a fitting example. Hardly any religion today will claim a monopoly on the name itself, even though it claims that its particular notion of divinity is the right one. Allah or YHWH cannot be confounded with the generic term of God, but few "enlightened" people belonging to the traditions in which those names occur will call the others "atheists" merely because they don't know the "true name" of God.

Or, to take a couple of current secular instances, *democracy* and *freedom* are two names with more mythical content than *logos*-content. The concepts of democracy and freedom vary, up to almost diametrically opposed views in different countries, while under the word *liberation* a broad range of concepts can be understood, from a mere disentanglement from earthly bonds to freedom from class or political or economic oppression.

---

[182] See the abundant literature, specially in Roman Catholic circles, about the 1940s, culminating in Pius XII's encyclical *Humani generis.*

[183] See my "La loi du Karma et la dimension historique de l'Homme" in E. Castelli, ed., *La Théologie de l'Histoire, Herméneutique et Eschatologie* (Paris: Aubier, 1971), 205–30. Vol. IX, book 1, *Opera Omnia.*

There is a certain ambiguity in all names, depending on the degree of balance being kept between their mythical and *logos*-content. There seems to be, further, a law of inverse proportionality between the mythical universality of a name and its logical-conceptual precision.

We can now apply this to our case, regarding "the Name outside which there is no salvation." Is it a proper or a common noun? It would be out of place here to make reference to etymology, explaining that Jesus means Yeoshua, "God is salvation,"[184] and Christ (Χριστος), that is, the Anointed One, is the Greek translation of the Hebrew word *Messiah* (*Mashiah, Mashiach*),[185] because the Name is not an abstract and general expression but denotes a concrete reality: a person, in this case.

In other words, a real name always expresses both myth and *logos*: the myth provides the context of which the *logos* is the text. Wisdom is the art of having a balanced view of both. Fanaticism destroys myth and imprisons truth in the *logos*. Agnosticism allows truth to escape and remains in an amorphous state in which not even myth can live.

Christians now monopolize a name in the knowledge of which alone there is said to be salvation? Is the saving name a proper or a common noun?

This is not quibbling. It is an effort aimed at fostering growth in Man's consciousness—that is, a development that does not break with the past, and allows continuity, identity and thus loyalty; and, at the same time, is not entangled in a stagnant view of Man, history, and religions.

If we are to take Christian Scripture and Christian religion seriously, we cannot bypass this issue lightheartedly, namely the issue that salvation as human fulfillment—in whatever sense we may take it—is linked with the recognition of a particular name, which requires faith in it.[186] Either (as traditional Christian belief says) the acknowledgment of a special name is required for salvation; or the "name under heaven," outside which there is no salvation, is a common noun, or rather a Supername in the sense that we explain below. In the first case, today Christianity would become a sect, and a dangerous one, for that. We say *today* because one of the contemporary underlying myths is the unity of humankind and the democratic constitution of Man. In other periods in history, when slavery was tolerated, the others were called barbarians, or castes were theologically justified. When the vertical dimension of human existence was considered to be the only real one, it was still possible to consider a selected group—the "born again"—as the only ones who would attain human fullness, and therefore only Christians (or Muslims, brahmans,

---

[184] Jesus, i.e., Yeoshua, was a very common name in Israel; the meaning "YHWH is salvation" is obviously implied in Mt 1:21 and Lk 2:21. See also "Emmanuel," i.e., "God with us," in Mt 1:23.

[185] From the verb *mashach*, to anoint.

[186] See the text and the context of the expression "on the faith of the name of him" (επι τη πιστει του ονοματος αυτου), and the "name of him and the faith through him" that performed the miracle at the Beautiful Gate of Jerusalem, according to Ac 3:16.

monks, etc.) would reach the fullness of life. This is no longer possible today, without meeting a general resistance and an ingrown human repugnance. The first alternative is a text that in our present-day context can hardly be accepted.

Since this point is central in the whole Christian economy, we cannot dismiss it by saying that it was a wrong conviction held by Christians in times past, but it no longer holds. You cannot change your fundamental convictions as you would change your clothes. If any continuity has to be safeguarded in the Christian tradition, the sentence on the necessity of the name, which epitomizes Christian revelation, cannot be dismissed so easily. Perhaps one of the major crises in Christian consciousness today is that Christians unconsciously try to evade this problem, with the consequent deleterious results.

Our aim is not to justify a tradition or to defend Christianity, but to understand a human situation of the past and of the present, and—in this case—to help modern Man to overcome his crisis. When millions of Christians used to say, pray, believe, and still are saying, praying, believing that Christ is the Savior, what do they mean? That He is one saving symbol among many? That He is the only one? But who is *He*? And this is again our problem. What is His real name? Who knows it? Can there be a monopoly on such a name?

The Transcendent Name

We may begin with another scriptural reference. Certainly, "There is no other name granted to men by which they may receive salvation,"[187] but this name is "a name above every name";[188] it is a name that transcends all names, even those of the angels,[189] a name that is above "every name that can be named, not only in this age, but also in the age to come";[190] it is a "new name, which no-one knows, except those who receive it."[191] This name is "called the Word of God."[192] To confess this name means to say that it is "Lord."[193] Jesus did not come for His own glory,[194] but to let us know the name of the One who had sent him.[195] "Jesus" is not the revealed name, but he reveals the Supername.

---

[187] Ac 4:12.

[188] Ph 2:9: το ονομα το υπερ παν ονομα. A literal translation would read, "the name above all name." The English language not allowing this, we have the alternatives "a name above all names" or "above every name." The former should not be understood as saying that there is *a* name above all other names, and the latter should not be read as saying that there is a name above every *other* name.

[189] See Heb 1:4.

[190] See Ep 1:21.

[191] Rev 2:17.

[192] Rev 19:13.

[193] Ph 2:11 and *passim.*

[194] See Jn 8:50, etc.

[195] See Jn 17:6, 26, etc.

We may suggest that the reason for this is precisely that "the names that can be named are not unvarying names,"[196] or again, because "it was from the nameless that Heaven and Earth sprang."[197] However, there is no need to draw from another tradition. We could equally well say that "the kingdom of God does not consist in word (εν λογω) but in power (εν δυναμει)."[198]

The verses preceding our main text affirm, thematically, that the reason for the Supername is that the Carrier of that name "emptied himself,"[199] not only from a moral standpoint by "becoming obedient unto death,"[200] but also ontologically by "bearing human likeness"[201] in spite of His being "in the form of God."[202] "Taking the form of a slave,"[203] He fell at the bottom of the human scale, so that His name could never be felt as an imposition. In point of fact, this "annihilation," this "emptying himself" made it possible to transcend the world of "forms and names,"[204] and have a name, certainly, but "which is above every name."[205] He is not the nameless, not the apophatic reality, nor sheer transcendence, not the unapproachable Godhead, not the disembodied principle of "the eternal archetype"; He is the enunciated mystery,[206] the revealed epiphany, which was concealed since the beginning of time.[207] There is no vagueness here, however. He is the *Logos* that was made flesh,[208] yet did not remain in a body of death,[209] but was changed into a body of life,[210] for he has overcome death,[211] and taken a spiritual body.[212] The Supername is the Word[213] and not just a name; it is *Logos*, not mere denomination.[214] "To all who did receive Him

---

[196] *Tao Te Ching,* 1 (translation by A. Valey, in *The Way and Its Power* [New York: Grove Press, 1958]).

[197] Ibid.

[198] 1 Co 4:20. The context suggests that *logos* here means "speech," or rather "talk."

[199] Ph 2:7.

[200] Ph 2:8.

[201] Ph 2:7.

[202] Ph 2:7.

[203] Ph 2:7: μορφην δουλου λαβων.

[204] See the Indic expression *nāma-rūpa*, meaning that which is not the ultimate reality.

[205] See Ps 138:2: "Magnificasti super omne nomen sanctum tuum," says the *Vulgate* (literally: "You [God] exalted your holy Name above every [name]"). The *New Vulgate* corrects it into "eloquium tuum" [You exalted your word above every name]. The RSV renders it as, "For thou hast exalted above everything thy name and thy word," but the text is uncertain (cf. *Jerusalem Bible*).

[206] See Rom 16:25.

[207] See Col 1:26.

[208] See Jn 1:14.

[209] See Rom 7:24.

[210] See Mt 26:26; Mk 14:22; Lk 22:19; etc.

[211] See 1 Co 15:55ff.

[212] See 1 Co 15:44.

[213] See Jn 1:1.

[214] See the Upaniṣadic saying quoted above.

[the Word], He gave power to become children of God, to those who believe in the name of Him."[215] But it is not mere *Logos*; it is the spoken *Logos*, and what is uttered is the Spirit,[216] the Spirit who will teach us all truth,[217] the Spirit that permeates the whole universe,[218] which has the knowledge of every word,[219] is mentioned in any authentic name[220] and makes everything new.[221] The Supername is not an empty word nor a mere label. Not only is it named, it also names.

We may try to formulate our problem in a philosophical way. The revelation of the name does not imply any freezing of the vital human activity of naming, as it would happen by favoring a particular name—which therefore will become frozen and dead, as happens sooner or later with all names. It is rather the affirmation that there is always a name, that there is no salvation without a name, without a saving name. The revelation of the name is precisely the revelation *of the name*, not only of the *word*. It is the revelation of the vocative, and it is the revelation of the maximum of concreteness—nothing is more concrete than a name—combined with the maximum of universality. A name is only such if it names something, if it has a content that is somehow intelligible. A name is more than just a sound, and yet it is concrete nonetheless. But a name, precisely because it names, is also universal. The name draws the so-named thing out of its isolation, out of its "hiddenness." A name is communication; it conveys a meaning, of whatever type. Moreover, a name is infinitely more than this. A name is also communion. A name is a real name only when it establishes communion, at least between the "namer" and the "named." Furthermore, this communion can be shared by whoever understands the name.

This is the reason for the power of names, and of the human wish to keep some names secret, because they are too intimate or too powerful. In fact, whoever shares the name does immediately establish a communion with the thing having that name. There is no need to give examples taken from the most ancient cultures up to the present day (from "you-ing" to calling "names," or education seen as familiarity with names, etc.).

A name is in itself concrete and universal, and has at the same time the tendency to become more concrete by being monopolized, dominated, used, or manipulated by a particular class, caste, culture, and so on. It also tends to become more universal by overflowing beyond its boundaries through translation, imposition (for domination), and so on. The revelation of the Supername seeks to keep the balance. We cannot

---

[215] See Jn 1:12. Significantly enough, the NEB translates: "to those who have yielded him their intelligence." The name here has clearly not yet been spoken. The subject of the sentence is the "true Light which enlightens every Man coming into the world" (v. 9).

[216] See Jn 7:37ff.; 14:15ff., etc. See also the theological controversy on the *Filioque* and the Greek Orthodox interpretation of it, which is implied in my words.

[217] See Jn 14:26; 15:26; 16:13, etc.

[218] See Ws 1:7 as it is used in the liturgy of Pentecost.

[219] Mt 10:20, etc.

[220] See the homology between the Spirit and the truth: Jn 4:23–24; 14:17; 15:26; 16:13, etc.

[221] See Ps 104:29–30 as it is used in the liturgy of Pentecost; Rev 21:5, etc.

do without names, nor, on the other hand, can we freeze names so as to confound the living name with a technical label.

We can exclude both extreme approaches as untenable—on the one hand, postulating *one* individual as universal Savior, and on the other hand, reducing Jesus to a mere abstraction or to a conventional sign for salvation.

Christ, the Lord and Savior, is for Christians the symbol of that Mystery that is unveiled in or through Jesus. The Christian act of faith in Jesus reaches far beyond a mere reliance upon historical memory, trusting in the testimonies of the elders. Ultimately, Christians do not worship Jesus, who is the Way,[222] but the Father. "Blessed are those who do not see and yet believe."[223] He who sees Him sees the Father.[224] He came in order that the life and unity that exist between Him and the Father might also exist between Him and the believers.[225] He did not want to be proclaimed "Son of God," lest some misunderstanding arose because of the wrong attitude of the believers.[226] Furthermore, it is good that He goes and disappears.[227] Otherwise, Man would make him king[228] or God, and forget that Jesus's name is like that of his ancient *typos*,[229] a truly admirable name,[230] an unnameable name.[231] No Christian prayer ultimately stops at Christ, but it always proceeds to the Father through the Son in the Spirit, or by the Son through the Spirit.[232] There is no need, however, to dwell on Christian tradition.[233]

---

[222] See Jn 10:7; 16:6.

[223] See Jn 20:29.

[224] See Jn 12:45; 14:9.

[225] See Jn 6:57, etc.

[226] See Lk 4:35, 41; Mk 3:11–12; etc. See also Lk 10:21 and parallel texts.

[227] See Jn 16:7.

[228] See Jn 6:15.

[229] See Gn 32:29 and the whole mystical tradition stemming from this passage.

[230] Many examples can be found in the Psalms, e.g., 8:2.

[231] See Christian commentators from at least Dionysius onward, describing God as *anonymos* (without a name), *polynomos* (with many names), e.g., Dionysius, *De div. nom.* VII.3; *De myst. theol.*, I,2, 3.

[232] *Per Dominum nostrum Jesum Christum in unitate Spiritus Sancti Deus* is, since time immemorial, the final line in Christian liturgical prayers.

[233] See this passage by Meister Eckhart in I *Expositio libri Genesis* (*Lateinische Werke* I.95–96), listing some of the most important biblical and Patristic texts about God's unnameable Name: "Cur queris nomen meum, quod est mirabile? Primo sic: Nomen meum est mirabile, Ps 8,2: Quam admirabile est nomen tuum; Is 9,5: Vocabitur admirabilis. Secundo sic: Nomen meum admirabile—quod est, quasi dicat: Hoc quod est, sive Qui est, ipsum est nomen meum mirabile, Ex 3,14: Ego sum qui sum; Qui est misit me; hoc nomen meum. Tertio sic: Cur queris nomen meum quod est mirabile? Mirabile quidem primo, quia nomen et tamen super omne nomen, Ph 2,9: Donavit illi nomen, quod est super omne nomen. Secundo, nomen est mirabile, quia nomen est innominabile, nomen indicibile et nomen ineffabile. Augustinus, primo De doctrina christiana, locutus de Deo, sic ait: Diximusne aliquid et sonuimus dignum Deo? Si dixi, non est hoc quod dicere volui. Hoc unde scio, nisi

Jesus Christ is the Mediator, the *medium quo*, although not an intermediary, because the *quo* is not separated or disconnected from the *quod*; because He is a person, and we also are persons; because we all are in the *quo*, at least as long as the pilgrimage lasts, "in regione dissimilitudinis."[234] His mediatorship is not primarily epistemological but ontological, and thus it is ultimately not necessary to see Him, provided that we see *through* Him; and one may dare to say that the more transparent He is, the clearer the vision is through Him. Otherwise the Paraclete, who will teach us the whole truth, will not come.[235] Jesus explicitly said that he had achieved and fulfilled the work entrusted to him[236] and repeated it in the most solemn and unmistakable way: "Consummatum est."[237]

Christ is not the *revelation*, nor the *revealed* name, but the *revealer* of the name. The name Christ reveals is a Supername, a name that was prepared even before the sun started to exist;[238] a new name, so new that to repeat it without applying one's mind and heart to it would mean to rob it of its saving power. And so secret that we cannot put it in front of us as an object, so saving that those who utter it (and the sounds and voices may be infinite) know for certain that in that name all the treasures of the Godhead dwell in the most corporeal manner.[239] They also know that that name has made its splashdown upon earth in innumerable tongues.[240]

---

quia Deus ineffabilis est; quod autem a me dictum est, si ineffabile esset, dictum non esset? Et sic nescio que pugna verborum, quoniam si illud est ineffabile, quod dici non potest, non est ineffabile, quod vel ineffabile potest dici. Que pugna verborum silencio cavenda potius quam voce pecanda [text variant: petenda] est. Quarto: Cur queris nomen meum? Quod est mirabile—scilicet te querere nomen meum, cum sim innominabilis; mirabile certe est querere nomen rei innominabilis. Secundo, mirabile querere nomen eius, cuius natura est esse absconditum, Is 45,15: Vere tu es Deus absconditus. Tertio, mirabile querere foris nomen eius, qui non extra sed intimus est. Augustinus, De vera religione: Noli foras ire, in teipsum redi, in interiori homine habitat Deus, veritas, ad quam nullo modo perveniunt qui foris eam [variant: eum] querunt."

[234] A traditional expression in Christian tradition to express the existential human condition after Adam's fall. See Augustine, *Conf.* 8.10,16; Bernard of Clairvaux, *Serm.* XLII.2 (*PL* 183.661), etc. On the rather interesting Platonic origin of this phrase, cf. A. E. Taylor, "Regio dissimilitudinis," in *Archives d'histoire doctrinale et littéraire du Moyen Âge*, VII.305ff. And E. Gilson, *La théologie mystique de Saint Bernard* (Paris: Vrin, 1934), 63ff.; V. Lossky, *Théologie negative*, 175ff., for a modern use of this expression.

[235] See Jn 14:26; 16:13, etc.

[236] See Jn 4:34; 17:4, etc.

[237] Jn 19:30 (see also v. 28).

[238] See Ps 71 [72]:17: προ του ηλιου διαμενει το ονομα αυτου, according to the LXX, and "ante solem permanet nomen eius" in the *Vulgate*. Both Jewish and Christian traditions interpreted this text as referring to the "preexistent" Messiah. See H. A. Wolfson, *The Philosophy of the Church Fathers* (Cambridge, MA: Harvard University Press, 1964), 1:157ff. Modern translations render it as "enduring as long as the sun" (*Jerusalem Bible*)," "may it live for ever like the sun" (NEB), "a name to endure while the sun gives light" (Knox), etc.

[239] See Col 2:9.

[240] See Ac 2:3.

Jesus, the Lord

To say, "Jesus is the universal Savior," means, therefore, that there is a universal salvation, but the Savior is not an individual, nor merely a historical figure, nor basically an epistemological revealer. Salvation—whatever it may consist of—is always a personal act, thus a personal experience and a personal encounter.

It is always in the Spirit that Man encounters his Savior: not a disembodied Savior indeed, but equally not a merely temporal or geographical individual. And yet, for Christians, the path leading to this encounter must pass through the historical manifestation of Mystery.

Jesus is the Christ because He was anointed by the Holy Spirit at His baptism, says Christian tradition.[241] Christ is the Anointed One, anointed with the *chrism* of universality; the *Mashiah* is anointed not only by God but also by men. Jesus, as the universal symbol for salvation, cannot be objectified and thus reified as a merely historical personage.

The Christian experience of salvation in Jesus does not carry with it a stamp of "contents examined: let pass," as if there were some superman who saves those who believe in Him—plus, some would add, those who do believe, but not explicitly. Nor does it only mean a subjective disposition, which could find any number of "symbols" meaningful. It means a personal discovery of the Mystery of life and existence, a personal encounter with reality, not as a faceless, cold Being, transcendent or not, but as an intimate and ineffable meeting with the Person, with God, the Mystery, Nothingness, the Ideal, Truth—in whatever manner and by whatever name we may prefer to express it.

The "normal way" of salvation, for Christians, passes through the revelation of the name given by Jesus, whom they believe risen. But Christians will not deny a priori that this encounter, experience, conviction (or by whatever term we may call it) may take any other form and epiphany. They will believe that the Mystery with which they are in communion through Jesus is the Mystery that saves, gives meaning to existence, hope to life, and love toward reality to any being capable of sharing this very experience in as many forms as possible. "Jesus is the Lord"[242] is the shortest way in which Christians may formulate this belief.

By saying, "personal encounter," we aim at avoiding a purely subjective and anthropomorphic feeling, as much as a merely objective and doctrinal approach. To reduce personal experience to a sentimental or subjective discovery of "another, personified" being would amount to degrading the person to a subjective bundle of feelings.

Personal encounter means a personal discovery by which the different, constitutive poles of the person become what they are, precisely because they respond—actively

---

[241] See the striking formula of Paul of Samosata referring to the baptism of Christ: "Having been anointed with the Holy Spirit, he was named Christ" (which anyway should not be interpreted in a "modalistic" way), in Wolfson, *Philosophy*, 593.

[242] Ph 2:11.

and passively—to the mutual stimulation from the poles themselves. The person is not the "I" alone (which would have no meaning whatsoever: there can be an "I" only against another personal pole), nor the "you" alone, but the constitutive *I-you-he/she* relationship, both in the singular and in the plural. Personal encounter is, then, the discovery of my personal being in and through the inclusion of the different poles of personal existence. This is far from being an anthropomorphic category in the usual sense of the word.[243]

The affirmation, "Jesus the Lord," would consequently mean, first of all, that I find out that my being is not exhausted in an isolated and almost solipsistic private self, nor in any egalitarian horizontal relation with similar selves, but it needs a Lord, a superior dimension that opens up the ultimate horizon where my person can exist. It means, further, that this Lord—whose Lordship can appear in innumerable forms—has taken an ultimate (for me) form that is indissolubly connected with Jesus of Nazareth.

We can now turn to a possible understanding of this classic Christian tenet from a point of view that takes other religious traditions into consideration. The language of a Hindū or a Buddhist is, obviously, very different from the language and word meanings of a modern secularist or atheist, for instance. We will try to address, first, a traditional religious language, then a more secular and modern parlance.

The Lord of Religions

For the sake of concentrating our attention on our single problem, we may assume that there is a common language regarding the meaningfulness of salvation or liberation (*sōtēria, mokṣa, nirvāṇa, . . .*) and the Savior, be it a person, grace, enlightenment, or whatever.

First of all, the meaning of traditional Christian tenets can only be understood by accepting the notions of time, history, Man, salvation, revelation, and so forth, which are peculiar to the Mediterranean cultural and religious area in which they were formulated. Second, they make sense only within that proper context.

Outside the Christian cultural area, the statement, "Jesus is the universal Savior," will almost forcefully be understood as, "Christians, because of their peculiar faith, personal experience, or limited horizon, believe that *their* Christ is the only Savior of the world, so that, if non-Christians are saved at all, they are by an alien Savior, namely the God of Christians"; or "the man Jesus of Nazareth, in the eyes of Christians, has become the only door of salvation."

If Jesus has to be understood as the only Savior, but in a way that does justice to both the experience of other peoples and the deepest Christian insights, he cannot be exclusively linked with the biblical tradition. In other words, the context in which

---

[243] The reflections from the French "philosophie de l'esprit," especially E. Mounier, L. Lavalle, R. Le Senne, G. Marcel, M. Nedoncelle, et al., should be remembered and incorporated here.

the text was inscribed is no longer tenable. The message of the Bible is valid but is not necessarily the only one. The basic function of the Bible is not to carry a cognitive message, but to play a strictly historical role—namely, that out of the people of Israel came Jesus, in whom the fullness of the Godhead dwelt in a corporeal manner.[244] Assuming for a moment that tomorrow all Bibles will be destroyed throughout the world, and even that no people will remember a single *literal* sentence of it, the fundamental function of the Bible would remain unharmed, because the historical genealogy of Jesus would remain unchanged, even though the existing records differ.[245] What has happened historically *has* happened historically, and so will it remain.

The history of salvation is not the salvation of history, but the acknowledgment of salvation through history, even for those who do not live in history, because salvation is ultimately not a historical fact, but a transhistorical act.

However this may be (it is not our purpose now to elucidate this problem), we may venture a series of sentences that we consider perfectly Christian—that is, acceptable for a Christian and not repugnant to other traditions of the world.

The first affirmation says that *there is a universal salvation*.[246] A Christian does not only believe that God wants every man to be saved,[247] but that He also provided the means for it.[248] A Christian can even quote Scripture[249] and tradition[250] to ground his hope in a universal reintegration (ἀποκατάστασις).

Furthermore, if the scheme of the history of salvation has to be applicable outside the peoples of the covenant, an almost immediate corollary follows: namely, that the different religious traditions of the world are the normal and ordinary ways for salvation, willed and provided by God, the term "religion" remaining in this case sufficiently vague and open to the future.[251]

The second affirmation is *the uniqueness of the Savior*. If Christians were aware of another Master speaking "words of eternal life,"[252] they would follow him; for they have learned that "who is not against you is on your side"[253] and understood the distinction between the sociological relativism of the visible groups following Jesus and the uncompromising ontological attitude vis-à-vis the Master.[254] They have been

---

[244] See Lk 3:22; Col 2:9.

[245] See Mt 1:1ff.; Lk 3:23ff.

[246] See Rom 5:12–21.

[247] See 1 Tim 2:4.

[248] See R. Panikkar, *The Unknown Christ of Hinduism* (London: Longman, Darton & Todd, 1964), 51ff., and the reviewed version, *Il Cristo sconosciuto dell'induismo* (Milan: Jaca Book, 2008), now in vol. VII, *Opera Omnia*.

[249] See Ac 3:21 and also Mk 9:12, besides the later qualifications given by the Church (cf. *Denz.*, 211, 429, 531).

[250] See *Lumen gentium*, VIII.28.

[251] See above, "Christianity and World Religions" in *Christianity*, ch. 1.

[252] Jn 6:68.

[253] Lk 9:50; cf. also Mk 9:40.

[254] See Lk 11:23; Mt 12:30.

made aware of the cosmic manifestations of the Lord,[255] so that the uniqueness they claim for the Lord is in no way an epistemological monopoly. Significantly enough, only when, in recent periods of Western Christian history, modern Man tried to get rid of metaphysics and ontology, has he fallen into the temptation of interpreting Christ's uniqueness in epistemic terms—that is, that those who do not take any epistemological notice of Jesus are outside the realm of salvation.[256]

Uniqueness belongs to the qualitative and not to the quantitative order. It belongs to the personal and not to the reified, merely objectifiable order. Every person is unique and, thus, un-interchangeable and incomparable. Uniqueness is the phenomenological characteristic of Mystery. Every mystery is irreducible to anything else. It is unique.

The third affirmation states, *Christians not only have no monopoly on Jesus, but no control, either, over the ways in which the Lord brings about salvation.* It is not only a matter of acknowledging that Jesus has other sheep[257] that the apostles themselves do not know,[258] but furthermore to affirm that His ways[259] are never our ways, nor His measure our measure.[260] Not even the Son of Man knows the mystery of the "hour."[261]

Fourth, *as to the issue of salvation, Christians should refrain from any theory being put forward as certain.* They should remember that neither those on the right of Christ nor those of the left were aware that what they were doing, they were doing to Christ, so that it earned them salvation or damnation.[262]

Furthermore, they should not venture to investigate—except tentatively and only on the level of theological speculation—the concrete ways in which the Lord is present and at work, though hidden and unknown, in any authentic form of religiousness.[263]

Fifth, as it should have become clear from the previous reflections, *when a Christian says "Jesus" in the Spirit, he or she does not only mean, or not mainly, the historical Nazarene, but the risen Lord,* whom he or she has encountered in his or her own Emmaus[264] or Damascus[265] or like Nathanael[266] or Thomas[267] or Magdalen[268] or any other

---

[255] See the already quoted passages from Jn, Col, Ep, Rev, etc., on the so-called cosmic or preexistent Christ.

[256] See the many works on the so-called salvation of unbelievers, especially just before Vatican Council II. See some bibliography in my book *The Unknown Christ of Hinduism*, 50–52, and the already mentioned bibliography (see above) on the problem of universal salvation.

[257] See Jn 10:16.

[258] See Jn 11:52.

[259] See Rom 11:33.

[260] See Jn 7:6.

[261] See Mk 13:32; see also Ac 1:7.

[262] See Mt 25:37ff.

[263] See again my Unknown Christ of Hinduism.

[264] See Lk 24:32.

[265] See Ac 9:5: "Who are you, Lord?"

[266] See Jn 3:1ff.

[267] See Jn 20:28: "My Lord and my God!"

[268] See Jn 20:16: "*Rabboni*!"; Mt 28:5: "Do not be afraid!"

experience.[269] And this forbids us to exclude other ways of meeting the Lord, even if we do not understand.[270]

There remains, sixth, *the historical dimension of Christian belief*. This constitutes both its strength or peculiarity and its weakness, or rather limitation. In front of types of religiousness that are not based on history, Christians feel that they are at a loss when trying to express their belief, because Christian understanding has not yet freed the text—that is, the Christian fact—from its interpretation within a certain context. They will stress the uniqueness of the historical fact of the "coming of Christ," but they will tend to identify the historical epiphany—however real—with the Mystery manifested in and through history.[271] They will not exclude the theoretical possibility of another interpretation of their belief, but they will have to confess that, until now, there has hardly been any serious attempt at understanding the Mystery of Christ in a context different from what we have called the Mediterranean worldview.[272] The understanding and reception of Christ have been Mediterranean ones. No wonder that outside that area there are only colonial Christian enclaves. This is a point in which pure speculation would not work, for we touch the very root of the Mystery of human existence: we have not fully lived our lives yet, nor exhausted the possibilities that reality offers us.

Christian speculation, like any other truly human activity, does not just mean to repeat past models, but to create new possibilities and paradigms. The present-day Christian consciousness of an emerging planetary context of human experience is ready to welcome any possible interpretation that accounts for the facts (which it believes have to be preserved in all their historical reality) and allows, at the same time, a really nonsectarian universality and self-image. This interpretation, however, does not concern a single historical event, which took place at Bethlehem or Jerusalem, but it interprets that event within the real, complex human tradition, encompassing not only the twenty centuries of the Christian church or the millennia of human history, but also all the eons of human experience crystallized in the depths of human life. Neither the purely mystical discovery of Christ nor the merely historical approach will do. The principle of growth underlying this method is as distant from mere continuity as from sheer discontinuity.

The seventh remark will recognize that *there are no "bare facts." Therefore, pure historicity is far from being the only criterion of reality, or reality as such*. The so-called historical fact, for instance, presupposes an understanding of history that in no way can be called the only possible interpretation of temporal reality. There are no bare facts, for the understanding and acceptance of any fact *already* belongs to the fact. So the question is not as simple as clothing reality with another conceptual garb, once we recognize that the old one is no longer fitting, because the garb, though not any specific one, belongs to reality itself.

---

[269] See H. A. Williams, *True Resurrection* (London: M. Beazley, 1972).

[270] See Lk 9:50, etc.

[271] See Rom 16:25–26.

[272] I, for one, had already suggested, almost two decades ago, that a Christian theology for India should not begin with creation, but straightaway with the Eucharist.

Can another interpretation of a so-called bare fact still be considered as just another reformulation of the same (hypothetical, nonexisting) "thing in itself"? Christians will have to recognize that they were and are superimposing structures that they cannot get rid of, but are not given with the unfolding of the Mystery, but only with the acceptance of it.

To recognize this does not imply that one will accept any other interpretation. It is one thing to accept that my vision is neither perfect nor universal, and another thing to accept another insight as the equivalent of what, so far, was considered incontrovertible. Who can decide whether it is a normal growth or a cancer? This is the place of dialogue—not as a means to "convert" the other, not even of gathering information about the other, but as a way of discovering oneself and, thus, growing together.[273] It would then be preposterous to plan beforehand, almost a priori, the finishing line of this new understanding. Here it is literally true that the path is made by going along it. Perhaps this "freedom of the children of God"[274] is the real "good news."[275]

What we are saying is that an authentic religious dialogue, in the true meeting of religious traditions, lays bare the modern Christian myth of history as the criterion and interpreter of reality.[276]

Our eighth observation will revert to the question of *whether it is possible to believe in Jesus in a non-Semitic way*, which at the same time may not be considered unacceptable for the Jewish-Christian mentality.[277] If Jesus has to be relevant to those who are spiritually outside the old and new Israel, he has to relate to them either through the mediation of Israel or through the common humanness of humankind.

In the first case, we have the present-day, widespread Christian interpretation of Christ. A Christian is, accordingly, not only a person who discovers the Lordship of Jesus, but who interprets this Lordship in a concrete, historical way, with reference to the unfolding of YHWH's alliance with His people and—through His people—with others.

The second alternative is offered by the notion of the so-called cosmic Christ. He then appears as a universal Savior, directly related to the history of humankind after having appeared and been active within the Jewish covenant, afterward fulfilled by the New Testament. Here Jesus, as the epiphany of the primordial Mystery,[278] relates Himself to the general human experience, and at the same time is connected

---

[273] See R. Panikkar, *Témoignage et dialogue*, in E. Castelli (ed.), *Le Témoignage* (Paris: Aubier, 1972), 367–88, esp. 376–79.

[274] See Jn 8:36; Gal 5:1.

[275] See Mk 16:15; 1 Th 3:6.

[276] See W. Taylor Stevenson, "History as Myth," *Cross-Currents* 20, no. 1 (Winter 1970): 15–28, showing that "what is commonly termed *history* is a mythic perception of reality" (17). The same author has written an entire book on the subject (*History as Myth* [New York: Seabury Press, 1969]).

[277] It is today well-known that this is one of the capital, thorny problems which the so-called young Churches of Africa and Asia hardly dare to put in this almost crude way.

[278] See Rom 16:25–26; Ep 1:9ff.; Col 1:15.

with one particular people and one of the phyla of Man's history. So, in order to be a Christian, one does not need to deny one's particular religious and cultural tradition, but joins the main phylum of world history and human development. The other traditions are here not excluded but subordinated.[279]

There is still a third hypothesis. Jesus would be here considered not only as the Jesus of history (first alternative) and the human manifestation of the cosmic Mystery (second hypothesis), but as the concrete anthropological symbol through which Christians experience the whole of reality and the fulfillment of human life. Here Jesus is conceived as the one who discloses the saving Supername, which in each case names the Savior of the particular believer or believing tradition.

The central Christian Mystery in the first hypothesis is incarnation. The Jesus of history is the incarnated *Logos*, and the stress is here on the *skandalon* of concreteness, the human condition and the cross.

The central Christian Mystery in the second hypothesis is resurrection. The cosmic Christ is the risen Jesus: the stress is on his universal Lordship as the cosmic center toward which everything converges.

As for the third hypothesis, the central Christian Mystery is Pentecost.[280] The descending Spirit is the Spirit of Jesus, allowing each person or tradition to speak their own language. They become aware that, although they may not understand one another, they nevertheless are exalting the same "great things."[281]

In this third hypothesis, Jesus relates Himself to those outside the Western Christian area not by means of the history of another people, or by virtue of a general cosmic experience, but thanks to their own human traditions. Jesus, in this case, would be one of the names of the cosmotheandric principle, which has received practically as many names as the authentic forms of religiousness, and which at the same time finds a historically sui generis epiphany in Jesus of Nazareth. Jesus is here the Man,[282] the *Puruṣa*,[283] or whatever symbol may open us up to the Mystery.

The three attitudes share the idea that Jesus is the Savior, but within different contexts. The first one will say that the historical Jesus is the only historical Savior of humankind. The second hypothesis will understand the same sentence as saying that the cosmic Christ whom Christians could know through the historical Jesus, and whom they identify with the risen Lord, is the universal Savior. The third hypothesis will also consider the statement as valid inasmuch as it says that the *who* whom Christians see in Jesus is the only universal Savior.

It must be added that, as soon as the mystery of the *who* is mistaken for the objectification of the *what*, the third hypothesis ceases to be such, and certainly it is

---

[279] See Jn 4:22; Rom 9:4ff.; 11:1ff.

[280] See, among other passages, Ac 16:7; Ph 1:19; Rom 8:9; 1 Pet 1:11; 2 Co 3:17–18; Gal 4:6, about the relationship between Jesus and the Spirit.

[281] See Ac 2:11.

[282] See Jn 19:5.

[283] See *Ṛg-veda* X.90.

no longer Christian. It does not say, in point of fact, that *what* Christians call Jesus is *what* Buddhists call Buddha, or Hindūs by other names. When the mystery of the name fades away, the Supername is reduced to a psychological or dialectical device, and our third hypothesis becomes a mere figment of eclecticism.

Finally, it would remain a major theological problem, this being our ninth remark, *to find an adequate theology of religion, capable of encompassing the whole range of Man's religious experience today.*[284] It could still be a Christocentric theology, even if the Greek name of Christ is not mentioned, for He does not only stand for one single event but for that cosmotheandric principle which, while being incarnated in Jesus of Nazareth, has not only spoken many times through the prophets[285] but did not leave Himself without witnesses in any moment of history[286]—to quote just one among the many sacred Scriptures of the world.

The Lord of History

The meaning of Jesus's universality may be even more difficult to understand in the current context, which some would call post-Christian or secular, than in the traditional religious world. The main divergence here does not concern Jesus as a symbol for universal salvation, but the interpretation of salvation itself. This is, however, a problem that we have excluded from our investigation.

If Christian experience must be open to different cultures from those in which it has been couched, it will have to be even more open to worldviews that come from the interaction of those various forms with itself.

The proper task of fundamental theology as a separate discipline is not to defend a priori a particular philosophy as more adequate than another for explaining the Christian belief, but to have such a deep and, I would add, mystical experience of Jesus, that one may express it by means of whatever cultural tools one may have at his disposal.[287]

In this context, unlike in the previous one, Jesus is not at odds with some other Savior. The question here is whether the whole language of salvation has any meaning at all, and, further, whether any Savior is needed. What is the sense of a Savior when the very notion of it appears to be meaningless? Shall we have to say that now the *kērygma* has first to create the need? The problem is complex and outside the range of this essay.

On the other hand, could Jesus be defined as a secular Savior? Has He anything to say to secular Man? Probably not that He is the Savior in a traditional way. In

---

[284] See R. Panikkar, *Philosophy of Religion in the Contemporary Encounter of Cultures*, in R. Klibansky (ed.), *Contemporary Philosophy: A Survey* (Florence: La Nuova Italia, 1971), 221–42.

[285] See Heb 1:1.

[286] See Ac 14:17.

[287] See R. Panikkar, "Metatheology or Diacritical Theology as Fundamental Theology," in *Concilium* 6, no. 5 (1969): 21–27.

fact, modern Christology is trying to argue that the concept of salvation and even of religion has to change, whereas the figure of Jesus towers perhaps greater than ever among men, precisely because He has been demythologized, removed from his divine pedestal, and turned into a Universal Brother.[288]

We may agree or not with the trends of many current theological schools, but we should understand them as efforts aiming at discovering the context in which Jesus is not only relevant but central for the quest of modern Man for happiness, love, community, justice, a better world, a more human life, and so on.

We may dispense with further references, because this constitutes one of the central problems of present-day Christological speculation: How to relate Jesus to history, both universal and personal history?[289] We simply recall the already mentioned shift from the cosmological to the historical myth, as well as the historical centrality reserved to the place of Jesus, the experience of history triggered by the Jesus event, and the caution in not superimposing one particular Jesus model on other cultures and worldviews.[290]

The Lord of Faith

This study should not be reduced to a theological reappraisal of the Christian claim. I think that there is a more positive and constructive approach to the question, without denying the part of truth contained in the cosmological reduction, as well as in the anthropological and epistemological interpretations. Some may call it the mystical approach, but perhaps it could be better defined as the approach of simple faith.

It may be another example of the paradox according to which the more personal a language, the more universally understandable it is. Concreteness is the way to universality, but hardly vice versa.

To say "salvation in Christ" or "Christ is the universal Savior" is an extremely general and objective statement, which has a meaning only within a particular context. And it is difficult to come down to the concrete from the universal. If I were to formulate my belief, I would not speak that way. I would simply say that I have the experience of a "new name," which is constantly new and renewed for me—a name that is hidden to outsiders, not because of any kind of esotericism or particularism, but because a name, unlike a term, is only such if it really names, that

---

[288] We could mention some extreme and interesting cases, such as Charles de Foucauld and the theologians of the "death of God": Th. J. J. Altizer, P. v. Buren, et al., or theologians like K. Adam, H. Cox, D. Bonhoeffer, and K. Rahner.

[289] Names like R. Bultmann, O. Cullman, W. Pannenberg, and in another sense, G. Vahanian, P. Berger, et al., and the innumerable followers of so-called Christian humanism, are contemporary examples of this trend.

[290] See the essays by K. Rahner, J. Ratzinger, G. Thils, W. Dantine, et al., in T. Michels (ed.), *Geschichtlichkeit der Theologie* (Salzburg: Pustet, 1970).

is, if it is discovered from within, if it is a name by which I am called or by which I call. This name challenges, makes, redeems me. In this name, both my Savior and myself are one because the calling belongs to the called and to the caller alike.[291] And yet, in the internal polarity of the person, the poles are neither identical nor interchangeable.

The name here is not a label, but a real symbol, and a symbol is neither object nor subject.

But this name, which is new and unknown—except in the act of naming (calling) it, otherwise it is only a term or a sound—is, at the same time, a Supername, a name above all names.[292] In discovering it as a Supername, I realize that I have no monopoly on that name, that I cannot objectify it without killing it, that it is a name only in the vocative, and that I do not know it fully (only the winner can eat from the tree of life[293]), for it is still veiled to me, because the name has not yet fully emerged, is still in a process of birth, of being spoken.

This Supername—this Mystery, as others may prefer to call it—is opening up in and through my life—my sensitivity, heart, and mind, in and through my dreams and feelings, as well as my dealings with others and all my actions. It is as an empty space and a virgin time that allows me to grow, to penetrate into both, so that my very entering becomes a new creation. This progressive revelation of the name, as some may wish to put it, always takes the form of a personal discovery, which amounts to a personal encounter. The disclosure of the saving name is, thus, not the discovery of a thing, as an object, not even as an "other," if by this we mean another "individual"; but it is the inner unveiling of another *pole* of that integral relationship that makes me truly *me*, because the same relationship also makes Him truly Him.[294]

This Supername cannot be discovered outside this living and loving constitutive relationship. This is the name that so many religious traditions have forbidden to utter in vain, or to pronounce in the third person, because such an exterioriza-tion or objectification would kill the living name, and it would no longer be the saving name. Only to him who overcomes in the struggle is the hidden manna given, and the white stone in which a new name is written, but which no man knows except he who receives it.[295] It is not only the name of God, or the name of the New City, but one's own new name that Man has to discover.[296] A name that nobody knows but the party concerned,[297] not because it is not uttered aloud or is kept secret, but because the name is only a name when it really names the named, the called.

---

[291]   See Jn 6:56; 17:6–8, 21.

[292]   See Ph 2:9.

[293]   See Rev 2:7.

[294]   See Song 2:16: "My beloved is mine and I am his."

[295]   See Rev 2:17.

[296]   See Rev 3:12.

[297]   See Rev 19:12.

I am aware that this experience of mine, this belief of mine, is linked with view-point and my understanding of it, but I am also fully aware that the name that is revealed to me is not in my power, nor can it be labeled by denominations of any kind. Furthermore, I will be uneasy about both questions, the one concerning the universality and the one concerning the particularity of the Lord, the saving process, the saving power, the Savior, grace, or in whatever form one may like to refer to it—not because I know no answer, but because I know no question. The Supername in fact cannot be named, because it is the source of all names and all naming. Since I experience myself as a person, I experience myself as unique, not in a solipsistic way but in a relational way. I am unique, not because I am a single individual in a series, but because I am a unique expression, an image, a mirroring of the entire reality—Creator and creation included, in the terms of a given tradition.

In other words, the question about the universality or nonuniversality of the saving power of Christ is not a valid question at this level, or rather no question at all, for it does not ask anything. The question is here a wrong question that forces me into a false perspective. It puts me under the "objectified" and "individualized" perspective, as if the Savior were an object and I an individual. The "Lord who saves" is not an independent, disconnected force, nor an absolute somebody unrelated to me, so that He may choose to "save" me or any other. He is not an object. In point of fact, this asked-for "thing," in the sense of an objectified, independent, unrelated Savior ("in itself"), does not exist: it is a purely mental construction, or rather a false mental construction, a mere extrapolation. Certainly I may confess that I am saved by Christ, but this Christ, my Savior, is neither an "other" nor my ego. No need to quote St. Augustine to recall that He is more interior to myself than myself;[298] we could also cite St. John speaking of the Eucharistic and Trinitarian identity[299] and a universal tradition, East and West, sacred and secular, modern and ancient.[300] What I am trying to say is that the process of salvation is not an extrinsic process, nor an automatic event we can bring about with our individual capacity alone. When the Lord saves me, when He discloses reality to me, He does it not to a private individual but to the whole world, microcosmically mirroring the macrocosmic process. Neither "He" nor "I" are individuals. Moreover, my person is saved in the same measure as my individuality is lost.[301]

One may feel that the saving power bubbles up from within, or comes from without. In fact, it is constantly both, transcendent and immanent, though some temperaments may be more sensitive to one or another aspect, and interpret it with more intrinsic or extrinsic categories.

One analogy may perhaps prove helpful. Just as the traditional philosophical proof for monotheism states that, even under the assumption that there were two or more

---

[298] *Confessions* III.6.11: "Tu autem eras interior intimo meo et superior summo meo."

[299] Jn 6:57; 17:21–23, etc.

[300] See R. Panikkar, *Misterio y Revelación. Hinduismo y Cristianismo* (Madrid: Marova, 1971), 213ff.

[301] See Mt 10:39; 16:25; Jn 12:25, etc.

Gods, those Gods would be ontologically indistinguishable, and thus would ontically have to be one and the same God, so—and this is only a metaphor—"salvation," in whatever form it may be conceived, and the "Savior," whatever image we may have of "Him," are respectively one and the same salvation and Savior.

The most common way, within the Christian world, to express this experience is to use the biblical context, but I do not exclude the possibility of accepting the Lordship of Jesus—to put it in still biblical terms—as referring to a Jesus who is not the monopoly of Christianity, and discovering Him at work, or rather present and effective, in any religious tradition, under whatever name and form.

Through Jesus, "handed down" by Christians or simply by history, I may attain a better comprehension of the riches of my own tradition, as, on the other hand, through my Buddhist or Hindū or whatever tradition I may be able to deepen the Christian understanding of the Ultimate Mystery (to call it some way). There is no convincing reason today why someone could not accept the person of the Lord as he appeared in Jesus of Nazareth and have sincere respect for the twenty centuries of Christian tradition, and at the same time, out of love for and faith in the same Lord, keep on following his or her particular religious tradition, insofar as there is no inconsistency in one's life and commitment.[302] There are, indeed, serious theological problems to clarify, and one cannot foretell whether the effort to create a theology of religion valid for more than one religious tradition will succeed; but it cannot be said that it is an a priori impossible enterprise, either.

The Word of the Spirit

We have gone a long way. We said that no statement has any valid meaning outside its proper context, that the context varies with the growth or change in human consciousness, and that traditional contexts today are no longer sufficient to sustain any claim to universality.

On the other hand, we tried to show that the claim to universality, in one form or another, is implied in any statement with a truth claim. Further, we also said that in the existential and real issue of salvation, the question of universality does not properly arise; it arises only under the assumption that there is a universal conception, that is, a universal understanding of universality, as in a platonic world of ideas, for instance.

We have further emphasized the fact that universality can only have an acceptable meaning if it is not separated from concreteness, which led us to the core of the problem, and to the core of the cosmotheandric constitution of that principle

---

[302] See Mt 23:13, and the significant modern cry of Roger Garaudy: "You who have been enjoying the great hope of which Constantine spoiled us, you, men of the Church, give Him [Jesus] back to us: his life and death belongs also to us, to all for whom that hope is meaningful, to all who learned from him that Man is created as creator," in "L'Homme de Nazareth," *Evangile aujourd'hui* 64 (1969).

that Christians call Christ. We suggested that our understanding of Jesus would rise to a more universal understanding if we widened the horizon against which we understand Him; this is true of any other *homologous* figure in the traditions of humankind. We also asserted, however, that this process cannot be planned or manipulated, but it corresponds to the historical situation and depends on the factual growth of the peoples of the earth.

We have hinted, further, at the distinction between individual and person, and suggested that a certain nominalistic tendency in interpreting names as mere labels has had the double effect, on the one hand, of alienating from the Christian message those who could not accept such a sectarian interpretation that excludes all those who do not join one particular denomination from salvation; and on the other hand, of hardening those who, under the umbrella of the "folly of the cross," could not accept any weakening of the name, here again understood as a particular denomination.

"The name which is above every name" is a Supername that cannot be identified with any particular sound nor any particular denomination. The ancient prohibition of Buddhism, Israel, and Islam, among other religious traditions, against any "idea" (picture), image, or representation of God could analogously be applied to the Supername; the only difference being that the Supername is indeed a name, has a body, is concrete, is (Christianly speaking) incarnated—not a simple reference or no-name-at-all. It *has* a name, which, however, is above all names. It could even be (as some traditions would prefer) No-Name, but a name after all. Utter silence cannot be contradicted, because it does not offer any "diction" to contradict.

There is a name without which there is no salvation. There is no salvation without a name. Salvation belongs to the level of the name, or properly speaking, of the Supername. It is the realm of the *Logos*, the sphere of the Word, the level of language, the kingdom of history. Outside this kingdom, besides the Word, in utter silence, transcending the *Logos*, there is no salvation. The fact that there is no salvation does not mean that there is condemnation—that is, nonsalvation—but that salvation has no meaning, no place. Salvation means salvation from the present human condition, redemption from the realm of the necessary verbalization of all things, of private self-consciousness. Salvation is salvation history, which amounts to the salvation of history, so that only the historical dimension of reality, so to speak, *can* be saved, because only that dimension *needs* to be saved.

When the Holy Spirit came at Pentecost, every people, tongue, and race praised in their different ways the great things of the Lord,[303] everyone speaking after their own manner and tongue. Certainly, they did not understand each other as if by a simultaneous translation. They understood, however, that they were exalting the same things, that they were involved in the same adventure, that they were in true communion, and that their sayings, words, and gestures were all directed toward the same goal, which they just worded differently.

---

[303] See Ac 2:11.

Religious traditions are not only complementary, they are supplementary: they support and enforce one another. Even more, they are interpenetrated and interpenetrating. Each of them represents a unique mirroring of the whole; they embrace each other in an intertwined, unique structure, so that each religious tradition contains the whole of human experience that is available to Man at a certain time and space, in spite of the fact that, each time, different moments or aspects of the whole are stressed. In other words, Jesus is unique because He represents and reenacts the mystery of salvation in a unique way.

Is this not the warning given time and again, that God has to be worshipped in truth and in the Spirit[304] that nobody is good but God,[305] whom nobody has seen[306] except in and through the Son,[307] the Way?[308] Is it not explicitly said that the risen One "is not here,"[309] so that to pinpoint Him to a space and place would mean to deny His resurrection? Did He not disappear from their sight exactly when they recognized Him?[310] Is not this the real recognition? That He disappears and is present in His constant absence? Were not those proclaimed blessed who believed while not seeing, so as to suggest that to believe is to not-see, to pierce through all seeing, all appearances?[311]

It was our concern to suggest an understanding of Jesus according to Christian Scripture and human contemporary tradition, an attempt to explore one of the central problems of fundamental theology: the awareness of a cosmotheandric principle, of an embodied *maṇḍalic* center, which could become one of the bases for a theology of religion (to use an expression sanctioned by custom).

In brief, we tried to unearth a little of that underlying myth that the world's peoples are beginning to rediscover: that the Word, that was at the beginning, had and still has the ten thousand echoes of a polyphonic symphony.

---

[304] See Jn 4:23.
[305] See Mt 19:17.
[306] See Jn 6:46.
[307] Mt 11:21; Lk 10:22; Jn 1:18; 6:44; 14:9, etc.
[308] Jn 14:6.
[309] See Mt 28:6.
[310] See Lk 24:31.
[311] See Jn 20:29.

13

SUPER HANC PETRAM

Two Ecclesiological Principles: The Rock and the Keys[1]

In my contribution to the debate provoked by a possible promulgation of a Fundamental Church Law, or *Lex Ecclesiae Fundamentalis* (LEF), I will view the problem from a different geographical, historical, cultural, and religious perspective than that normally presented. Without posing as a spokesman for two-thirds of mankind, but merely as a "voice in the wilderness," I would like to propose the following alternative: either the church in general, and the Roman Church in particular, remains restricted to the Mediterranean world and its cultural colonies (with or without the colonialist hope that one day this world will cover the face of the earth), or it completely gives up trying to formulate any kind of fundamental law.

I do not say that the first part of this alternative is not a possible, valid, even Christian solution (in keeping with the awareness of being the remnant of Israel, the little flock, and so on). All I am saying is that it is not possible to do both—to claim to be universal, not bound to any particular sector of mankind, and then promulgate a fundamental law that, regardless of its content, only has meaning on the basis of the presuppositions of the so-called Western conception of Man, society, religion, God, and so on. No one can serve two masters, and the church, which loves to confront people with certain choices and options, is perhaps now also finding itself faced with a fundamental choice.

I would like, if I may, to expound on this subject using the very tools of the Latin and Roman tradition and, at the end of my arguments, to use the definition of law given by Thomas Aquinas (*Sum. theol.* I–II, q.90, a.4). Let me make it clear from the start that I am not dealing with the subject of the need for a discipline, a rule, or a law in general but the specific need for an LEF. This is not to say that rules are unnecessary or that any human activity can proceed on its own without them. I do not claim, for example, that we have no need for traffic control or laws that give a certain order to human relationships. I believe that traffic control is necessary, even though the growing number of cars on the road is not the result of a basic general law.

Quidquid recipitur ad modum recipientis recipitur: This is a well-known and fairly widely accepted saying. It is a fact, and may be considered a blessing, that the Greek

---

[1] *"Super hanc petram" Due principi ecclesiologici: la roccia e le chiavi*, in *Legge e Vangelo. Discussione su una legge fondamentale per la Chiesa* (Brescia: Paideia, 1972), 135–45. Translated by Geraldine Clarkson.

genius and the Roman *forma mentis* molded quite impressively the first Christian *kērygma* as soon as it emerged from the "circumcision." A blessing can turn into a curse, however, just as a liberator can turn into a dictator if he does not acknowledge the "signs of the times" and change or pull back in time. It seems obvious, and might be considered a motive for joy and gratefulness, that the juridical or, rather, the ethical charisma of Rome took the lion's share in forming the church, especially the Catholic Church, up to today.

A great deal has been said about the post-Constantinian period of the church, but the debate has mainly taken place within the structures of a Constantinian mentality; ultimately, in fact, it is not power, pomp, or money that characterizes this age, but rather a particular vision of the world and a special juridical form of thought. We can well understand the disappointment of the people on both sides of the barricade when they see that the so-called reform goes no further than replacing an emperor with a president or a rigid, hardened organization with a more liberal and less centralizing secretariat, or when they discover that there is still the intention to preserve world leadership (today theoretically without violence or means, but in reality with the money, influence, and means of other powers) or that a given collection of rubrics has been replaced with a mass of more or less flexible regulations.

From a certain point of view, a juridical constitution may, in actual fact, still be necessary in guiding a society through all these reforms. However, today the question that urgently demands serious ecclesiastical reflection is whether acceptance (necessary in any human institution) of the horizontal principle *ecclesia semper est reformanda* should be integrated with the pneumatological principle of a constantly updated work of "information" on the part of the Spirit: *ecclesia semper est informanda. Ecce nova facio omnia.*[2]

The hypothesis of an LEF rests on the predominant ecclesiology, previously dormant in the Roman genius and manifest from Constantine onward, according to which a fundamental *lex* or charter is needed for the very existence of the church. It is easy to comprehend and respect the distress of those who, unable to conceive of any other type of ecclesiology, come to the conclusion that it is not a question of formulating a better *lex* and taking into account the voice of the minorities, but of doing without it altogether. Within the framework of Constantinian ecclesiology the church needs a law; this is practically a dogma. This may be why many opponents of the *lex* argue that such a law already exists in the Gospels or the New Testament and the entire Bible; the supposition in both cases is that a certain LEF is necessary. How else, they would say, can an efficient organization or a sound organism exist? If this were true I would bow to both sides, suggesting that they gather as much as possible from the Gospels, and I would withdraw. Yet it appears to me that not only does two-thirds of mankind fail to see the problem in this way, but in the remaining third there is a growing awareness that struggles to give shape to something that is not necessarily anarchy or chaos or license. Can a society, or even just a religion, exist

---

  [2] Rev. 21:5 ("Behold, I make all things new").

without a basic juridical order, a constitution, a charter, a *lex fundamentalis*? My answer, which is (a) based on the lesson of the science of religions; (b) confirmed by philosophical considerations; and (c) supported by theological reflection, is yes, without a doubt. The church, religion, society, a population, and therefore, order and even efficiency can exist without any *lex fundamentalis*. In other words, the foundation and basis of a stable order does not necessarily have to be a law, a juridical set of rules, or an order, either self-imposed or enforced from without.

I will go so far as to suggest that to speak of an LEF, if we are to avoid abusing the language, is a contradiction in terms.

(a) After almost fifteen centuries of one single, rigid theology, it may prove difficult to imagine that a church can exist without a certain basic law as a principle of cohesion and unity. We might convince ourselves that this may be possible by observing, first of all, the greater part of natural societies. These are not based on any laws. The family existed as an institution even before it was institutionalized; the clan, the sect, the nation, and so on are natural units whose origins in most cases are not based on any kind of social contract but, rather, on more profound and less voluntaristic anthropological motivations. Spontaneity is still a positive value in many parts of the world (and its theological equivalent could be related to the Holy Spirit); only artificial bodies demand the preeminence of the law.

Natural societies do not need a *lex fundamentalis* to live and exist in order and efficiency. They need a myth or a basic belief, which disintegrates as soon as it is transformed into law. It is not necessary to discuss here whether the church is natural or supernatural, but in any case, if the church is to be not an artificial society but the product of a precise and conscious human project, it cannot have a charter. This argument finds consolation in the fact that the heritage of liturgy and tradition has no founder (the Messiah is certainly not the founder of the kingdom), much less a basic charter. It is a mistake and an abuse, with regard to both form and content, to consider the books of the New Testament as a juridical expression of the church, or even in the broadest possible sense as a *lex fundamentalis*. I am not disputing the right of an authority to promulgate laws, even fundamental laws; I am saying that the origins of the church are not based on a fundamental law, and that it is now too late to give it one.

The absence of a basic law or central constitution is born out not only by the so-called primitive religions or natural societies but also by the example of Christianity itself; in the consciousness and awareness of millions of people, in fact, it has no basic law whatsoever. These people could not consider the good news that frees Man as another law substituting a previous law. The Bible can have religious authority as far as it remains a myth; the first ecumenical councils retain a certain superior regulatory character because they now belong to a mythical *in illo tempore*. There is no need here to quote St. Paul or emphasize the fact that the Constantinian spirit never succeeded in permeating the entire ecclesiastical Christian consciousness.

By way of example, let us turn our attention for a moment to the case of Hinduism, which is almost forty centuries old and exists, survives, and even expands without any of the structures that in Christianity may be called fundamental law, central organization, unified discipline, universally accepted juridical authority, and suchlike. There are laws, certainly, but there is not one law; there are authorities and group leaders, but there is no central organization or single authority, not even theoretically, just as in Christian Protestantism, for example. The *śruti* is not the Bible. It is something much freer and more spontaneous, based on being and not on the will, on existence rather than essence, on a certain tangible and existential faithfulness rather than a doctrinal agreement; it is orthopraxis rather than orthodoxy. The common creed is an existential faith, not an intellectual conviction. The purpose here is not to compare or judge, concluding that, after all, Christianity is not Hinduism, but to discover a model that works and recognize the existence of a religion in the full sense of the word, as opposed to any type of church in the juridical sense.

One does not go in and out of Hinduism as if joining or leaving a club. The experience of facts such as this can also help us understand the following philosophical observations.

(b) The question of a *lex fundamentalis*, if the semantics are taken seriously, means that there is or will be a *lex* that must be considered as the foundation and basis of any further legislation and, indeed, the whole structure of the church. This is as far as *fundamentalis* is concerned. As for *lex*, suffice it to say that, as the Code of Canon Law itself recognizes (c. 8), the promulgation of a law belongs to the essence of a law.

Here I would like to make a couple of considerations, one general and one concerning the nature of the church.

The *first* general consideration is that every instance of promulgation implies that the authority is fully aware of what is being promulgated and considers itself capable of formulating the contents of the given law. Apart from the attitude of condescendence, which is reflected in the etymology of the very word "promulgation," founding something on a law implies accepting that this something is the work of Man, that Man can manipulate it or at least define its nature; it implies the destruction of the myth, a mistrust in spontaneity or in any kind of natural or ontic reality that cannot be reduced to formulas by the human *ratio*.

Physical nature exists and has its own order whether or not Man is acquainted with it or its basic laws (although the word "law" is used here only analogically). No living reality can be established in laws, nor can any human action carried out in obedience to the law be said to be perfectly free (as Aristotle and Augustine would agree). True Christian obedience increases human freedom because it transcends the law. In fact, the very awareness or discovery of a "natural" law or formulated purpose not only destroys authenticity and innocence but alters the very action or attitude itself. We cannot love by law, and the mere recognition that there exists a certain "law" of love causes the loving encounter to be altered.

Our main interest here, however, is not of a psychological nature. It regards a certain vision of the world that refuses to surrender to the total control of *logos* that leaves no room for "myth," love, spontaneity and the absence of schemes, play, and joy that confidently welcome the ever-unexpected new.

The second consideration I would like to express concerns the specific problem we are examining here. If the church succeeds in giving itself a fundamental law, this will destroy its nature as Mystery and leave no room for the Holy Spirit as its vital principle; it will no longer be able to claim to be an institution of divine origin. The original myth would become so reduced by the human formulation, so consistently elaborated by human logic and so clearly and distinctly formulated (otherwise it would not be a law), that it is difficult to see how this law (that would claim to express the foundation and lie at the basis of any other ecclesiastical rule) could be compatible with "faith," indeed, with love.

A church that can be juridically *defined* ceases to be a part of the sphere of faith; a church that can identify a juridical (or even philosophical or theological) principle on which to found its entire life ceases to be a living organism. It becomes a consistent Cartesian system, a society that is so well ordered that sin is no longer the *mysterium iniquitatis* but an error or a transgression of the law. The word "Phariseeism" has every right to reclaim prestige and dignity, since the Pharisees were not always the grotesque figures that the Christians tend to portray them as; nevertheless, here the term may be used in its pejorative colloquial meaning. The promulgation of a fundamental law, in fact, would open the way to the worst kind of Phariseeism and officially consecrate it. Once a *lex fundamentalis* has been established, all authority can be done away with, since the law and the exegesis experts are all that is needed; it is simply a matter of applying *lex fundamentalis* appropriately. The church can then become a model institution, an example for all other human societies—but certain of the basic characteristics of twenty centuries of Christian life and tradition would disappear. From this point of view it is surprising what a secularized mentality and profane attitude this project reveals. Those who would like to see the church as a social body abreast with human progress may rightly ask for a *lex fundamentalis*; anyone else, however, should be invited to consider the possibility that this law disappoints and contradicts their expectations.

(c) It is not necessary to analyze all the theological implications relating to the attitude of those who defend a *lex fundamentalis*. We can understand the origins of this attitude by referring to the classical place from where the ecclesiology underlying the project took its stratagems for developing the doctrine of Peter as the foundation of the church and the power of the keys given to him and the apostles. Here again we find the same principle that the mind receiving the message in a text, as far as its comprehension is concerned, is as important as any "objective" content the message may have. *Quidquid recipitur . . .*

Considering now the text[3] traditionally regarded as the act by which the church was established and founded, we find ourselves faced with the surprising fact that, in order to express the idea of establishing His church, Christ apparently used Simon's change of name and the metaphor of the keys.

---

[3] Mt 16:18–19.

These two words (*rock* and *keys*) may represent the symbols of a twofold ecclesiology. The first, based on the symbolism of keys and interpreted in a certain way, became established in the period of Constantine, or perhaps even earlier. Having the power to bind and release is certainly a juridical power—although we should carefully consider the fact that power is bestowed on a man and not on a constitutional charter or a set of rules, so that if we admit that Peter's successor has equal right to this power, it should also be granted to each consecutive successor. Therefore, a *lex fundamentalis* promulgated by one of these successors will only be valid to the extent that another successor recognizes it as such—a fact that is distinctly in contrast with the idea of *lex fundamentalis*. If the concept of *causa sui* is a contradiction in terms, a "legislator of itself," even though it is conceivable, it is doomed to fail in its purpose.

The power of the keys is a power given to Man; it is an act that manifests an extraordinary trust in Man. If the power to release and to bind is also granted to the successors of Peter and the apostles, this power seems to us to be the power to pass and to promulgate every kind of law, except a *lex fundamentalis*, since it would be difficult to define as basic a law that can be changed by a successor according to the power given to him. In other words, the metaphor of the keys is itself much less juridical than it may seem at first glance. It is not the pen of the scribe, but the keys held by the administrator or the mother, as mistress of the house (to remain in the literary genre).

It is quite interesting to note that the main, and crucial, metaphor of the passage in the Gospel (that of the rock) is rarely given the importance it might have, apart from the aspect of immovability, "solidity," and the guarantee of stable permanence despite the onslaughts of the "gates of hell." Peter was given a new name—it is difficult to overemphasize the significance of this fact—*cephas*, *petra*, rock, and we might continue to read: stone, earth, chthonic values, myth, that which resists *logos*, that which cannot be manipulated or exhausted by knowledge. You are rock, stone, earth. The foundations of the church are no different from the foundations of any building on the earth, and of the earth itself; the church does not stand on special ground but on the very basis of creation. You are Peter, beyond all the vagaries of men, especially when they see themselves as legislators, reformers, intelligent, and gifted with superior knowledge. We might also mention here the *humilitas* of the Magnificat[4]—the earthly aspect of the church of Christ, which rests not on human or man-made laws (though they aim to interpret divine commandments) but on the *humus*, on the rock of mother earth. You are Peter; that is, you are not just an individual, a man, but also a "thing," a being, rock, stone, earth. Why this human excommunication from the rest of the world? Why this *hybris* and this rather forced interpretation of Genesis, as if Man were the "king" of creation, as if he came from another planet, and alone had power over the animals, plants, and the entire material world, regarding them as exclusively in his service?[5] What about the sacraments? What about the new earth?

---

[4] Lk 1:48.
[5] Gn 1:28.

On this rock I will build my church. A rock is not transparent; it retains its peace however it is used, for good or evil. A church founded on the supremacy of being over doing; of silence over words; on fundamental, indeed material values before those of a "spiritual" and sophisticated nature; on ground on which the common man and also the animals can strive to move, will grow up to the sky, though it is built on the earth and stands on the earth, like the tree to which the kingdom of God is resembled. It grows up to the sky so that the birds of the sky may rest on its branches, yet it continues to be rooted in the ground.

Rather than expounding further on these considerations, however, let us turn our attention back to the alternative mentioned above.

I am not saying that African and Asian civilizations do not have their own laws, casuistries, and Machiavellis. For this I do not think they need the church. What I am saying is that it will be difficult to eradicate the (well-founded) suspicion that, after so much talk about the independence of the church from every specific cultural context, about genuine service and *kenōsis*, if the peoples of the world have not received the "blessing" of so-called Western culture, they will come to see the church as it appears today—the ideal incarnation of clear, methodical, well-balanced Roman law, first sacralized and now secularized. Here again, strength is weakness, and weakness is the glory of God—a church built on the rock has no need of anxious vigilance and watchfulness in order to be sure to resist the onslaughts of time and the corrosion of history.

On the subject of the power of laws, I would like to end with a story from the *Purāṇa*. A king asks his minister, who has made considerable progress in his spiritual life and discipline, to teach him his mantra—his life and his way of praying distilled into a formula that is effective if proffered in ontological truth, that is, when there is mutual adaptation between the subject and the object. The minister turns down the request, and the king insists. The minister then tells a page who is standing by to seize the king, but the page does not move, despite the repeated orders of the minister. Finally the king becomes angry and tells his page to seize the minister, and the boy immediately obeys. The minister then bursts into laughter and says to the king, "Our orders, our laws, were the same and so was the person carrying them out; yet in one case the order did not work and in the other it did. It is not possible to make laws work by magic. Everything depends on the authority that is granted us, on the orders we give and the persuasive power of the law."

To say the same thing in academic terms, if a law is to be truly such, it must not only be promulgated but also accepted and recognized as a law. Today, the body of the church does not appear very eager to adopt a fundamental law, old or new, and even less does it seem willing to accept it. And a fundamental law without the essential approval and acceptance of those to whom the law is directed would certainly not be a *lex* fundamentalis; it would be without a purpose. This might be the last consolation—at least to Oriental sensitivity—if the law it to be effectively promulgated.

The letter kills . . . itself.

14

Christians and So-Called "Non-Christians"*

> "But God has been showing me that we ought not to
> speak of any manas profane or unclean."

Ac 10:28

Introduction

Our problem is today an acute and unavoidable one. In past times, a certain religious instinct made the followers of different religions avoid mutual contact and dialogue, lest the purity of their respective doctrines and the steadfastness of their adherence to their faith be endangered. Today this attitude can no longer survive, either in practice or in theory. However, it is not my purpose to deal with the general problem of the encounter of religions. I will do my best to limit myself to the theme of this paper, which I mean to approach from an anthropological point of view. *Theological anthropology* is, in fact, necessary to solve this problem, as it is for many other present-day problems, because the new degree of consciousness that is emerging in the present stage of the evolution—or involution—of Man toward his goal makes a reflection on himself indispensable. We can no longer enter into contact with "things" themselves without our subjective attitudes biasing our judgment.

I say this because, although the ideas I will put forward are not new (they are quite traditional, in fact), they spring from that new and deeper degree of consciousness that humanity at large, and the church in particular, is acquiring in the present encounter of peoples, cultures, and religions that has been made sociologically possible by modern technological developments.

I first analyze the meaning of the title, then I develop some leading principles, and finally I offer some practical reflections on the fundamental Christian attitude in so-called non-Christian surroundings.

---

*   Original edition: "Christians and So-Called 'Non-christians,'" *Cross-Currents* 22, no. 3 (1972): 281–308. A previous publication, "Bases teológicas para la cooperación de cristianos y no cristianos," appeared in *Criterio* 31, no. 1319 (1958): 806–08.

Non-Christian Surroundings

This is a somehow ambiguous and perhaps even misleading phrase, for nowhere on earth are there situations that can be said to be independent from or unrelated to Christ (see Col 1:17).

Obviously, the phrase is not supposed to suggest a condition of sin or intellectual error; neither does it mean that kind of environment in which religion plays hardly any role in the people's lives. It rather means a situation created by the existence of so-called non-Christian religions, in the midst of which a Christian may happen to live.

What we cannot accept is the very expression "non-Christian religions" and, even more, the underlying concept, because

(a) It is offensive and unacceptable for so-called non-Christian religions to be described only by a negative feature, which merely distinguishes them from the Christian religion. I am afraid that this expression is nothing more than an unconscious outcome of what we may call "theological colonialism." In any case, it leaves a bad taste in the mouth to divide people up in such a way.

(b) Neither is this distinction scientific. It cannot stand up to any historical, philosophical, or even theological criteria. We cannot indiscriminately lump together all types of religions that, from a certain point of view, may differ much more from one another than any of them differs from the Christian religion.

(c) In the minds of those who hold Christianity to be the only true religion, the expression "non-Christian" amounts to saying that other religions are false. If Christianity stands for truth and the fullness of truth, a non-Christian religion will necessarily be false; thus, either Christianity is not *the* truth, or world religions cannot be called "non-Christian." Moreover, if the "other" religions are "non-Christian" religions, then Christianity is merely one religion among many; and if this is the case, it is arbitrary to consider one specific religion as the point of reference.

(d) In fact, so-called *non*-Christian religions cannot be described like that, because, from a Christian point of view, one should honestly recognize not only that Christ is *already* there but also that, in different ways and degrees, those religions do belong to and fit into the Christian economy of salvation.[1]

This is why we understand the expression "non-Christian surroundings" as the situation of a Christian living in a world where Christ is not explicitly acknowledged as the Lord.

What Is a Christian?

We now have to clarify the other word in our title. From an anthropological viewpoint, we have, first of all, to dispel three vague misconceptions that, though not explicitly affirmed, do put the problem of the relationship between Christians and non-Christians in a wrong perspective.

---

[1] See, as regards Hinduism, R. Panikkar, *The Unknown Christ of Hinduism* (London: DLT, 1964).

(a) Christians have no *monopoly on goodness*, either at the so-called natural or the supernatural level. History in general, and the history of religions in particular, clearly shows not only that sin is everywhere but also that goodness flourishes all over the world. Even what is sometimes specifically called "the Christian moral doctrine of universal love, and love for our enemies"—that is, the attitude returning a blessing for a curse and recognizing the existence of a human-superhuman dignity everywhere—can be found in many other religions, with almost the same wording as in the Gospels, and that at least five centuries before Christ.[2]

The modern world, even in the West, cannot accept the Christian claim to a monopoly on goodness. In fact, the struggle for justice in our times can by no means be said to have been made under the leadership of Christians. We must get rid of oversimplified apologetics about the human achievements, or the civilizing power of the church, and the like, even if the civilizing action of many churchmen cannot be denied. It is even methodologically wrong to credit Christianity with all the good that Christians have done, and to their "humaneness" all the harm they have caused. The Christian fact lies elsewhere. Only God is good, but He lets His goodness be shared by all His creatures.[3]

(b) Christians have no *monopoly on truth*: neither human truth, for Man's reason is a valid means of true knowledge everywhere, nor religious or supernatural truth. Most so-called Christian truths can be found in other religions.[4] The Christian church's claim to be the custodian of divine revelation, even while admitting that

---

[2] For example, "Do not hurt your neighbor, even if he provokes you; do not harm anybody by thought or action, do not proffer words which may be painful to others" (*Laws of Manu*, 161). "Do not despise anybody; suffer calumnies with patience; do not get angry with the angry man and bless him who curses you" (*Laws of Manu* VI.47–48). "This is the summit of all virtues: deal with others as you would wish that others dealt with you; do not do to your neighbor what you do not want him to do to you. When you please others, or displease them, when you do good or give hurt, you will follow the just norm, if you consider your neighbor as yourself" (*Mahābhārata*, XIII.5571). "Rejoice over the welfare and prosperity of others, even if you yourself are poor" (*Mahābhārata*, XIII.3889). "Even to the foe, if he asks from you hospitality, do not deny it; do not even the trees offer their shade and shelter to those who cut them?" (*Mahābhārata*, XII.5528). "Suffer insults patiently, do not fall into wrath with the wrathful man; to one who curses do not answer with curses, nor should you hurt him who harms you" (*Mahābhārata*, V.1270). And again: "Never in this world can hatred be subdued by hatred; it will be stilled only by non-hatred. This is the everlasting *dharma*" (*Dhammapāda*, 5). "When Confucius was asked about the meaning of *jen*, the Master replied: Do not do to others, what you would not like others to do to you" (*Analecta Confuciana*, XII.2 [or similarly in VI.28]); or again: "Do not treat your enemy badly; repay him with goodness who does evil to you, and let justice prevail over your enemy" (old Assyrian proverb). As for the Old Testament, see, among other passages: Lv 19:17–18; Pr 24:17; 25:21; Ex 23:4–5, etc.

[3] See Gn 1:10; Mk 10:18; Mt 19:17; Lk 18:19, etc.

[4] See, e.g., the three volumes edited by F. König, *Christus und die Religionen der Erde* (Freiburg im Breisgau: Herder, 1951).

the fullness of revelation is to be found in Christianity, does not mean at all that Christianity exhausts the whole of God's self-disclosure to humankind, and that Christians can reserve the right to enjoy all that God has done out of His divine care for Men. Who are we to limit the works of God, or to prescribe to Him what He has to do?[5] Nowhere in Christian Scriptures is it said that God has not spoken to "others," or that He has not been looking after His "other" children (Jn 10:16). There is no evidence of where to ground this claim to exclusiveness. The fact that God may choose one person or elect a particular people for a special function does not imply the rejection of others. Even more: God's dealings with every creature are, by definition, *unique* and admit no comparison. The very fact that at the *end of time*, after having sent and inspired so many prophets, God has spoken to us in His Son (Heb 1:1) does not exclude but rather presupposes the cosmic covenant and His universal providence.[6]

(c) Finally, Christians have no *monopoly on salvation*. If we take seriously the dictates of our conscience, the light of our reason, and the Christian doctrine of God's universal saving will (see 1 Tim 2:4, etc.), we cannot doubt for a moment that salvation is offered to every man who comes into this world (see Jn 19). It is, therefore, improper to try to justify the Christian missionary activity only in connection with the salvation of people. As a result, we cannot speak of *ordinary* or *extraordinary* ways of salvation. We lack any criterion for such a discussion: neither numbers, nor quality, nor facilities, nor anything regarding personal salvation is disclosed to us. Christ Himself rejected such a question as an idle pretense (see Lk 13:23). It would be nonsense to say that the whole of humankind was in utter darkness and doomed to damnation, then suddenly the Creator realized the weight of human misery and decided to save men—but only a numerically negligible part of them. The justification of Christian missions lies elsewhere.[7]

A Christian is simply a *conscious* collaborator with Christ in His threefold function of creating, redeeming, and glorifying the world. Perhaps only mystics are aware of their sharing in the work of creation and divinization of the world, but every Christian is aware that he or she is called to be a Christian precisely in order to participate in the redeeming function of Christ. We speak of a more or less conscious collaboration (see 1 Co 3:9) because we do not exclude an ontic collaboration on the part of all those whom today some would like to call "anonymous Christians,"[8] or others would prefer to consider as "men of goodwill." In fact, any human being in ontological union with Christ, the Firstborn of all creation and the head of his Body, the church (Col 1:15–18), collaborates with Him in building up the Body of Christ (Ep 4:12).

---

[5] See Is 40:13; Ws 9:13; Rom 11:34.

[6] See R. Panikkar, "Eine Betrachtung über Melchisedech," *Kairos* 1 (1959), 5–17.

[7] See Masson's paper in J. Neuner, ed., *Christian Revelation and World Religions*.

[8] See K. Rahner, *Schriften zur Theologie* (Einsiedeln, 1962), 5:155; A. Röper, *Die anonymen Christen* (Mainz: Matthias Grünewald, 1963).

Christian theology has traditionally developed the function of Christ in His redeeming action as threefold by considering Him, on the basis of Scriptures, as king, prophet, and priest.[9] Thanks to baptism, confirmation, and Eucharist, the Christian participates in that threefold function. In this perspective we could explain the mission that is entrusted to every Christian, starting from the very fact of his or her Christian vocation. Nevertheless, in order to shed light on this problem from an anthropological point of view, we will follow (1) the line that originates from Man himself, once he has received his Christian calling, and (2) that which derives from Christ Himself as Pantocrator.[10] We only aim at complementing the other traditional line of thought, which we have just mentioned.

In what follows we retain the idea that a Christian is a man who has received, as a free gift, the personal call of Christ to perform, together with Him and really *in* Him, the task of redeeming the world. We leave aside, but only to simplify our exposition, the two other and deeper sharings—that is, in the intra-Trinitarian mystery of the creation and divinization of the whole cosmos.

Principles

From the Point of View of Christians

The principle that rules the specifically Christian attitude toward the world cannot be different from that which guides the Christian relation with God. If God the Creator is not different from God the Redeemer, if the Christian is not to be a split personality, if his Christian calling is not to ruin his human vocation, he cannot indulge in two loyalties, as it were: one to God and another to the world. He cannot be truly a citizen of two kingdoms, that of God and that of Man. He cannot have two ultimate ideals, one natural and one supernatural, as he does not have in fact two goals or two final destinations. In short, he cannot serve two masters (Mt 6:24). The call to be a Christian is a special and personal one indeed, but it is not the only call coming from Christ. It is not an exception, but a fulfillment (Mt 5:17). Moreover, Christ the Redeemer is not different from the Christ through whom all things were made and in whom all things subsist (Col 2:17). Therefore, the Christian calling is not in contradiction to the specifically human vocation—this also coming from Christ, not as a general character of being a creature—the whole created existence being nothing else than a *Christophany*.

Because of an education not completely free from Manichean, Puritan, and Jansenistic influences, Christians are sometimes inclined to consider their relation with God as an altogether different thing from their relation with the world, as if the world could exist independently and be apart from God; as if creation were only ex nihilo, and not also—and even primarily—*a Deo* and *in Deo*, from God and in

---

[9] See Y. Congar, *Lay People in the Church* (London, 1959).
[10] Rev 4:8; 11:17; 16:7, etc.

God. Analogically, as God the Father by the one and the same act by which He begets the Son and breathes the Spirit also "creates" the whole cosmos,[11] so the Christian by the one and the same act by which he "reaches" God also "embraces" the world.

Now, the fundamental, simple, integral Christian act, albeit structurally three-fold, is the supernatural act of faith, hope, and charity, all in one: the setting into motion of our whole being by the exercise of the theological virtues in the simple unity of our fundamental act—for which we currently have no proper name, since each expression, be it faith, hope, love, or even worship, surrender, intuition, and so on, can convey only one aspect of that act, the simplicity of which precisely makes it so rich. Let us now briefly analyze this fundamental Christian act by which the Christian is united to Christ, and is saved by so doing.

It has been the sad fate of the Western tradition that a distinction between God and the world has been so carefully worked out, this sometimes leading to the *separation* of God and the world, and, finally, even to the *negation* of that "element" (God) that, once separated from the *datum* (the integral realm of our experience), becomes more and more superfluous. Once God is set "over there" just to supervise the deeds of men or control the working of the laws of nature, this *Deus ex machina* becomes unnecessary as soon as the human mind becomes adult. Man no longer needs a "prime mover" to put the world into motion and then retire, or a "mind" just to cover the gaps in human knowledge, until Man discovers, behind the events, the real reasons he had been ignoring until then. God is not like the joker in a deck of cards, to be used instead of what we momentarily need.

It is not by chance that modern atheism, an almost unique phenomenon in history, has appeared within Western culture. As an example of this trend we could take the attitude that has made its way into the very heart of Christian spirituality (perhaps love being the only exception)—that is, that of considering God as an *ob-iectum*, as an object separated from the world. The result is that, when He becomes the object of our act of faith, hope, or charity, we have faith *in* (the direction of) God, we hope *in* Him and love Him, but without completely realizing that, if this faith, hope, and charity are really theological virtues, they have to reach the living God, who includes (with)*in* Himself the whole of His creation. In other words, the authentic act of faith, hope, and charity does not only "reach" a transcendent Godhead, but includes our whole and innermost relationship with the world as well. Otherwise we fall into a dualistic, anti-Christian position, removing God from His creation. Creatures are not only *the* way to reach God (see Rom 1:19–20); they are also *in* Him (see Ac 17:28), so that any deep contact with God cannot exclude what He has created.

Any real contact with the Godhead is always—consciously or unconsciously—Trinitarian, so that a lifeless or monistic absolute is only an illusion. Likewise, a real union with the absolute includes, one way or another, the relative: the relative of the absolute, that is, in other terms, the world—not, indeed, in the fragmentary form in which it stretches its being in space and time, but really as it is, a cosmos, *in, from,*

---

[11] "Pater dicendo se dicit omnem creaturam" [The Father, by "saying" Himself, "says" every creature], medieval Scholastics taught.

and *of* God. A separated Godhead, in fact, does not exist. Nor has a separated cosmos any consistency whatsoever. We may define *existence* as the tension of the creature "between" God and nothingness, as the "sistence" *extra causas*. It is not enough to say that the world is *in*, *for*, and *of* God, as if it were something, a substance, a being in itself that only happens to be in the bosom of another (God, to begin with, is not an-other). It is the world itself which is *in-God*, *from-God*, *of-God*, *to-God*, and the like; we could even say the world is *God-in*, *God-from*, *God-of*, etc., which is far from being pantheism. For this reason, the act that "ascends" to God also lingers on the shore of creatures. In a word, the authentic theological virtues are by this very fact *cosmological* virtues also.

Let us now briefly analyze the three moments of that simple integral act in its *cosmological* dimension.

Act of Faith

We cannot properly say that we *have* faith. One does not *have* faith as one possesses an object or masters a situation. Faith is "something" that by its very nature cannot be "had," and for this reason it can be neither stored nor kept, as it were, without "using" it. We just "have" faith by believing—that is, by performing that actual act of faith, which we cannot possess, because it is mightier than ourselves. If a possession occurs, then it is rather faith that possesses us; we are possessed by a God who lets us share in His "knowledge," "vision," and "light," or by whatever name we may call that participation in the act by which God (re)cognizes Himself as God.

The integral act of faith does not mean a belief in an "isolated" God, but in the living Godhead, which includes God's creation also, and especially, for our purpose, the human race. The Christian, by the same act by which he believes in God, also believes in Man as God's children. A man of faith is a man who also trusts his fellow beings—a man who, precisely because he believes that God is what He is, is not overanxious about the fate of men and does not usurp the place of God by trying to replace His providence or to imitate His justice. A man of faith assumes in his very faith the faith of his fellow-beings, and even the unbelief of the human world. Faith always plays a vicarious role: it does not only enjoy a "vision," it also believes *for* others, while believing *in* others. For this reason, real faith is contagious, and experience shows that the presence of a saint creates an atmosphere of holiness around him or her. A true Christian is not only one who loves "for" those who do not; he also believes for those who do not believe—believes for them in such a way that "they" do not even need to believe. Real faith is not so much concerned with making others believe as in believing, and by doing so, it also trusts so-called nonbelievers. Faith, as it were, believes in the nonfaith of others. If we have faith, we share God's worldview, we discover why the sun shines on the good and the evil alike, and the rain falls on the just and on sinners; and if God allows the wheat to grow together with the tares, the man of faith "sees" that this is neither due to a legislator's caprice nor to a cosmic necessity, but is the expression of the real and divine order of things.

The more supernatural the act of faith is, the more natural it is—not only as regards the subject who performs that act without, as it were, forcing his "nature," but also concerning the subject matter of faith, which includes the whole of creation as it really is: *of, in, for*, and *through* God. The paradox, well known to saints and theologians, that the more divine a person or a situation is, the more human it appears, can also be applied to the Christian act of faith. Moreover—and this seems of capital importance to me—real faith is not something that divides men; it is not something that cuts humankind up into groups and factions, but something that unites them and leads them to find a deep unity. By and through my personal faith I take part in the faith of another believer, and even shoulder the "nonfaith" of an "unbeliever." It is because I have faith that I can understand—and assume—others' faith and even "no faith" at all. Real faith is just the opposite of what people "without faith" seem to think it is: it is not something that divides people, but something that unites them—not a cause of separation, but of union. Only from a merely rational point of view does the plurality of beliefs look like a scandal, because it is incomprehensible, whereas, from a higher point of view, true plurality has a fundamental place.[12] If faith is what it claims to be, it should be as tolerant as God Himself: a man of faith, precisely because of his faith, will trust the God who so wonderfully trusts Man and the cosmos (see Ws 12:18).

We will describe the *cosmological* aspect of the act of faith in the following way, and we think this has a certain relevance for the present problem of the relationship between the church and the world.[13] By the modern mind, the old dilemma about the apparent incompatibility between the world and God could be expressed like this: either God does not exist, or the world as it *appears* does not exist.

Either there is no God (because there is evil, suffering, and sin, and all this cannot be outside or independent of God, in which case He would no longer be good or almighty), or there is no "world" as we see it. But faith implies the purification of our seeing powers, so that we discover God on the one hand and the real face of the world on the other. Faith is not so much the discovery of God as the discovery of the world, of the real world, of God's world, as it really is; it is not so much an extra-mundane awareness (of a transcendent Godhead) as rather an inner-worldly insight into the true reality of this world. A man of faith is not so much a man who believes in God, as a man who believes in God's world—or to be more precise, a man who, because of his insight into the Godhead, discovers God's creation, the real world, just there. It is so true that faith is this inner-worldly "vision" that faith is necessary for our earthly pilgrimage, but no longer necessary in heaven. There, we will not need faith, because the world will no longer be an opaque screen.[14] Faith is required here on earth in order to pierce the screen of the world and see it from the other side, the real side.

---

[12] See Ps 44:10 in the allegoric interpretation of the Church Fathers, and down to Benedict XV, *Acta Apostolicae Sedis* (1919), 98.

[13] See, for instance, the well-known discussions on *Schema 13* during Vatican Council II.

[14] See 1 Co 13:9–13, etc.

The consequence is not only an attitude of positive tolerance, but also the purification of any *superiority complex* on the part of Christians toward their "non-Christian surroundings." They will not look down upon others as inferior beings, or as if they were in a lower stage of awareness: the Christian, on the contrary, will realize that the others, to begin with, are not "others," mere opponents or enemies, because he understands and accepts them without ulterior motives.[15]

Act of Hope

Similarly, the act of hope is an act of hope in the world, as far as the whole universe is in God and sustained by Him, and on its way back to Him.[16] This is why the Christian is always an optimist, with a positive outlook on the world, because he hopes in God and God's almighty power, which can raise up out of stones children to Abraham (Lk 3:8), and make the whole of humankind go back to its own Source. To hesitate in believing in the salvation of the world or in the power of redemption is a sin against hope: "Just as *all* have died with Adam, so with Christ *all* will be brought to life."[17]

If I hope in God and in God's salvation, my act of hope embraces, as it were, the whole world; or, at least, the more hope includes the world, the deeper it is; but in any case the act of hope always includes something more than hope in one's own private salvation. This would not only be presumption and blasphemy, it would also be a contradiction in terms, as it would no longer be hope in God, but mere confidence in oneself. If I hope to be saved, not because of myself, but because of God, I cannot make any distinction between the hope that God will save *me* and the hope that He will equally save *others*. The act of hope in God is an act that hopes in God as the goal, end, and aim of every being. The real act of hope excludes any shadow of self-justification; I hope in God precisely because I realize that I cannot hope in myself, and I have no ground whatsoever to doubt the salvation of others more than my own. Therefore, a man of hope is not distressed about the problems of salvation. He *knows* himself to be in God's hands, but he equally well knows that everybody is in the same situation, and that his being allowed to hope in God does not make him a privileged person (see Mt 7:21).

A Christian not only believes in God; he has, at the same time, hope in God. He, as it were, stretches his whole being toward the future, and "touches," in hope, the *eschaton*, the end of everything. That famous passage in the Scripture—"And when all things will be subdued to him, then the Son also himself will be subject to

---

[15] See "He who is not against you is for you" (Mk 9:40).

[16] "Should we say *yes* to any particular moment, then we have said it not only to ourselves but to all existence," wrote Nietzsche in his *Wille zur Macht* [Will to Power], IV.1032.

[17] 1 Co 15:22. See *Denz.,* 319: "Sicut nullus homo est, fuit vel fuerit, cuius natura in illo [Christo] assumpta non fuerit, ita nullus est, fuit vel erit homo, pro quo passus non fuerit" [As there is, there has been, there will be no Man whose nature has not been taken by Christ upon himself, just so there is, there has been, there will be no Man for whom He did not undergo the Passion].

Him who put all things under him, so that God may be all in all" (1 Co 15:28)—is the Magna Carta of the supernatural theological virtue of hope. Christian "hope" brings with it the cosmic optimism that Christ has conquered death, that in him all will live as all died in Adam.[18] He overcomes death, and after having integrated everything into himself, he will subject himself to the Father.

All this implies a positive openness toward the world: a Christian is not one who shuns the world or negates it. He has no *inferiority complex* when dealing with the world; he *knows* that the whole cosmos is on its way back to God, nor does he hope in a "God" disconnected from the world, but in the real living God, including God's saving power. Morphologically viewed, faith could be somehow independent of the rest of the world: one could have faith in God and not be explicitly aware of the world, for faith is that special awareness that God is as He is, and, in a way, one could put in brackets the fact that He *is* the Creator. But hope cannot even morphologically subsist without including creation; for hope is indeed hope in God, but as savior, as principle and end, as the goal of the cosmos. Faith is a theo-anthropological virtue, while hope is strictly a theo-cosmological one. There would be no hope if there were no world and no other people. It is through the supernatural act of hope that the Christian links the world with God and finds a basis for service and love.

The attitude of a Christian toward his "non-Christian surroundings" is an attitude of hope—that is, an inexpressible joy and peace because God is the Lord of all, the end of everything, the magnet of every being. It is out of his authentic hope that the Christian overcomes a sort of crypto-heresy that would make us "believe" that God's creation was somehow a "fiasco" and Christ's redemption an utter failure, so that we have now to fill the gaps and, in some way, correct His plans. Christian hope gives us the right perspective and corrects that distortion of the real situation that has been the cause of so many wrong approaches to the world in general, especially in the missionary field. God has created and *is creating* the world—as it is—and Christ has created and *is redeeming* the cosmos as it exists. God did not create only in the past, nor will He redeem only in the future. Both belong to the present, and Christians are not people brooding over the past or dreaming of the future (in order to conquer the world, in case), but they are directly concerned with and engaged in the present. It is through hope that modern man gets rid of that anxiety that crept into a certain type of Western-Christian mentality as a result of an anthropocentric culture: the *fear of being.* Let us remember that to be frightened to *be* amounts to being frightened of being God. Yes, the fear of being is actually fear of being God.

Act of Love

This point has been sufficiently developed in Christian tradition, so we just need to mention that we love God and love our neighbor by one and the same theological virtue. The Christian is neither a split personality, nor has he a double principle of action or a double standard of truth: one for God and another for the world. His

---

[18] 1 Co 15:22. Note the change of verbal tenses from past to future.

surrender to God implies and demands a dedication to the world; his love of God includes a love of God's creation; his devotion to the transcendent is manifested in his service to the immanent structures of reality. It is so much one and the same love that, on the one hand, theology shows and experience confirms that we cannot love God if we do not love our neighbor. How can we really consecrate ourselves to God if we despise what He loves? And He loves all that exists, as existence itself is nothing but, as it were, a crystallization of a divine act of love. Experience also confirms that any fictitiously exclusive love of God, which excludes humankind, degenerates into false religiousness and odious selfishness (1 Jn 4).

On the other hand, theology and experience equally show that there is no possibility of love for our neighbor without the love of God. No human love is worth its name if it does not pierce the external veil and penetrate into the very core of the person we love, where God dwells and sustains him or her. No love is real love if it does not enter the inner chamber of our beloved—where God already is—and love him or her for what he or she really *is*. But even without further considerations, daily experience shows that we cannot keep real love for our neighbor if the love of God is not there; nobody can love everybody. When human love stops short of divine love, then we discriminate according to psychological factors. Further, nobody can have a lasting love if divine love does not give it endurance. Who can keep on loving—really loving everybody—after the shortcomings and limitations of our fellow-beings have been discovered and suffered?

It is this theological love that prevents us from falling, on the one hand, into pure *sentimentalism* and, on the other, into a sort of *paternalistic* attitude, both of which kill real love.

The Christian's relation with his "non-Christian surroundings" is therefore a relation of love: not only sincere love, but a supernatural, divine love. The Christian loves the world, and especially his fellow-beings, with the same love with which he loves God, that is, with his whole heart, mind, strength, and being. Love, as with every truly supernatural act, is primarily an answer, a response to the primordial act of God's love, who has loved us first.[19] When we love God, we are simply mirroring His love for us; when we love our neighbor, we are simply sharing the divine love for all things; we are united with God, who does not want the death of the sinner, but his conversion and life.[20]

So, the Christian's relationship with the world is a relationship with God's world, and as a consequence, it is guided precisely by the supernatural act of faith, hope, and love *in*, *to*, and *for* the world as it ultimately is: God's creation, not only in the sense of a property of God, but also in the sense of God's own (here just one word would be inadequate) "being," "creation," "body," and so on. Any deep relationship with the world cannot exclude its Maker, the *logos* through whom every thing has come to be.[21]

---

[19] See Jn 3:16; 13:34; 15:12: and especially 1 Jn 4:10, 19; etc.
[20] See Mt 9:13; 12:7; 18:11; Lk 5:31–32; 15:7; 19:10; etc.
[21] Jn 1:3; Ep 2:10.

The achievement of this fundamental Christian act in its integral, theandric dimension is not brought about by merely *extending* it, in a halfhearted way, also to the world, but by *deepening* it into God, so that it finds God's action *ad extra*, too, as it were, on the outer shore of the Godhead. This theological attitude toward the world has another specific feature, which is at the same time a criterion for its authenticity: it is a real, mystical act that *reaches* God as well as the world, and therefore it is an end in itself, not biased by ulterior motives or preconceived ideas. The Christian has faith, hope, and love in the world as he has in God, and because of this, he does not mean either to "convert" or "transform" or "change" the world. It goes deeper than this. His action is really *naiṣkarmya*,[22] a disinterested action, because there is no particular "interest" behind it. The relationship of Christians with their "non-Christian surroundings" is a truly *theological act*, that is, an ultimate action that has its own justification in itself and does not need to aim at further ends or hidden intentions.

This is the "embrace" a Christian gives. This is the *mystery* of faith, hope, and charity by which the Christian takes part in God and in God's world, that is, in God's native action. A Christian creates, redeems, and deifies, together with the Blessed Trinity, that "part" of God that is still on pilgrimage, "on the way": this world of ours as it returns to its Source. Only this threefold and integral act of faith, hope, and charity will give the full measure of the Christian calling and set us free from all kinds of complexes and anxieties, as well as from prejudices, grudges, and jealousies regarding the world. Only this primordial act of any true Christian existence will overcome that surreptitious discouragement that today affects a great part of the missionary body of the church. After having consecrated everything to the work of evangelization, the missionary discovers that the theological foundations of his work were not accurate enough to sustain and justify his missionary activity. There is sometimes a false and bitter zeal that hampers the authentic Christian liberty and curtails Christian joy. A missionary, after all, is not someone who threatens and foretells punishment, disaster, and vengeance, but an envoy—an "angel"—who proclaims the glad tidings of the liberation, salvation, and love that Christ—not he or she—brings to the world.

From the Point of View of Christ

What we keep on underscoring, in so many different ways, is that God is the God *of* and *for* all, not only the "our God" of believers. And Christ is equally universal, not an *idol* for the worship of a particular clan or a mere *avatāra* for the private benefit of Christians. Christ, the only-begotten Son of God (Jn 1:14), is also the Firstborn of all creatures (Col 1:15), in whom all things took their being (Col 1:16), and in whom all subsist (Col 1:17), the Alpha and Omega of everything (Rev 1:18; 21:16), slaughtered since the foundation of the world (Rev 5:6), and thus the only mediator

---

[22] See *Bhagavad-gītā* II.47ff.; III.4, 17, 19, etc.

between the creation and the Father (1 Tim 2:5). He is the light that enlightens everyone who comes into this world (see Jn 1:9).

If every being qua being is a Christophany, there is no real relation outside or independent of Christ; there is no communication without Christ and, as a consequence, no "human relation" from which Christ is absent. Wherever two or more people are gathered in his name, there he is present (Mt 18:20); wherever there is a suffering human being, there Christ is present and receives our works of mercy (Mt 25:40); wherever there is real love, there is Christ.[23]

This leads us to deal with an important question of contemporary philosophy, because the problem of communication has become an urgent one for the man of our time. Modern Man, after discovering and taking refuge in his reason, perhaps in the same way that prehistoric humans took shelter in caves in order to survive and to protect themselves against the wilderness (now the wilderness is the jungle of opinions, feelings, and perspectives of our fellow beings . . .), perceives himself as an isolated being, and now tries to bridge the gulf that he himself has created between his own being and his fellow Man. Paradoxically enough, human reason, which was supposed to be the most universal and common denominator, proves itself totally inadequate to bring about that communication. We may all know that 2 and 2 make 4, or that nuclear war is a fearful threat, or that it is unjust that two-thirds of humankind have not enough to eat, and so on, but it seems that a shared rational truth does not foster any personal communion or effective action.

Here we can barely sketch out a thesis—to be developed and justified else-where—according to which a true communion is possible in Christ, and only in the realm of the sacred can a personal exchange take place. The only deep human communication is the *communicatio in sacris*: only when people pray together, or perform a sacred action, is there real communion. Human relations, when reduced to the sphere of the profane, are neither deeply human nor really relations, but only cultural conventions, surface smiles, shallow contacts, and polite manners. Our relations with other people cannot be reduced to the *pro-fanum*, cannot stop by the threshold of real communion.

Perhaps one should come into closer contact with the world religions to regain the sense of the sacred that part of the modern "civilized" world has almost lost, or at least very often distorted. Let us remember that real human relations, starting from the ways of greeting (such as *shalom, namaste*, "God bless," "good-bye" . . .), forms of eating (*agapē*, the partaking of the bread and the salt, mystery cults, etc.), down to feasts and the main events in human life (birth, adolescence, marriage, death, etc.) are all sacred categories and religious actions. If we exclude from human relations that sharing in the sacred, nothing remains but superficial scratchings. Even commerce, in which an oath in God's name was an essential element, and contracts and treaties have been religious forms of communication until not much time ago.

---

[23] See the traditional *ubi caritas et amor, ibi Deus est.*

It goes without saying that *communicatio in sacris* does not mean, here, any indiscriminate full participation in the rites of other religious confessions, when it carries with it a real danger of scandal or *negatio fidei* (which is intrinsically wrong).[24] And yet a new conception of the canonical *communicatio in sacris* is emerging nowadays in the Church, which, while maintaining the core of the traditional teaching, opens a door so as to find a place for that deep communion that already exists among people belonging to different confessions.[25]

Our thesis that every real human relationship is a sacred communication finds its justification in the fundamental religious conviction that God is indeed distinct, but not separated from the world. God is our mutual link. Anyway, we are not going to justify our affirmation now, but only to apply the thesis to a particular case.[26]

Christ, the *Pantocratōr*, is not only the universal *redeemer* but also—from the Father—the *creator* of everything, and—together with the Spirit—the glorifier or *deifier* of the cosmos. This threefold function of Christ provides the triple foundation for the relation of the Christian with his "non-Christian surroundings."

Koinōnia

To be a Christian is neither a privilege nor an excuse to refuse to work in the world and to collaborate with all our fellow Man—with whom we share the same "human nature" received from Christ, through whom all things have been created.[27] We all have a common human "nature" coming from Christ.[28] There is no difference or exception on this secular level between Christians and non-Christians. The Christian shares the whole burden of human endeavor for the betterment of this world; he is present in it without fears, complexes, or mixed motives. Whatever further mission the Christian may have received, this does not exempt him from fulfilling his human vocation up to the last "iota," because this is his first and fundamental calling.[29] Our first duty is to be human, and being such, we communicate (*in*, *through*, *for*, and *from* Christ) with our fellow beings. This is a *Christian* and holy

---

[24] See *Codex Iuris Canonicis* § 1258, where the word "active" means, according to all commentaries, *formalis*, i.e., so totally identified with the others' rites that it amounts to a denial of the Catholic faith.

[25] See Vatican II, decree *De Oecumenismo*, n. 8: "licitum est, immo et optandum, ut catholici cum fratribus seiunctis in oratione consocientur" [It can—it should, indeed—be done, that Catholics join their separate brothers to pray].

[26] As far as I know, there are very few studies on this problem. The few essays that set out to cover the new situation seem to me to overemphasize the autonomy of canon law. See K. Kappel, *Communicatio in sacris. Die gottesdienstliche Gemeinschaft zwischen Katholiken und Nichtkatholiken* (Winterthur: Keller, 1962); and the valuable remarks by J. Neumann in *Una Sancta* 19, no. 3 (1964): 283–86. See also B. Schultze, "Das Problem der communicatio in sacris," *Zeitschrift für Theologie und Glaube* 51 (1961): 437–46.

[27] Jn 1:3; Col 1:16; Heb 1:2, etc.

[28] See, as a typical example, Irenaeus, *Adversus haereses* V.18.1.

[29] Gn 1:15; 3:23, etc.

communion. We may know it and the others may not, but it comes to the same as regards the communion as such. Any relationship on this level is already a religious relation, even a Christian one, and yet does not need to bear the "Christian" label or to have a "religious" flavor. All men *are* brothers *in* Christ. We are not only Adam's children, we are also Christ's brothers; the action of the second Adam is by no means less universal than that of the first.

We cannot limit Christ to a historical figure. To do this would imply denying His divinity. To begin with, Christ is not a historical *person*: His person is the divine one, who takes upon Himself all history, but is not "exhausted" in time. Christ really appears in history,[30] and even becomes real flesh (Jn 1:14), and thus gets "entangled"—becomes "sin" (2 Co 5:21)—in the temporal rhythm of the cosmos, in order to "disentangle" it from mere temporality; but he cannot be identified with any *avatāra*, with a mere "incarnation" of the divine, that is, a descent of God at a given moment for a particular or universal purpose. The Christian conception of incarnation is essentially linked with the Trinity. Were the Absolute not Trinity, then Christ could be nothing more than an *avatāra*, not the *alpha* and *omega*, the beginning and end, the only mediator, He through and for whom all has been made, and in whom all things subsist.[31]

Only if Christians are aware of this can they, in their relation with the so-called non-Christians, behave so as not to abandon or whittle away their Christian faith, on the one hand, nor, on the other, impose their own structures on the rest of humankind, or live in this world as "aliens" and foreigners, with other aims and ambitions. The fellowship of the Christian with the "non-Christian world" is neither a non-Christian nor a neutral relation, nor an artificial make-believe, but an ontic reality based on the *koinōnia* of every being in Christ.[32]

Diakonia

Nobody can go to God the Father, or, in Indic terms, nobody can become or reach, and thus be, the Absolute, except in and through Christ, irrespective of creed, place, and time. That is to say, the mediatorship of Christ is total and unique, and

---

[30] *"Ante luciferum genitus* [unigenitus], *et ante saecula* [primogenitus], *Dominus Salvator noster* [in multis fratribus] *hodie* [quia tempiternus] *mundo apparuit* [epiphania]" [Begotten before the morning star (only-begotten Son) and before the eons (Firstborn), the Lord, our Savior (among many brothers) today (as tempiternal) *appeared* (epiphany) to the world], sings the Latin liturgy during the feast of the Epiphany. See the collect: "Deus cuius Unigenitus in substantia nostrae carnis apparuit" [O God, whose only-begotten Son *appeared* in the substance of our flesh]. Nothing is more real than this manifestation of the Real, but it is nevertheless the *appearance,* just the real and true appearance of the Savior: *Apparuit benignitas et humanitas Salvatoris nostri Dei* (the benevolence and humanity of our Savior appeared—Tt 3:4).

[31] See my "La tempiternidad" in *Actas del V Congreso Eucaristico Nacional,* Zaragoza, 1961, 73–93.

[32] See the traditional thesis of the cosmic effects of Christ's redemption, which corroborates all that I am trying to say.

this by definition, so that, if anything or anyone happens to be the link between God and the world, this is the Christ. The novelty of Christian faith does not lie in denying anything of the world religions, but in affirming that *the* Christ, which all religions acknowledge, in one way or another (Īśvara, Tathāgata, Lord, . . .), finds his full, or at least his main, *epiphany* in Jesus, the son of Mary. What I mean is that this ontic mediatorship of Christ is independent of the religion an individual may profess, and from the place and time of one's existence on earth, whether inside or outside Christianity, within or without the historical and visible church. What Christ claims to be and to perform is valid for the animist, Hindū, Muslim, and so on, as well as for the Aztec, Mongol, Greek, European, and others, as also for the Cro-Magnon Man, for those who lived fifteen thousand years ago, and for the man of our time. If we lose sight of this catholic Christic perspective, we may easily falsify all relationship among Christians and so-called non-Christians.

Now, for human history, or—in biblical terms—after the original sin, the return to the Father through Christ is a way of redemption. This is why the specific and historical character of Christ is that of a redeemer. He has redeemed humankind and the whole cosmos, and not only Christians, that is, those who consciously acknowledge him. Christ's sacrifice is universal also for nonbelievers,[33] and the opinion that non-Christians cannot receive Christ's redeeming influence has been explicitly condemned by the Church.[34] From this standpoint, history is nothing else but the temporal adventure of the family of Man, and, together with him, of the whole cosmos toward the new heaven and the new earth, that is, toward the total union with the Absolute, by means of continuing and applying, collectively and personally, the redemption of Christ. The ultimate meaning of human life in this historical context is to work out, to continue, to apply, to realize . . . the redemption of the world. And again, this is a common task for Christians and so-called non-Christians, for a common calling concerns both—the calling of the *diakonia*, of the *service* in the redemption of the world. Christians might have a fuller awareness of what they are striving for or called to, and might even have received better tools for this mission; but neither are so-called non-Christians just passive receivers of the redeeming mercy. They also have to collaborate actively in the work of co-redeeming themselves, with that part of the cosmos that is connected with them. In other words, all human activities that somehow have redemptive value offer a common ground for cooperation between Christians and so-called non-Christians; both have to work together, though the degree of awareness may be different in the two cases. The so-called non-Christian, thanks to an unknown "grace" from Christ, is working for the welfare of his fellow-beings. The Christian is engaged in the same "beneficence," according to the classical meaning of the word (to do good), witnessing to Christ and enabling Him to act in the world for the fulfillment of redemption—in a way that we describe in the third part of this study.

---

[33] See *Denz.,* 1294.
[34] See *Denz.,* 1295.

This level of *diakonia* is the *sacramental* level par excellence. Certainly, the so-called non-Christian partner may not have the sacramental fullness of the New Covenant—although there is a "baptism of desire"—but he shares the *cosmic sacraments* of the first pact God made with humankind just after the fall. Setting aside the question of the specific sacraments of other religions, we here especially refer to the "sacrament of suffering," through which every man who comes into this world receives, at least, the chance of purification. It is the right and the duty of Christians to be the ministers, the deacons, of this primeval sacrament. This amounts to saying that Christians have the right, because they have the duty, of practicing the works of mercy and of collaborating with all those who have been inspired to do the same. Where mercy is active, Christ is already there, and the Christian has the right and, even more, the duty to collaborate. He is at home wherever love is at work.

On the first level of cooperation, the "non-Christian surroundings" can be, in a sense, already Christian; but on this second level, we do not exclude a really non-Christian milieu. In this case, cooperation has little meaning, but *service* still retains its value. The relation of a Christian with a non-Christian world remains always a relation of service. It may sometimes be an unwelcome service, as when someone refuses to be cleansed of his filth, but it has anyway to be a true service, not forcing the other to do what he or she does not wish to, even if it may objectively be a good thing. It is this *service* to the person, and not the *work* done, that matters; real ministering is demanded of a Christian, not organizing welfare services or solving social problems. Christian *diakonia* is not a "service to the cause," overlooking differences and overruling discrepancies, but a service to the person, even at the risk of harming the "cause." This may sometimes lead to almost tragic conflicts—for example, a worker priest standing by his fellow workers and the situation being exploited by a communist trade union—but nothing is so dangerous as the authentic Christian *diakonia* that requires laying down one's life for one's friends (Jn 15:18), and to be obedient unto death.[35]

Kērygma

The relation of the Christian to his "non-Christian surroundings" is not exhausted by the discovery of the *koinōnia* on the grounds of our common nature received from Christ, nor is it completed by the performance of the *diakonia* on the basis of Christ's universal calling to collaborate in the redemption of the world. The Christian has received, further, as a sovereign, free gift of God, a specific calling to announce the emancipating news of Christ's wonderful action in deifying Man.

---

[35] Ph 2:16. Thrilling examples of this Christian attitude were seen recently in the reactions of Christian to the persecutions they suffer in communist countries. The prayer, understanding, and love for their persecutors is always stressed, as well as their desire to be obedient to the laws of the society in which they live. See O. Clément, *La situation de l'Eglise Orthodoxe en Union Soviétique* (1964); N. Struve, *Les chrétiens en U.R.S.S.* (Paris: Seuil, 1963); *Contacts* 45 (1964): 67–78.

In other words, Christians have received the injunction to announce the gospel, that is, to spread the glad tidings of Christ with their whole life, and to announce to the peoples of the world the joyful message of salvation: real liberation from every shackle, chain, and law. Christians have not primarily to teach *morals*, or even to preach a doctrine, or to make propaganda for a church, nor always to proclaim the name of Christ outside whom there is no salvation (Ac 4:12), but they have to proclaim God, his Fatherhood, his kingdom, the love that Christ the Lord taught his disciples to spread.[36]

The relation of a Christian to the so-called non-Christian milieu is always a witnessing, a proclamation, a preaching, a challenge—but not something esoteric or foreign, or even totally uprooted. It is an active injunction; it is a positive message; it is something very effective, dangerous, and real; but it is at the same time something that is already there, that is at work before the messenger came (Ac 10:4ff.), something of which the Christian, as a useless servant (Lk 17:10), has only to reveal the true manifestation, the real face. *Re-velation* means lifting the veil that was hiding or perhaps distorting the image (*eikōn*) of the living God and the saving truth. It is not a question of *bringing Christ in*—He who is the Light enlightening every person who comes into this world (Jn 1:9) and who has sheep that do not belong to the sheepfold or are even unknown to the shepherd[37]—but of *bringing Him forth*, of helping the full growth of Christ there, of really continuing the incarnation of the Son of God, of revealing His true name, His actual deeds, His wondrous message.[38]

To take a classic example from Indic philosophy: what the Christian has to do is to reveal that there is no snake there, and to tell the people that they should not be afraid and should cast off all fears and anxieties;[39] to say that it only *looks* like a snake; that the *appearance* may sometimes be that of Kṛṣṇa, or of society, or Man, or an idol, but *that* in reality is a rope, a simple rope—in fact, a rope of salvation.[40]

---

[36] See the far-reaching distinction of Karl Barth between *Ankündigung* (the bare message) and *Verkündigung* (an elaborate doctrine).

[37] See Jn 10:16; Mt 9:37.

[38] See how this spirit has been translated into ecclesiological language: "Moreover, in becoming, as it were, the life-blood of these people, the Church is not, nor does she consider herself to be a foreign body in their midst. Her presence brings about the rebirth, the resurrection of each individual in Christ, and the man who is reborn and rises again in Christ never feels himself constrained from without. He feels himself free in the very depth of his being, and freely raised up to God. And thus he affirms and develops that side of his nature which is noblest and best" (John XXIII, *Mater et Magistra* [May 15, 1961]).

[39] See Ps 54:23; Mt 6:25; 1 Pt 5:7.

[40] This way of using such an example is far from being new in Christianity. On the contrary, it represents the catholic trend of a Christian mind tending to assimilate everything and to interpret on a deeper level what is already existing. One interesting instance: Plato in *Timaeus* 36B–C, with reference to the soul of the universe, says that it has the form of the Greek letter "X," because he sees it is somehow folded. According to Justin (*Apologia*

A whole theology of religions is needed in order to see how this *kērygma* can be announced. A complete treatise on the cosmic sacraments, on the holy Scripture of the world and their fuller meaning in Christ, and so forth, are urgent requirements of the theology of our times, which can no longer live in splendid isolation or in proud or shy apartheid.[41]

Here we can only say: Christ did not come to found a religion, much less a new religion, but to fulfill all justice (Mt 3:15) and to bring every world religion to its fullness.[42] Christianity is, sociologically speaking, certainly one religion; it is the ancient paganism, or to be more precise, the complex Jewish-Greek-Latin-Celtic-Gothic-modern religion *converted* to Christ, more or less successfully. Christianity in India, to take one example, should not be an imported, fully fledged, and highly developed religion, but Hinduism itself *converted*—or Islam, or Buddhism, whatever.[43] It must immediately be added that this converted Hinduism would substantially be the same as the old one, and yet something different, a new creature.[44] The process of conversion implies a death and resurrection; just as the risen Christ or the baptized person is the same as previously, and yet is a new being, likewise, converted Hinduism is the true, risen Hinduism, the same and yet renewed, transformed. In one word, the church brings every true and authentic religion to its *fulfillment* through a process of death and resurrection, which is the true meaning of conversion. Real Christianity is the *fulfillment through conversion* of every religion, and the mission of the church that of being salt, light, leaven, which gives taste, enlightens, and raises the whole mass without claiming to be identified with—neither separated from—the whole cosmos.[45] Wheat and weed must grow together (Mt 13:29).

The Christian *kērygma* is thus neither an intrusion coming violently from without, nor a mere immanent evolution emerging linearly from within: the seed comes from heaven, descends from God Himself, but it is the earth that brings forth the Savior.[46]

---

prima 60) this symbol had been borrowed from Moses and foreshadowed the mystery of the cross: "In the discussion of the nature of the Son of God in Plato's *Timaeus*, when he says: *He placed him like an X in the universe*, this was similarly borrowed from Moses" (*I Apologia* 50.1). He goes on: "Plato, reading this and not clearly understanding, nor realizing that it was the form of a cross, but thinking it was the letter *Chi*, said that the power next to the first God was placed X-wise in the universe" (*I Apologia* 50.5–6). Interestingly enough, in this passage the snake of Nb 21:6–9 is also mentioned; cf. Jn 3:14.

[41] See some suggestions in R. Panikkar, *Die vielen Götter und der eine Herr*.

[42] Mt 5:7; Heb 1:1, etc.

[43] "But I may be permitted to say that Jesus preached not a new religion, but a new life," said Gandhi with his usual acuteness (*Harijan*, June 12, 1937).

[44] See 2 Co 5:17.

[45] For concrete principles of action, see R. Panikkar, "The Theological Basis for Christian–Non-Christian Co-Operation in Social Thought and Action," *Religion and Society* 5, no. 1 (March 1958).

[46] See 1 Co 15:47–49; Is 45:8; Tt 2:11; 3:4, etc.

The Christian Attitude

Among the many possible ways of describing this attitude, I choose, first, to discard a *negative approach*; second, to describe a *psychological position*; and, third, to explain the *ontological-mystical attitude*.

Overcoming Negativism

Christians should not condemn the "non-Christian surroundings" in which they have been called upon to live. They have today, before their eyes, the example of the very hierarchy of the Catholic Church, which, while recognizing the "signs of the times" (Mt 16:4), follows the teaching of the old Law and of the New Covenant: not to destroy but to fulfill (Mt 5:17), not to quench the smoking flax,[47] not to throw the first stone (Jn 8:7), but to have patience (Lk 21:19), to tolerate, that is, to welcome the world,[48] to imitate the heavenly Father,[49] and not call "profane" anything that God has created (Ac 10:28). Christians, like their Master, are not here to condemn or judge the world,[50] but to serve and save it.[51] This attitude is also extended to so-called non-Christian religions.[52] This we could call the attitude of *true ecumenism.*[53]

The Christian has neither to condemn nor to judge; moreover, he must not be an obstacle or a scandal to his brothers.[54] He has to constantly remember the immense

---

[47] Is 42:3; Mt 12:20.

[48] See my *Pluralismus, Toleranz und Christenheit* (Nuremberg: Abendländische Akademie, 1961), 117–42.

[49] Mt 6:14; 18:35, etc.

[50] Jn 3:17; 12:47; etc.

[51] Lk 22:27; Mt 20:28, etc. One example among many others: "Let the world know this: the Church looks at the world with profound understanding, with sincere admiration and with the sincere intention not of dominating it, but of serving it; not of despising it, but of appreciating it; not of condemning it, but of strengthening and saving it" (Paul VI at Vatican II [English text from *Council Speeches of Vatican II* (London, 1964), 155]).

[52] See the remarkable texts of Vatican II on world religions.

[53] See the human touch in these words of Augustine quoted by Pope John XXIII and remembered by the Vatican II in its *Schema de Oecumenismo*: "Sinite fratres et filios dulci nos desiderio appellemusṇ Velint, nolint, fratres nostri sunt. Tunc esse desinent fratres nostri, si desierint dicere: Pater noster" (Augustine, *Enarrationes in Psalmos* 32.II.2.29 [*PL* 36.299]): in John XXIII's encyclical *Ad Petri Cathedram* (June 29, 1959): "Let us call them brothers and children, as we sweetly long to. Whether they like it or not, they are our brothers. They will stop being such if they stop praying: Our Father." We could add: "si desierint *esse* filii Patris nostri" [if they stop *being* children of Our Father], which is, however impossible, for God would cease to be God if He were not our Father.

[54] See 1 Co 8:13. Significantly, Gandhi appealed to this text to encourage Christians in India to be vegetarians.

power he has received[55] and that, while having the keys of the kingdom, he can close the doors to those who would like to enter (Mt 23:13). It is a frightening thought, and at the same time a divine lesson of immeasurable importance to be aware of that self-surrender of Christ into the hands of his church, that *kenōsis* of the Lord in the lives of Christians. We then discover that one of the main obstacles to the real growth of the church is the unworthiness of Christians.[56] This is a responsibility that is not only true in our times.[57] The grace of Christ does actually flow through the channels of the church, but the church is not an abstract entity. It has a sacramental structure in which the material as well as the human world is included. If Christians do not behave according to their vocation or—as older times used to stress—live up to their true dignity,[58] the living waters of Christ will be stemmed by obstacles put in the way by those who have freely received the gift of their Christian calling in order to believe, hope, and love *for* the whole world.[59]

Witnessing

The Christian simply has to witness to Christ, without mixed motives. It would be both theoretically false and practically wrong if the Christian told his non-Christian neighbor, "You (already) are a Christian" or "you are *not* a Christian." Both statements do not correspond to the true situation. We touch here the mystery of Divine Providence, which is not given to us to understand in individual instances. Not even Peter was given an answer to his question about John, other than to follow Christ (Jn 21:22). "He who is not against us is for us," taught the Master.[60] Perhaps our categories do not apply here. Hinduism, to take an example, is neither Christianity nor non-Christianity. The relationship is of another type, and we have already mentioned that Christ is hidden and unknown, but really present in all the authentic religions of the world. The Christian is simply witnessing to a

---

[55] Mt 16:19; 18:18; Jn 20:23, etc.

[56] See the famous book by N. Berdjaev, *De la dignité du Christianisme et l'indignité des chrétiens* (Paris, 1931), and the similar expression of Mahātma Gandhi; or another example by him: "If I had to face only the Sermon on the Mount and my own interpretation of it, I should not hesitate to say: Oh yes, I am a Christian," *Young India* (December 8, 1927).

[57] "Those who come to me in order to believe are frightened by the wretched life of lukewarm and false Christians. How many, my brethren, are there who would like to become Christians, but who are hurt by the bad behavior of Christians?" (Augustine, *Enarrationes in Psalmos* 30.II.2.6 [*PL* 36.243]).

[58] See the famous and often repeated sentence: "Agnosce o christane dignitatem tuam" (Leo I, *Sermo 1 de Nativitate Domini* [in the Roman Breviary], December 25).

[59] See the reason St. Cyprian gives when he calls on the persecuted Christians of Carthage to minister to the sick and dying Gentiles in time of plague: *Respondere nos decet natalibus nostris* [it behooves us to be worthy of our birth], Ponzio, *Vita di Cipriano*, 9.

[60] Mk 9:40.

new dimension, hidden or unknown, of the same reality. He has neither to condemn nor to escape, but to assume and to go deeper.[61]

Much has been written recently on Christian witnessing, and even specific religious congregations have been founded in the church in order to witness to Christ in the ordinary ways of life. We do not need to pursue this theme further. Only one aspect we would like to stress, which can provide an answer to those who think that witnessing is only a preparation or a strategic move toward "conversion," or those who think that witnessing means nothing more than mixing with "non-Christians."[62]

To begin with, we may remember that the Greek word for "witness" is *martyr*, and there is no witnessing apart from laying down our own life for those whom we love.[63] To be a witness does not mean to "give an example," or even to "preach silently," or to "show" how one can live a concrete human life (either of a poor villager or a rich industrialist) and still be a Christian.[64] There is much more to it than this. The concept of Christian witness is a mystical and, thus, a Trinitarian one. To witness means to give testimony of the Father, to reveal Him, to lead to Him, to manifest Him.

Now, only the Holy Spirit can do this. There is no witness outside or independent of the Holy Spirit. Only the Spirit can witness to the Father. The Christian can only be a witness if he is identified with Christ, united with him (Jn 6:57), so that the Spirit in him is free, is able to speak, to pray, to glorify, and to witness to the Father.[65] Being a witness is not the same as being a public relations officer, or even an apostle, that is, an envoy under orders to perform a mission. Witnessing is not propaganda but the very act of faith, hope, and love. There is no witness but the Spirit. Christian witnessing consists in becoming transparent, as it were, so as to allow the Spirit to shine, to act, to witness through us. The Christian witness has no mission of his or her own, nor has he or she received a special injunction for a

---

[61] See some sentences of Gandhi: "I want you [a Christian missionary] to complement the faith of the people instead of undermining it" (*Young India*, August 11, 1927); "I shall say to the Hindus that your lives will be incomplete unless you reverently study the teachings of Jesus" (*With Gandhi in Ceylon*, 143); "I believe that he [Jesus] belongs not solely to Christianity, but to the entire world; to all races and peoples, it matters little under what flag, name or doctrine they may work profess a faith, or worship a God inherited from their ancestors" (*Modern Review*, October 1941).

[62] "To be a witness does not consist in engaging in propaganda, nor even in stirring people up, but in being a living, and I should add a loving, mystery." Cardinal E. Suhard.

[63] See first chapter.

[64] Well known is the example given by Mahātma Gandhi, which he repeated time and again, often applying it to Christianity: "The rose transmits its own scent without a movement" (*Young India*, January 19, 1928); "I have a definite feeling that, if you want us to feel the aroma of Christianity, you must copy the rose. The rose irresistibly draws people to itself, and the scent remains with them" (*Young India*, October 15, 1931); "Therefore I should do without any preaching at all. A rose does not need to preach. It simply spreads its fragrance. The fragrance is its own sermon" (*Harijan*, March 29, 1935).

[65] See Rom 8:15; Gal 4:6.

particular task. Not every Christian can be a preacher or an apostle in the precise meaning of the word, and yet every Christian is called upon to be a witness, because his or her being a Christian means precisely to have been called to become Christ, whose Spirit is the only testimony.[66]

The practical consequences are obvious.[67]

Redeeming

Not so long ago, Christian circles used to discuss what should be the specifically Christian attitude toward the world. As a reaction against the so-called *mystique of transcendence*—that is, an attitude underscoring the eschatological and supernatural aspect of Christianity, they stressed the *mystique of incarnation*: an attitude that advocates the Christian presence everywhere in the world and the duty of Christians to share all problems of society.[68] Both attitudes develop a fundamental Christian aspect and correct each other. Pure transcendentalism would lead to a kind of mono-dimensional supernaturalism, which is the opposite of Christian revelation. On the other hand, mere "incarnationism" would turn into sheer naturalism and fall into an inner-worldly activism that would kill all that Christianity, and even religion, stands for.

We can find the synthesis between both attitudes in what we may call the *mystique of redemption*. In fact, there is no redemption without incarnation, but neither would redemption have any meaning at all if it did not lead toward transcendence.

This seems to be the fundamental Christian attitude toward the so-called non-Christian surroundings, or in a broader context, vis-à-vis the world: not that of *co*-existing with the world, but one of *pro*-existence for the world;[69] standing for the whole cosmos before God in action, contemplation, and love. The church has not to convert the world, before time comes to an end, but to stand there before God as a "sign raised up among the peoples,"[70] and redeem the cosmos.[71]

---

[66] See Jn 5:31–32, 36–37; etc.

[67] See Dunas, "Le témoignage de la foi," in *Contacts* 12, nos. 35–36 (1961): 207–28; O. Clément, *Remarques d'un laïc sur le témoignage de la foi*, in *Contacts* 12, nos. 35–36 (1961): 235–45. But the whole issue, dealing with *Approches au Mystère de la Foi*, is worth reading.

[68] See, e.g., G. Thils, *Transcendence ou Incarnation?* (Louvain: Publications de l'Université de Louvain, 1950).

[69] Words used by Hans Küng.

[70] See Is 11:12 and the application of the text by the Church to herself in Vatican I, Sess. III, chap. 3.

[71] The apparently difficult saying of Christ, "Many are called, but few are chosen" (Mt 19:12), can be, in fact, quite easily explained. "Many are called," to be sure, *all* are called ("the many" being a Hebraism, as in Mt 26:28); all are called to be united with God, to be saved, to reach their destination, "but few are chosen" to help the Redeemer consciously to bear the burden of the day and the heat, to lay down their lives for their brethren, to be eunuchs for the kingdom of heaven, to perform the priestly act of offering the whole world to God,

This is the priestly vocation of every Christian (1 Pet 2:9), sharing the one, only priesthood of Christ (Heb 7:21, etc.). This is the vocation of the whole Christian people as chosen people.[72] We should not forget this mission of the church as the chosen people of God, as the convocation of believers (*ekklēsia*) pursuing a common mission. Just like Israel, which had—and has—a mission on earth, a command from the Lord, and a covenant with YHWH, the church today has another pact; it has received another mission. The church is the people of the new and definitive covenant, that of the last *kalpa*, of the final period at the end of time.[73] And this mission is not just an individual task, or a mission entrusted to the hierarchy or to specialists (call them missionaries, religious congregations, or clergy); it is entrusted to the people of God as a whole, as a family and a unit. It is to the church as a whole that this priestly mission is entrusted and with whom this new covenant is sealed. And, incidentally, this is the reason why pioneers have to hold back or, putting it the other way around, why traditionally Christian peoples have to hasten, so that they can fulfill the will of God according to the signs of the times. There are reforms in the church that cannot be carried through yet, because the *ekklēsia* as a whole is not yet ready for them. The effort to bring every religion to its fulfillment through an authentic conversion provides an example of what we are trying to say.

We will now see two aspects of this priestly "corporate" act of the church that will shed light on the problem of the relationship between Christians and the rest of the world.

The Offering of the Sacrifice

"So much attempted, so little attained"[74] could perhaps summarize the atmosphere of disillusion of more than one missionary group in the church today. But this feeling of disenchantment betrays an attitude deriving from a certain mentality of a not too distant past, which considered the mission of the church as being the "conversion" of all *individuals* and not the redemption of the *world*. Christ has not failed to redeem the universe. He has in fact redeemed it. He has entrusted his church, his Christian people, with the task of applying and actualizing His redemption. This is the mission of the Christian: to offer the sacrifice that creates, redeems, and glorifies the world.[75]

The Christian is the priest of the whole creation as well as of the entire humankind, his primary priestly action being that of gathering the materials for the sacrifice, collecting the broken pieces (Jn 6:12) of all the actions, sorrows, joys, prayers, virtues, sins, and so on, of his surroundings. Therefore, the Christian can

---

to perform the sacred act in the marriage feast of the Son of Man with mankind. Little flock, seed, leaven, etc., are all metaphors to express the same concept.

[72] See Dt 26 and its liturgical application on Ember Saturday of Lent.

[73] See Heb 1:2; 9:26; Gal 4:4; Ep 1:10, etc.

[74] See the book of the prophet Hag 1:9.

[75] See, for the whole underlying problem, my *Kultmysterium in Hinduismus und Christentum.*

offer them to the Father, placing them on the paten of the Only Victim who, as he offers himself to God, takes with him all that he himself inspires his collaborators to gather, so that all may ascend to the final goal through the one and only Mediator (1 Tim 2:5).

The prayer and the action of Christians are, first of all, a priestly and liturgical action of extending their arms to embrace that part of the cosmos—without excluding themselves—of which they are aware, and offering it to God the Father *per Dominum nostrum Jesum Christum in unitate Spiritus Sancti* (through our Lord Jesus Christ, in the unity of the Holy Spirit). It is Christ, through the action of his Spirit in Christians, the one who offers the whole cosmos to its Source. The whole life of a Christian is a journey, as he or she walks through the world collecting the human and cosmic materials to be incorporated into the sacrifice of Christ, so that they may all rise up with the Absolute and reach their destination. Here, action and contemplation meet in a deep unity.[76]

If only this point were taken seriously, the "missionary crisis" we mentioned could be overcome. The underlying Marxist tendency of projecting into a temporal future that which, according to Christian faith, happens in the vertical line ("The kingdom is coming") is all too obvious. It is not a Christian answer, however, to say that the world has not yet been converted because Christians have not been holy enough, or that, if we redouble our efforts, a "brighter" future may appear, as if the kingdom of God were in the horizontal future, and not *within* us and *above* time. It is not true that the "missionary" failed to convert the world: rather, he will perceive himself as a failure when he forgets that his "mission" consists precisely in offering the whole world to Him who has *already* conquered and redeemed it.[77]

---

[76] See a summary of this authentic spirituality: "Il importe, dit saint Maxime [le Confesseur], de s'assimiler en les imitant les rythmes et les leçons du *liber mundi*, de se conformer, a l'instar du soleil, à tous les événements . . . sans rien abandonner se de propre identité illuminatrice, de recueillir des *logoi* spirituels des êtres, non point pour se les approprier, mais pour les offrir à Dieu comme dons *de la part* de la création. L'oraison devient ici participation à l'existence universelle . . . où le cœur s'enflamme pour toute creature (St. Macarius); où la conaissance s'épanouit en charité cosmique; où la présence d'habitation s'amplifie en présence d'Immensité à mesure que l'univers devient plus trasparent a la lumière incréé du Verbe invoqué dans le coeurs" [What matters, says St. Maximus (the Confessor), is to assimilate oneself by imitating the rhythms and teachings of the *liber mundi*, to conform oneself, like the sun, to every event . . . without abandoning at all one's own enlightening identity, to gather the spiritual *logoi* of Being, not in order to take possession of them, but to offer them to God as on behalf of the whole creation. Here, prayer becomes a taking part in the universal existence . . . where the heart burns with love toward all creatures (St. Macarius), where knowledge expands into cosmic charity, where the inhabiting presence turns into presence of the Infinite, insofar as the universe becomes transparent to the uncreated light of the Logos being invoked in the hearts] (J. A. Cuttat, *Rencontre des Religions* [Paris: Aubier, 1957], 121).

[77] Jn 16:33; 1 Jn 5:4, etc.

Receiving the Sacrament

The history of religions shows, and Christianity itself confirms, that the fundamental religious act involves a twofold movement: the *upward* movement of surrendering to the Absolute, of offering oneself, of lifting up the creature to its Creator—in a word, *sacrifice;* and the *downward* movement of the divine response, the descent of the transcendent, God accepting the offering of Man, and the meeting of both, as it were, midway—in one word, the *sacrament.*

Christians do not only offer the sacrifice, they also receive the sacrament; and likewise, as they offer the sacrifice *of* and *for* the whole world, they receive the sacrament for themselves and for the entire cosmos (Jn 17:19).

This applies in a special way to the Eucharist, the sacrament of sacraments. The liturgical renewal of the Church has made Catholics aware of the truth that Christ does not come in the Eucharist just to be adored in the monstrance, but in order to come into our hearts and remain in our whole being and transform it. The "natural" place of the Eucharist is not a golden tabernacle, but the flesh and blood of the individual human being. Christian consciousness is today realizing, more and more, that Christ "became" Eucharist not only for the Christians who receive it, but for the entire world, which receives it through the Christians who take Holy Communion. This Communion is not only a private devotion or an exclusively individual act of Christians: it is a cosmic act.[78] It is the final stage in a growth that begins at the level of the electron and rises to the supernatural assimilation brought about by the Eucharist.

This last stage, indeed, does not belong to the "natural" order, but it is nevertheless the final—gratuitous and supernatural—consummation of the cosmic law of growth and assimilation: from the physical tendency to form stable electronic orbits, down to the holohedral crystallographic formation, to the biological forms of assimilation, both vegetable and animal, up to the intellectual identification in the process of knowing and the integration of love! All this culminates in that divine and supernatural metabolism by which, through eating the flesh and drinking the blood of Christ (the expressions might sound crude, but are essentially Christian: Jn 6:53–56), the Christian receives eternal life and is assimilated into Christ (Jn 15:1ff.).

But this is not all. This process of divine assimilation also involves the people who do not believe explicitly in Christ, thanks to the sacramental action of Christians who, having "received" Christ, are subsequently "received" by others in the stresses and strains of daily life.[79] The Christian receives Christ and, as it were, brings Him down to other people, who enter into contact with the Eucharist through the contact with their Christian brothers. We are not suggesting mere passivity, a purely mystical

---

[78] The public celebration of the sacrifice and conferring of the sacrament before the whole world and in the presence of all religions, as took place in the Eucharistic Congress of Bombay, seems to symbolize the deep meaning of this Eucharistic Congress—and of those in the future.

[79] Mt 10:40; Jn 3:20.

attitude. On the contrary, the mission of Christians is a *theandric* integral vocation calling them to a most active life, although in the spirit of contemplation.

The Eucharist is of absolute necessity for salvation, according to the traditional theological conception, and we can easily discover the ontological reason for it. Salvation means union with God, and this is only possible through our incorporation into Christ, Christ being the only possible cause of our resurrection. Now, how can this sacramental contact take place for those who neither believe nor even know anything about Christ?

We should here develop two points, but we are only going to state the respective theses: the first is that the Eucharist is not only the *sacramentum sacramentorum* in the order of the New Testament, but is also the sacrament of sacraments in the cosmic covenant. It is not only the sacraments of the New Law, which culminate in the Eucharist and receive their efficacy from their reference to it; this is also true, though obviously in a different way, in the cosmic sacraments, so that they also tend toward the Eucharist. The second point has already been expounded, that is, the eucharistic/sacramental role of Christians, who are the bearers of the Eucharist to all those who enter into relationship with those who believe in Jesus Christ.

Consequently, the relation between Christians and so-called non-Christians belongs to the sacramental order, and even enters into the "Eucharistic economy." Non-Christian surroundings are not only sanctified by the offerings and prayers of Christians; they are transformed by the sacramental action of Christians, who work as Eucharistic channels for those who do not receive it. The parables of Christ concerning the kingdom of God and the function of Christians do not say that everybody has to become a Christian, but that His disciples are the light, salt, seed, and leaven, whose duty is to enlighten, to flavor, to die, to grow, and to leaven the whole mass, not just for themselves. Christians have not received from Christ a calling to believe in Him for their own sake only, but also for the sake of their brothers.

Christians are sent forth to be among others; they are sent to all nations—but like lambs among wolves,[80] and we wonder what service a lamb can do to a wolf, other than to allow himself to be eaten.[81] But this, to be sure, is a continuation of the Eucharistic law of being eaten *for the life of the world* (Jn 6:51).

---

[80] Mt 10:16; Lk 10:3.

[81] See the amazing passage from the *Gospel of St. Thomas*: "Blessed is that lion which the man will eat, and the lion will become man; and abominable is that man whom the lion will eat; and the lion will become man [*sic*] and the man will become lion."

15

THE CONTRIBUTION OF CHRISTIAN
MONASTICISM IN ASIA
TO THE UNIVERSAL CHURCH*

I have learned from you, in these past days, to follow the rhythms of a naturally unfolding understanding, and carefully avoid causing unnecessary shocks in dealing with any issue. I will begin, then, by presenting both my credentials and my apologies.

I speak to you as a monk of the *human congregation*, a member of the religious family of Man, who for over twenty years has been present at most attempts to start new monastic communities in India. I am here recalling not only those foundations that have been successful or, at least, are still alive, but also those that, by human standards, have failed, disappeared, but whose contribution I dare to say is not less important. Anyway, my main credential is obedience to Bishop D'Souza, who "daringly" asked me to talk to you, if not in his name, certainly in his place.

We have had "animators" all these days. My role this morning may perhaps be that of a "stimulator." I will not speak about Asia, but about a problem perceived by a man who has tried to integrate into his whole being the Asian dimension of Man, and who at the same time has "undergone" an incarnation in Western and Christian soil. Speaking, then, in and from Asia, I will not elaborate on the *ora* and the *labora* about which we have heard these days, but will try to develop the *et* that both connects and distinguishes them.

The Waking State: A Contribution

Done and Dreamt

The origins of monasticism, at least in the Indo-European world, lie most probably in the proto-Jaina ascetic movements of India. The Asian spirit is at the root of monasticism. In the Christian church, however, although until the sixth century

---

* In *Cistercian Studies* 9, nos. 2–3 (1974), they published as much material as possible from the second Asian Monastic Congress, organized by the ALM and held at Bangalore in October 1973. The present article comes from the same Congress; this was my closing address as the chairman.

most monastic contributions came from the "East," it was about quite another East from what we today call Asia.

When we come to more recent times, especially since the so-called period of Christian expansion, the contribution of Christian monasticism to the church in Asia has been minimal, not to say practically nil. Christian monasteries, where they exist, have been almost "air-lifted" *ante litteram*, so that they have become enclaves, colonies of Western Christianity. In spite of strenuous efforts, immense goodwill, and even holiness, the history of monasticism in Asia is a sad chapter in the life of the Christian church, over which there is no point in lingering now.

It will be more profitable for us to consider that, given the present situation, unless a radical conversion occurs, the possibilities of any contribution are minimal. Perhaps the closest and most blatant illustration of this is the report of our first Congress, at Bangkok. Many wonderful and practical things were said, many instructions and directions given, yet hardly one has been implemented. The reason was not ill will, or lack of freedom, but mainly the fact that all those beautiful *desiderata* did not find a proper and propitious soil in which to take root and blossom. We should take this example seriously, meditate on the Bangkok Report, and react from the vantage point of the five years that have passed since then. It would no longer do to dream of possibilities. The greatest obstacle is perhaps the fact that there are no external obstacles now.

Transplantation and Implantation

Now let me point out some contours of Indic spiritual geography, which represents at least a part of the Asian continent. I refer to those aspects of Indic spirituality that, apparently, either choked the Christian monastic seed or made it impossible to sow it.

Traditionally, in India, monasteries are small autochthonous units, little *āśramas* on a human scale, so much so that the person, or the idiosyncrasy, of the *guru* is much more decisive than any idea or ideal deriving from a set of values or principles. The person, with all his warmth and all his defects and limitations, is at the core of traditional monastic institutions, rather than any ideology or rule. It is not its mission that identifies an *āśramas*, but simply its being there. Further, Indic monasticism is centered on the inner and outer pilgrimage of the monk. The important thing is not *stabilitas* but a double pilgrimage: an inner one, which is reflected in an outer one. This implies a mobility that, under different conditions, may sound, or even be, a chaotic anarchy. I am obviously forced to oversimplify.

Therefore, the utmost stress is laid upon the simplification of needs, upon a simplicity of life perhaps impossible to follow or understand from another anthropological or cultural point of view. We are all children of our times, and human time is not synchronous. There is perhaps a diachronical gap, which calls for careful investigation. Transplantation requires a certain contemporaneity or synchronicity, which has sometimes been taken for granted when in fact it was not the case.

This time gap is not only cultural and historical, it is also anthropological. The Indic monastic ideal begins (as Śaṅkarācārya beautifully puts it) by discriminating between the temporal and the timeless. This involves the vexed question of temporary or permanent commitment. In fact, the word "vow" has in India a queer, not to say weird, sound. The monastic vocation is neither temporary nor nontemporary. To begin with, time cannot be transcended, but it has—at least—to be overlooked. The monastic urge does not concern the *time being* but the *being in time*, as long as this time lasts.

Something similar could be said about the basic conceptions of space underlying the average Western and the traditional Indic experience. Without now raising the question of sacred space, the Indic intuition sees and feels space, by and large, as the place created by our being in it, filling it, and not vice versa. We do not choose a space, we do not look for a place in order to install an *āśramas*: the place of the *āśramas*, the space, comes from the very placing of the *āśramas* there.

Finally, each monk in India (I speak of Indic asceticism in general, and of that bundle of religions that is called Hinduism) is, as it were, an institution in himself rather than a "juridical" member of a congregation; he is a species out of the genus, rather than a member of the species. I hope I will not be misunderstood. I am not saying that there is no casuistry in India, or no rules and binding traditions. I am only trying to describe a basic attitude built into the Indic tradition, in order to underscore that, under such conditions, a Western/Christian monastic *transplantation* cannot easily be done. Did not many, especially in the past century, dream that a complete transplantation from Europe would "take" faster, grow more quickly, and solve—thus making them obsolete—many of the unresolved theological problems in the encounter of religions? Were not abbots and other superiors reluctant to let individual members go to the East? They strove for a complete transplantation, as perfect as possible. We should not despise the loving concern of superiors, but if the grain does not die. . . .

Perhaps we can now more easily understand why full transplants did not succeed, and will not. The appropriate kind of soil, of humors, sap, blood, or whatever, is simply lacking.

It is therefore a good sign that this meeting occurs under the aegis of a different effort, not that of transplant, but the *aide à l'implantation monastique*. This effort is concerned with implantation, with letting the seed go into the soil, not only letting it die (and there must be no manipulation of dying, if resurrection is to be real), but also letting it grow in a different way. Implantation requires a double confidence: confidence in the vital power of the seed (the Christian monk) and in the productivity of the soil (Hindū monasticism). A word on this may fit here.

Kenōsis and Pluralism

Such a trust in the vitality of the seed requires—from both those who go and those who stay at home—to be confident that a Western monk may well wander to Asia without the sandals of his rules and ways, without the purse of his riches and traditions, and without the walking stick of his companions and the security of being backed by superiors and authorities. It is indeed the nature of the seed to die, the destiny of the monk to live in enclosure, that is, to close the doors. It is the vocation of the Christian not to look back.[1]

This is what could be called the principle of *kenōsis,* the total emptying of oneself in order to embody a higher principle. Does it not belong to the calling of the monk to be so well-rooted in the transcendent that he does not fear to be *monachos,* alone? Of course, this is quite easy to say, but so difficult to do.

Implantation cannot succeed if there is no confidence in the productivity of the soil, no trust that the seed falls into good soil, "in which others have already toiled,"[2] that is, if there is not the conviction that the autochthonous religions are good, that the Holy Spirit is not bound by any limit, that not only we but also others are a new creation in Christ,[3] and that those fields are not just heaps of stone and thorns, but good and fertile earth.

This could be called the principle of pluralism. It does not only imply a great respect for variety, it also entails the belief that God's ways are not our ways, that we do not need to understand everything, and that we are "useless servants"[4] because usefulness is not what matters. Pluralism does not belong to the domain of the *logos,* but to that of myth. It entails the conviction that other forms that we cannot understand, nor even sometimes approve, may be equally acceptable in the eyes of God, or play a decisive role in the necessary interaction of secondary causes. It implies a whole theology of religions, one of the most urgent imperatives of our times.

It it not up to me, now, to examine in detail how far this implantation has gone, how deep its roots, to what extent there are, in Asia, autochthonous forms of spirituality that are in explicit communion with the Christian Mystery. We must keep in mind the wishes and *desiderata* Bishop D'Souza expressed in his introductory words.[5] He asked monks to embody the values that I will summarize in the six following phrases:

An eschatological sign for a world in the process of secularization
Liturgical creativity (which requires daring humility)
Serenity reflecting the Absolute
Simplicity of life and culture
An example of Christian life
Hospitality without discrimination

---

[1] Lk 9:62.
[2] Jn 4:38.
[3] See 2 Co 5:17.
[4] Lk 17:10.
[5] See *Cistercian Studies* 9 (1974): 318–19.

Are we simply going to see these points as good wishes, or as prophetic orientations? The Western mind, which loves to linger on dilemmas and to delegate decisions, may now perhaps take this alternative seriously: either accomplish the program or "shut down the shop" in Asia.

Further, this is not merely the wish of a few people. The All-India Consultation on Evangelization, held two weeks ago in Patna, wrote a message to our Conference: it was not officially published by the Consultation because they did not want to interfere with our decisions. In this brotherly spirit, I think it should be read and reflected on.[6]

The Nightmare: Christian Monasticism in Asia

While reflecting and meditating on this, and wondering what "contribution" could be given, I fell into a *trance* (with the body or without, in heaven or in hell, I don't know . . .[7]), but, instead of having a dream, I had a nightmare.

Will you listen to it?

A Suspicion and a Suffering

A suspicion lies at hand. Are we going to be satisfied with minor reforms? Are we going to engage in mere patchworks? Are we going to understand the challenges of our times only in terms of a moral improvement on our part, marred perhaps by a concern with the image we project around us? In a word, is there not a danger of an unconscious desire to justify the status quo by just polishing it up?

Now, having liberated myself of the suspicion, I may give expression to the suffering. Can we jump over our own shadow? Can we really perform the task? Is it not all wishful thinking, once again the fruit of an in-built Christian superiority complex? Are we sufficiently aware of both the earnestness of this hour and the importance of the possibilities it offers?

On the one hand, my suffering comes from the nightmare of seeing what a monk is. Is he not the successor and substitute of the martyr? Is he not the man of courage who can perform the most astounding deeds, precisely because he is neither entangled with or bound by any vested interest, any personal gain? Does not the monk have a leverage outside the field of historical gravitation, so that he can radically change the course of events? Is he not the perfect Christian? Does not history teach us about the cultural revolution that monasticism performed down the ages?

On the other hand, my suffering increases because I cannot help seeing how much, under the pretense of humility and the cloak of prudence, the wings of man and the power of faith have been cut, and almost reduced to mediocrity. The big

---

[6] The message can be found in ibid., 329.

[7] See 2 Co 12:2.

picture fades in the shadow of historical conformism. In a word, are monks today equipped for the task, for the formidable historical mission they, and perhaps only they, can still perform? You can understand that I sweated out of my nightmare.

The Monk

A monk, indeed, is no minor figure among human beings. He is an almost constant and ever-present institution in human life. To speak of a "Buddhist Jesuit" stretches words beyond their permissible limits, whereas to speak of a "Buddhist monk" makes as much sense as to speak of a Christian or a Hindū monk. We could even speak of "monks," ancient and modern, without any further garb or name. The monk is a primordial religious figure, before the split into religious confessions. In a word, the monk is not a Christian specialty, or the monopoly of any single religion or tradition. The monk is not a specialist for a particular task, a specific apostolic mission. He is not defined by what he or she does, but by what he or she is.

The monk is the man who has taken seriously and uncompromisingly his vocation to become fully and totally man by transcending his "humanness." The monk is the man who wants to be essentially and substantially man, because he believes that the core of Man is to become more than human. He is the man who aspires to become God, precisely because he believes that divinization is the destiny of Man. He is the man who tends with his whole being to the fulfillment of this *real* being, even if this means "exploding" his human condition by deconditioning himself of all the limitations of temporality, *saṃsāra*, *avidyā*, and the like. And again: the monk is the man who tends toward the radical perfection of his being, in whatever way the different traditions may have interpreted this perfection.

We could perhaps put this in a more anthropological way, in tune with the trend of our times. In that case, we could speak (as I did elsewhere) of the monastic dimension of Man as a constitutive human dimension—though not the *only* one, because Man is more complex than his deepest core alone. To be a monk is not the monopoly of a few. Every human being has a "monastic dimension," but this is realized in different ways and cultivated in different degrees of purity and awareness by different people. The monk, properly, is the one who does not only cultivate this dimension in a peculiar way, but also commits himself publicly, therefore in a more or less communitarian way, to develop his human vocation. It goes without saying that this dimension can be understood differently, and unfortunately it has too often been interpreted and lived as being *against* genuine humanity and humane values.

The Western tradition has a theistic, Christian understanding of this fullness, and thus we find the *re vera Deum quaerit* (he actually/sincerely looks for God) of St. Benedict in practically all Christian monastic ideals. The quest for God, the search for the Absolute, the concentration on essentials, elimination of superfluity, attention to the substantial, and the vertical path—to mention some metaphors from different contexts—are central to the monastic vocation. The *et* to which I referred at the beginning of this essay is precisely the connecting link between the two fundamental human activities: the doing (*labora*) with one's hands (mind and heart guiding), and the being (*ora*) by sharing in the redemption of the world. The *et* uniting *ora et labora* is the symbol that unites the *being* and *doing* of Man, at the same time letting the *having* evaporate, because the private owner has it sublimated into the cosmotheandric *being* and *doing* of the universe.

If there is in every man a monastic dimension, what does the strictly called "monastic vocation" mean? Or more specifically, what is the place of the monastery?

The Monastery

Having spoken of the "spatial insight" of Indic spirituality, I may now sum up the whole complex problem and say that a monastery is neither a spot in which to dwell, nor a building within whose walls the life of the monk has to unfold, but a place in which to *live* in order to develop and cultivate the monastic dimension of Man. It is a place where a person can come and go, in and out, as he or she pleases, not by whimsy but by vocation, in order to foster that universal dimension, the vertical one, in his or her own life. To speak in Indic terms (for tradition corroborates what I say), a monastery is a place of *bhakti, jñāna*, and *karman*. It is a living institution, with which dedicated members are entrusted, under the radiant influence of a real *guru* (alive either in a physical or a mythical way), which fosters a life of love, dedication, prayer, knowledge, and real work.[8]

I am sketching all this not in order to develop a theory of monasticism—that would be preposterous in your presence and impossible in a single talk—but in order to illustrate my nightmare about the contribution of Christian monasticism in Asia. Unless these ideas become more alive in Christian monks, and until this view (imperfect as it may be) is seen as relevant for Christian monasticism, we can hardly speak of any contribution. But I now come to what, in another context, I would have called a reflection on a monastic theology of history.

The Threefold Mystery

By following the *Bhagavad-gītā*, St. Paul, and many other sacred texts, we could speak of the threefold mystery of reality. We may word it, in Christian terms, as the mystery of *creation*, the work of the Father, the unfathomable Source and groundless Ground of all that is; the mystery of *incarnation*, the action of the Son, the field of history, the place of the *Logos*; and the mystery of *glorification*, the mission of the Spirit, the sacred, struggling action in which Man and cosmos are transfigured—the process of enlightenment, the divinization of all that has come out of God.

---

[8] This is how "liturgy" should—etymologically—be understood: the *ergon* (*ourgia*, work) of all the *people* (*laos*) in order to collaborate in the running of the world; or, to use two rich traditional words, the *synergeia* of all forces, human, cosmic and divine, for the *lokasaṃgraha*.

Could we not discover here the calling of the three main continents of our planet?

Is it not the genius of Africa, so often misunderstood, to be sensitive to all the values of creation, to the transcendentally indwelling origin that makes words and any other expression secondary? Is it not the mission of Africa to stress this first moment of the mystery of reality?

Is it not the terrific achievement of the West to have discovered the unique value of history, the world-transforming power of the *logos*, the place of incarnation? Is not the West (Jewish, Christian, Muslim, and post-Christian) the natural *locus* for the dialectical encounter, for the struggle with the *logos*, for the divine and satanic power of science and technology?

Do not most experts agree in telling us that the apophatic dimension of the real is what best characterizes the Asian soul? The field of the Spirit, the experience of realization, the ever-present presence of the *eschaton*—not in terms of eschatology, but of epiphany.

We should not oversimplify or compartmentalize; we should avoid neat theories. Yet, speaking of monastic contribution, we could not but underscore the Asian vocation as that of sensitizing the world, "conscientizing" Man to his transcendent, vertical reality. Could we not envisage a real synergy, a collaboration among the different gifts of humankind? The contribution of Christian monasticism in Asia is not, and cannot simply be, to embellish what the West has already done, but rather to complement it, to enrich the *katholikon,* the universal experience of Man, with values that would otherwise not exist. The time is ripening for this really universal and catholic cooperation. I do not say it will be easy, but I suggest it is imperative.

The Coming Revolution

This was the last phase of my nightmare, and I have already hinted at it. It is true that we live in different worlds and cultures, and that we can try to understand, and in this sense justify, different worldviews. But my nightmare came to its acme when I began to surmise that it may be *too late*. Time is pressing. Is not the situation so urgent that any dream of a harmonious synthesis will be made ineffective by the avalanche of the coming revolution: human, ecological, and political? Are we still blind? Don't we detect the signs of the times, the writing on the wall?[9] Is not another epoch already emerging, irrupting? Is not a much more radical *metanoia* required today?

It is not that monks have to change their monastic structures; the dilemma is not a private monastic problem. The world and Man himself are changing. The very foundations of human life on earth are in question. Not only secularism, socialism, technology, science, ecology, and so on, but Man himself, and the entire cosmos, in as much as it is reflected in human consciousness, is at stake today. To "think

---

[9] See Dn 5.

small" is to betray our own vocation. Today's problems are not to be seen merely as being those of church reform or a post-Vatican discussion, but in the context of a ten-millennial human experience. Any other measure is now too small. The changes are not only sociological, political, and economic, but really anthropological in the deepest sense of the word.

The era of the Gods is over, and the era of God is waning. Certainly, the Gods are real and God is alive, but in a deeper and transformed sense. Perhaps the crisis of the Gods can help us understand the eclipse of God. And here again my dream turns to the monk, whose vocation is transhistorical, whose mission is that of being not a sign but a martyr, a witness, a leader. According to an Arab saying, the world belongs to God, but He rents it to the most courageous. In this transit, in this *pascha* to another degree of consciousness, the monk is needed, his transtemporal perspective is required, his serenity is necessary. When the acts of the Gods become doubtful and the image of God blurred; when any word is vague and contains more lie than truth; when any value is ambivalent, unsatisfactory, and inadequate, then the challenge becomes to bring out the impossible! "How can this happen, for I do not know man?"[10]

And here I woke up.

The Hangover: The Universal Church

To express things once again by concept and name, I may attempt to sum them up briefly under three headings.

The Overall Situation

The monk is a man of prayer, and prayer means awareness of our whole condition. Therefore, the man of prayer will be the first to open his eyes to this hunger for justice, liberation, and bread, which is, all at once, entirely permeating the world. This hunger is sometimes highly sophisticated, but it most often occurs in an immediate, literal way. The immense majority of the human beings walking on this cracking earth are falling victim to a situation created by Man, yet insoluble by Man alone. The real situation appears to me as that of a suffering mankind thirsty for liberation. Perhaps the first task of the monk is not to try to solve the problems by himself, but to create the climate for a universal human collaboration. Is not the monk the man who is always available, precisely because he is open to the Absolute, and constantly free?

I am not advocating the idea that monks should be tossed into social work and political involvement, for which they are at present unprepared. I am not excluding it, either. I rather promote a human solidarity, a planetary consciousness, to break

---

[10] Lk 1:34.

all the barriers and shackles, to abolish every factional privilege. We have too often mistaken solitude for isolation. It is the monastic solitude, I submit, that breaks the terrible isolation of our times. Does not a true experience of God break our isolation and yet respect our solitude?

The Ecumenical Ecumenism

I am not saying that the monk has to be everywhere, a sort of jack-of-all-trades. I only defend the idea, the ideal, of the monk as universal Man, precisely because he is not at the periphery but in the center, where the primordial dimension of being a man originates. In other words, I am emphasizing the mystical factor, the hidden vector, the underlying thrust in all human endeavor. It is not on the doctrinal, ideological, or even theological level that mutual inspiration and deep understanding will primarily emerge, but on a previous, more humble, more fundamental level.

I call it the "mystical" level, for lack of a better word, but I hope not to be misunderstood, at least by monks. The enormous popularity of mysticisms and nonconformisms of all sorts, and rebellions on every level, is both a distressing and a hopeful sign of our times. *Intelligenti pauca.*

The Other Dimension

Let me now stress another dimension, where the monk may especially contribute to humankind in general, and to the church in particular. The global revolution is coming; the transformations are deep and real. The change needs grassroots support, yet nothing will be lastingly done if that deeper dimension is lacking—a dimension that, paradoxically enough, seems to go against all that the world prima facie prizes. It is the manifestation of the constitutive polarity of reality.

I may sum it up in three paragraphs.

1. The monk is not a man of the past. But he is not a man of the future either. He belongs to the "timeful" present: he has a transtemporal vocation that neither escapes nor denies time (this is important) but does not get entangled in it either. His transtemporal vocation frees him from the burden of the past and from the paralyzing fear of responsibility for the future. He can plunge himself fearlessly into the present. He is our contemporary. He neither treasures past knowledge nor entertains hopes for the future: he is pure contemporaneity. No charisma can be manipulated or utilized for ulterior motives, edifying as these may be. The monk, the *monachos*, is a "freelancer" and may be an uncomfortable person to live with, as any prophet is destined to be.

2. The monastic vocation is not only transtemporal, it is also silent. The monk *is* the man of few words. There is a wordless contribution to be made. There is something in the world that defies being put into words. Not everything need be articulated, said, conceptualized. There is a wordless action that the world expects from monasticism, an authentic act.

3. I do not wish to be paradoxical, but there is no need to mention the *Bhagavad-gītā* again, or the Gospels, to stress the actionless being, the immobile center around which everything revolves. To know when to stop and think; even to stop thinking, so that being may be all the more pure . . . not of bread alone,[11] not of action alone, not of words alone, nor of God alone, or the monk alone . . . The mutation that is taking place needs the quietness of the monk no less than the activity of those who bear the burden of the "first hours."[12] In a total human and cosmic solidarity does it lie the contribution of the monk to the universal church.

So, we may fall into that deep prayer which is silent because it does not know what to say.[13]

Varanasi, India

---

[11] See Mt 4:4.

[12] Mt 20:1–16.

[13] See Rom 8:26.

16

SOCIAL MINISTRY AND MINISTRY OF WORD AND WORSHIP

*Some Considerations from the Asian Background**

Three assumptions form the backbone of this paper.

First, *ecclesiologically*: There seems to be a consensus among experts in this field that the theology of ministry today needs a radical and fundamental rethinking. Mere patchwork, adaptation, and reform is insufficient.

Second, *culturally*: A feature common to most of the traditional Asian cultures is an a-dualist and nondialectical approach to reality. There seems to be a certain unanimity here, also, in that neither a merely rational worldview nor any kind of dualism is satisfactory.

And third, *existentially*: Unless our reflections come from an experience arising from the actual world situation and from a praxis leading to a more fruitful and insightful ministry, they are useless and even wrong. That *scientia inflat*[1] should also be noncontroversial among an immense majority of our contemporaries.

A combination of these assumptions will furnish the background for the following reflections. I am not suggesting recipes for instant implementation or making recommendations for immediate action. Rather, I am calling for fundamental research and radical meditation, which should hardly be foreign to those who have committed themselves to a sincere and constant *metanoia*. Only such an ongoing radical conversion may be able to face the formidable difficulties involved in reconsidering a central Christian question that pierces the crust of twenty centuries of history.

The Radical *Metanoia*

In almost every church today, but much more in the churches outside the Western world, the need is felt for adaptation and *aggiornamento*.[2] The old colonial period in world history is collapsing, and in spite of the neocolonialistic attitudes of the

---

* Original text: "Social Ministry and Ministry of Word and Worship (Some Considerations from the Asian Background)," in P. S. de Achútegui (ed.), *Asian Colloquium on Ministries in the Church* (Hong Kong: FABC, 1977), 1–20.

[1] 1 Co 8:1.

[2] Italian word meaning "updating," often used with reference to Vatican Council II.

technocrats and the dearth of signs of a new order, the old order can certainly not be restored. Whether the new will be a postcolonial, post-technological, or post-Christian order remains to be seen. In any case, it will be "postmodern."

In the Christian ecclesiological field, the issue no longer seems to be one of, say, "Africanizing Roman Catholicism,"[3] but one of reenacting the incarnational act of Christ in time and space. The question is no longer how to explain the historical status quo, and the problem is not merely one of sociological change; rather, it is entirely a question of a basic *Christo-pneumatic* approach, and ultimately a mystical issue. In other words, the pinpoint of departure for a genuine Christian reflection in Asia on the issue of the Christian community should not be just a sociological consideration about the ecclesiological status quo, but a Christological reflection, a mystical insight into the nature of the fundamental Christian fact. The churches in Asia now face this challenge: whether continuing to exist as parasites on the main body of Christianity, or instead creating a symbiosis that—although not breaking the fundamental Christian unity—will allow for their own potentialities.[4]

The problem of a fundamental Asian response to the Christian fact is complex and delicate. We should not overstep intermediate situations and ignore the status quo: we cannot start from a nonexisting point zero. Yet I submit that genuine Christian thinking here cannot simply be reduced to socio-historical considerations, because there is another factor to take into account: the belief in the transtemporal character of the Christian vocation. The continuation, or rather the reenactment, of the Mystery of Christ on earth is governed by this belief-factor as much as by all the other behavioral components of any human group. In theological terms, Christian identity does not need to mean sociological homogeneity or doctrinal uniformity. Christians in Asia should be convinced of their right—indeed, their duty—to rethink and to reenact the Christian fact, certainly without ignoring twenty centuries of Christian history, but also without forgetting that Christ is living yesterday, today, and forever[5] so that they are not constrained to repeat, annotate, or simply adopt the creative achievements of their Western brethren, either "Greek" or "barbarian."[6]

If we do not start from the living Christ, who was before Abraham, who is the Firstborn of all creation[7] and the fullness of reality,[8] we will betray both our Christian calling and our ancient heritage. If Christian life in Asia is to have a vitality of

---

    [3] See M. Singleton, "New Forms of Ministry of Africa," *New Forms of Ministries in Christians Communities—Pro Mundi Vita* 50 (1974): 33. The whole dossier of the international colloquium held in Louvain-Heveries in September 1973 is an important document.

    [4] See R. Panikkar, "The Category of Growth in Comparative Religion: A Critical Self-Examination," in *Harvard Theological Review* 66, no. 1 (1973): 113–40. Now in vol. VI, book 2, of this *Opera Omnia*.

    [5] Heb 13:8.

    [6] Rom 10:12; Gal 4:28; Col 3:11.

    [7] Jn 8:58.

    [8] Col 1:15.

its own and not just one imported from abroad, it has to draw its force both from the universal sunlight and from the native soil of the millenarian Asian culture.

If the first Christians of the diaspora could abolish circumcision,[9] if the Patristic age could formulate the central Christian Mystery in Hellenic categories, if the Scholastic period could go so far as to equate God with Being, and if Western modern times have so utterly transformed the Christian self-understanding as to make it a Christian humanism, should we deny Asia the right to its own creative contribution to the crown of the *Catholica*? This, then, is the background.

The Christian Ministry

Jesus said that he came to serve and not to be served,[10] and the first apostles elected some helpers for the service of the tables.[11] The New Testament is full of descriptions of ministries: from a ministry of death[12] to a ministry of reconciliation,[13] of condemnation,[14] righteousness,[15] of the Spirit,[16] of the Word,[17] to a ministry to the Lord—also called office, service, and so on.[18]

There are excellent monographs on the Christian ministry, which we only need to study. What has been less often remarked, however, is the connection of the New Testament *diakonia* with the cosmology of its time, and the change that the concept has undergone since the disappearance of the cosmological background from which it originated.

The Christian ministry has undergone a certain negative evolution whereby being *ministry* became being *magister*, and *ministration* became *administration*[19] (a negative evolution that in no way denies the other side of the stupendous works of Christian ministry) and has often fallen into the temptation of prescribing to others the way in which they are to be served, thus converting *servus* (service) into *dominus* (domination). I submit that this degradation of ministry or its transformation into domination has its ultimate ground not in any desire to command, but in the disappearance of the myth of the world as an organized and ordered cosmos.[20]

---

[9] Ac 15.

[10] Mt 20:28; Mk 10:45.

[11] Ac 6:2–3.

[12] 2 Co 3:7.

[13] 2 Co 5:18.

[14] 2 Co 3:9.

[15] Ibid.

[16] 2 Co 3:8.

[17] Ac 8:4.

[18] See the many Hebrew expressions for ministry in the Old Testament.

[19] No need to recall the *magis* (from *maius*) lurking in the *magisterium*, against the *minor* (from *minus*) hidden in the *ministerium*.

[20] The confidence that "heaven and earth will pass away, but my words will not" (Mt 24:35), the Chinese trust in ultimate harmony, or the Indic-Vedic trust in *ṛta* imply a belief

We should not overlook all the historical factors after Constantine, Charlemagne, the Crusades, Boniface VIII, and others, but from the perspective of a thousand years and thousands of miles we may find a deeper explanation, which would not exonerate individuals or periods of their responsibility in creating a gospel of domination, but it may explain in more than ethical terms this passage of *Christianity* into *Christendom*. Only with a kind of cosmic confidence in the natural forces of creation, the ultimate meaningfulness of reality, and the nonexistence of absolute evil could the servant serve the master without any hindsight, suggesting that he may destroy the very meaning and purpose of service.

Only when the suspicion dawns that the ultimate structures of the world may be chaotic, that the universe may in fact be chaos and not cosmos, that evil can get the upper hand, that divine Providence seems not to care for truth and justice and the like, can the preoccupation arise that perhaps to serve the other's desires is not the best thing to do, since he may be in the grips of that chaos, and my service to him may then ultimately be a disservice. In other words, in a world not immediately directed by the Divine but by "second causes," we are not satisfied with just serving the other, but begin to speculate about the service he needs. Christian missions could in fact exemplify "servers" who claim to know what is needed better than the "served" themselves.

The service then becomes not the duty of the slave or the inferior but the right of the master and the superior. We then teach, become masters: *magistri*, not *ministri*; we organize kingdoms, crusades, and empires. This is "higher" service indeed, as the very words in most Western languages still betray: ministers, administrations, ministries of any kinds are words that designate authority. Up until not much time ago, the *servus servorum Dei* had three crowns and a *sedia gestatoria*—and justifiably so, given the evolution of Western history. What I am hinting at is that, with the fall of the colonial period, a new epoch may begin, even in ecclesiology. I am not suggesting that the silver trumpets should not sound any longer; I only note that Tibetan rituals use long horns, and the Swiss Guards alone may not be able to handle them.

What I am saying is this: The transmutation of all values, proper to the Christian message ("to serve, not to be served"; "the first will be the last, and the last the first"; "those who want to be the superiors, let them be the inferiors"; the sinner is justified and the just Pharisee proves to be sinful; "those who have loved much have been forgiven much"; "the rejected stone is made the foundation";[21] and the like), either goes on constantly transmuting old values into new (i.e., the servant has to be allowed to be served again; he who is now the first, because he was the last, has to go back to the last place; the inferiors who have become superior will have to be superseded in their turn; the publican aware of being such is the real Pharisee; the

---

in a divinely created world and the experience of an ordered cosmos. We modern people have lost—irretrievably—that innocence, the belief that Goodness will prevail.

[21] See, respectively, Mt 20:27; 20:16; Mk 9:35; Lk 18:9ff.; Lk 7:47; Mt 21:42.

sinner confident in divine mercy will not be forgiven; the successful foundation stone will have to be replaced by another rejected stone, etc.), or the message becomes "frozen" and thus subject to the very judgment that first justified the new values. Once the servant has become master, or the "minister" obtained authority, he will have to be replaced if the gospel is to have any living value: the ministries of today have to be displaced tomorrow precisely because their ministry has been successful. *This* is the Christian paradox. Redemption is a constant process precisely because the Redeemer did it once and for all.

One of the most powerful examples of this constant *Umwertung aller Werte*[22] is certainly the entire Sermon on the Mount, which, in this light, does not appear as a bucolic ideal or some unrealizable dream, accompanied by the excuse that human nature is wounded if not corrupted.[23]

And in that sermon, the flat statement of the Lord, "Do not resist evil,"[24] seems to be the most scandalous of all. It only makes sense under the assumption of the Easter mystery: that the world has already been redeemed, and that the struggle with evil is not dialectical, but the mystical action of charging ourselves[25] with the sin of the world, like the symbol of the Lamb . . . for only through our tolerance, patience, endurance, and assimilation of evil shall we win our lives.[26]

If the Christian tradition has reserved all these lofty ideals to a few selected people (segregated from the world in monasteries and convents), may it not be the calling of Asia to reincorporate these insights into the mainstream of Christian life?[27] The rejected stones may now become cornerstones for the time being. The Body of Christ is constantly under construction.[28] In speaking of Christian ministry, these fundamental questions cannot be bypassed. In other words, Christian ministry cannot be reduced to doing what an almighty God could do without effort, but He "prefers" to entrust to our responsibility. It cannot be reduced to giving a helping hand to the agencies that, being without the burden of theological ideologies, can be much more effective in eradicating poverty, injustice, hunger, sickness, and so on. Must the church give up her self-awareness of being the aim and goal of creation,[29]

---

[22] "Trans-valuation of all values": expression coined by Nietzsche.

[23] See the Scholastic, then Catholic/Protestant controversy about the *vulneratus in naturalibus, spoliatus in praeternaturalibus* (after the original sin, Man is wounded in his natural qualities and without his former supernatural gifts).

[24] Mt 5:39.

[25] This is the original meaning of the Latin verb *tollere* (*peccata mundi*).

[26] See Lk 21:19. R. Panikkar, "Tolérance, Idéologie et Mythe," in E. Castelli (ed.), *Démythisation et idéologie* (Paris: Auber, 1973), 191–206.

[27] We should here pay tribute to the many Western Christians who moved to the East to live the Gospel, really serving, without penning a bill for their services.

[28] See Ep 4:12, etc.

[29] See H. de Lubac, *Méditation sur l'Église* (Paris, 1935); F. Holbock and T. Sartory (eds.), *Mysterium Kirche* (Salzburg, 1962).

and become just another society for the welfare of humankind—and not a very successful one, for that matter?

What, then, is Christian ministry? I have no other answer than saying that it is a sharing in the redemptive function of the living Christ,[30] *in stultitia crucis*.[31]

The Undivided Ministry

There is one and a unique Christian ministry, as there is only one Spirit, although manifested in many gifts.[32] Let us remember, incidentally, that unity is not a privilege of the Spirit, for there is also one Body, though with many limbs.[33] Perhaps we have somewhat lost sight of the forest for the trees. These recalling to oneness, which should not be confused with uniformity, may belong to an Asian Christian reflection.

If Christ is the universal Redeemer, the unique High Priest of the Last Covenant, and the only Mediator[34]—in whatever sense we may interpret this[35]—we should stress the oneness of this ministry. "Ministry of reconciliation"[36] could perhaps be the most appropriate term for the kind of service toward the fragments of reality, whether those formed at creation, or those sundered by the power of Man or the work of time.[37] The reconstruction of the dismembered body of the Divine, according to this intuition, could be another way of expressing it.[38]

Now I will specify what I consider this central Christian service to be by enumerating a few of the dichotomies that divide our world, which should be rediscovered and thus reconverted into *creative polarities*, instead of being allowed to become antithetical foes or to collapse into an amorphous monism. I stress here that the a-dualist and *advaitic* intuition I am propounding is neither dualism of some sort nor a monism of any kind.

1. The first dichotomy that should be overcome is that between God and the world. A certain Christian dualism has made of most of Western Christianity a mere continuation of Semitic and Iranian religiousness. Yet dualism, I submit, is

---

[30]   See the above chapter.

[31]   1 Co 1:18.

[32]   1 Co 12:4.

[33]   1 Co 12:12.

[34]   See 1 Tim 2:5–6; Heb 5:10.

[35]   It seems to be a Christian duty, nowadays, to defend a nonexclusivist and nonimperialist conception of the Christian Fact. To break monopolies does not mean to water things down.

[36]   2 Co 5:18.

[37]   See R. Panikkar in the proceedings of the II International Symposium on Belief, Vienna 1975, "The Cosmotheandric Vision: An Emerging Consciousness for the Third Millennium AD."

[38]   See R. Panikkar, "La faute originante," in E. Castelli (ed.), *Le Mythe de la peine* (Paris: Aubier, 1967), 65–100; Panikkar, "The Myth of Incest as Symbol for Redemption in Vedic India," in R. J. Zwi Werblowsky and C. J. Bleeker (eds.), *Types of Redemption* (Leiden: Brill, 1970), 130–43. In vol. IX, book 1, *Opera Omnia*.

ultimately foreign to the central Christian intuition. If Christ is the central symbol, he is first of all *one*, and thus equally human as he is divine: the entire reality is a Christophany—*in fieri, in potentia, in spe*.[39]

2. In a world artificially divided into believers and nonbelievers, Christians should be the real mediators, who make religious wars obsolete, and the dreams of a humanistic paradise impossible. This applies not only to the strictly religious sphere, where Christians bear a great deal of the burden (I spoke of *metanoia*), but equally to the religiously inspired mutual excommunications in force between political blocs, economic systems, and ideological denominations. Sectarianism, of all kinds, is antithetical to a God who lets the rain fall on good and bad people alike, and the sun rise for both just and sinners,[40] and antithetical to the Spirit, who has the knowledge of any word.[41] I may be allowed not to elaborate.

3. In a time of encounter with civilizations in which spirit and matter seem irreconcilable enemies, the Christian *diakonia*—as deriving its intuition from Christ—should again stress that distinction does not mean separation; that there is no matter without spirit; and vice versa: "In Him we move and live and are."[42] Again, *intelligenti pauca*.

4. A fourth dichotomy is that existing between the world and a certain notion of church. A superficial Christian view has often turned the church into a sect, and forgotten the Patristic intuition according to which the entire dynamism of history is in its transit, the *pascha*[43] from *kosmos* to *ekklēsia*.

Christians are not just the members of one particularly social, political, or religious—let alone ethnic or cultural—group. We should be aware that the borderlines pass amid ourselves, our lives, our own existences, so that "Christian" is not a label for a sociological group, but a name for a pilgrim's conscious acceptance of the human condition on his or her way to a goal that can be seen either as fullness or emptiness, since it is ultimately beyond description.

There is a dominant trend in Western theology today, which, having lost sight of that mystical intuition and in no way wanting to endorse Christian imperialism or the church's exclusivity, tends to reduce the church to the small "remnant of Israel," with a "humble" function alongside the many other human and divine groups striving toward the same goal of furthering Man's life. If "outside the church there is no salvation" was the motto in an imperialistic ecclesiology, this theological trend will add, "which should be buried and forgotten." In full sympathy with the aim of such a new reflection, a more mystical and less historicist Asian approach could stress, in greater consonance with the Christian tradition, that the church is not primarily a "club" or compact visible group, but a communion and a Body

---

[39] In progress, potentially, in hope.

[40] See Mt 5:45.

[41] See Ws 1:7.

[42] Ac 17:28.

[43] Etymologically: passing (pass-over).

of another order altogether. "Outside the Church there is no salvation," precisely because the church is, by definition, the *locus* of salvation, wherever this place may be and whatever form it may take.[44] This is not mere semantics, attributing to the church what others would apply to the kingdom. I am speaking of a consciousness of Christian identity not being exhausted by sociology and history, and I am appealing to a Christian reflection more akin to Asian thinking.

We could proceed with further dichotomies: male/female, cleric/lay, rich/poor, and so on, but we have said enough to stress the need for a ministry of "ontological reconciliation."

The Ministries of Karman, Jñāna, and Bhakti

In meditating on the links between the three ministries (the social one and those of Word and worship), their intrinsic connection with the three traditional *mārgas* or ways of human spirituality appears strikingly. We will not elaborate on the many ministries that the church could and should exercise on the social level (*karman*), on the level of the Word (*jñāna*), or on that of worship (*bhakti*). I would like instead to stress their relatedness and internal unity. This internal unity reflects my general thesis about the oneness and specificity of the church's *diakonia*. Needless to say, what follows is strictly a theological reflection. It does not supersede sociological and pastoral considerations, but functions rather as their basis, if we are to speak of a Christian *diakonia* at all, and not just of the obvious commonsensical and ethical imperative of service to humanity.

My first observation regards the "division of labor" as an answer to the problem of the diversity of ministries within the church: it may be a diplomatically prudent device and a sociologically wise refuge, but theologically, as an answer to the problem, it is insufficient. It is often formulated as follows: "There are many vocations, skills, and idiosyncrasies in the church: let each follow his own tendencies, and we—the theologians, or the hierarchy—will find a justification a posteriori. . . . Who are we to forbid social action, intellectual research, artistic creativity, pure contemplation, struggle for justice, political agitation, liturgical celebration? Who are we to impose a rigid pattern on everybody and say that Christians should not engage in such activities? Christian pluralism is a necessity today." Certainly, and nothing is more contrary to the intention of this paper than to put straitjackets on people in the name of the gospel. All the examples cited are ministries that our contemporaries feel a need to perform—and, to be sure, Christians should not and cannot be forbidden to engage in these and similar human activities. On the contrary, it would be a sign of spiritual anemia to be unable to take up such services in the name of Christ, to leave them to others because Christians are afraid to soil their hands in such profane activities.

---

[44] In the words of St. Ignatius of Antioch, who possibly employed the adjective "catholic" for the first time: "Where Jesus Christ is, *there* is the catholic (*katholikē*) church" (*Epist. ad Smyrnaeos* VIII.2 (*PG* 5.724).

Freedom and pluralism are the very conditions for a genuine Christian attitude.

What I am, however, criticizing is the conversion of pluralism into a strategy, the cloaking of the problem under the pretense of tolerance. What I am chastising is a possible hypocritical complacency, which starts from the fact that there are Christians in good faith in all the different fields of human activities. If the church has "members" among the leftists and rightists, she will never lose. Against this attitude of not daring to take stances, I would say that merely relying on a division of labor neither does justice to those who have put their souls at stake working for one concrete cause (and who would feel manipulated and betrayed if the hierarchical church would equally justify their opponents), nor takes sufficiently into account the nature of the Christian *diakonia*. "Nobody can serve two masters."[45]

In other words, the church is not above the human and secular struggle. To say that "we" need Christian authorities and Christian revolutionaries, Christian activists and Christian contemplatives, and then wash our hands when we see the "children of Man" in distress and on the verge of being crucified . . . this could never be a theologically sound answer, or even an ethical human attitude. In short, taking refuge in the supernatural character of the church in order to justify Christian pluralism does justice neither to the seriousness of the secular world nor to the truth of the real nature of the church. In simpler words, not to take sides in the stresses and strains of the human condition is already to have taken the side of escapism.

It is no excuse to say that "there are many mansions in the Father's house,"[46] because there is also hell, Gehenna, the "outside," where there is darkness and the gnashing of teeth.[47] The church cannot avoid her responsibilities. Here again, the Asian theological contribution could indeed be relevant, both as a historical perspective and as a way of theological thinking.

Historically speaking, Asia in general and Christian Asia in particular have been practically absent in the development and growth of Christian self-awareness. The main tensions, struggles, defeats, and victories have taken place in the West. The East has only suffered the repercussions of the Christian wars, schisms, and theological controversies. Not only money and personnel, but ideas also have been a one-way traffic. If anything, Asia is a Christian appendix. It leads nowhere to try to hide this, in order to show sympathy for Asia or to give a sense of dignity to Asian Christians. Now, precisely because of this peripheral position, Christians in Asia today may gain a historical perspective that would be difficult to find outside the Asian vantage point. The false dilemma of communism vs. anticommunism could be a case in point. The conflict may appear to be one of heresy rather than apostasy.

The visible church—inseparable from the invisible one, but not identical with it—should perhaps regain a more integrated vision of herself in the global context in which she is now only a minor factor. Or, coming back to our point, the ministries

---

[45] Mt 6:24.
[46] Jn 14:2.
[47] Mt 25:30.

of the church should be placed in the more sober perspective of collaborating with the work of the Spirit, which blows in and from all directions.

Or again, the "ministries" of the church should no longer be considered ministries of the church exclusively. The church has *a ministry*, but no specific and proper *ministers*: they belong to humanity as a whole. As for services, Christians in particular and the church in general should join hands with all the other human agencies presently trying to improve the human condition.

And here also a more typically Asian way of thinking—with all the qualifications that should accompany such an expression—may prove of help. I am referring to the a-dualist and dialogical, rather than dialectical, approach to reality. I may be allowed to use a very traditional Christian language to express my view on the nature of Christian ministry: one Spirit, one Body, one High Priest, one Redemption, one Resurrection.[48]

The act of Christ, done once and for all[49]—not because of a privileged moment in history (the Western, even Christian myth), but because it has a *tempiternal* significance—is not primarily one of alleviating the sufferings of humankind. Christ did not (nor did the Buddha, incidentally) promise a universal panacea, or to establish an agency for the relief of the ills of humanity. If that, indeed, was His intent, He would have failed miserably, and we should awaken to this reality after twenty centuries. But Christ's unique contribution, to use an awkward parlance deliberately, was not to tell us that we should love our neighbor, bless our enemies, or be obedient to the laws of heaven. Humankind was awake to this much before Jesus appeared on earth.[50] Christ's unique performance was the event of His life—or rather, of His death and resurrection—which revealed in history the Mystery hidden but effective since the beginning of the world.[51] The event is trans-historical and tempiternal, and for this reason not limited in space and time, but historically made manifest in what Christians call "the Mystery of Christ."

The Christian *diakonia* is Christian discipleship, witness to and collaboration in that event in which every human being has been invited to participate, in one way or another. The Christian service to the world is to reenact the Memorial, to be in communion with Christ, the Alpha, the Omega, the Lamb, the Bread, the Son of Man—and from that center, not to be mere spectators of the cosmic display, but actors, as well, in this cosmotheandric liturgy.

Once this center is reached, once this communion is established, the manifestations in space and time can be as manifold as human beings and human activities. Any field in which Christians believe they have to perform a service to the world is a legitimate field of *diakonia*, however subject, of course, to all the tensions, limita-

---

[48] See Ep 4:4; Heb 7:27; 1 Tim 2:5–6; 1 Co 15:12–13.
[49] Heb 7:27.
[50] See Lv 19:18–19; Pr 20:22; 24:17; 25:21; as well as *Manu* II.161; VI.47–48; *MB* XIII.5571; Confucius, *Dialogues* XII, etc.
[51] Rom 16:25; Col 1:26; 2 Tim 1:10, etc.

tions, and contradictions to which any human activity is subject. The Christian, in his field, is as limited and fallible as any other human being or group.

"Omnia propter semetipsum operatus est Dominus,"[52] said the Bible, at least in the Latin version used by the Christian Scholastics.[53] "Ad maiorem Dei gloriam" was not only the motto of Jesuits: Calvin as well as most Christians until very recent times would consider it the ultimate purpose of human existence. "*Yoga* is not for the sake of humanity, but for the sake of the Divine," Śrī Aurobindo used to say in order to shift theocentrically the balance against modernistic and humanistic trends.[54] "First see God and then open your dispensaries," was Śrī Ramakrishna's advice.[55] "Seek the kingdom first."[56]

The Triune Ministry

As a direct outflow of the preceding insights, I may venture some suggestions for discussions.

1. The visible church, as a sociological group, should take at least as much care as the individual Christian in not allowing her ministry to split into disconnected specializations. The link should not be external but constitutive.

The sacred is not the profane, but they are mutually interrelated, so that the profane becomes deconsecrated if severed from the sacred, and the sacred becomes profaned if disconnected from the profane. In simpler terms, workdays spent working for the exploitation of others and Sundays for the parish, being a political coward who then takes the initiative in liturgical celebrations, helping the rich and praying for the poor, or preaching justice and living selfishly, and so on, are all inconsistencies inherent in such a dichotomy.

In concreto, the Christian service has always to be a (w)holistic and integrated one. To be saved is to be made *whole*. And this unity works both ways; that is, there must be no mere social service that is not at the same time a service of praise and contemplation, of love and celebration; but also no religious or worship service that is not at the same time a ministry of justice, with all the political and corporeal ramifications.

Second, the social ministry should not be severed from the ministry of Word and worship, so that any absolutization of temporal concerns becomes impossible. The social order is not an ultimate order. Human life can be lived in its fundamental fullness even in unjust and oppressive sociopolitical structures. This implies that a pluralistic service is of the nature of the Christian involvement in the world, and

---

[52] "The Lord has made everything for / because of Himself."

[53] Pr 16:4 (*Vulgate*); cf. Thomas Aquinas, *C. gentes* III.17; IV.34.

[54] Quoted by D. K. Roy, *Yogi Sri Krishnaprem* (Bombay [Mumbai]: *Bharatiya Vidya Bhavan*, 1968), 158.

[55] Ibid., 145.

[56] Mt 6:33.

that only in the fair play and interaction of conflicting views can a really positive service emerge.

This does not contradict what has been said against a false prudence. It is a pledge against idolatry. I am not advocating that church authorities shrewdly balance Christian ballots and distribute their subjects among all fields of human activities (which would be atrocious). I am suggesting, rather, that those who are engaged in one particular social service should not, in spite of their wholehearted and total commitment to the cause, see the salvation of the world or of individuals as *depending* on the eradication of, say, apartheid, capitalism, socialism, weapons, dictatorship, poverty, slavery, or whatever.

I am not advocating a "strategic" involvement in social services. On the contrary, I am defending a total plunge into human affairs and, for this very reason, a total purity of heart and nonattachment.[57] I am only warning against all types of fanaticism, the result of absolutizing human values.

2. The ministry of the Word should not be disconnected from the concrete social milieu in which this ministry is performed. To keep silent in Christian worship, for instance, in front of patent social injustices, economic disorder, or political abuses may amount to a mockery of worship and a prostitution of the service to the Word. We should not exclude *real* prudence, but we are reminded to beware of the "prudence of the flesh."[58]

The ministry of the Word cannot be reduced to mere exegesis of stereotyped texts. God has not only spoken in old times and spoken unto us in His Son,[59] but He is still a living God, constantly speaking to us, and He is mighty enough to raise up children to Abraham even from stones.[60]

3. The ministry of worship cannot be a cheap consolation, amounting to alienation, for the social ills of a particular time and place. We cannot praise the Lord if meanwhile we prepare strategical wars; we cannot sing in the congregation if we have silenced other voices.

The Real Ministry

When all this is said, still nothing is done—and ministry means *doing*. In other words, giving a glass of water or a simple smile is more valuable than all these theological considerations. One of the greatest traps of human thinking—and thus for intellectuals, theologians, and others—is that the purely mental level does not lead to action. And action cannot wait for the guidance of the mental level, though the

---

[57] See the concept of *asakta* in the *Bhagavad-gītā* (chs. III and V), with the basic distinction among an inhumane, and ultimately hypocritical, detachment, and a serene, and ultimately more effective, nonattachment to our work.

[58] See 1 Co 2:6; Jas 1:15.

[59] Heb 1:1–2.

[60] Mt 3:9.

former presupposes the latter. If we have to wait for refined, balanced, 100 percent correct answers, and injunctions taking all the complexities of human situations into account, we shall never come to any action, to any service. Ministry cannot wait until we have an entire theory about it and a mature theology for our times. There is something rhetorical in saying "theology *of* ministry." What we need is ministry *itself*: service, action, involvement.

All too often the church has kept silent because the intellectual answer to the practical challenge was "too complex." It did not need to speak, but only to act. And this applies not only to great political issues like those raised by Hitler, Pinochet, communism, apartheid, racial discrimination, and social injustices; it also applies to problems such as mental health, overpopulation, divorce, and so forth. The people in the middle of these agonizing situations cannot wait for universally valid answers and spotless theories, whether on birth control or civil resistance. Furthermore, no working solution is going to come from the isolated studies of a theoretician. We need involvement as much as distance, action as much as contemplation.

A reflection about the ministries in the church cannot be a mere deductive speculation from lofty principles. It has to proceed from a personal and suffering experience in our own flesh and in the shared anguish of our fellow beings. Only afterward may we try to put it in the best possible theoretical way and give it a garb as fitting and universal as possible—well aware, however, that though this is not useless and unimportant, it is certainly secondary. These reflective and theoretical efforts exist only for the sake of communicating to others. Our solutions are provisional and imperfect, as they must be, also as far as the problems of ministry are concerned. *Caritas Christi urget nos.*[61] Without this sense of urgency, all our talk will be "tamquam cymbalum tinniens."[62] What can we do *with* and *for* the people who suffer, and who suffer from man-made injuries—today perhaps a majority of the human family? We think, we organize, we even pray. All this is very good if it comes from our own service and leads us toward a better service; otherwise, we know what is written of those who abuse their privileges....[63]

Not only is there something rhetorical in theorizing about ministries as an end in itself, there is also something hypocritical and methodically false. Any theory about ministry that is not aware of its secondary, provisional nature and shortcomings will tend to a certain self-justification, thus converting the *ministerium* into a *magisterium*, and making it impossible for the left hand to give full freedom to the right.[64] To speculate, comfortably ensconced, on what others have done following the example of the Master, to submit their strengths and weaknesses to theological scrutiny, is as painful as it is inconsistent. We may find faults in what some "sisters of charity" are doing somewhere, because they are preventing a social awakening

---

[61] 2 Co 5:14 in the *Vulgate* version.
[62] 1 Co 13:1.
[63] See Lk 12:42ff.
[64] Mt 6:3.

(and we may even be right, from a certain point of view), but the moment we *speak* about it instead of *doing* what we believe we also should do, we begin to monopolize the Spirit, who cannot be subordinated to the *Logos*.

Each ministry is a free gift.

Glossary

abba (Aramaic): Father; as Jesus called God.

Abgescheidenheit (German): "detachment"; an expression coined by Eckhart in his treatise *On Detachment*; represents one of the central points of his mystical conception, implying both an active and a passive attitude.

abhavyatva (Sanskrit): the inability to attain liberation; used in Buddhism and Jainism.

abhimāna (Sanskrit): vanity, presumption, deceit, attachment.

Abhinavagupta (*Abhinavaguptācārya*) (Sanskrit): a tenth-century Śivaite mystic.

Abhiṣiktānanda (Sanskrit): monastic name of Henri Le Saux (1910–1973), a Hindu-Christian monk who sought to synthesize both traditions in his work and his life.

ab intra (Latin): from within.

ācārya (Sanskrit): teacher of *Veda*, spiritual guide who imparts initiation. The term is anterior to *guru*.

acosmism: doctrine that denies reality and/or the value and ultimate sense of the world (*cosmos*).

actio (Latin): activity, action.

adam (Hebrew): man, the first man, as prototype, according to the Bible. Only later it became a man's name. Etymologically related to "red" and "earth," "ground."

ad-extra (Latin): outward.

ad-intra (Latin): inward.

advaita (Sanskrit): nondualism (*a-dvaita*). Spiritual intuition that sees ultimate reality as neither monistic nor dualistic. The recognition that the merely quantitative problem of the one and the many in dialectical reasoning does not apply to the realm of ultimate reality. The latter, in fact, possesses polarities that cannot be divided into multiple separate units; not to be confused with *monism*.

advaitin (Sanskrit): followers of *advaita*, who profess *ātman-brahman* nonduality.

agapē (Greek): love.

Agni (Sanskrit): the sacrificial fire and the Divine Fire, one of the most important Gods or divine manifestations, the mediator or priest for Men and Gods.

agnihotra (Sanskrit): the daily fire sacrifice performed morning and evening in all homes of the high castes, which consists of an oblation of milk sprinkled on the fire.

agnostic: a recently coined philosophical position that claims that there is no such thing as certain knowledge, especially with regard to God and ultimate questions.

agōn (Greek): fight, struggle, battle; the agonic sense of life.

agora (Greek): public square where the townsfolk gathered and held meetings in ancient Greece.

aham (Sanskrit): "I"; first person pronoun. *Aham* as ontological principle of existence is generally distinguished from *ahaṃkāra* as a psychological principle.

aham asmi (Sanskrit): "I am"; a formula of spiritual creation or *mahāvākya*, deriving from the *Bṛhadāraṇyaka-upaniṣad*.

ahaṃkāra (Sanskrit): the sense of the ego.

ahiṃsā (Sanskrit): "nonviolence," respect for life, not killing and not wounding, not desiring to carry out violence against reality. A moral and philosophical principle based on ultimate universal harmony. The root *hiṃs-* from *han-* means "to wound," "to kill." This is not exactly a Vedic notion; it appears only a few times in the *Upaniṣad*; it was developed in Jainism and Buddhism.

Ahriman (Persian): principle of darkness and evil, according to Mazdaism; a noun deriving from Angra Mainyu (evil spirit), used by Zoroaster.

aiōn (Greek): cosmic time, eternity; also a period of life.

aisthēsis (Greek): perception, sensitivity, sense, knowledge.

ākāśa (Sanskrit): air, sky, space, ether, the fifth of the primordial elements (*mahābhūtāni*), which is the element of sound. It is all-pervading and infinite, and therefore often identified with Brahman.

aliud (Latin): the other, neutral.

alius (Latin): the other (other I).

amerimnia (Greek): absence of anxiety.

'am ha'aretz (Aramaic): "people of the earth," lower classes, the disinherited, the poor, the untouchable, the ignorant, those who do not know the *Torah*.

amplexus (Latin): embrace.

amṛta (Sanskrit): immortal, imperishable (*a-mṛta*); refers mainly to the Gods; noun, neutral: immortality, absence of death, and nectar of immortality, *soma*, the sacred drink (ambrosia).

anakephalaiōsis (Greek): summary of all things (in Christ); used by St. Paul.

ānanda (Sanskrit): joy, bliss (cf. *sukha*), the delights of love, and especially the highest spiritual bliss; *sat*, *cit*, and *ānanda* represent three possible attempts at defining *brahman* or absolute reality.

anātman (Sanskrit): absence of *ātman*, of the substantiality of an individual ontological Self.

anātmavāda, nairātmyavāda (Sanskrit): mainly Buddhist doctrine of the insubstantiality of the *ātman* or Self.

anātmavādin (Sanskrit): follower of the doctrine of *anātman*.

anima mundi (Latin): soul of the world; as an analogy of man, the earth is conceived as the body of expression of a planetary Consciousness or Soul.

animus-anima (Latin): masculine (in the woman) and feminine (in the man) image or characteristic, as psychologically thematized by C. G. Jung.

anitya (Sanskrit): impermanence.

antarikṣa (Sanskrit): that which is "between," the space of air between the sky and the earth, atmosphere, intermediate space (cf. *dyu* and *pṛthivī* as two other terms for *triloka*).

anthrōpos (Greek): man, in a general sense.

anubhava (Sanskrit): direct experience, knowledge deriving from immediate spiritual intuition.

apatheia (Greek): impassibility, indifference, calm, imperturbability (complete liberation from all emotional stress produced by the events of life).

apokatastasis pantōn (Greek): restoration of all things at the end of the world, or of a period of time, according to Christian Scripture.

aporia (Greek): difficulty that prevents one from going beyond reason, dead end.

arhat (Sanskrit): ascetic, saint, the highest and most noble figure of Theravada Buddhism.

asat (Sanskrit): nonbeing; denial of being; as opposed to *sat*, being.

asparśayoga (Sanskrit): yoga without intermediary, without mental content, stopping of the mind, "nonmind."

āśrama (Sanskrit): state of life, the four traditional periods in the life of the "twice-born": student (*brahmacārin*), head of family (*gṛhastha*), inhabitant of the forest (*vānaprastha*), and itinerant ascetic (*saṃnyāsin*). Also the hermitage of a monk and, therefore, the title of an ascetic. Also indicates a spiritual community, generally under the direction of a *guru* or spiritual teacher. Also refers to a stage in human life.

asura (Sanskrit): spiritual, incorporeal, divine. In *Ṛg-veda* the highest spirit, God (from *asu*, life, spiritual life). Varuṇa is considered an *asura*. Later the meaning changes completely and *asura* (now analyzed as *a-sura*, or "non-God") takes on the meaning of demon or evil spirit constantly opposed to the *deva* (*Brāhmaṇa*).

atha (Sanskrit): here, now, furthermore; particle translated according to context.

ātman (Sanskrit): principle of life, breath, the body, the Self (from the root *an*, to breathe). Refers to the whole, undivided person and also to the innermost center of man, his incorruptible nucleus, which in the *Upaniṣad* is shown to be identical to Brahman. The Self or inner essence of the universe and man. Ontological center in Hinduism, which is negated in Buddhism.

ātmānātma-vastuviveka (Sanskrit): discernment between real and unreal.

ātmavāda (Sanskrit): doctrine that accepts the existence of the Self, the *ātman*, as the essential, incorruptible center of being.

ātmavādin (Sanskrit): follower of the *ātman* doctrine.

ātmavid (Sanskrit): he who knows the Self (*ātman*), who has fulfilled his innermost being.

atyāśrama (Sanskrit): the state beyond the four traditional states of a man's spiritual being (cf. *āśrama*), which transcends them in complete spiritual freedom.

Aum (Sanskrit): cf. Oṃ.

autarkeia (Greek): self-sufficient.

avatāra (Sanskrit): "descent" of the divine (from *ava-tṛ*, descend), the "incarnations" of Viṣṇu in various animal and human forms. Traditionally, there are ten *avatāra*: *matsya* (the fish), *kūrma* (the tortoise), *varāha* (the wild boar), *narasiṃha* (the lion-man), *vāmana* (the dwarf), Paraśurāma (Rāma with the axe), Rāma, Kṛṣṇa, Buddha, and Kalkin at the end of time. In general, any personal manifestation of the Divinity, descended into this world in human form; descent as antonomasia.

avidyā (Sanskrit): ignorance, nescience, absence of true and liberating knowledge, often identified with *māyā* and a cause of illusion and delusion.

āyus (Sanskrit): vital force, vitality, life, temporal existence, the length of life granted to man. Cf. Greek *aiōn*, aeons.

bandhu (Sanskrit): bond, connection, relation, friendship, friend.

Bhagavad-gītā (Sanskrit): The "Song of the Glorious Lord," the "Song of the Sublime One"; a famous ancient Indian didactic poem included in the *Mahābhārata* (often called the "New Testament of Hinduism"), the most well-known sacred book in India.

bhakti (Sanskrit): devotion, submission, love for God, personal relationship with God, devotional mysticism. One of the paths of salvation through union with the divinity.

bhakti-mārga (Sanskrit): the path of love and devotion, one of the three classical spiritual paths (cf. *karma-mārga, jñāna-mārga*).

bhārata-nāṭyam (Sanskrit): divine dance.

bhāṣya (Sanskrit): commentary.

bhikṣu (Sanskrit): he who begs for food and leaves home, the monk.

bios (Greek): existence, biological life, length of life.

bodhisattva (Sanskrit): the enlightened one. In particular, in Mahāyāna Buddhism, he who, having attained liberation on earth, makes a vow to help all other beings attain liberation before they enter *nirvāṇa*.

Brahmā (Sanskrit): the creator God (cf. the "Trinity," later Brahmā, Viṣṇu, Śiva). It is not important in the *Veda* but in later periods it inherits many of the characteristics of Prajāpati.

brahmacārin (Sanskrit): student of Brahman, i.e. of *Veda*; novice who lives a life of chastity and purity. He who lives in the first of the four *āśrama*.

brahmacarya (Sanskrit): life of a student of Brahman, also of the chastity and education of Brahman. The first of the four *āśrama* (cf. *gṛhastha, vānaprastha, saṃnyāsa*).

brahman (Sanskrit): prayer, sacrifice, the inherent power in sacrifice; the Absolute, the ultimate reason underlying all things; in the *Upaniṣad* it is identified with the immanent Self (*ātman*). Also, one of the four priests who perform the sacrifice or the clergy in general.

Brahma-sūtra (Sanskrit): traditional Hindu text; one of the bases of the Vedānta.

Bṛhadāraṇyaka-upaniṣad (Sanskrit): one of the most ancient and important *Upaniṣad*.

buddhakāya (Sanskrit): lit. "body of Buddha," universal solidarity, the behavior of the Buddha.

buddhi (Sanskrit): the highest faculty of the intellect, also comprehension, thought, meditation.

cakra (Sanskrit): center of energy in the subtle body of man (related, perhaps, to each plexus); lit. "wheel."

capax Dei (Latin): capacity of the soul to perceive and receive God.

cela (Sanskrit): disciple.

cenobitic: relating to the monastery (*cenobium*).

Chāndogya-upaniṣad (Sanskrit): one of the most ancient of the *Upaniṣad*, which deals with the mystic value of sound, song and the identity of *ātman-brahman*.

chara (Greek): grace, joy, cheerfulness.

circulus vitiosus (Latin): "vicious circle," bad reasoning, which states what is still to be proven.

circumincessio (Latin): compenetration of the three Persons of the Trinity. Corresponds to the Greek *perichōresis*.

cit (Sanskrit): root noun (from the root *cit-*, to perceive, to comprehend, etc.), meaning "consciousness, intelligence." One of the three "characteristics" of Brahman (cf. *sat, ānanda*).

civitas Dei and *civitas terrena* (Latin): "city of God" and "earthly city"; theory formulated by Augustine (354–430), according to which there are two citizenships or "states."

cogito (ergo) sum (Latin): "I think (therefore) I am."

coincidentia oppositorum (Latin): coincidence of the opposites.

colloquium salutis (Latin): dialogue of salvation.

complexio omnium (Latin): integration of all things.

comprehensor (Latin): one who truly comprehends; one who already possesses the beatific vision, the fulfilled man.

compunctio cordis (Latin): repentance, heartfelt sorrow, the essential attitude of monastic spirituality.

consecratio mundi (Latin): consecration or sanctification of the world; the secular is sacralized, contemplated in its sacred dimension.

contemptus saeculi (Latin): contempt for all that is temporal and worldly.

conversio (Latin): change or transformation, generally religious; one of the translations of *metanoia*.

conversio morum (Latin): change in customs, way of living.

cosmotheandric: the nonseparation between World, God, and Man.

creatio continua (Latin): "continuous creation"; doctrine of the continuous creative force of God in the sense of the preservation of the universe and universal government.

Christianity: religiosity based on the experience of Christ.

darśana (Sanskrit): from the root *dṛś*, to see, to observe; hence vision, sight; philosophy, *Weltanschauung*. In a religious context it means the vision of a saint or God, hence also meeting, audience, visit.

Dasein (German): being here; real, existing man; a term used mainly by M. Heidegger; human existence.

deva (Sanskrit): connected with *div*, sky, light (Latin *divus, deus*), celestial, divine. Also God, divinity, heavenly being, cosmic power. The *deva* are not on the same level as the one God (sometimes called also *deva*, in the singular, or *īśvara*) or the absolute (Brahman). They are powers that have different functions in the cosmos. Subsequently, the human sensory faculties are also called *deva* in the *Upaniṣad*.

Dhammapāda (pāli): collection of 426 Buddhist verses of the Pāli canon.

dharma (Sanskrit): cosmic order, justice, duty, religious law, religious and social observances transmitted by tradition; "religion" as a collection of practices and laws. That which holds the world together. One of the four "human purposes" (cf. *puruṣāsartha*).

dharmakāya (Sanskrit): mystical body of *dharma* in Mahāyāna Buddhism.

dhyāna (Sanskrit): meditation, contemplation.

diachronic: that which extends through time.

diakonia tou logou (Greek): ministry of the word.

diatopic: that which extends through space.

digambara (Sanskrit): ascetic of the Jain religion who walks naked as a symbol of detachment and purity.

dīkṣā (Sanskrit): initiation; the preliminary rites; consecration of one who performs the sacrifice, such as that celebrated, for example, at the beginning of the *soma* and leads to a "new birth." Out of the context of sacrifice *dīkṣā* is the initiation of the disciple by the *guru* into *saṃnyāsa*, the life of the errant monk.

dipsychos (Greek): one who has a double soul.

discretio (Latin): discernment, discretion, prudence.

docta ignorantia: classic term used by Nicolaus Cusanus to denote supreme innocence, ignorance of one's own knowledge.

doxa (Greek): glory.

dualism: vision of a basic split within the being into two principles, each irreducible to the other, particularly spirit and matter, soul and body.

duḥkha (Sanskrit): disquieted, uneasy, distress, pain, suffering, anguish (lit. "having a poor axle hole," i.e., that which does not turn smoothly), a basic concept in Buddhism and Hinduism. Opposite of *sukha.*

Dulosigkeit (German): absence of all reference to any "you."

dvandva (Sanskrit): pair of opposites, e.g., cold and heat, pleasure and pain.

dvija (Sanskrit): one who is born a second time into the life of the spirit, the initiated.

dynamis (Greek): power, energy, capacity.

ecclesia (Latin): church, assembly, reunion.

eidetic: relating to knowledge; from *eidos,* idea.

eidos (Greek): idea, form, appearance.

ekāgratā (Sanskrit): concentration in one spot; hence simplicity and purity.

ekam (Sanskrit): one; generally the primordial oneness, the origin of all, later identified with Brahman.

enstasis (Greek): entering fully into one's self: through concentration and meditation one attains a state of absolute identification (absorption) with the contemplated object, with the Self.

epektasis (Greek): dilatation, expansion, extension; man's trust in his divine destiny, according to St. Gregory of Nyssa. Hope.

epistēmē (Greek): science.

erōs (Latin): love.

ersatz (Ger.): substitute.

eschatology: from the Greek *eschaton*, which refers to the ultimate, both in relation to time (the last things that will happen, the end of this life), and in ontological importance (the ultimate reality).

exclusivism, inclusivism, pluralism: terms indicating an attitude toward non-Christian religions, which (a) considers the latter as being excluded from the salvation of Christ, (b) absolutizes the salvation of Christ by granting a place to non-Christian religions, and (c) recognizes that the different visions of the world are mutually irreducible.

esse sequitur operari (Latin): being follows action.

extasis (Greek): ecstasy, "outside of itself."

extra ecclesiam nulla salus (Latin): "outside the church there is no salvation."

fanum (Latin): temple, sanctuary. Cf. *pro-fanum*.

fides quaerens intellectum (Latin): "faith seeking understanding."

fuga mundi (Latin): escape from the world; an attitude indicating a departure from the things of this world to focus on a world beyond that is considered the "true" world.

Gautama (Sanskrit): family name of prince Siddhartha, who became the Buddha.

Gītā (Sanskrit): cf. *Bhagavad-gītā*.

gnōsis (Greek): saving knowledge, liberating wisdom. Cf. *jñāna, prajñā*.

gopī (Sanskrit): shepherdess full of love and devotion for Kṛṣṇa; symbol of the soul united with the divine being.

guhā (Sanskrit): cave, grotto, secret place (human heart).

guṇa (Sanskrit): the three qualities or attributes of being: *tamas*, darkness; *rajas*, desire; *sattva*, being.

guru (Sanskrit): cf. *ācārya*; usually refers to one who has attained fulfillment.

hamartia (Greek): sin.

haplotēs (Greek): simplicity, naïveté; *h. kardias*: simplicity of heart.

hara (Jap.): center, place of vital energy in man; area of the belly.

hen (Greek): one, unit.

hermeneutics, hermeneutic: "the art of interpretation"; the theory and method of understanding and interpreting writings.

hiranyagarbha (Sanskrit): "the golden germ," a cosmological principle in the *Veda*, later identified with the creator (*Brahmā*).

holistic: that which considers reality in its entirety.

homeomorphic: that which performs a similar function.

homeomorphism: theory used in comparative religion to discover functional equivalence in two or more religions.

humanum (Latin): the basic human; that which is specific to all humanity.

hypomonē (Greek): patience, perseverance.

ihāmutrārthaphala-bhoga-virāga (Sanskrit): renouncement of the reward for good deeds done.

inclusivism: cf. *exclusivism*.

Indra (Sanskrit): the great divine warrior who wins all battles in favor of his worshippers, both against opposing clans (*dasyu* or *dāsa*) and against demons such as Vṛtra and Vala. His virile power is irresistible and is the *soma* that provides him with the energy needed for his mighty exploits. He is the liberator of the compelling forces; he releases the waters and the light. His weapon is the *vajra*, the lightning bolt.

Īśā-upaniṣad (Sanskrit): one of the shortest of the *Upaniṣad*, which deals with the presence of the divine in all things.

Īśa, Īśvara (Sanskrit): the Lord, from the root *īś-*, to be lord, to guide, to possess. Although a generic term for Lord, in posterior religious systems it is more often used for Śiva than for Viṣṇu. In the Vedānta it is the manifested, qualified (*saguṇa*) aspect of Brahman.

itivuttaka (Pāli): "so I have heard"; traditional form of passing on the teachings of Buddha and the heading of a text in Buddhist writings.

Jainism: post-Vedic ascetic tradition organized by Mahāvīra (fifth to fourth centuries BC), path of purification emphasizing the importance of *ahiṃsā* (nonviolence). Religion slightly anterior to Buddhism.

jīva (Sanskrit): living being (from *jīv-*, to live); the soul in its individuality, as opposed to *ātman*, the universal soul. There are as many *jīva* as individual living beings.

jīvanmukta (Sanskrit): "liberated while alive and embodied," the highest category of the holy or fulfilled person who has reached the destination in this life and, therefore, in the human body; he who has fulfilled his *ātman-braham* ontological identity; he who has reached his own being, becoming totally integrated.

jñāna (Sanskrit): knowledge (from the root *jñā-*, to know), intuition, wisdom; frequently the highest intuitive comprehension, the attaining of *ātman* or *brahman*. *Jñāna* is the result of meditation or revelation. Cf. *jñāna-mārga*.

jñāna-mārga (Sanskrit): the path of knowledge, contemplation, and intuitive vision; one of the three classic paths of spiritual experience, generally considered superior to those of *karman* and *bhakti*, although many *bhakta* regard *jñāna* as merely as form of *bhakti*.

jñānavādin (Sanskrit): person who claims that supreme knowledge (*jñāna*) is in itself sufficient for liberation. Actions barely count.

kaivalya (Sanskrit): isolation, solitude, detachment; one of the spiritual states of supreme freedom.

kairos (Greek): time, opportune moment, crucial point at which the destiny changes phase, epoch.

kalpa (Sanskrit): a period of the world, a cosmic time of variable length.

kāma (Sanskrit): the creative power of desire, personified as the God of love; one of the *puruṣārtha*.

kāraṇa (Sanskrit): cause.

karma, karman (Sanskrit): lit. "act, deed, action"; from the root *kṛ*, to act, to do; originally the sacred action, sacrifice, rite, later also moral act. The result of all actions and deeds according to the law of *karman* that regulates actions and their results in the universe. Later also connected with rebirth, it indicates the link between the actions carried out by a subject and his destiny in the cycle of deaths and rebirths.

karmakāṇḍin (Sanskrit): refers to those who emphasize the importance of the action, in occasions of ritual, for salvation/liberation.

karma-mārga (Sanskrit): the path of action; one of the three classic paths of spirituality (cf. *bhakti, jñāna*). In the *Veda* it refers to sacrificial actions viewed as the way to salvation; later includes also moral actions, or all actions that are performed in a spirit of sacrifice.

katachronism: interpretation of a reality or doctrine with categories that are extraneous or posterior.

kāya (Sanskrit): body.

kāyotsarga (Sanskrit): the abandoning of all bodily activity; spiritual exercise in which even the possession of one's body is renounced.

kenōsis (Greek): annihilation, emptying of oneself, overcoming of one's ego.

kērygma (Greek): message, proclamation (of the word of God), from the Greek *kērysso* (to proclaim), corresponding to the first level of the evangelical teaching.

keśin (Sanskrit): "long-haired" (*keśa*), he who has long hair, ascetic, monk.

kleśa (Sanskrit): affliction, impurity of the soul.

koinōnia (Greek): community, communion.

kosmos (Greek): order, the ordered universe, the wholeness of the world.

Kṛṣṇa (Sanskrit): *avatāra* of Viṣṇu (lit. "the black one") and one of the most popular Gods. He does not appear in the *Veda*, but he is the revealer of the

Bhagavad-gītā. He is the divine child and the shepherd God of Vṛndāvana, the incarnation of love and the playful God *par excellence*.

kṣetra (Sanskrit): "field," both in a metaphorical and literal sense. Knowledge begins with the distinction between the field and he who knows the field, i.e., between the world (as the object) and the knowing subject.

kunamnama (Sanskrit): rigid, inflexible; the feminine form *kunamnamā* also indicates a feminine divinity.

kurukṣetra (Sanskrit): the battlefield where the war of the *Mahābhārata* was fought and where Kṛṣṇa revealed the *Bhagavad-gītā* to Arjuna.

lama: head of Tibetan Buddhism.

laukika (Sanskrit): natural, worldly, temporal.

leitourgia (Greek): activity of the people, liturgy.

līlā (Sanskrit): divine game, the world as the amusement of God. This concept is not Vedic but Purāṇic.

liṅga (Sanskrit): characteristic feature of Śiva; phallus.

lingua universalis (Latin): universal language.

locus theologicus (Latin): the proper and legitimate place of theological activity.

logos (Greek): word, thought, judgment, reason. In the New Testament Christ as the word of God (Jn 1).

loka (Sanskrit): "world," open space, place, kingdom. Cf. *triloka*.

lokasaṃgraha (Sanskrit): the "keeping together, maintaining of the world" by the wise man and the saint through the sacred or liturgical action (concept of *Bhagavad-gītā*).

madhyama (Sanskrit): central position, middle.

madhyamamārga (Sanskrit): the middle path taught by Buddha.

madhyamika (Sanskrit): the school of the "middle way" in Mahayana Buddhism.

Mahābhārata (Sanskrit): epic poem that tells the legendary story of the Indian people and expounds its prescriptive values.

mahātma (Sanskrit): "great soul." Name of the founder of the Jain religion (fifth to fourth century BC).

mahāvākya (Sanskrit): "great saying." Refers to great expressions of the *Upaniṣad* that express very concisely the content of the experience of the Absolute.

Mahāyāna: "great vehicle." Branch of Buddhism established in India two thousand years ago.

maithuna, *mithuna* (Sanskrit): union, mating, copulation both in a sexual and metaphorical sense.

Maitreyī (Sanskrit): wife of the sage Yājñavalkya. Was considered a "knower of Brahman."

manas (Sanskrit): mind in its broadest sense, heart, intellect, the internal organ that is the seat of thought, comprehension, feeling, imagination, and will. In Upaniṣadic anthropology *manas* is one of the three constituent principles of man (cf. *vāc, prāṇa*).

maṇḍala (Sanskrit): lit. "circle." Mystic representation of all reality; a pictorial illustration of the homology between the microcosm (man) and the macrocosm (the universe). Also a book of the *Ṛg-veda* (a "circle" of hymns). The *Ṛg-veda* is made up of ten *maṇḍala*.

mantra (Sanskrit): prayer, sacred formula (from the root *man-*, to think), sacred word, a Vedic text or verse. Usually only the part of the *Veda* consisting of the *Saṃhitā* is called a *mantra*. As it is a word of power it may also take the meaning of magic formula or spell.

Manu (Sanskrit): the father of humanity, the man par exellence; also the first priest to establish sacrifices.

mārga (Sanskrit): road, path, way.

martys (Greek): martyr; one who gives testimony for his own life, even through death.

maṭha (Sanskrit): monastery.

mauna (Sanskrit): silence, practiced by the silent itinerant monk; cf. *muni*.

māyā (Sanskrit): the mysterious power, wisdom, or ability of the Gods, hence the power of deceit, of illusion. In the Vedānta it is used as a synonym of ignorance and also to indicate the cosmic "illusion" that shrouds the absolute Brahman.

mederi (Latin): to heal, to treat.

metanoia (Greek): transformation, change of mentality or heart, conversion; going beyond (*meta*) the mental or rational (*nous*).

metron (Greek): measure, meter.

mikrokosmos (Greek): the entire reality reflected or concentrated in the individual; "man as *mikrokosmos*" refers to man as compendium of the cosmos.

mimaṃsa, mimaṃsaka (Sanskrit): one of the six classic systems of Indian philosophy which deals mainly with the rudiments and the rules for interpreting the Vedic writings. From the root *man-*, to think. The two main schools are the *purvami maṃsa*, which focuses on the ritual interpretation of the *Veda* (cf. *karmakaṇḍin*) and the *uttarami maṃsa*, which gives a philosophical and spiritual interpretation.

mokṣa (Sanskrit): ultimate liberation from *saṃsāra*, the cycle of births and deaths, and from *karman*, ignorance, and limitation: salvation. Homeomorphic equivalent of *sōteria*.

monism: from Greek *monon*, unique; concept by which all things are traced back to a single active principle.

monos (Greek): one, unique.

monotropos (Greek): alone, solitary, he who lives in one place only.

morphē (Greek): figure, form, apparition.

morphology: the study of form, especially the forms of development of the living and of culture.

mu (Jap.): nothing, nonbeing.

mumukṣutva (Sanskrit): desiderative form of the root *muc-* (cf. *mokṣa*); desire for salvation, and yearning for liberation, the necessary prerequisite for embarking on the path of liberation.

muni (Sanskrit): a silent monk, ascetic; an ecstatic. One who practices *mauna*, silence.

mythos (Greek): the horizon of presence that does not require further inquiry.

Nachiketas (Sanskrit): name of a young brahman who descends into the realm of Yama and discusses ultimate questions with him (in the *Kaṭha-upaniṣad*). Some have interpreted his name as "he who does not know," i.e., the novice, the seeker.

nāda (Sanskrit): sound, original vibration in the emanation of the word; an important concept in Tantric cosmogony (cf. also *bindu*).

nāma-rūpa (Sanskrit): "name and form," the phenomenic world that constitutes the *saṃsāra*.

neti neti (Sanskrit): "not this, not this" (*na iti*), i.e., the negation of any kind of characterization of the *ātman* or *brahman* in the *Upaniṣad*; pure apophatism.

nirguṇa-brahman (Sanskrit): Brahman without attributes and qualities, the unqualified, transcendent Absolute.

nirodha (Sanskrit): halt, destruction.

nirvāṇa (Sanskrit): lit. "the going out (of the flame)," extinction. The word does not refer to a condition, but indicates liberation from all dichotomy and conditioning, whether it be birth and death, time and space, being and nonbeing, ignorance and knowledge, or final extinction including time, space, and being; the ultimate destination for Buddhism and Jainism.

nirvikalpa (Sanskrit): certain, beyond doubt.

nitya (Sanskrit): the eternal, permanent, real.

nitya-anitya-vastu-viveka (Sanskrit): discernment between permanent (eternal) and temporal things.

nomos (Greek): custom, rule, law.

nous (Greek): mind, thought, intellect, reason.

ob-audire (Latin): to listen, to obey.

Ohrmazd (Persian): or Ahura Mazdā; God of light and truth in the Medo-Persian religion and that of the *Avesta*.

oikonomia (Greek): science of the management of household affairs (of the human family). Stewardship of the human *habitat*, home economics.

Oṃ (Sanskrit): the sacred syllable, formed by three letters A-U-M. Also means "yes," "so be it" (*amen*). Used also at the beginning and end of every recitation of sacred writings and is believed to have a mystic meaning. The highest and most comprehensive symbol of Hindu spirituality, which is also used as a *mantra* in Buddhism. Manifestation of spiritual energy, which indicates the presence of the Absolute in the world of appearance.

ōn (Greek): participle of the verb "to be" (*einai*); being, that which is higher, entity, that which exists.

ontonomy: intrinsic connection of an entity in relation to the totality of Being, the constitutive order (*nomos*) of every being as Being (*ōn*), harmony that allows the interdependence of all things.

operari sequitur esse (Latin): "acting follows being."

orthodoxy and *orthopraxy*: "correct doctrine" and "correct action."

pan (Greek): all, everything.

Pantokratōr (Greek): the Sovereign of all; designates Christ and also God.

paramahaṃsa (Sanskrit): "sublime swan," i.e., the supreme soul, a liberated person who enjoys complete freedom, a class of ascetics.

pāramārthika (Sanskrit): ultimate level, ultimate reality, true reality.

paredra (Greek): female companion.

parigraha (Sanskrit): tendency to possess, hoarding.

parousia (Greek): the return, the presence, the second coming of Christ.

pars in toto (Latin): the part in the whole.

pars pro toto (Latin): the part that represents the whole.

pati divina (Latin): passive attitude of man toward the "touches" of the divine; synonym of mystic experience.

penthos (Greek): repentance, sadness.

perichōresis (Greek): notion of the early Church Trinitarian doctrine describing the interpenetration of divine persons. Corresponds to the Latin *circumincessio*.

phainomenon (Greek): phenomenon, that which appears, that which shows itself.

phaneros (Greek): bright, from *phanos*, light.

plerōma (Greek): fullness, the full, complete.

polysemic: having several meanings.

pluralism: cf. *exclusivism*.

polis (Greek): the city-state of ancient Greece.

politeuma (Greek): belonging to the social body, political unit. Cf. *conversatio*.

Prajāpati (Sanskrit): "Lord of creatures," the primordial God, Father of the Gods and all beings. His position is central in the *Brāhmaṇa*.

prajñā (Sanskrit): understanding and awareness, consciousness, wisdom. Cf. *gnōsis*, *jñāna*.

pramāṇa (Sanskrit): means for attaining valid knowledge.

prāṇa (Sanskrit): vital breath, life, the breath of life, the vital force that holds the body together. In the *Upaniṣad* one of the three constitutive principles of the human being (cf. *vāc, manas*). It is made up of five types of breath (*prāṇa, apāna, vyāna, samāna, udāna*). The cosmic equivalent of *prāṇa* is *Vāyu*, air, wind.

prasthānatraya (Sanskrit): term referring to the three principle texts of the Vedānta (*Upaniṣad, Bhagavad-gītā*, and *Brahma-sūtra*).

pratiṣṭhā (Sanskrit): foundation, support, base.

pratītyasamutpāda (Sanskrit): Buddhist doctrine of the "conditioned genesis" or "dependent origination," which claims that nothing exists for itself but carries within itself the conditions for its own existence, and that everything is mutually conditioned in the cycle of existence.

primum analogatum (Latin): the point of reference for every analogy.

pro-fanum (Latin): pro-fane; outside the temple (*fanum*).

psychē (Greek): soul, psyche, heart, animated being.

pūjā (Sanskrit): worship, reverence, adoration. The concept is more closely related to the *bhakti* cult than the Vedic cult.

purohita (Sanskrit): priest, liturgy.

Purana (Sanskrit): ancient history, narrative, myth; a class of literature incorporating Hindu mythology.

Puruṣa (Sanskrit): the Person, the spirit, man. Both the primordial man of the cosmic dimension (*Ṛg-veda*) and the "inner man," the spiritual person existing within man (*Upaniṣad*). In the Sāṃkhya it is the spiritual principle of reality (cf. *prakṛti*).

quaternitas perfecta (Latin): the perfect quaternity.

qui/quid pro quo (Latin): substitution of one thing for another; error consisting in the mistaking of one person (*qui*) or thing (*quid*) for another.

rāhib (Arabic): instructor, teacher, monk.

Rama (Sanskrit): *avatāra* of Viṣṇu and one of the most popular of the Vedic Gods. Son of Daśaratha and husband of Sita, Rama is a model of uprightness and the great hero of the *Ramayaṇa*.

Rāmāyaṇa (Sanskrit): Indian epic poem.

ratio (Latin): reason.

res cogitans / res extensa (Latin): thinking thing / extended thing, division of reality, according to Descartes.

res significata (Latin): signified thing.

Ŗg-veda (Sanskrit): the most ancient and important of the *Veda* texts.

ṛṣi (Sanskrit): seer, sage, wise man; the poet-sages to whom the *Veda* were revealed. Regarded as a special class of beings, superior to men and inferior to the Gods. According to one tradition there were seven *ṛṣi*, probably the seven priests with whom Manu performed the first sacrifice and the seven poet judges in the assembly. Their identification with the names of ancient seers and with the stars of the Ursa Major occurred later (*Brāhmaṇa*).

ṛta (Sanskrit): cosmic and sacred order, sacrifice as a universal law, also truth; the ultimate, dynamic, and harmonious structure of reality.

Saccidānanda (Sanskrit): Brahman as Being (*sat*), Consciousness (*cit*), and Bliss (*ānanda*).

sadguru or *satguru* (Sanskrit): eternal teacher, teacher archetype, universal *guru*.

sādhaka (Sanskrit): one who practices a spiritual, yoga discipline.

sādhana (Sanskrit): spiritual practice or discipline.

sādhu (Sanskrit): straight, leading straight to the goal, good, just. A good person, renunciant, monk, or ascetic.

sādhvī (Sanskrit): female ascetics in Hinduism and especially Jainism; feminine form of *sādhu*.

saeculum (Latin): the human age, era, century; also spirit of the day.

saguṇa-brahman (Sanskrit): Brahman with quality, corresponding in the *Vedānta* to *Ùśvara*, the Lord.

śaivasiddhānta (Sanskrit): religion, philosophical/religious school pertaining to Hinduism; dominant Śivaism in Tamil Nadu.

śakti (Sanskrit): energy, potency, divine power, the creative energy of God. The active, dynamic—feminine—aspect of reality or of a God (generally of Śiva). Personified as the goddess Śakti, consort of Śiva with a creative function.

salus (Latin): health, salvation.

śama (Sanskrit): calm, tranquility, method of mental appeasement.

samādhi (Sanskrit): state of deep concentration, compenetration, immersion, perfection (enstasy); the last of the yoga stages; also the tomb of a saint.

saṃgha (Sanskrit): the (monastic) community of those who follow the path of the Buddha.

saṃnyāsa (Sanskrit): renunciation, the fourth stage of life spent as an errant monk (from *samnyas-*, to suppress, to renounce, to abandon).

saṃnyāsin (Sanskrit): renunciant, ascetic; pertaining to the fourth stage or period of life (*āśrama*), to some the superior stage.

sampradāya (Sanskrit): tradition, religious system and community that follows a tradition.

saṃsāra (Sanskrit): the impermanent phenomenic world and the condition of identification with it, the temporal existence, the cycle of births and deaths, of conditioned existences; state of dependence and slavery.

saṃskāra (Sanskrit): "sacrament," rites that sanctify the various important stages and events in human life. Also karmic residues, physical impressions left over from previous lives, which in some way influence the individual existence of a person.

samudaya (Sanskrit): origin.

Śaṅkara (Sanskrit): eighth-century Hindu philosopher and teacher; one of the most famous exponents of nondualist Vedānta.

śānti (Sanskrit): peace, tranquility, quiescence. The closing *mantra* of many prayers and oblations.

śānti-mantra (Sanskrit): introductory invocation or prayer of an *Upaniṣad*, which is generally common to all the *Upaniṣad* of the same *Veda*. Recited at the beginning and usually also the end of an Upaniṣadic reading, although not actually part of the text.

sarvam duḥkham (Sanskrit): "all is suffering," a classic Buddhist statement.

śāstra (Sanskrit): precepts, orders, rules, authoritative teachings; body of traditionally authorized texts.

sat (Sanskrit): essence (present participle of *as-*, to be), existence, reality. Ultimately, only the Brahman is *sat*, as pure Being is the Basis of every existence. In the Vedānta one of the three "qualifications" of the Brahman (cf. *cit, ānanda*).

Śatapatha-brāhmaṇa (Sanskrit): "*Brāhmaṇa* of one hundred paths," the most complete and systematic of the *Brāhmaṇa*.

satori (Japanese): experience of enlightenment in *Zen*.

satyāgraha (Sanskrit): active nonviolence of those who live for the truth.

satyasya satyam (Sanskrit): true truth, true reality, the being of the existent.

schola Domini (Latin): school of the Lord.

secularity, secular: of this world, being-in-time, being-in-the-world (from Latin *saeculum*).

semper maior (Latin): always greater.

septuaginta (Latin): "the Seventy" (translators); translation of the Hebrew Bible into Greek, carried out in the third to first centuries BC in Alexandria.

simplicitas cordis (Latin): simplicity of heart.

śiṣya (Sanskrit): disciple (cf. *guru*).

Sitz im Leben (German): vital setting, context.

Śiva (Sanskrit): propitious, gracious, pleasant, benevolent. He who is of good omen; in the *Veda* it is Rudra who is known to the *Śvetāśvatara-upaniṣad* as Śiva, one of the most important Gods of Hindu tradition. He is the destroyer of the universe (cf. also *Brahmā, Viṣṇu*), and also the great *yogin* and model of ascetics. His consort is Pārvatī or Umā.

Śivaism, Śivaita (Sanskrit): one of the two great families of the Hindu religion, whose God is Śiva.

sobrietas (Latin): sobriety, moderation.

sola fides (Latin): "the one faith," the response of Scholasticism to philosophically unsolvable theological questions; the central doctrine of Luther.

soma (Sanskrit): the sacrificial plant from which the juice of the *soma* is extracted through elaborate rituals, hence the sap or drink of immortality (*amṛta* is another name for *soma*); a divinity ("Soma the king"). *Soma* was used ritually for entering a higher state of consciousness. Later it also took on the meaning of "moon."

sōma (Greek): body.

sophia (Greek): wisdom.

sōteria (Greek): salvation, liberation, redemption.

śraddhā (Sanskrit): "faith," the active trust (in Gods or in the rite itself) required in every act of worship; confidence (in the teachings of the *Veda*). In the *Ṛg-veda* (X.151), *śraddhā* is invoked almost as a divinity.

śrāddha (Sanskrit): rite of homage to deceased relatives; offering to ancestors generally made by the son of the deceased and repeated on certain occasions. Consists in oblations of food to the ancestors and a meal for relatives and priests.

śrī (Sanskrit): splendor, brilliance, glory, beauty, preeminence; used as a title for Gods, saints and respected persons; the consort of Viṣṇu.

śruti (Sanskrit): "that which has been heard," the Vedic revelation, an expression mainly used in sacred texts, *Veda* and other authoritative Hindu scriptures, which reveal to the human spirit the entire corpus of the *Veda* transmitted orally.

stūpa (Sanskrit): sacred place or sacred mountain in Buddhism.

sui generis (Latin): "of its own kind."

sukha (Sanskrit): happiness, pleasure, joy, bliss.

śūnya, śūnyatā (Sanskrit): void, vacuity, nothingness, the structural condition of reality and all things; represents the ultimate reality in Buddhism (cf. *nirvāṇa*).

suṣupti (Sanskrit): deep, dreamless sleep; one of the four states of consciousness, along with wakefulness, dreaming, and the state of conscious enlightenment.

sūtra (Sanskrit): lit. "yarn, thread of a fabric." Short aphorism in a sacred text that generally cannot be understood without a comment (*bhāṣya*). The literature of the *sūtra* is part of the *smṛti* and is conceived to be easily memorized.

Śvetaketu (Sanskrit): son of Gautama; in the *Chāndogya-upaniṣad* a famous disciple of Uddalaka, to whom is imparted the highest teaching on the *ātman* and the *brahman*, which ends with: *tat tvam asi* ("that is you").

Śvetāśvatara-upaniṣad (Sanskrit): one of the principles of the last *Upaniṣad*, frequently cited in the Vedānta, which tends to personify the supreme principle (Brahman) and identify it with the God Śiva or Rudra.

symbolon (Greek): symbol.

synechēs (Greek): continuous, uninterrupted, persevering, solid: that which keeps something in cohesion.

Taboric light: the light that illuminated Jesus in the transfiguration; this light may be regarded as the visible character of divinity, the energy or grace by which God allows himself to be known; Man may receive this light.

taṇhā (Pāli): thirst; thirst for existence; origin of all suffering, according to Buddhism. Cf. *tṛṣṇā*.

Tantra (Sanskrit): lit. weave, weaving, loom; religious system not based on the *Veda*, consisting in secret doctrines and practices that give access to hidden powers; accentuates the interrelation between body and soul, matter and spirit; the development of special powers. The Tantric tradition has practically permeated the entire spiritual tradition of Asia. The basic assumption of all Tantric practices is the interrelation between body and spirit, matter and soul, *bhukti* (pleasure) and *mukti* (liberation).

tao (Chinese): "way," a central concept in Chinese philosophy, especially Taoism.

Tao-te Ching (Chinese): "the book of the way and its power," a fundamental work of philosophical Taoism in China, attributed to Laotzi (sixth century BC), historically demonstrable from third century BC.

ta panta mataiotēs (Greek): all (is) vanity.

tapas (Sanskrit): lit. heat; hence inner energy, spiritual fervor or ardor, austerity, ascesis, penitence. One of the forms of primordial energy, along with *kāma*.

tat (Sanskrit): demonstrative pronoun: "that." Opposite of *idam* (this), refers to Brahman. When isolated, it refers to the ultimate reality without naming it.

Tathagata (Sanskrit): lit. "the one thus come, who has attained being, who has extinguished himself," an appellative of Buddha.

tattva: essence, true nature, reality; philosophical principle.

tat tvam asi (Sanskrit): "that is you," an Upaniṣadic expression meaning that *ātman* is ultimately Brahman. One of the four Great Sayings (*mahāvākyāni*) of the *Upaniṣad*, as taught to Śvetaketu.

technē (Greek): art, ability, handicraft.

tempiternity: nonseparation between time and eternity.

theandric: "divine-human" (from Greek *theos* and *anēr*).

theanthropocosmic: " divine-human-cosmic" (from Greek *theos*, *anthrōpos*, and *kosmos*).

theōreia (Greek): theory; originally in the sense of "contemplation."

ṭīkā (Sanskrit): commentary, generally of the *sūtra*.

tīrthaṅkara (Sanskrit): line of great sages/saints in Jainism.

tonsura: preparatory religious rank for receiving the minor orders in Christianity; special haircut as a distinctive mark of the clerical status that distinguishes it from the secular and signifies separation from the world.

triloka (Sanskrit): the "triple world," totality of the universe, consisting in three realms: earth, atmosphere, and sky, or earth, sky, and the nether regions (later called hell); the inhabitants of the three worlds are Gods, men, and demons..

tṛṣṇā (Sanskrit): thirst; cf. *taṇhā*.

tvam (Sanskrit): you (personal pronoun, second-person singular).

tyāga (Sanskrit): renunciation, abandonment of possessions and attachments.

umma (Arabic): the community of believers; church.

Ungrund (German): bottomless, without foundations, abyss.

Upaniṣad (Sanskrit): fundamental sacred teaching in the form of texts constituting the end of the *Veda*; part of the revelation (*śruti*) and basis of posterior Hindu thought.

upekṣā (Sanskrit): equanimity, detachment, benevolence.

utrumque (Latin): the one and the other.

vāc (Sanskrit): word; the sacred, primordial, and creative Word; sound, also discourse, language, the organ of speech, voice. Sometimes only the *Ṛg-veda* and other times all the *Veda* are referred to as *vāc*.

vairāgya (Sanskrit): estrangement, renunciation, indifference; one of the requisites of the spiritual path.

vānaprastha (Sanskrit): inhabitant of the forest, hermit; the third stage of life or *āśrama*, when the head of family withdraws into solitude, with or without his wife, after having fulfilled his earthly duties.

Varuṇa (Sanskrit): one of the main Gods of the *Veda*; Varuṇa is king, commander, and supervisor of the moral conduct of men. He is Lord of *ṛta*, cosmic and moral order. He is often invoked together with Mitra. Due to his close association with water he later became known simply as a God of water, the Lord of the ocean.

vāyu (Sanskrit): air, wind, personified as a God in the *Veda*.

Veda (Sanskrit): lit. knowledge (from the root *vid-*, to know); the sacred knowledge incorporated in the *Veda* as the entire body of "Sacred Scriptures" (although originally they were only passed on orally). Strictly speaking, "*Veda*" refers only to the *Saṃhitā* (*Ṛg-veda, Yajur-veda, Sāma-veda, Atharva-veda*); generally, however, *Brāhmaṇa* and *Upaniṣad* are also included. In the plural it refers to the four *Veda*.

vedanā (Sanskrit): sensation, feeling.

Vedānta (Sanskrit): lit. end of the *Veda*, i.e., the *Upaniṣad* as the climax of Vedic wisdom. In the sense of Uttaramī māṃsā or Vedāntavāda, a system of Indian philosophy (Advaita-vedānta, Dvaita-vedānta, etc.) based on the *Upaniṣad*, which teaches a spiritual interpretation of the *Veda*; one of the last schools of Hindu philosophical thought, of which the most renowned representatives include Śaṅkara, Rāmānuja, and Madhva.

viator (Latin): traveller, novice, aspirant, disciple.

vidyā (Sanskrit): knowledge, wisdom, also branch of knowledge; a section of a text in the *Upaniṣad*.

vihāra (Sanskrit): monastery, generally in Buddhism; Buddhist or Jain temple.

vinaya (Sanskrit): collection of moral rules and practices in Buddhism.

Viṣṇu (Sanskrit): important God in Hinduism, featured in the ancient *Veda*; his name means "the all-pervading one." Associated with the sun, he is famous for his three great strides with which he measured the three worlds. He later became the second component of the *trimurti*, the preserver, and is mainly worshipped in his *avatara* (cf. *Kṛṣṇa, Rāma*).

viveka (Sanskrit): discernment, discrimination.

Vivekacūfāmaṇi (Sanskrit): "jewel/diadem of discernment," an important work of the Advaita-vedānta, written by Śaṅkara, which deals with the distinction between true reality and the phenomenic world.

vrata (Sanskrit): vow, religious observance.

vyāvahārika (Sanskrit): "relating to earthly matters, to mundane life," i.e., the earthly way of seeing, the practical perspective; the relative level.

wu wei (Chinese): "nonaction" in Taoist philosophy.

xeniteia (Greek): the state of being a stranger,

yakṣa (Sanskrit): spiritual, semidivine, supernatural being; beings belonging to a higher level than the physical.

Yama (Sanskrit): the "twin" of Yamī, the first man and the first to pass through death and obtain immortality; hence the predecessor of men on the path of death and he who commands in the realm of the dead. Later became the personification of Death and the Lord of the nether regions.

Yamī (Sanskrit): the sister of Yama, with whom she forms the first couple of humans on the earth. Although her brother attempts to commit incest with her, she (according to some texts) does not yield.

yang (Chinese): the solar, celestial, masculine aspect in the yin-yang polarity.

yin (Chinese): the lunar, earthly, feminine aspect; complement of *yang*.

yoga (Sanskrit): from the root *yuj-*, to yoke, to join, to unite, to prepare, to fix, to concentrate; union; method of mental, physical, and spiritual union; concentration and contemplation, which also uses bodily posture (*āsana*), breathing control (*prāṇāyāma*) and spiritual techniques. Yoga appears to be an extremely ancient Indian practice that was developed into a system by Patañjali (*Yoga-sūtra*) and made to correspond to the philosophical system Sāṃkhya. Yoga as a method has become a fundamental factor in practically all religions of Indian origin.

yogin (Sanskrit): the ascetic, one who practices self-control, a follower of the path of yoga.

zen (Japanese): from the Sanskrit *dhyāna* (deep meditation); school of Buddhism that claims to be the purest and most direct path to enlightenment (*satori, nirvāṇa*).

INDEX OF NAMES

INDEX OF ORIGINAL TEXTS IN THIS VOLUME

Introduction, revised version of "La posizione della Sacra Scrittura nel Cristianesimo," in Maya e Apocalisse. L'incontro dell'induismo e del cristianesimo. Abete, Roma 1966, cap. 6, 157-164. Translated by Geraldine Clarkson.

Humanism and Cross, orig. text Humanismo y Cruz, Rialp, Madrid 1963. Translated by Carla Ros.

"The Mass as Consecratio Temporis and Tempiternity," orig. text "La Misa como consecratio temporis. La tempiternidad," in Sanctum Sacrificium. Zaragoza 1961, 75-93. Translated by Carla Ros.

"Christianity and World Religions," in M.P. John et al., Christianity. Punjabi University, Patiala 1969, 78-127.

Salvation in Christ: Concreteness and Universality, the Supername (Inaugural Lecture at the Ecumenical Institute of Advanced Theological Study Tantur, Jerusalem), Santa Barbara, CA, 1972, 1-81.

"Super hanc Petram: Due princìpi ecclesiologici: la roccia e le chiavi," in Legge e Vangelo. Discussione su una legge fondamentale per la Chiesa. Paideia, Brescia 1972, 135-145. Translated by Geraldine Clarkson.

"Christians and So-called "Non-Christians," in Cross Currents 22, no. 3, 1972, 281-308.

"The Contribution of Christian Monasticism in Asia to the Universal Church," in Cistercian Studies 10, no. 2, Spencer 1975, 73-84.

"Social Ministry and Ministry of Word and Worship (Some Considerations from the Asian Background)," in P.S. de Achútegui (cur.), Asian Colloquium on Ministries in the Church, FABC, Hong Kong, 1977, 1-20.

About the Author

An international authority on spirituality, the study of religions, and intercultural dialogue, Raimon Panikkar has made intercultural and dialogical pluralism one of the hallmarks of his research, becoming a master "bridge builder," tireless in the promotion of dialogue between Western culture and the great Oriental Hindū and Buddhist traditions.

Born in 1918 in Barcelona of a Spanish Catholic mother and an Indian Hindū father, he is part of a plurality of traditions: Indian and European, Hindū and Christian, scientific and humanistic.

Panikkar holds degrees in chemistry, philosophy, and theology, and was ordained a Catholic priest in 1946. He has delivered courses and lectures in major European, Indian, and American universities.

A member of the International Institute of Philosophy (Paris), of the permanent Tribunal of the Peoples (Rome), and of the UNESCO Commission for intercultural dialogue, he has also founded various philosophical journals and intercultural study centers. He has held conferences in each of the five continents (including the renowned Gifford Lectures in 1988–1989 on "Trinity and Atheism").

Panikkar has received international recognitions including honorary doctorates from the University of the Balearic Islands in 1997, the University of Tübingen in 2004, Urbino in 2005, and Girona in 2008, as well as prizes ranging from the "Premio Menéndez Pelayo de Humanidades" for his book *El concepto de naturaleza* in Madrid in 1946 to the "Premio Nonino 2001 a un maestro del nostro tempo" in Italy.

Since 1982 he has lived in Tavertet in the Catalonian mountains, where he continues his contemplative experience and cultural activities. There he founded and presides over the intercultural study center Vivarium. Panikkar has published more than fifty books in various languages and hundreds of articles on the philosophy of religion, theology, the philosophy of science, metaphysics, and Indology.

From the dialogue between religions to the peaceful cohabitation of peoples; from reflections on the future of the technological society to major work on political and social intelligence; from the recognition that all interreligious dialogue is based on an intrareligious dialogue to the promotion of open knowledge of other religions, of which he is a mediator; from his penetrating analysis of the crisis in spirituality to the practice of meditation and the rediscovery of his monastic identity; from the invitation of colligite fragmenta as a path toward the integration of reality to the proposal of a new innocence, Panikkar embodies a personal journey of fulfillment.

Among his most important publications with Orbis are: *velo della realtà* (2000); *L'incontro indispensabile: dialogo delle religioni* (2001); *Pace e interculturalità. Una riflessione filosofica* (2002, 2006); *La realtà cosmoteandrica. Dio-Uomo-Mondo* (2004); *L'esperienza della vita. La mistica* (2005); *La gioia pasquale, La presenza di Dio and Maria* (2007); *Il Cristo sconosciuto dell'induismo* (2008).